ALISON C. AYRES

ON A RAFT OF DREAMS

AN AUTOBIOGRAPHY

PAGE PUBLISHING
Conneaut Lake, PA

First originally published by Page Publishing 2023

ISBN 979-8-89157-356-7 (paperback)
ISBN 979-8-88793-290-3 (hc)
ISBN 979-8-88793-287-3 (digital)

Printed in the United States of America

Have you ever noticed,

that while the sky and sea meet at the horizon,

if you journey towards it,

it opens before you,

leaving you face to face with a new horizon?

Well...all those who have,

will never understand why those who haven't

feel trapped by the sky and the sea.

So...journey bravely towards the horizon.

If your destiny is of your own making,

YOU ARE INDEED ALIVE.

PROLOGUE

My life always revolved around my immediate family, especially my single parent mother and older brother; my gifts of art and creative writing, especially songs; and the sport of football (soccer in the United States). My daughter and my girlfriend, who became my lifetime partner, eventually completed my life portrait. It is a journey that began on the Caribbean Island world famous for its Steelpan, Calypso and Carnival; and with a burning desire to pursue one of my life ambitions, inevitably took me to "The Land of The Free and The Home of The Brave", where today I reside as a citizen.

From a very early age I was never really enthusiastic about school. As a matter of fact, it would be fair to say that I hated attending school except for the friends I made, art classes and a period when football was on the agenda. My natural gift of art and my love for music were readily recognized and acknowledged within my home circle from very early on. My song writing talent on the other hand, though also there from a young age, would only come to the fore much later in my life. As for football; it was an instant love affair after I was introduced to the sport at the age of eight.

With not much enthusiasm for school during my very early years, there were no expectations for success in my future. Being also very stubborn and short-tempered, which might be difficult for those who would have come to know me to imagine, did not help to alleviate that concern. In fact, those very early childhood character traits saw predictions of an inevitable stint behind bars from some elders within the household back then.

Growing up in households where there was a deep sense of contentment, especially financially, with the mantra "if yuh doh have it do without it" engrained by the elders, I never harbored the dream of having financial and or material success later on in my life; and as such, as an adult I never pursued either one. However, I did harbor other dreams, which were born out of the undeniable love I had and passion I felt, for the things around which those dreams revolved; namely, art, football and writing and composing songs. Dreams of one day becoming a full-fledged Commercial Artist; of one day becoming one of the top football players in my homeland, which would somehow lead to me meeting my childhood football idol Edson Arantes do Nascimento "Pele"; of one day becoming a successful songwriter, not just in my homeland, but also beyond.

Living in abject poverty over the course of my very early childhood, and into and during my teenage years, I witnessed my mother's never-ending struggle to raise and provide life's most basic necessities for her children, which would have been made doubly difficult for her, being that she was born deaf. I personally wanted more than anything else to repay my mother for her lifetime of unconditional love, sacrifice and profound dedication to us. As such, I also harbored perhaps the most significant dream of all, which was to make her proud and happy one day, so that she would know that her tireless efforts were not in vain.

I felt I could achieve that ultimate dream through the realization of any one of two of my other childhood dreams. More specifically, those related to me becoming a successful Commercial Artist or songwriter, since I felt that I could earn a decent income through either of them as I didn't view football as such. My mother came to represent my "Primary Positive Source of Motivation" towards achieving that goal. And so, during my mid and late teens, I became purpose driven by my ultimate dream to make my mother proud and happy one day. During those years I began focusing on developing my talents in the areas of commercial art and song writing, knowing that any significant level of professional and by extension personal achievement during the course of my lifetime, would most likely come through either of them.

Achieving some degree of success in those two respective areas, as well as on the football field at the ordinary levels during those teenage years, instilled a significant amount of self-belief and self-worth. My aspirations grew. And so, I launched my raft built of dreams and set out on my journey towards the horizon, on the turbulent sea of life, in relentless pursuit of my ultimate dream. I have included the lyrics to some of the songs that I have written over the years but were not recorded, which were inspired by some of my life experiences, some of which I assume some readers may be able to relate. The lyrics to those songs would appear at the very end of the passages of the chapter in which I share those respective experiences.

I accept the probability that my decision to write and publish this book, might be viewed as somewhat audacious by some and perhaps even daring by others, especially in and from my homeland. And particularly those who are the subjects of some of my life experiences. But as audacious and or daring as writing and publishing my life story up to its most recent past at the time of completion and publication may be perceived, for whatever it is worth, I simply felt compelled to share it with not only those in and from my homeland, but also with the world.

As the simple truth is; whomsoever we were, are, or become, relative to any personal, social and or professional statuses we assumed in the past; currently assume or will assume in the future, we were always, are always, and will always be human beings first and foremost. And as human beings and individuals, we all have our own respective life experiences and stories that we wish the world would know. We all have our respective goals, dreams and aspirations...through which we find hope and the will to live; and through the pursuit, achievement and or realization of which we discover not only who we are, but perhaps even more importantly, why we are who we are. Furthermore...what are our life experiences truly worth, if we simply choose to keep them to ourselves?

THIS BOOK IS DEDICATED TO MY WIFE ALICIA

TABLE OF CONTENTS

CHAPTER ONE

THE SIXTIES

MY VERY EARLY CHILDHOOD:
GROWING UP WITH NO FATHER AROUND

I was born Alison Cecil Ayres Jr., to Helen Rosanna Andrews and Ethelbert Alison Ayres Sr. on the 14th day of August 1959, at the district hospital in the southern village of Princes Town on the island of Trinidad, the main island of the twin island Republic of Trinidad and Tobago, which is the southernmost islands of the Caribbean chain of islands.

My mother was born on another Caribbean Island, Grenada, on December 22nd 1931 to Monica Theodorine Thomas who was of African descent, and was also born in Grenada, and Samuel Ignatius Andrews, who was Caucasian. My grandfather Samuel lived in Grenada with other members of his family during that time.

My father, Alison Sr., who departed this life on September 11th 2010 at the age of 80, was also born in Princes Town, Trinidad. My grand-mother Monica immigrated to Trinidad in the late 40s, where she took up residence on the island's oil rich countryside village of Point Fortin, which is in the deep-south of the island.

Sometime thereafter, a teenage Helen also made the journey across to Trinidad from Grenada by sea on a small schooner to join her mother. Several years later she met the man who would be my father. He was a Policeman when they met; and after a period of courtship, they got married.

My mother and father lived together as a married couple in Point Fortin for a while before moving to Princes Town, where my father's father, Samuel Cyrenius Ayres who was also born there lived, until his death in the mid-70s. My father's mother was Evelyn Simon. She was born on the island of Barbados, and immigrated to Trinidad.

I had six siblings; two brothers and four sisters. My brothers are Evans and Brian Ayres, both by mother and father. Evans is my mother's second child, and is four years older than I am. Brian is my mother's last child, and is two years younger than I am. My four sisters were Cheryl by mother, who was her first child and who was five years older than I am, and Sandra, by both mother and father, who is my mother's third child, and who is three years older than I am. Cheryl departed this life on January 15th 2003.

My other two sisters are by father. They were both also born in Trinidad. They are Carol Mason, who lives in New York and another Cheryl, whose last name is Mclawrence, who lived in London for many years, but has since returned to our homeland and now resides in Tobago, Trinidad's sister island. I first met my sisters Carol Mason and Cheryl Mclawrence sometime during the mid-80s and early 90s respectively. They are both older than I am.

I would eventually discover that "Alison" was not a very common name for a male, when teased at times about having "a girl name" during my Trinidad school days. Then there is my last name "Ayres" that many jokingly interpret as "ears". Still, I really did not mind my name at all; that is, until I grew to absolutely resent and despise my father. I regretted having my name then, because it was also his.

And since "Lewrick", a very unique and distinctly male name, which I really like, appears as my first name on my Baptismal certificate, I had thoughts of changing my first and last names at times during the course of my adulthood, using my mother's last name to become Lewrick Cecil Andrews. But in the end, I decided to live with my birth name.

Naturally, I cannot recall most of my very early childhood experiences. However, I have somehow managed to retain vivid memories of a few. Most of what I would come to learn about the very early period

2

of my life was revealed to me by my mother and a very close relative. No reference could be made to my father with regards to the aforementioned.

And that's because while I heard quite a lot about him, I never did hear about anything from my father, since he was not around while I was growing up. Even through adulthood up to the time of his death in 2010, I had not heard much from my father.

I personally have not retained any early childhood memories of my mother and father living together under the same roof with us kids, but I understand that they actually did at times during my infancy, and into and during my toddler years when we lived in Princes Town.

While he did not do so almost throughout its entirety, in fairness to Alison Sr., he did in fact make a quite significant contribution to my life at a critical stage; details of which are revealed in a later passage. It is a contribution for which I will remain eternally grateful.

And while there will always be an undeniable biological bond between us, our father and son relationship never went beyond that biological bond. I cannot honestly say that I ever felt any real emotional connection with my father during his time on this earth, at any time during the course of my lifetime. So much so that I felt no significant degree of distress or sadness, upon hearing the news of his sudden passing back in 2010.

The one thing that was very clear about my very early childhood is that it was rough; extremely rough. Of that period, I would learn of my father's infidelity, with the other female being the priority in his life. It resulted in him spending the majority of his time at her residence with her and her kids, none of which were his, while neglecting his own biological offspring.

Not having heard much about anything from him while he was alive, I never got his side of that story or any other family related matters. He never ever volunteered any such information and I simply never inquired. Therefore, my personal opinion of my father, while formed to some degree on what I had come to learn about him from my mother and some close relatives from both sides, is in the final analysis, based on what I had come to learn through my personal experiences with him.

Those experiences were in the form of limited personal interactions that I had with him over the years during short, infrequent visits to his places of work; initially, when he became a new car salesman, subsequent to him resigning from the police service; and when he eventually became the owner of his own car rental company, with locations in both San Fernando in the south and in the capital city of Port of Spain in north Trinidad. There were also short, infrequent visits to his home subsequent to him becoming a business owner.

My visits to his workplace during the period when he was a new car salesman, would have been when my mother would have sent me to him for financial assistance, which would have been desperately needed at the time. I always left empty-handed. There were about a half dozen visits to his home in Chaguanas central Trinidad, during my adult years.

What I would learn about my father through my limited conversations and interactions with him over the years was that he was quite intelligent and articulate, self-assured, had a love for fast cars and listening to music; and he most definitely loved living in luxury. So, given that what I would personally come to learn about him was more in general terms, I cannot honestly say that I really knew the man in the true sense of the word.

Our address while living in Princes Town during my infancy and toddler years was Ayres Avenue. It was so named because my father's father owned much of the land along that geographical stretch, which was connected to the street named Lothian's Road, which was connected to the main thoroughfare.

Of those very early childhood years, I would learn that we were literally knocking from pillar to post. And because of my father's neglect, and usually without money since she was a housewife, my mother really struggled to provide for us on her own.

4

She told me that she often had to visit the Canteen at the Police Station in San Fernando where my father was stationed at the time, to seek sustenance for us kids; and that his colleagues always obliged her, as they were fully aware of our family's state of affairs as it related to our father.

She also told me that when the situation became too overwhelming, she would drop us off at my father's other residence in San Fernando where he lived with the other female, which is about a 30 to 40 minutes drive from Princes Town. She would then head down to her mother's countryside residence in Point Fortin to seek solace, which was over an hour's drive by car from San Fernando.

I understand that in anger, most of the times my father would then simply drive us and drop us off to where he knew our mother would be, which was at our grandmother's Point Fortin residence. Our grandmother's residence served as our house of refuge then, and would continue to serve as such over many years.

One of those occasions when our father drove us to Point Fortin after our mother had dropped us off at his San Fernando residence, is one of the few very early childhood memories I have managed to retain. My sister Cheryl, the eldest of my mother's five children, had been living with our grandmother since her very early childhood. My mother had dropped off my two other older siblings Evans and Sandra and me, at the San Fernando residence where my father lived with the other female.

As he usually did, my father became enraged by our mother's action. With absolutely no concern for our safety whatsoever, my father then drove us down to Point Fortin and simply dropped us off at the side of the road in the dark of night, in front of one of our grandmother's friend's house some distance from our grandmother's, with our suitcase (also called a Grip back then) containing our clothes and drove off.

Our grandmother's friend, one Miss Murray, who knew us, upon hearing the commotion came out and upon recognizing who we were, took us to our grandmother's house. That event, as vividly as I remembered it, was corroborated by a very close relative who was also living with our grandmother at the time. I was about to turn 3 years old at the time.

On August 31st 1962, just 2 weeks and 3 days after my 3rd birthday, my beloved homeland, the twin island nation of Trinidad and Tobago, gained independence from Britain. One Dr. Eric Eustace Williams, would become the then newly independent nation's first Prime Minister.

At that time my grandmother, having since been married for many years, shared the Point Fortin residence with her husband Septimus Bowen, Patricia or just "Patsy" the youngest of her three children who were all girls, my sister Cheryl and my cousin Michael, aka "BoPeep", the son and oldest child of my grandmother's first daughter Rita, who passed away in 1993.

They occupied what was originally a one-story house, and thereafter occupied the three-bedroom top floor of the new two-story house after the original one-story was renovated. The ground floor was divided into two separate apartments, which my grandmother rented out. Like my mother, both Aunty Rita and Michael, aka BoPeep, were also born in Grenada and immigrated to Trinidad.

My mother also told me about a very serious incident, that occurred during one of the occasions when she had dropped us off at my father's other residence, of which I have no recollection. According to my mother, I was pushed down a section of the flight of concrete stairs leading up to the one-story concrete residence, by one of my father's stepchildren, and hit my stomach and was seriously injured.

My mother revealed that upon her return to the residence to pick us up that evening, which was not very long after the incident had occurred, I complained about stomach pain and told her what had happened. Upon checking, she discovered a bruise on my stomach that felt even more painful when touched. She immediately took me to the San Fernando General Hospital.

I had suffered abdominal trauma. My mother in relating the story, told me that the Doctor who attended to me at the hospital explained to her that the injury may have been too severe for such a small child like myself to overcome and therefore, there was a chance that I might not survive it. But by the will of "The Higher Power", I did.

One of the other memories I have managed to retain from my very early childhood, may simply be because it was a severe undeserved "cut arse" (beating) I received with a Tambran whip (a thin branch cut from a Tambran (Tamarind?) tree) while attending kindergarten. I say undeserved because I was totally innocent of what I had been accused of.

I had just turned 4 years old on August 14th. Two months later in October 1963, my mother would leave Trinidad for New York on what would be her very first overseas trip, to seek work so she would be better able to provide for her children. With Cheryl already living with her since very early childhood, our mother left the other four of us, that is, Evans, Sandra, Brian, and I with our grandmother in Point Fortin.

Before my mother left, in a move initiated by my grandmother, I was enrolled at one Miss Thomas' kindergarten, which was located in Mahaica, which was about a 20 minutes walk from my grandmother's residence.

Miss Thomas operated her school from the ground floor of her two-story concrete residence. It was not uncommon for such early learning institutions to be housed on the ground floors of private residences back in those days in my homeland. There was a football field located directly across the street from Miss Thomas' residence.

I could not actually see it from the schoolyard, because there was the combination of a 7 feet and a 9 feet high wire and bamboo fence around it, with the 9 feet bamboo fence on the inside of the 7 feet wire fence. But one could have seen through both fences in some spots from the street. Unknown to me at the time, in addition to the Point Fortin Roman Catholic Church, that very football field would become my second place of worship.

Miss Thomas was an extremely strict teacher. I was terrified of her. I received the undeserved and "unforgettable Tambran whip cut arse" one day during a recess period. There was an almond tree in the adjoining neighbor's yard to the right of Miss Thomas'. It was close enough to Miss Thomas' boundary line wire fence, that some of the branches hung over into her yard.

That day, some of my classmates were "pelting (throwing) stones" at the tree trying to pick off almonds. One of the stones that were thrown, went all the way through the branches of the tree and found its way to Miss Thomas' neighbor's window and "pliting!"; a glass pane was shattered.

Miss Thomas, who was upstairs inside her residence at the time, apparently heard the sound of the shattering glass, and upon hearing the commotion between us kids that followed, "fly outside" (to come in a rush). Upon discovering what had occurred, she asked in a most furious tone, "who pelt dat stone?" Acting on impulse, knowing exactly what was to follow, the boy who threw the stone pointed directly at me.

That was all Miss Thomas needed. She rushed down the stairs and into the class room, quickly emerging with Tambran whip in hand as she walked briskly towards us, but with her eyes trained on me. I instantly burst into tears while repeatedly pleading my innocence. But it was to no avail. In a fit of rage, Miss Thomas put what was an unforgettable "cut arse" on mih (me).

And as if that wasn't enough, Miss Thomas called her over the telephone and reported the incident to my grandmother, who everyone in the household affectionately called "Nennie". Apparently, they knew each other well and were cut from the same cloth so to speak.

Nennie gave me a second "cut arse" upon my return home from school that evening. Back in those days, getting licks, justified or not, whether at home or at school, was a normal part of disciplining children during the growing up process.

Back then, it was also quite normal for incidents of misbehavior involving kids to be reported by any adult or heads of any household who would have witnessed such, to any adult or heads of other households, to make the other respective adults or heads of households aware of what the kids from the respective households were up to, if they would not have become aware otherwise.

I was about to turn 5 years old when my mother returned to Trinidad in July of '64 after spending 9 months in New York. Not long thereafter, we had another change of address. Our relocation took us to La Romaine, San Fernando, which was some distance on the outskirts of the center of Trinidad's second city. San Fernando as mentioned prior, was then over an hour's drive by car from Point Fortin. Our sister Cheryl, then 10 years old, continued to live with our grandmother in Point Fortin.

Our new residence was one of two small one-bedroom ground floor apartments of the two-story concrete dwelling located on a street named Peter Trace. There was a cinema located on the corner of Peter Trace and the main thoroughfare. The cinema was owned by one Mr. Chandru, who lived in a house situated on the premises. He also owned several animals including a monkey, which provided a mini spectacle and entertainment for us kids.

There was only one bed in our apartment on which my mother slept with my sister Sandra. Evans, Brian, and I slept on the bedroom floor on very old, mostly torn clothing that couldn't be worn anymore. Except for when we were at Nennie's, sleeping on the floor was normal throughout my early childhood.

Our mother did hair dressing inside the small living room to try to make ends meet after completing a hair dressing course. In those days, to create her hair-styles she used two metal hot combs and curling irons, which were kept hot by the fire of a small one burner kerosene stove, that remained lit throughout the entire hair styling process. So, while one was in use the other would always be hot and ready when the one in use got too cold to affect the style she was creating.

During our time living in La Romaine, Evans, Sandra, and I attended St. Paul's AC Primary School in San Fernando. At some point, Evans then attended a school called Southern Academy, which was not far from

St. Paul's. Brian, my other brother and the youngest of my mother's 5 children, attended pre-school in the immediate vicinity of Peter Trace.

He and I went to Church almost every Sunday with our mother. A gentleman with a car who befriended our mother usually took us to and from church. The church was called The Open Bible Church and was located very close to the St. Paul's AC School. Back then, going to church on Sunday mornings was almost second nature. We also attended Sunday school immediately after church. I remember my mother teaching Sunday school classes on a few occasions.

With no father around and being the big brother, I naturally looked up to Evans. He and I developed an extremely close bond from very early on. Brian and I were close as well. My sister Sandra and I had less of a close bond.

I remember her as being a bit of a bully during those early years, with vivid memories of occasions when she would cover my head with a pillow and lie on top of it, at times when I would be lying down on our mother's bed. While I would be literally stifling and frantically trying to escape in desperate need of air, she would be laughing until eventually getting off the pillow after several seconds, which to me seemed like an eternity at the time.

There were no public transportation buses on a regular schedule on our route. With our mother unable to afford the cost of two-way transportation by taxi on a regular basis, my two older siblings and I usually had to walk the approximately 4 to 5 miles return journey from St. Paul's AC Primary School on Harris Street in San Fernando, back to our Peter Trace La Romaine home. On much more than a few occasions, we had to walk to and from school. I was just 5 years old at the time.

And with my mother also unable to afford timely replacements, it was normal for me to do so while wearing my Bata "Crepe-soles", with gaping holes at the bottom as a result of the wear and tear from the many miles they covered. They were the absolute cheapest sneakers on the market in those days.

My socks would have also gotten holes as well. So, to protect the bare balls of my small feet from making direct contact with the ground, and possibly being injured by pebbles and other sharp objects as I walked over them on the journey to and from school, my mother would usually cut pieces of cardboard from boxes with a scissors in the same shape and insert them as in-soles. That worked okay in dry weather, but did not stop my socks and feet from getting completely soaked when the ground was wet, whenever it rained.

On the occasions when my mother could have afforded it, we would enjoy the absolute welcome luxury of traveling to and from school by taxi. I usually sat on Evans' lap to avoid our mother having to pay the fare for all three of us. At other times we got "a drop" (a lift) to school from the gentleman with a car who had befriended her.

On our walks back home from school, we took a route along the train line for a short distance, where the trains transporting sugar cane in those days ran, en route to the factory. If a train was passing at the time and stopped or slowed down almost to a halt on the track for whatever reason, oblivious to the danger, Evans and I would run up to it and hurriedly pull pieces of sugarcane from the car that was closest to us, which we then shared with Sandra and consumed on the walk home.

Back then, Fry's Cocoa, or cocoa that was grated to make cocoa tea, sugar-water (water sweetened with brown sugar) and "bush tea" (tea made from shrubs, including one I remember called shining bush, which grew wildly in the yard), served with fried or roast bake or home-made bread with Blue Band butter and sometimes with Smoked Herring or canned Sardine was breakfast and dinner. Rice porridge or flour porridge was also on the breakfast or dinner menu.

While the fried or roast bake were made in an iron pot, the "home-made bread" was baked in a small portable oven. The oven was made of galvanize material and had one steel-wire shelf inside, on which the dough in the baking pans were placed for baking.

The bottom of the oven was fully opened with a small glass window constructed into the door at the front to monitor the baking process. My mother baked the bread by placing the oven directly on the small lighted two burner kerosene stove she cooked on. And there was hardly any buying of snacks. So, my mother would usually make local delicacies like Kurma, Fudge and Sugar-Cake to serve as such.

The lunch menu on any given day was either yellow split peas and rice, split peas soup with flour dumplings, saltfish and rice, Ochro and rice, Bhagi and rice, Dasheen bush and rice with pig tail, Bodi and rice, Corn Beef and rice, breadfruit and saltfish, ground provisions or flour dumplings served with saltfish. Apart from the split peas soup, the Corn Beef and rice, the ground provisions and the dumplings, the other menu items didn't really appeal to me. So, on many occasions, just boiled white rice with Blue Band butter, which melted into the hot rice was usually my preferred lunch meal.

Lunch for me at school at St Paul's AC was usually a slice of what was known as "belly-full cake"; so named because said slice was quite filling. It was usually washed down with a sweet-drink (soda). The two items together would have cost a total of around 12 to 15 cents, if my memory serves me correctly.

Sometimes lunch would be just the slice of belly-full cake with water. And at least once a week, students received a glass of milk with three sweet biscuits (vanilla cookies) courtesy of the school at no cost. I always looked forward to that weekly treat.

From that very early age I really did not take a liking to the solid, hot, lunch meal. I much preferred consuming what was called "Dry Stuff", especially anything made with flour. And there was also a very early trend of not wanting to consume chicken, most types of red meats and sea foods, when they were available, which would continue into and during my teenage years and into adulthood.

On the occasions when I did consume any of them while growing up, I usually had to be forced. Much later on in my life, I would come to learn that not consuming lots of red meat from an early age may not have been such a bad thing after all.

In addition to products made with flour, as an adult, the foods I prefer include fruits and vegetables, most milk drinks and plain milk with or without a variety of specific Cereals, and porridges including Cream of Wheat and Corn Meal in particular. I could go days without consuming the so called "solid hot lunch meals" and have regularly done so over the course of my lifetime.

When I do consume the solid meal, which I have been more consistent doing since my mid to late 30s, Tuna, ground turkey, boneless chicken or Shrimp served with rice, most pasta dishes or ground provision, especially dasheen, green fig, eddoes and potatoes with mixed vegetables, lentil or pigeon peas or red beans is preferable.

So, it is therefore more than likely that my very early childhood eating habits and preferred diet, which more or less continued into my teenage years and more than it should have throughout my adulthood, would have accounted for my relatively small physical stature.

While living in La Romaine, we got a few visits from my mother's older sister Rita. She usually brought along my cousin David, the fourth of her then five children. David and I grew very close during our earlier stints in Point Fortin. Of all my relatives, I shared the closest relationships with brothers David and Michael, aka "BoPeep".

The period for which we lived in La Romaine was not very long. And we would relocate on two more occasions within the geographical area of San Fernando. St. Andrews Avenue Cocoyea Village, just on the outskirts of the city center was our next stop.

I distinctly remember the Trinidad visit of Haile Selassie, the Emperor of Ethiopia during that time. I got to see him in person, as I accompanied my mother as one of the thousands who lined the streets to get a view of him during a motorcade in his honor.

But there is another experience that stands out in my mind from the time when we lived in Cocoyea. And it was a horrible one. It was the day that I witnessed my mother being physically abused by her gentle-man friend, who sometimes gave us lifts to school when we lived in La Romaine and had since been around.

What I saw him do to my mother that day, filled me with extreme anger towards him; more so as I was totally helpless to do anything about it, being that I was just a kid at the time. It was the very first and only time that I had witnessed any type of physical abuse of my mother by any male companion. Many years later, apart from mental, emotional, and verbal, I would learn that my father had also been physically abusive to my mother.

Our third and last address in San Fernando was St. Vincent Street, which was just about a 15 to 20 minutes walk to the heart of the city's main shopping area. Back then Batman, with his side-kick Robin, was one of the hit TV shows and one of the favorites for us as kids.

With our mother unable to afford a television, I remember Evans and I would immediately stop whatever we were engaged in at the time, upon merely hearing the very distinct guitar riff at the very beginning of the Batman theme song from a neighbor's television.

We would then make the 100 meters dash for his then best friend Garth's house up the street, hoping to get there before the other kids who also did not have TV sets in their respective homes did, in order to get preferred seating.

A television set, though only showing in black and white, was then a major luxury item that mostly the well-to-do could have afforded. Garth's parents apparently fell into that category, and so allowed most of the kids in the immediate vicinity that had no television sets in their homes, to view our favorite shows from through their living room ventilation parti-tion, while sitting outside in the yard.

Garth also reared homing pigeons. Being around them, I developed a love for that species of bird; and in addition to tropical fish, would rear some myself together with ordinary pigeons during my teenage years. There was also a neighbor who lived directly across the street from us whose name was Allec who had a pet Python, which he allowed us to pet or hold.

I distinctly remember our respective apartments being without electricity during our years residing in San Fernando and environs. A Kerosene Lamp and or candles were the source of lighting at nights. During those days we also had no inside toilet or bathroom.

While I never took night time baths back then, if I needed to move my bowels during the night, I used a white enamel utensil called a "posey". A "posey", which looks like a hugely oversized tea-cup, was indeed a very popular utensil among the local poor like ourselves back then. Wiping my butt with a damp piece of Gazette paper after moving my bowels was normal back then.

As indicated in the prologue, I was always extremely close to my mother. So close that I remember that during those early years, I would always start crying on almost every occasion that my mother would be getting dressed to go out, just so that she would take me along with her, which was usually into San Fernando's city center itself, or just on its outskirts to visit one of her friends.

Sometimes she did; other times she did not. When she did, and at times when it was affordable, I suppose, she would take me to Woolworth, which was located at Library Corner, and buy me my then favorite snack, which was an Oh Henry nuts and chocolate bar. When she did not take me with her, I usually threw a tantrum and continued crying long after she had left.

During those years, which were defined by economic and domestic hardships and instability, sometime during one of the annual 2 months long July to September school holidays, Evans, Sandra, and I spent some time at my father's San Fernando residence with his mother. She lived in a self-contained one room lodging on the ground floor of what had long since become my father's permanent residence, where he lived with the other female and her children.

The address was 10 Dasent Street, Les Effort East, San Fernando. I knew my father's mother only as Miss Simon and addressed her as such. She had a different accent than that of a Trinidadian, which I later learnt was Barbadian.

I remember she, Evans, Sandra, and I having to sleep crossways on her bed, as it could not accommodate all four of us lengthways. I also remember Miss Simon having to put a wooden stool with a cushion on top to rest her feet on to sleep at nights, otherwise they would hang off the edge of the bed. Meanwhile, my father lived in luxury on the top floor with his female companion and her children.

I have however, retained some fond memories of the time we stayed with Miss Simon, who treated us quite well. She was making ends meet by baking and selling pastries; namely Currents-Rolls, Coconut Tarts, and Beef Pies. They were all very tasty, and I practically lived on them while we stayed at her residence. Then there was a huge drain across the street from the house that we played in, when the water level was very low or when it was completely dry.

And as she herself could not afford one, and with our father not seeing it fit to provide one, Miss Simon used to take me with her to one of her friend's residence once or twice a week, during the very early hours of the night for some television viewing entertainment.

Then there were also the fun-filled evenings Evans and I spent at Skinner Park, which was about a ten to 15 minutes walk from the residence. There we were learning to play lawn tennis. Sometimes we watched the cyclists train on the cycle track encircling the football field.

Before that time spent at Miss Simon's, and in between our early stints at Nennie's Point Fortin residence, I remember me staying for relatively shorts periods elsewhere, including Marabella just outside of San Fernando with a really nice relative named Rita Fredrick, who then lived with her husband Joseph and their son Jude.

I also spent time at 11 Bhaggan Avenue, San Juan Port of Spain with one of my father's sisters Eileen, who was one of my favorite Aunts. I remember also having had very short stints in Prizgar Lands Laventille at the residence of one of Nennie's sisters Cynthia Hercules, who we called "Aunty Cynty". She lived at the residence with her six children.

An effort to also have me stay with my Godfather Trevlin Lovell and his wife Gloria for a period of time, did not work out, because I cried continuously from the minute my mother dropped me off late that evening and left. My Godfather even had me ride around on the veranda on a tricycle during the course of that night to try to stop me from crying. But even that did not work. My mother had to return to pick me up the following morning. At the time my Godfather and his wife lived in Vistabella, which was the town just before Marabella.

At the very beginning of August 1967, just 1 week and a few days before my 8th birthday, having spent about 3 years living in the nation's second city of San Fernando and its environs, and out of necessity I suppose, we made what turned out to be a permanent move back to Nennie's Point Fortin residence.

For me that meant both great and not so great news. The great news was that I was once again reunited with my cousins. The not-so-great news was that I was then back in Nennie's clutches. She was strict without compromise when it came to dealing with any of the kids in the household. She struck a certain degree of fear in most of the kids, but struck a special fear in me.

For example, if Nennie felt that I did something wrong, or if I perhaps forgot to attend to some daily household chore and found myself playing outside with friends, then I most certainly had punishment coming. She would literally try to "twist-off" either of my ears while squeezing either of them extremely tightly between her thumb and index finger. At the same time, she would mumble words only she could understand as she bit her bottom lip with rage. She had many rules, one of which was that you had to attend church every Sunday morning. But regardless of her being an extremely strict disciplinarian, Nennie most certainly loved and was loved by us all. She was indeed the family's matriarch.

Nennie's address was 10 Adventure Road Point Fortin at the corner of Lyle Street, which was only a short distance from the villages' shopping area. And as it was with most of the Point Fortin community, our neighbors were made up primarily of blacks. But they also included East Indians and Chinese.

To the left of us on Adventure Road were the Maharajs', and next to the Maharajs' were the Katticks; diagonally across from us to the right on Adventure Road were the Mulchars, and living diagonally across the street from us on Lyle Street were the Singhs; all families of East Indian descent.

Directly opposite to us on Lyle was a Chinese shopkeeper and his family. His name was Stanley. I remember he had a daughter whose name was Moy Moy. Not very far up on Lyle were the Laws who were also of Chinese descent. And in the vicinity, there was another Chinese shopkeeper Wong and his family.

It was at both Chinese shops where my cousins David and Annmurie, my younger brother Brian and I, after each chipping in with a few cents, would buy skimmed milk, which was then mix with brown sugar and shared among ourselves and enjoyed as one of our favorite treats.

But, Africans, East Indians, Chinese and others who were of mixed race, were not the only races residing in the community. There were also Caucasian families living in Point Fortin at the time. They however, did not live among the general community. They all lived in the exclusive, strictly residential area called Clifton Hill, where there was the beach, a golf course and a swimming pool. And there was a fairly large open field next to the swimming pool, for any other recreational activities they chose to engage in.

The Caucasian families were all foreigners, whose heads of the respective households were Management or other Senior level employees of the then community-based U.S. Oil Company, Shell, which was the primary employer of residents. Nennie's husband Septimus Bowen, who was affectionately called "God-Seppie" within the household, was employed with Shell and held a senior position. Back then, Point Fortin was a major contributor to the local economy as a major producer of crude oil.

While generally the Point Fortin community was socially diverse, Clifton Hill was best known for its white residents, its golf course and its swimming pool, which was for the exclusive use of said residents. And although located in their immediate vicinity and only a very short distance away for most of them, I personally cannot recall ever seeing any of Clifton Hill's then white residents at the beach, which was open to the public. And boy, did we frequent it.

One of my cousins, the late Anthony James, aka "Sinaman", another of BoPeep's brothers and my older brother Evans, actually started working on the Golf Course as caddies during their mid to late teens. And while Evans eventually left for greener pastures (no pun intended), Sinaman continued caddying into and during his 20s, and developed into a decent golfer.

Within the Point Fortin community, there were at least three gas stations. One was located just at the beginning of the shopping strip called Frisco Junction where there is a round-a-bout; and where there was a black owned furniture store named Mackie John's.

There was a Hospital, Police Station, Fire Station, Post Office, two commercial Banks, three Super Markets; namely, Peiping's, Chang's and Hi Lo, and at least two Pharmacies that I can remember. Peiping's and Chang's Supermarkets were owned by two other Chinese families who were also residents. Close to Hi Lo there was a second round-a-bout.

There were three cinemas, Strand and Metropole and a Drive-In Cinema; a Hardware Store, Bakery, several Bars and or Rum Shops and two other furniture and appliances stores that I can remember; namely American Stores and Huggin's. Bata is the only shoe store that I can remember.

There were several clothing and cloth stores with one called Kallicharran's the most popular among them. There were also several A class tailors and seamstresses, with tailor and seamstress made clothing being very popular back then. There was a Record Store and one sports store called Thompson's, which were also black owned. There were also a few Barber Shops, with Peck's being the most popular, and where I got my haircuts.

Then there was the Market that was always a-buzz with patrons especially on Saturday mornings. There residents could buy a variety of fresh sea foods, meats, fruits, vegetables, ground provisions and naturally grown seasonings and other ingredients, that they needed to prepare that special Sunday Lunch the following day. That menu usually included that favorite weekly national staple of Callaloo, with or without crab, Macaroni Pie, and Potato Salad, which is usually served with rice, which is prepared according to the household's liking.

There was but one place that one could get Fast Food. That was at a family-owned establishment called Comissiong's. On the menu was fried chicken with fries (called chicken and chips in Trinidad back then), which was usually served with the patrons' choice of alcoholic or non-alcohol beverages. Comissiong's was primarily a night spot.

And with the tasty curry delicacy Roti being another favorite local staple, there was the then extremely popular Khan's Roti Shop. And I simply cannot forget Rainbow's Café, that would for many years be my go-to place for another of my favorite milk drinks Peanut Punch. I usually had it with a Biscuit Cake or a Milk Cake, and would have been served by either Joyce, Margaret, or Tara, the Café's three employees, who were always very pleasant and nice to me.

I remember Point having just one restaurant called Kim Far, which was owned by another Chinese family, who were also residents. There was also a park with a fountain as you went past Frisco Junction, where residents could hang out day or night. There were several schools and churches, a Mosque, a Mandir, two cemeteries and a family-owned funeral home called Elite's Funeral Home. There was also a Library, which I used to visit to burrow books to read.

There was also the Dunlop tyre factory, which employed many of the residents. Most of those different business establishments and or landmarks were located on or just off a 1 mile stretch along the main road, which also included the community's shopping area.

And of course, Point Fortin had its fair share of unique characters as well. There are three that comes to mind. The first, who everyone knew as "Pringay", was a fairly aged Special Reserve Police Officer who patrolled the main road. He often used to be teased by the much older boys, since he was too slow to catch any of them. The second is "Melda", a woman, also fairly aged, whose mode of transportation was a donkey cart.

The third is "Selvon". He was a grave digger, who it was said was possessed by an evil spirit after he went to perform some ritual at the cemetery at the midnight hour one night. He roamed the streets of the community and always had a bottle of Bay Rum in hand. He would enter unsuspecting residents' home and steal food from their pots, if they were unaware of his presence.

Upon our relocation from San Fernando to the tranquil Point Fortin countryside, my cousin BoPeep introduced me to the sport of football, in the form of the street version known on the island as "small goal". Little did I know then, the tremendously positive impact the game would have on my life.

I was enrolled at Point Fortin Intermediate Roman Catholic School. I entered in September 1967 in Standard 2 of the established 5 or 6-years attendance structure of the Trinidad and Tobago primary school system, with promotion each year from Standard 1, with Standard 5 or Standard 6 in some instances being a student's final year at the primary school level. My sister Cheryl and my cousin David, who is just nine days older than I am, were already attending what was commonly known as RC School when I was enrolled.

I was fortunate enough to have landed in the class that was being taught by one Miss Cynthia Mungo, who counts as one of two of my all-time favorite teachers during my time in the Trinidad and Tobago school

21

system. Disliking school as much as I did, I thoroughly enjoyed the experience under Miss Mungo's tutelage, and will admit that I sometimes took advantage of her mild-mannered approach.

For instance, if I did not feel like participating in a particular class subject or subjects on any given school day, I would simply feign illness. Miss Mungo would then allow me to lay my head on the desk until I felt better however long it took, which was usually after she was finished teaching the said class subject or subjects on the day. I remember her as always having a bright smile on her face.

Within a year of our relocating permanently to Point Fortin, sadly, Nennie's husband Septimus passed away. I would eventually come to learn that he was always there to assist my mother financially when we were in need, which was very often. I still remember the image of his body lying in the coffin, which was placed in the living room of the residence for public viewing. Being that he was the primary breadwinner during those times, God-Seppie's death brought about major changes within the household, with Nennie leaving for Canada sometime in mid-1969.

With BoPeep already residing there, Aunty Rita, the eldest of Nennie's three daughters and her husband Phillip (last name Charles), who was born in St Vincent, then moved into Nennie's residence with my other cousins David, Anthony aka "Sinaman" and their sister Annmurie, who was Aunty Rita's youngest child at the time.

Before then, they lived in Mahaica, very close to the Mahaica Oval and equally close to where the Drive-In Cinema was located. We often visited them during the day and fairly regularly at nights, when both our families would all sit on a hill a very short distance from where they lived, where we had a clear view of the Drive-In Cinema screen and viewed movies from that location. One movie I remember seeing, if only for the scene where a head was completely chopped off was titled "Beckit".

A total of 14 of us were then occupying the 3-bedroom top floor of Nennie's residence. Her three daughters, Aunty Rita the oldest, my mother and Aunty Patsy the youngest and Aunt Patsy's then infant daughter Valarie; Aunty Rita's husband Phillip; my cousins BoPeep, Anthony, aka "Sinaman", David and Annmurie, who were all Aunty Rita's children, together with my sisters Cheryl and Sandra, brothers Evans and Brian and me. Reynold, Aunty Rita's third child of a then total of five, aka "Broko" because he walked with a limp as a result of Polio, did not live with us at Nennie's residence. I got along extremely well with all my cousins.

Aunty Patsy owned a piano that sat in the living room, which she played fairly often before her father God-Seppie died, but hardly ever played it thereafter. Nennie loved listening to music, and would regularly play records of two of her favorite singers Mariam Makeba and Jim Reeves, on her small portable record player, which also had a radio.

Apart from listening to our very own local Calypso music on the radio, all types of American artistes and their respective genres were also being played. Motown Records recording artistes of the day were really burning up the local radio airwaves and music charts.

The Jackson 5 was my absolute favorite. And like a lot of other kids back then, I idolized Michael. The Jackson 5 and Michael in particular, and the other Motown recording artistes would be my musical influence and inspiration. One Dave Elcock, the then extremely popular local radio DJ, had a weekly Top 10 countdown on Sunday evenings, that I always looked forward to listening to.

While everyone else within the household was Catholic at the time, Uncle Phillip was a Spiritual Baptist. I can remember at least one occasion when my cousins David and Annmurie and my younger brother Brian and I participated in one of his Church's activities. It was an Easter concert event, where we played out the crucifixion, with Uncle Phillip himself, portraying Jesus Christ.

Uncle Phillip also liked to sing a lot and owned an acoustic guitar, with which he accompanied himself. He provided the musical accompaniment for us kids when we would often engage in our own singing competition. It was a version of a then extremely popular local talent

23

show for kids in those days, which was named after its host, who was popularly known as "Aunty Kay". There was most definitely a newfound sense of domestic stability and total sense of happiness since we relocated to Nennie's residence.

I was then beginning to explore and develop my gift of art, and would draw quite often on any clear pieces of paper I could find. My football skills were also quickly developing from the small goal games that were played almost daily on Lyle Street or Baptist Road. BoPeep, or sometimes just simply "Peep", who is 12 years older than I am, became my mentor. At the time he played competitive football in the community minor-league at a field very close to Nennie's residence named Cobo Park.

I remember going to see him play when the games then moved to another field nearby, where the Point Fortin Police Station now stands. It was an absolute quagmire of really thick, heavy, smelly mud when it rained; and a hard bumpy surface when it was dry. The name of the team he played for was Flamingoes. Their kits were red, reflecting the color of the bird itself.

I also remember a couple of the other teams by name; one being Spartacs and the other Egyptian Tigers. They wore green and black and yellow and black respectively, if my memory serves me correctly. Some of us youngsters would eventually play on that football field, usually on a Saturday morning.

Back then, the Point Fortin based Shell Oil Company had a football team that participated in the Southern Football League (SFL); a league for teams based in south Trinidad; and the deep south country side community was producing players of the very highest caliber.

Players such as Leroy "Dilly" DeLeon, Warren "Archie" Archibald, Steve "Smell" David, Anthony "Crapo" Douglas, Wilfred "Bound-To-Score" Cave, Leo "Twinkle-Toes" Brewster, Sydney "Pusher" Augustine, Dick Furlong, Kenny "KJ" Joseph, Henry Quanvie and Keith Douglas, the older brother of Anthony among others. Most of them represented the

Trinidad & Tobago senior men's national football team, with Dilly first doing so as a 17-year-old. They were all my local idols.

I have retained vivid memories of Dilly dribbling past opponents at will, numerous times during a game. Often times, he would also freeze an opponent by standing on his left foot while shaking his right ankle and foot over the ball, daring his opponent to try to tackle it. Any such attempt usually left said opponent embarrassed, as Dilly would quickly shift the ball away from the lounging feet of the said opponent.

Memories of Archie dribbling at top speed towards a defender, then slowing almost to a stop, then with an outward burst of deep breaths which were released from his nostrils, which spectators could hear, blowing past said defender with his explosive burst of speed.

Memories of Crapo unleashing his thunderbolt shots from outside the box, stinging the goalkeeper's palms or ending up in the back of the net; of Twinkle Toes flying down the wing, skipping past defenders, his fleet-footed propulsion distorting his big afro hair style into all different shapes as it blew wildly in the wind; of Wilfred running on to through passes and hitting one time low and hard into either corner of the net with either foot; of Dick taking the ball on his chest and turning in one motion, then shaking off defenders as he dribbled down the right wing. Oh, what memories.

Leroy DeLeon, Warren Archibald, Steve David, Anthony Douglas and I believe also Leo Brewster, all went on to play professionally and excel in the North American Soccer League (NASL). During that time, the NASL was also graced with the presence of players such as the king himself "Pele", Germany's legend and icon Franz Beckenbauer, George Best the Northern Ireland great, and other top players of that era.

Most of the youngsters within the Point Fortin community who played football, including myself of course, aspired to emulate those local legends. Apart from what I was taught by my cousin BoPeep, it was from watching them in action and on a few occasions playing among some of them, that I learnt more of the skills and how to play "The Beautiful

Game". BoPeep would himself play with some of them in the national football league for our community-based team Point Fortin Civic Center, which was formed after the Shell team was eventually dissolved.

As mentioned earlier, my initial introduction to the game came in the form of the street version known on the island as "small goal"; the reason being that the goals that are used are very small. They were usually made with two 3 to 4 pounds stones (rocks) placed approximately 3 feet apart in the middle of the narrow street.

The size of the playing area extended beyond the actual width of the street (about 13 ft.), to include the shallow drains on both sides, and was up to 25 to 30 meters in length. We eventually changed the goals from the two stones to a single empty grapefruit or orange juice can, which was approximately 5 inches high x 3 1/2 inches in diameter, which players had to hit with the ball to register a goal. BoPeep would sometimes play with all the youngsters against the older fellas.

The youngsters included my cousin David and me, Ronnie Brathwaite, Shawn Bea, Dane Myers, Kerl Lewis and brothers Anthony, aka "Sugars", and Russell Monroe, the nephews of Steve David. Sugars, though an extremely talented player with blinding speed and a powerful shot, chose athletics over a football career, and developed into one of Trinidad and Tobago's top 100-meter sprinters.

While games were played almost every evening, the big "Small Goal" games usually took place on Saturday and Sunday evenings, when all the older fellas came out to play. And that would be after we all watched superstars like George Best and others on Star Soccer (the then English First Division) on Saturday mornings, albeit on black and white television. Thankfully, Nennie owned one. There were very few Black players playing in the English First Division then.

The participants for our big "Small Goal" games included BoPeep, my older brother Evans, the John brothers, George, aka "heads", Trevor, aka "Popeye" and Ronald, aka "Sluggo", "Tony Sis", Keith "SanJuanman" Alexander, "Sinaman", Dion Miller, David, and I and some of the other youngsters.

The games were extremely competitive and went on for up to two hours. The then ball of choice was a black and white Wembley brand rubber ball, named after the famous Wembley Stadium in England. It was extremely bouncy on the hard asphalt road surface, which served to improve our ball control and technical skills immensely.

Point Fortin during the 60s and 70s, was a community totally consumed by and obsessed with sports in general and football in particular, with the Mahaica Oval being the hub. The little deep south Trinidad community would have then been well known for its crude oil production.

But it was at the time, also producing some of the twin island nation's top athletes in track and field, basketball and especially in football as mentioned earlier. Victor "Voot" O' Garro and Larry "Engine" Belfon were among the outstanding basketball players, who then also represented the Trinidad and Tobago national basketball team.

During those days, while football was my absolute favorite sporting activity, I also participated in several other sporting disciplines together with my cousin David and the other youths from the immediate area, which the older fellas named "Georgia".

Although we were under British rule before gaining our independence, the Georgia naming of our immediate neighborhood was indicative of the strong American influence from very early on. They actually installed a sign on a lamp post that read "Welcome To Georgia" at the corner of Lyle Street and Baptist Road, which was also their usual "liming" spot at nights.

So, apart from playing football, which we did the majority of the time, we would also play wind-ball (tennis ball) cricket, basketball and run races in the street. Flying kites and riding scooters and box-carts, all of which we made ourselves, pitching marbles and spinning Tops and Yo-Yos were also our other pastimes.

Some of the sporting activities and pastimes took place in someone else's yard. The basketball ring for instance, was constructed in a next-door neighbor's yard that was not fenced. His name was Robert Bernard, but most people called him by his nickname, which was "Dub". He lived in a small wooden house on Lyle Street, directly behind Nennie's residence, which was fenced.

His was also the official marble-pitching yard for the youngsters living in the immediate vicinity. However, if you ever became good enough, you would finally graduate to one Mr. London's yard on Baptist Road.

That was our neighborhood's "Marble Pitching Mecca". That was the place where one matched their marble pitching skills against the very best; including Mr. London himself, who, though already considered a relatively old man by the youngsters then, was the absolute king.

The marble ring in Mr. London's yard was at least 3½ to 4 feet in diameter. It was the biggest marble pitching ring you would have seen anywhere. The pitching area was surrounded by about three to four relatively small wooden houses including Mr. London's. There was always a crowd of onlookers on hand, especially when Mr. London himself was in action.

His sons Michael aka "Wylo" and Ken were also extremely good at pitching, the latter and younger of the two with whom my cousin David and I had many duels. Then there were the other top dogs like Popeye, my cousin Sinaman, Krishna Singh and Dion Miller, just to name a few.

Two other favorite community pastimes were going to cinema and going to the Clifton Hill beach, where most would have learnt how to swim. In fact, going to the Clifton Hill beach was much more than just a community pastime. Like sports, going to the beach, especially over the weekends, was an integral part of the Point Fortin lifestyle. It was another one of those places where we had lots of fun, including honing our skills playing beach football.

There were two different routes to get to the Clifton Hill beach. One route took you through the residential area that was exclusive to the white folks. The other route took you past the Shell oil refinery, with some of the huge tanks that stored the oil, scattered across the landscape on both sides of the road.

When taking the route through the residential area you were well advised to stay on course. Any diversion off course, usually drew the attention of the Shell "Guard Force" who policed that particular area 24/7, for the purpose of providing round-the-clock security for the white folks who were then residing there.

The members of the Guard Force were known to most, since they lived within the Point Fortin community and environs. During those days, any so called "trespassing" anywhere in Clifton Hill by the so called "residents from the outside", was usually met with stern warnings from the Guard Force.

Sometimes, depending on the level of the so called "trespass", one might be detained. However, that did not stop residents, including our crew, from trespassing anyway to pick mangoes, which grew in the Clifton Hill area.

I usually accompanied my older brother Evans or BoPeep, sometimes together with some of the other older boys from the block to the beach, on regular occasions during the July to September school holidays, and on Saturdays and or Sundays otherwise, until I became old enough to go alone. Sometimes we went to the beach as early as 4:00 a.m. On occasions, most of us from our household went together, which was usually on the weekends.

Clifton Hill's white residents eventually left sometime in the early to mid-70s, when the Trinidad and Tobago government acquired the local operations of Shell Trinidad Limited, and formed the Trinidad and Tobago Oil Company Limited (TRINTOC). Today there is still a beach although not the one I frequented while growing up. As for the golf course and the swimming pool; I have no idea if they still exist.

And what I remember as being just an open playing field back in the day, was converted into a football field. I had the absolute thrill of playing in a game there in the late 70s, in the community minor league competition for the team from the community which was called Self-Help, when it was still a bit of a novelty to play on that particular football field. The captain of the Self-Help team was popularly known as "Big Rich". I actually scored a goal (never mind it was just a simple tap in from close range) as we achieved victory on the day.

I had then been enjoying a quite normal childhood since we relocated permanently from San Fernando to Nennie's Point Fortin residence. Christmases were then being celebrated with not just one, but with at least two gifts that were affordable of course. My gifts were usually a Wembley football with either a drawing pad and water color paint with paint brush, or a Xylophone, or a Cap Gun with a Gun Sack, for which I would engage in another pastime of "Stick 'em up", with friends from the immediate vicinity.

My temper tantrums were also being quelled into dormancy; and my personal eating habits improved some. So, for me, Point Fortin's country and sporting lifestyle was offering the things that I was not able to enjoy while we resided elsewhere. I even had my first early childhood girl crush during my Point Fortin years of the very late 60s. Her name was Gail.

I attended Point Fortin Intermediate Roman Catholic School for four years. Some of my class mates during that time whose names I can remember include Peter "Brain" James, Gregory Graham, Christopher Smith, Learie Daniel, Timothy Abraham, Donald Emmanuel, Errol James, David Dawson, Andrew Hamilton, Nicky Williams, Eric Farrell, Garvin Chacon, Arnold John, Clive Romeo, Rawle De Freitas, Marlon Bennett, Eric Caberra, Michael Baptiste, Deane Bowen, Mathew Alexander, Gem Mc Donald, Lila Rodriguez, and Charmaine Foster.

I was closest with Peter James, since we met almost every day after school at the venue, when I eventually graduated football-wise to the lush green fields of the Mahaica Oval. There, the young aspirants engaged in small-goal games, which we would play with leather footballs.

I did not own a pair of football boots during those days because my mother couldn't afford to buy me one. So, I played barefooted as did some of the other players, with my then treasured pair of rubber flip-flops, either being held one in each hand, or left sitting on the grass off to the side of the playing area. The pair of sneakers I would have owned at any time then was strictly for school. I could have only used it to play football when it was replaced with a new pair when it became too worn out for me to wear to school.

Peter "Brain" James, Neville "Villa" Fredrick and Barry Hackett were the standout youth players of the day among my age group. I was most certainly talented, but not as talented as they were at the time.

Like those played on the streets and on the Clifton Hill beach, the small-goal games at Mahaica Oval were also extremely competitive. They were played off to the side of the football field in front of the main Pavilion or behind either of the goal posts, while the Civic Center senior team players practiced on the main playing area, in preparation for their Southern Football League (SFL) and eventually National Football League (NFL) games, when the NFL was introduced. The NFL games were usually played on Wednesdays and Saturdays, in the established home and away format.

Back then, Mahaica Oval used to be absolutely buzzing with football and various other sporting activities, including basketball, the community's then second most popular sport; and cricket and athletics when in season, from around 4:00 p.m. to 6:30 p.m. on week days.

Basketball activities, which took place on the court built right next to the football field, usually went deep into the nights since there were flood lights. Unfortunately, there were no flood lights for the football field during those days.

At best, I was a C grade student while attending Point Fortin Intermediate RC School. For me, the high points were my friendships, art classes, my very first stage performance ever when I sang at a school concert; and when my class represented the school at a regional school's recitation competition led by my then Standard 3 teacher, one Ms. Joan

Rush. Our recitation piece was called "Key to the Kingdom". I still remember some of it today.

The low point would be the time when I decided to "break Biche"; meaning to leave home for school, but intentionally cut school on the day, for whatever reason and go elsewhere to pass the time. I was in Standard 5 then, and in my 4th and final year at RC School. My teacher was one Mr. Brown.

The school had given a deadline for when all students needed to be in full uniform after the new school term had begun that September. At the time of the deadline, I still did not have my full uniform, for which the teacher promised that there would have been punishment. I was still without my school tie. Afraid of facing punishment, which I assumed would be licks, I did not want to attend school.

But I had no choice in the matter as my mother forced me to go, saying, "jus' tell the teacher that yuh mother doh have de money right now tuh buy the tie," assuring me that the teacher would understand and not punish me. I did not take her word for it, and therefore decided to "break Biche".

Being that it was my first time, I did not really know where to go to hide to pass the school hours. So, I ended up sitting on the stairs behind the concrete hand support wall attached to it, that led up to the entrance of Kim Far, the Chinese Restaurant, which was located on the Point Fortin main road, where there was constant vehicular and foot traffic. I paid the price for my inexperience.

Someone who knew me saw me; and without my knowledge reported it to one of the adults in my household. I was subsequently picked up by one Mr. Philbert in his green Victor Vauxhall vehicle. He was an SRP (Special Reserve Police) and had a daughter whose name was Lystra. They were close friends of the family. When Mr. Philbert and I arrived home, my mother instructed him to, and he gave me a good "cut arse", after which I got another one from my mother.

Mr. Philbert then dropped me off to school. In the given circumstances, I was not punished by my teacher either for being late or for not having my school tie. That was the very first and very last time that I ever attempted to "break Biche".

And it would be through Mr. Philbert that I would have the absolute honor, even as a youngster, of personally meeting Trinidad and Tobago's most famous Union leader, Tubal Uriah "Buzz" Butler, who for years fought for the cause of the Oilfield Workers of the day.

On that momentous occasion, Mr. Philbert took me along for the ride on what I would learn was one of his frequent visits to the man who was his friend cum national hero. Upon our arrival at his home, Mr. Butler was perched on a chair on the platform at the top of the back stairs, outside the door leading into his residence. He lived in Gonzales Village, Guapo, which was about a 10 to 15 minutes drive from Nennie's residence.

He was wearing a vertically striped calf length burgundy and brown bathrobe and brown bedroom slippers. Upon reaching the top of the stairs Mr. Philbert introduced me to him. He greeted me with a broad friendly smile, put his left hand on my right shoulder and firmly shook my same hand with his right. Behind his distinctively powerful, aggressive, confrontational, and defiant public persona, I found that he had a very peaceful and respectful disposition.

For me that was a most special day, for which I have obviously retained a very vivid recollection. I subsequently drew a pencil portrait of that great man in tribute to him and that extra special occasion. I still have it in my possession today.

CHAPTER TWO

THE SEVENTIES

MY TEENAGE YEARS: ENTERING SECONDARY SCHOOL: COMETH THE BLACK POWER MOVEMENT

In early 1970, my mother followed Nennie's lead and traveled to Canada. She left for the same reason she did when she traveled to New York in 1963, which was to seek work to enable her to better provide for her children. Arrangements had been made for my Aunt Rita and her husband Uncle Phillip, to look after me and my siblings in my mother's and Nennie's absence.

As she did during her New York stay, my mother sent clothes and shoes etc., and ensured that everyone in the household received something. I remember she also sent confirmation clothes for me and my cousin David, as we were both confirming together.

During my mother's and Nennie's absence, my temper tantrums that were more or less dormant, resurfaced, and when triggered, would at times escalate into threats of violence. That resulted in me being told time and time again by certain adults within the household, that one day I would end up in "Rayman Yard", meaning remand yard (jail).

Because of my short temper, my mother and certain other adults within the household often referred to me as "ah little beast". "Ah eh able with you dis Alison nah. You is ah little beast. Ah doh know wey yuh get dat temper from," my mother would say in resignation, whenever I exploded into one of my intense tantrums.

I remember one occasion when my sister Sandra, with whom I was having a verbal altercation in the kitchen, had to run and lock herself inside the toilet, after I snatched a knife from the dish drainer to stab her.

I sat right outside the door, knife in hand, waiting for her to show herself to attack her.

She only came out after my cousin BoPeep intervened, took the knife away and calmed me down. Only my siblings and those very close relatives on my mother's side, who also shared Nennie's residence, would have first-hand knowledge of that side of me, which most definitely came out during those early years.

Thankfully, I would find purpose to my life during my late teenage years in the form of my mother, who was continuing to struggle to provide for her children and herself. I wanted to make a better life for my mother. That ambition would then see me control my explosive temper, which could have otherwise led me down a dangerous, self-destructive path.

It would be that ultimate life goal, that would see me totally avoid verbal confrontations with others as I grew older; even in instances which would call for me to stand up and or speak up for myself. So, in situations that would arise that would lead to such confrontations, that could possibly trigger my short temper and escalate, I would make the conscious decision of responding with silence and or simply walking away.

It would be an approach to my life that would give most the impression that I was a walk over, so to speak. And it would in fact be an approach that would allow many the opportunity to walk all over me; and they did. But I made that choice simply because I did not want my short temper to get in the way of any progress that I could have made in my life; and further, of me achieving my ultimate life goal.

Apart from our mother leaving for Canada and though just a formality then, 1970 was also the year that my parents were officially divorced. That year there were two other events that were also significant to me personally.

One was the FIFA World Cup, which Brazil won for the third time at the Azteca Stadium in Mexico City, with my then football idol Pele scoring the first goal in Brazil's 4-1 victory over Italy. The other goals were scored by Gerson, Jairzinho and Carlos Alberto. That third World Cup Final victory allowed Brazil to permanently keep the Jules Rimet Trophy.

The other and more significant event that year was the "Black Power Revolution", which was the culmination of a black power movement on home soil. Ours was led by local activist Geddes Granger, during which period, like with the U.S. Civil Rights Movement, there were also several marches throughout the country in protest of social injustices against black citizens. I have retained a vivid memory of one such protest march, which took place through the streets of my hometown village of Point Fortin.

I distinctly remember standing on the second-floor veranda at the front of Nennie's house and seeing what to me seemed like thousands of black protesters streaming down Adventure Road. They all wore red head and or arm bands made from strips of cloth. With folded fists held above their heads, they chanted protest phrases as they marched by on the street below, directly in front of the residence. At just 10 going on 11 years of age at the time, I stood on the veranda in awe.

The image of those black protesters marching by with folded fists held above their heads and chanting phrases of protest, was indelibly etched in my mind forever. Mr. Granger and others usually wore African styled attire, including Dashikis, which then became a popular mode of dressing among many local blacks for a period of time. I actually owned a few, which was made by Nennie who was a seamstress.

I came to fully understand what the then movement and revolution were all about as I grew older. Its purpose was to bring about change, since the economic system in which skin color dictated a person's employment opportunities and upward mobility was still firmly in place, even after the country had gained independence from Britain, its former colonial masters in 1962.

Like Tubal Uriah "Buzz" Butler, Geddes Granger, who later became Makandal Daaga, also became one of my national heroes. And like Butler before him, I would have the absolute honor of also personally meeting him, but much later in my life.

The 4 years that I attended Point Fortin Intermediate RC School, were all in preparation for the most important day in the life of a Trinidad & Tobago primary school student. That was the day that students took what was then called the "Common Entrance Exam".

The Common Entrance Exam held a great deal of academic significance, since it determined whether a student would enter a five-year college / secondary school, where, similar to the primary level, a student's education was free. Success at the secondary school level equipped a student with the academic foundation, that made getting ahead in life a bit easier, so to speak.

A student usually took the Common Entrance Exam when he or she was about the age of 11 or 12. In my case, I was going to be turning 12 just 2 months after taking the exam. A student usually got to select 3 choices of secondary schools they wished to attend, should they be successful at the exam. But many parents usually made those selections for their children, hoping that they would end up in a so called "prestige" school.

A few months before I was scheduled to take the Common Entrance Exam, my mother returned to Trinidad from Canada after spending about a year. Nennie had since returned from Canada as well sometime before my mother did.

To prepare for the exam, I got extra lessons from my cousin Reynold aka "Broko", a few weeks before it was scheduled. He had been successful at the exam years before, and had since completed his 5 years in Secondary School. The extra lessons were usually two or three nights per week, with each session lasting about an hour.

I was extremely motivated to pass the Common Entrance Exam for two main reasons. The first reason was that my mother had made a promise to me and to one Earl "Boots" Jones, the then steel-pan tuner and one of the senior members of the community-based Dunlop Tornadoes Steel

Orchestra; with Dunlop, the tyre manufacturer that was based in the community being the then sponsor of the band.

The promise was that if I passed the exam, she would allow me to join the band, which was something that I wanted to do for quite a while. Boots had been asking her over a period of time on my behalf, knowing that I badly wanted to join although being still very young.

The second reason that I was so extremely motivated to pass the Common Entrance Exam, was because my success was going to see "a first" from my father. That first was him actually buying me something. That something was going to be a Chopper bicycle, which he said would be my reward if I passed the exam. Chopper bicycles were extremely popular back then; so of course, as a kid I was ecstatic about the prospects of actually owning one by way of passing the exam, because I couldn't own a bicycle otherwise.

I took the Common Entrance Exam in June 1971. The results were usually published in the daily newspapers several weeks later, making provisions for the necessary preparations for a student's early September entrance into Secondary School, if he or she was successful. Awaiting the published results was nerve-racking to say the least, especially for parents who knew what was at stake. When the day finally arrived, a Trinidad Guardian newspaper was bought and the search for my name began.

Throughout the household there was huge anticipation, excitement, and continued anxiety all at the same time, as multiple eye balls followed the index finger that ran from the top to the bottom and across the pages of the newspaper, where the names of my 3 selected school choices were listed; but my name was nowhere to be found.

The non-appearance of my name in the newspaper listing meant that I had failed the exam. Suffice it to say that my mother and I were both devastated, albeit for vastly different reasons; my mother because she would have reasonably assumed that my future would not have been looking very bright then.

I was devastated because I knew then that I would not have been allowed to join the Dunlop Tornadoes Steel Orchestra, and that I would also not have been receiving the reward of the Chopper bicycle from my father as promised.

My failing, also excluded my mother from experiencing the initial feeling of overwhelming pride and joy that all parents do, upon learning of their child's Common Entrance Examination success, through its publication in the newspapers. And thereafter, from continuing to experience the said feelings that then extends into minutes, hours, days, weeks, months and years, during the time that their child attends secondary school.

About two weeks before the new school term was to begin in early September, a letter addressed to my mother arrived in the mail. It was from the Ministry of Education. I was at home when the letter arrived. My mother anxiously tore it open and read it. Lo and behold, the letter informed her that I had in fact passed the Common Entrance Exam.

Our then lingering feelings of deep disappointment, instantly turned into total elation. My mother simply could not contain herself, as come early September 1971, her second son and the fourth of her five children would be attending secondary school; more specifically, Vessigny Antilles Government Secondary School, located in Vessigny Village La Brea, the home of the world-famous Trinidad Pitch Lake.

I remember my mother's reaction as if it were only yesterday. Standing in the corridor in between the doorways that led into the dining room and the kitchen respectively, with the torn envelope and opened letter in her left hand, she made the sign of the cross with her right. She then fell to her knees on the very same spot and made another sign of the cross.

She then lifted her head and looked up at the ceiling, opened both arms to the imaginary heavens I supposed, and with the utmost sincerity in her voice she said "thank yuh Lord Father," which she repeated several times, as tears filled her eyes.

Right then and there, I fully grasped what the achievement meant to my mother. She then had some semblance of hope, that it would probably serve as the catalyst that would see me achieve further academic success. And therefrom, propel me to the success in life that such academic achievement promised, and that every parent wanted for their child or children. And so, a next chapter of my life was about to begin.

Unknown to me at the time, upon my mother receiving the letter from the Ministry of Education informing her that I had passed the Common Entrance exam, she had contacted my father not only to share the good news, but also because she could not afford to purchase the books that I needed to attend classes. So, she made a request to him to do so, and got a copy of my book list to him after obtaining it from the school. In response, my father agreed to purchase just one particular book that was on the list.

In an act born out of total desperation, my mother then went back to the school where she met with the Vice Principal, one Mr. Bally. She explained our predicament to him and requested his assistance. Thankfully, our plight did not fall on deaf ears, as the Vice Principal willingly obliged her and provided all the books that he was able to. When those events were eventually revealed to me years later, it justifiably served to increase the resentment, that I had by then been harboring towards my father.

September arrived, and while I had no idea as to how my mother was able to obtain my school uniform, which consisted of long khaki pants and black belt; white short-sleeve shirt; black sneakers and socks; and a navy blue and yellow tie, I was off to Secondary School, entering Vessigny, also known as VSS, in Form 1.

The class structure in the Trinidad and Tobago Secondary School system generally goes from Form 1 to Form 5, with students spending 1 year in each Form. Back then, at the end of the 5th year, students took the University of Cambridge (England) General Certificate of Education (GCE) Ordinary Level (O Level) Exam.

Passing no less than 5 subjects, which was the minimum amount out of the maximum 8 or 9 that students were allowed to take at the ordinary level exam, was then the benchmark for obtaining a decent job, if one chose to enter the job market at that time. With English and Math being compulsory, it was then up to a student to choose the other 3 or more subjects they wanted to take at the exam.

The option of continuing to attend Secondary School for an additional year (6th Form), was also open to students who were successful at the O Level Exam. At the end of that 6th year of studies, students then took the University of Cambridge General Certificate of Education Advance Level (A Level) Exam. They would have chosen the specific subjects that they wanted to take. Further success at the Advance Level Exam, served to land the student a better paying job than he or she would have secured with only Ordinary Level Exam success.

My Secondary School journey started the second week in September of '71. And with several weeks already having passed since receiving the news of my Common Entrance Exam success, I was then anxiously anticipating the imminent delivery of my Chopper bicycle from my father as promised.

Then on the weekend following the week that school began, my father suddenly showed up at Nennie's Point Fortin residence. Because he never did otherwise, I immediately assumed that the purpose of his visit was to deliver on his promise. I was extremely excited.

But my unbridled joy quickly turned into what was a monumental disappointment, because as it turned out, that was not the purpose of his visit. He instead came to deliver the one item that he had agreed to purchase from the book list that my mother had sent to him. It was a big, thick, heavy text book, which was for my Physics class. It cost TT$52.00.

Given that he expended that huge amount of cash on just that one item, and then made such an effort to deliver it personally, I thought maybe he was trying to tell me that he wanted me to be a Physicist, Scientist, or something of the sort. Not only would that have been simply laughable, but it would have also indicated to me that the man was delusional.

I stood right next to my father looking up at him anxiously with bright sparkling eyes, anticipating the news about my Chopper bicycle, as he chit-chatted with the adult members of the household who stood around him. But he never even mentioned as much as one word about it. He simply showed up, delivered his Physics package, chit-chatted a bit; then he left.

That second Saturday in September 1971, I gathered that my father would have undoubtedly felt extremely proud of himself for not only purchasing it, but to have personally delivered what he obviously considered an invaluable educational item, in the form of a $52.00 Physics text book, which, as far as I was concerned, was totally useless to me.

Thankfully, my mother kept her promise and allowed me to join the Dunlop Tornadoes Steel Orchestra, much to my excitement and to the delight of Boots and the other Stage-Side members of the band. In the aftermath of that major disappointment by my father, joining the band certainly lifted my spirits. I was so short then, that initially, I had to stand on a box to reach my instrument to play it.

I would play with the band for 8 years from 1971 to 1979, during which time we played in the annual south steel band Panorama competition, when the champion band of the south was determined each year. The preliminaries of the event usually took place on a Sunday, from morning into the night at Skinner Park in San Fernando, about 2 to 3 weeks before the annual Carnival celebrations.

It was an absolute thrill to play for the many thousands who flocked to the park. The bands, with instruments mounted on numerous separate steelpans stands that were made from welded iron pipes that were mounted on wheels, were pulled and pushed around the sloping Skinner Park cycle track by devoted supporters, with other supporters and hundreds of steelpan lovers enjoying themselves to the fullest, jumping up in front and behind the bands, as the bands played their respective Calypso tunes of choice.

Other supporters occupying the football field and those in the stands followed suit where they were. Tornadoes also participated in the even more prestigious annual National Panorama competition, which were staged at the Queen's Park savannah, referred to as "The Big Yard" in the nation's capital. Oh, the memories.

At the time I entered VSS, the principal was a Mr. Chatoor. And there was one thing that was immediately established by some of the students who were already there. Be afraid...be very afraid of Principal Chatoor, because he was an extremely strict disciplinarian.

I was told of his famous "Tambran Whip", which was the whipping tool of choice back then, with which he inflicted punishment on those students guilty of indiscipline, or who dare to break any of the school rules, academically or otherwise. I was told that he unleashed his strokes with such force, that it continued to induce pain long after they were delivered.

I found that out first hand within the first couple of months of my attending Vessigny, after there was a verbal altercation between me and a female classmate which turned physical after she had put her hands on me, and I having had to defend myself. Her initials were ZK. Back then, you wouldn't have seen me shying away from such.

I can't quite remember exactly what started the verbal altercation between myself and ZK, who was of a different race and fair skinned. But I remember that during the argument, which took place in the classroom, she called me a nigger. She had some weird looking eyes that looked like those of a cat, so I responded by calling her "Cat Eyes", which she took offense to.

That's when it turned physical, with ZK initiating the action by pushing me. I fell backwards between some desks and chairs to the floor, receiving a few bumps in the process. I retaliated, although I was at a distinct advantage, since she was much taller and heavier than me. The fight ended when a teacher quickly appeared on the scene after hearing the uproar of our on-looking class mates.

The teacher immediately took us to Principal Chatoors' office, where we each received punishment, which was 6 strokes each from his much feared "Tambran Whip". ZK received her punishment first, after which she was ordered back to class. As all the female students did, she received her strokes in the palms of both hands with a far less amount of force than I would, for the obvious reason.

Then it was my turn. I was told to bend over and put both hands against a file cabinet. As all the male students did, I received my 6 strokes across my buttocks from Principal Chatoor with full force. What I was told about his famous Tambran Whip was most definitely not a lie. Upon receiving the first stroke, I cried out in pain and stiffened straight up on my toes, as my both hands flew off the file cabinet and grabbed both sides of my buttocks, which were then on fire where the stroke had landed. Stoned faced, Principal Chatoor quickly ordered me to assume my original position.

The second stroke, which landed on almost the same spot, seem to then send a heat through my entire body. I cried out even louder, as I repeated my entire sequence of action that ended with the second buttocks grab. My entire body was then trembling uncontrollably, as Principal Chatoor unmercifully repeated his order for me to assume my original position.

The other 4 strokes I received increased the pain and heat that I felt tenfold. By the final stroke, my butt cheeks then felt almost totally numb when I grabbed on to them. By that time the tears from my eyes and "snat" (snot) from my nostrils were also flowing uncontrollably. After a very stern warning from Principal Chatoor, I was then ordered to return to my classroom. I never had a friendship with ZK at any time thereafter during our entire 5 years at VSS.

I would come very close to having a more serious physical altercation during my time at VSS, when I got into a heated argument with a male classmate that time around. He was one of my closest friends. On that occasion I was prepared to use a dangerous weapon from my Geometry Set. It was called a Divider. The presence of the weapon ended the argument, and we got back to being friends a few days later.

There would be more visits to Principal Chatoor's office to receive strokes, up to the time of his eventual retirement, which was a couple of years into my five years term at VSS. But on those occasions, my punishment was for not meeting the expected academic standard at the end of a given school term.

It was referred to as "Mark Period", where students took a term test, and was not allowed to fail more than three subjects out of about the eight or nine that were being taught. I always failed more than the benchmark three subjects; as apart from Art, English and History, I was never really interested in any of the others. And thus, my 6 strokes from Principal Chatoor were a guarantee, come every Mark Period.

My Art class was then taught by the second of my two all-time favorite teachers, while I was in the Trinidad school system. His name was also Mr. Bally; not to be confused with Mr. Bally the Vice Principal.

That said however, I simply cannot forget Mr. Forbes, our Physical Education teacher and football team coach, who led us to a famous 1-0 victory over then powerhouse Naparima College of San Fernando. That game was played on the Lake Asphalt football ground in La Brea. My other VSS teachers that I can remember include, Ms. Phillip who taught Spanish, Ms. Bartholomew and Mr. Dookie (can't remember what subjects they taught).

Throughout my time at VSS, my mother usually prepared lunch meals for me to take to school. Those meals consisted of either 2 cheese-paste sandwiches or 2 slices of Coconut Sweet Bread or Sponge Cake that she would have baked over any weekend, which came with a bottle of Cool-Aid, which was always first on the drinks list, for the obvious reason.

On occasions it would be Orange, Grapefruit or Passion Fruit juice, or homemade Chocolate Milk. During that time, there was a Chocolate

Milk on the market named "Flip", which I kept asking my mother to buy for me. But since she couldn't afford it, she simply provided me with the homemade version.

At times my mother gave me money to buy lunch. I bought what met the lunch budget, which was usually a pack of Domino biscuits, which had 4 Oreo type cookies in the pack, and a Solo or Canning's sweet-drink (soda). I bought those items at Chinese shopkeeper Archie's shop, which was located directly across the street from the school.

And there were many occasions when my mother had no money to give to me for bus fare to travel to and from school, which was about a 35 to 40 minutes drive one way. So, she would send me already dressed for school to Mr. Philbert the family friend for the bus fare. His residence was a relatively short distance from Nennie's.

He used to be still in his pajamas when I got to his house, which was usually around 7:00 a.m. I actually woke him up from his sleep on quite a few occasions. Mr. Philbert always gave me twice or three times the amount that was needed. The bus fare at the time was 30 cents return. When she could have afforded it, my mother would have me purchase a weekly bus ticket, which was known as a season ticket. I even remember that it was pink in color.

Prior to my entering VSS, Nennie had started spending her time between Point Fortin and Port of Spain in the north eastern community of Curepe, as she was then looking after her sister's house there. That sister, whose name was Louise Alexander, was one of two of her three sisters that had been living in the United States for many years.

The house was located on Watts Street. My sisters Cheryl and Sandra and my older brother Evans all eventually relocated to Curepe from Point Fortin at some point. Curepe would also eventually become my home away from my then Point Fortin home.

My very first visit to Curepe was in 1972. It was also the year that one Edson Arantes do Nascimento, "King Pele" himself, would make an historic first ever visit to Trinidad, as a member of the world-famous

Santos Football Club of Brazil. Santos was going to be playing a friendly game against the Trinidad and Tobago Senior Men's National Team.

There was absolutely no way that I was going to miss out on that once in a lifetime opportunity to see my then football idol in action in person, and when there might have even been the slightest possibility of fulfilling one of my childhood dreams, by somehow getting to meet him.

The game was played on Tuesday September 5th at the Queen's Park Oval in the capital city of Port of Spain. My cousin BoPeep took me to see the game. On our journey to the Oval from Point Fortin, since we left very early, we made an in-transit stop to pay a quick visit to Nennie and my siblings in Curepe, which turned out to be my very first visit there.

Upon our arrival in the Oval, it was literally overflowing with spectators, who like myself, was eager and overly excited to see the man they called "The King" in the flesh. Queens Park Oval was so over crowded, that some spectators were almost encroaching onto a certain part of the playing field itself. The atmosphere was absolutely electrifying.

There was extremely high excitement and anticipation to see the man himself emerge from the dressing room, and for the game to start to see him in action. However, an unexpected delay in the arrival of the Santos team at the ground, got some pockets of the reported 40,000 spectators restless, including the pocket that were almost encroaching onto the field. They started to act up.

I remember I was standing right next to BoPeep, just in front of what is known as the Carib Stand. The Carib Stand was situated some distance from the southeastern corner flag on the field, where the restless pocket of spectators who started to act up were seated, a short distance away from the touchline.

A couple of Policemen on horseback were trying to keep the situation under control, and began using their horses to keep those spectators from encroaching too close to the playing field. In doing so, their horses trampled on some of the spectators. That triggered a reaction from the spectators, who began throwing missiles at the Policemen. The situation escalated.

With the Policemen seemingly losing control, tear gas was released. It was then that all hell broke loose. In a desperate attempt to escape the tear gas, spectators started stampeding in all directions. Many were also jumping from the front of Carib and other adjoining stands that were approximately 15 to 20 feet off the ground at their lowest point, as they were in the direct path of the tear gas, as the wind blew it in theirs and our direction. In all the chaos, BoPeep and I got separated.

In a state of absolute panic, I ran with a large group of male spectators underneath the Carib stand, and down some stairs that led into the car park inside the facility. We kept on running towards the car park exit, but the gate to the exit was padlocked with no one present to unlock it.

Desperate to get out, many then began climbing onto the top of a ticket booth inside the compound adjoining the high wall that enclosed the entire facility. From atop the ticket booth, they were then climbing onto the top of the wall, then jumping to safety onto the pavement (sidewalk) below, that adjoined the wall on the outside of the facility. I followed suit.

As I jumped from atop the wall, a young adult male with no shirt on, scampering by eastbound on the sidewalk below, suddenly veered off to his left closer to the wall, to get past someone who was running in the same direction ahead of him. Veering off his original path, then put him directly beneath me on my landing spot at that precise moment.

My feet landed directly on his shoulders and upper chest. On contact, his quick forward momentum flipped me upside down. I slammed face first into the concrete sidewalk and fell into a semi-conscious state. I can't really say for how long.

When I regained full consciousness, I sat on the sidewalk with my back against the Oval wall. I felt an immense amount of pain that was emanating from my head and from my mouth. My lips were busted and I was bleeding from the inside of my mouth, and could taste my own blood.

With a sweep of my tongue, I immediately detected that some of my teeth were broken.

The individual upon whom I had landed apparently kept on running, as did others who were also scampering by at the time. No one ever came to my assistance. I guess with all the chaos and panic, everyone was simply looking out for themselves.

I eventually got to my feet and made it across the street (Tragarete Road) into a Chinese fast-food outlet. Upon seeing my condition, a Chinese woman behind the counter quickly handed me a large Styrofoam cup of water. Since there were no washroom facilities and not thinking clearly at the time, I remember attempting to wash out my bloody mouth in a corner right inside the outlet, when the Chinese woman shouted in very broken English, "no wus ere! No wus ere! Wus utside! Wus utside!" I complied.

I then flagged down a taxi right outside the Oval that was surprisingly empty at the time, to take me to downtown Port of Spain, where I would have then gotten another to take me back to Curepe.

The driver, who was actually off duty at the time, thus his taxi being empty, said he stopped after he noticed blood stains on the shirt I was wearing. After he got a close-up view of my busted lips and broken teeth, he realized that I was badly injured from the Oval chaos. So, he took me directly to the Port of Spain General Hospital instead of downtown at no charge.

When I got to the emergency department, there were already quite a number of adult casualties from the Oval awaiting treatment for their respective injuries. Being just a child, I was treated as priority. After explaining to the attending doctor what had occurred and the amount of head pain I was experiencing, I was given painkillers.

And after checking out my injuries, the doctor told me that I was extremely lucky, as I could have suffered even more severe injuries, including being paralyzed. Or even worst, I could have possibly died instantly from hitting my head on the concrete sidewalk. Surprisingly, I was then discharged after being given some more pain killers to take at home over the next few days. I then made my way back to Curepe.

All except for one individual within the Curepe household displayed compassion and expressed that they were hoping and praying that neither BoPeep nor I got injured, as they watched the chaos unfold on television. But obviously, their worst fears were realized upon my arrival at the house. Not surprisingly, there was one older sibling who showed no compassion. "Ent yuh want tuh see Pele. Eh. Yuh want tuh see Pele. Look how yuh nearly dead fuh Pele," she stated, while laughing at me. While that sibling chose to laugh, there was really nothing funny about my situation.

So, sadly, I never got to see my football idol in action in the flesh at the famous Queen's Park Oval cricket ground that day, or at any time thereafter during his illustrious playing career. I simply had to settle for seeing him display his sublime football skills on television on recorded replays of the FIFA World Cups he played in, and on recorded replays of the time he played club football. Still, I never gave up hope of realizing my dream of meeting the king of football face to face one day.

The following year, 1973 to be more specific, should have been historic for Trinidad and Tobago's football. Late that year, our Senior Men's National Team would participate in CONCACAF's final round of qualification for the 1974 FIFA World Cup Finals, which was being hosted by Germany.

I would turn 14 years old a few months before, and was overly excited because we had a squad of players that gave us a very good chance of qualifying. Adding to my excitement was the fact that 6 of the 22 members of that 1973 World Cup qualifying squad, were from my Point Fortin hometown. Namely, Warren Archibald, Steve David, Wilfred Cave, Leo Brewster, Anthony Douglas, and Sydney Augustine.

I then found out that the team was having a live-in training camp on the Campus of the University of the West Indies (UWI), which was about a 10 to 15 minutes walk from Nennie's Watts Street Curepe location. The camp was being held over a period during which it was the final week of the July to September school holidays. So, I found myself back at Nennie's Curepe abode, just so I could have attended the team's training sessions, which I did do during the said week. The team's coach was an Englishman named Kevin Verity.

That final round tournament for qualification for the 1974 FIFA World Cup in Germany was being hosted by Haiti. There were six participating teams; Trinidad and Tobago, Mexico, Guatemala, Honduras, The Netherland Antilles, and the host nation. They would all play each other in a one round, round-robin format, with the team finishing at the top of the group, qualifying for the 1974 FIFA World Cup Finals in Germany.

And while it was a year that I would remember for a life changing domestic event, I would also come to remember 1973 primarily as the year of football heartbreak, as my beloved Trinidad and Tobago, were denied making football history, at that Haiti qualifying tournament.

We had lost our first game against Honduras 2-1, with games against Haiti, Guatemala, Mexico and The Netherland Antilles to follow, in that order. However, we were then flatly cheated out of what would have been a well-earned victory in our game against Haiti.

In that game, which was played on December 4th 1973, Trinidad and Tobago actually scored 5 legitimate goals. But to the total bewilderment of all, except the then Haitian President I suppose, 4 of the goals were unjustly disallowed by the referee, and we ended up losing the game 2-1.

Having been flatly cheated out of the win in that game against Haiti, victories against Guatemala 1-0, Mexico 4-0 and The Netherland Antilles also 4-0, still saw us miss the chance to make football history, as the then smallest nation at the time that would have ever qualified for a FIFA World Cup Finals. I remember crying my eyes out after that Haiti game, which I listened to on the radio.

Mexico had beaten Haiti, which was the only game Haiti ended up losing. And because of their bogus victory against us, Haiti then had a chance to qualify. But they needed assistance from the Trinidad and

Tobago team who needed to whip Mexico and did so 4-0, to open the door for Haiti who then beat Guatemala 2-1 in their final game, to reach the FIFA World Cup finals in Germany.

It was later discovered that the Salvadorian referee who had officiated the game between Trinidad and Tobago and Haiti, had taken bribes from Haitian officials to officiate the game favorably for Haiti. He was subsequently banned from officiating for life by FIFA. But oooh; what pain he caused; not only to the players themselves, but to the entire twin island nation of Trinidad and Tobago.

Meanwhile, more than 2 years had since past, and my father was yet to deliver on his promise of the Chopper bicycle, which was to have been my reward for my Common Entrance Exam success. I was then harboring even more resentment towards him than I had already been. I decided to write my father a letter. In my letter I informed him that if he wanted me to get on my knees and beg him for the bike that I never asked him for in the first place, that would never happen.

In my letter I vowed to be the one child he had, who will never ever run after him or beg him for anything. I had no intentions of ever kissing his behind for any reason whatsoever. Not kissing anyone's behind for anything or for any reason, is a guiding principle that evolved because of my father. And it would be one to which I would remain steadfast throughout the course of my entire life, even if it meant losing out on significant personal and professional opportunities that would have been beneficial to me.

I also vowed then, that I would strive to accomplish something major in my life related to my dreams, that would see my father feeling most proud that I was his son. Yet, he'd have to think twice before he could ever utter anything to that effect to me, as I would ensure that he could never in good conscience, absorb and enjoy any of that parental pride as a result of my said achievement.

While he had already established long ago, that he would always be more concerned about and interested in the welfare of any stepchildren he might have inherited, than the welfare of his own biological off spring, he reinforced that fact when he inherited two new, then very young step-children, Jimmy and Felecia, from a second marriage, sometime after he and my mother were officially divorced.

So much so, that even during our relatively short conversations during my sporadic visits to his Chaguanas residence over the years, as short as those conversations were, I was certain that there would be a seg-ment, where my father would proudly boast about Jimmy's and Felecia's academic development and achievements etc. etc.

He also did so to his two older biological children, and even on the occasions when we were all present at his home. I only wished that my older siblings would have, but they said absolutely nothing to him about it to his face, but would talk about it behind his back.

The manner in which he spoke to us about his two inherited step-children, one would have sworn that we were not his biological children. And he did not even seem to care if it was affecting any of us. Such occur-rences most definitely contributed to the resentment that I felt towards my father.

I however, made a personal decision to channel those negative, potentially self-destructive feelings into positive thoughts and actions. And so, with the vow that I made to myself uppermost in mind as a result of his neglect, I became more driven. And so, with my mother's ongoing struggles being my "Primary Positive Source", my father then came to rep-resent my "Primary Negative Source of Motivation", to relentlessly pursue and achieve my dreams.

Having then set that goal, which bottom line was to create a better life for my mother, I began to focus on developing my artistic, football and musical talents. It helped that I was then around family, close relatives and friends. Life for me continued to be the most enjoyable it had ever been.

Sometime during early 1973, the Nelson family, who lived about 150 meters or so from Nennie's residence on Adventure Road at the time, moved into one of her downstairs apartments that became available.

The father, who was black, had immigrated to Canada. So, their mother who was of East Indian descent was raising three of her four children, Junior her second child, Ricky the third and Ann Marie the youngest. Patty, the oldest of the four, had stayed at their original residence, which was their grandmother's.

Junior, who was closer to my age, joined the football fold almost immediately. He was a left-footed player and learnt the skills of the game rather quickly. And while all the kids became very close friends with each other, Junior and I became best friends. He had a big afro. And like my cousin David, he and I became more like brothers, and his mother did in fact treat me as if I was her own son.

Contributing significantly to my musical development, was me being introduced to playing music on Tin-Cans (homemade musical instruments made from tuning empty Powdered Milk tins and juice cans) by one John Davis, who is the father of Canadian based Calypsonian Connector. Mr. Davis, as we kids respectfully addressed him, occupied the other ground floor apartment of Nennie's residence with his then wife Marge.

He was then a schoolteacher and bodybuilder, who also played tenor pan with Dunlop Tornadoes Steel Orchestra, before I became a member of the band. Mr. Davis eventually taught me how to burn and tune the empty Powdered Milk tins and juice cans myself. It did not take me very long thereafter to start my own "Tin-Can" orchestra, made up of Junior, his brother Ricky, my cousin David and me, with tin-cans I burned and tuned myself.

We composed our own music. Today I still remember the melody of the first musical piece that I ever composed, which was unnamed. Junior also composed his very own musical piece which he called "Saltfish

Water". Junior's vocal rendition, always provided a source of laughter for the rest of us. I still also remember the melody to Junior's piece.

It was around that time that I also wrote my very first song. I was 13 going on 14 years old. It was a love song about my first childhood crush, who had since immigrated to the United States with her family. The title of the song was "You Are the One", in which I was professing my undying love for her. I still remember the melody and most of the lyrics today.

Creating the said melody, together with writing the lyrics seemed to come naturally for me. The ease with which I had written that first song, and feeling and capturing the emotion at such a tender age, it seemed like songwriting was in my blood, and I became really passionate about it.

But for me writing songs wouldn't be a hobby, nor would the primary purpose be for financial gain. For me, as a fellow human being and inhabitant of the earth, who would never be immune from the effects of such, it would be the medium through which I would express my innermost thoughts, feelings and beliefs about socio-political issues.

And critically important, writing songs would provide a necessary outlet that would help me to deal with life's never-ending trials and tribulations, as well as provide one for me to share other real-life experiences, both painful and joyful, as I grew into early, middle and late adulthood. Equally critical, for me songwriting would also be both cathartic and therapeutic.

I would allow my songwriting style to develop naturally on its own, without conforming to the usual rules of cord progression and song structure etc. And while there would be breaks over the years, some longer than others, I never stopped writing songs of all different genres after I had written my very first one. And I guess I'll keep on writing songs until I no longer have the ability to do so.

Around that same time when I was inspired to write my very first song; age 13 going on 14, I was also introduced to the field of Commercial Art. That introduction came through Ronald "Sluggo" John, the oldest of the John brothers small-goal football crew I referred to much earlier.

Sluggo and my sister Cheryl had attended RC school together. He had already been paying visits to our home, since he was also courting her. My sister knew he was an excellent Artist from their RC school days and told him that I liked drawing a lot. So, after he asked me to and I showed him some of my pencil drawings, he decided to be my tutor. Suffice it to say that doing so worked out perfectly for all three of us. I got a Commercial Art tutor; and they were then able to see each other more than usual.

Sluggo had successfully completed a U.S. Commercial Art correspondence course sometime before, for which he received reference materials. The course involved cartooning, lettering and newspaper advertising design. He passed on all his acquired knowledge to me. He also gave me most of the reference materials, so that I could have continued developing my skills.

Ronald "Sluggo" John is hereby being credited as the individual who first introduced and exposed me to the world of Commercial Art, which at the time was a career I was merely dreaming about. I did not forget to thank him personally for the part he played, when I did in fact embark on my Advertising / Graphic Design career many years later. Sadly, Sluggo passed away in 2006, while watching the FIFA World Cup Finals in Germany on television.

Though we played other sports, with it being the one that we played most and regularly, my football skills were developing rapidly. However, my cousin David was the best all-round athlete among our age group. He was most definitely the best basketball player, wind-ball cricketer, and fastest runner. His sister Annmurie, who is a few years younger than David and I, ran races with us sometimes and was quite fast. I believe that she could have been a successful track athlete had she chosen that path.

Unfortunately, from those that lived among us, there were two senior citizens in particular who weren't very pleasant, and had a negative impact on our sporting activities. They were Miss Dora, who had her young grandson Tony and even younger grand-daughter Angela living with her; and Mr. George who lived alone. And perhaps fittingly, they lived facing each other at the corner of Lyle Street and Baptist Road, which was one block up from Adventure Road.

The center of the Lyle Street and Baptist Road intersection, served as the center spot for the countless amount of small-goal street football games we engaged in. Whenever we played either football or wind-ball cricket in the streets, and the football or tennis ball were inadvertently either kicked or hit into their respective yards, which were totally fenced, Miss Dora and Mr. George took possession of them and refused to give them back. The games then ended abruptly, since we usually had no immediate replacements. Tony, who most came to know as Tony Dora, usually gave us back the footballs and cricket balls that his grandmother confiscated when he located them.

BoPeep and some of the other older boys used to throw stones on top of the roof of Mr. George's house while he was asleep late at nights as retribution for his misdeeds. However, Miss Dora was spared. She was so mean that she never even allowed Tony, who is a few years younger than I am, to even venture outside the fenced yard to play with the other kids.

Like myself, Tony was also a very promising artist. Being that he was not allowed to join us to play in the streets, I would often visit him and we would sit on their veranda and draw portraits from reference material, or we would play the out of tune tenor pan he owned and played as a means of entertaining himself.

He eventually broke free from his grandmother's clutches during his secondary school years, whereupon he joined in the activities we participated in, including playing football. But basketball was his preferred sport and true passion, and he developed into an excellent basketball player with a wicked jump shot.

With Tony as a witness, with my very first attempt, I once lobbed a shot with my right foot with my Wembley football from on the street in front of his house, through the basketball ring in Dub's yard, about 20 meters away. In today's world, it is a feat that would have certainly been recorded and gone viral on social media.

Tony and I became close friends. He and Junior my best friend, also became members of the Dunlop Tornadoes Steel Orchestra, where they also played the tenor pan. Tony currently lives in Australia, where he owns and runs a successful carpet cleaning business with his wife. And not surprisingly, he also coaches a youth basketball team there.

Meanwhile, although life seemed just fine, unknown to us kids at the time, behind the scenes there was trouble brewing in the household. My mother had switched her allegiance from the Catholic faith, and became a member of a Spiritual Baptist group. Nennie apparently did not approve.

I remember at least one occasion, when my mother took my younger brother Brian and I, to a prayer meeting held by her Baptist group at a very small worship space, located along the stretch of road called Egypt Stretch.

What added fuel to the fire was that on the invitation from my mother, the then leader of the said Baptist group, whom I would refer to only as Mr. P, came to Nennie's residence one day, and conducted a Bible class session in the yard with the kids from the household.

If there was any doubt about Nennie's disapproval of my mother's involvement with the group, the presence of Mr. P on her premises erased it completely. It made her furious, and as a result, Nennie threw us out of her house. So, after having enjoyed what was a quite normal life over what was a 6-year period at that point, the situation was about to change dramatically.

It was late evening that day in July 1973, during that year's 2 months July to September school holidays, when it happened. All of the clothes belonging to my mother, Brian, and me, which wasn't a whole lot really, were deposited on the 7ft x 5ft platform, that joined the front and back concrete stairs at the bottom, that led up to the front and back entrances of the top floor of the residence. Our belongings were covered with 2 short sheets of galvanize in the event that the rain fell I suppose. It is another childhood image that remain indelibly etched in my mind.

Our mother was not at home at the time. But upon her return just before nightfall, she appeared to have had some sense of what was happening upon seeing our clothing covered at the bottom of the stairs, and immediately left again. She returned after about an hour or so, as night fell. We each grabbed our then bagged belongings then promptly hit the road.

That night, we ended up in a small apartment of a friend of one "Mother Muriel", who is one of the subjects in SuperBlue's 1991 Road March winning song "Get Something and Wave". She was a relative of ours. She lived in an adjoining apartment with her two then very young daughters Annmarie and Bettyann. The house was located on Agard Road, which was not very far from Nennie's residence.

We were then in an apartment with a tenant who was a man who we did not know, and who I came to know only by the nickname "Sando". He had an organ in the apartment, which I would try to play when he wasn't at home during the course of the day.

It turned out that Sando was actually an organist at a local community church, and the one he had in his apartment was what he practiced on. However, our then newest house of refuge was only short term, and after a couple of weeks we relocated again.

We then found ourselves at the home of a family in the community of Self Help, which was referred to in an earlier passage. I did not know the family, but they were very hospitable. The head of the household was a man whose name was Mr. Ralph.

He was a single parent who shared the 3 bed-room residence with his then young daughter and son, Ruth and Brent, who could have been around the same ages as Brian and I. It was a very comfortable, well-kept house with all the necessary amenities etc. They made us feel at home. But theirs was also only another temporary house of refuge. And so, after another couple of weeks, we were on the move once more.

My mother was somehow able to secure a very small one-bedroom apartment. She was also somehow able to furnished it with the bare essentials, including a small bed on which she slept with my sister Sandra, who, together with Cheryl, had since relocated back to Point Fortin from their stint in Curepe. Sandra had remained at Nennie's, while our mother, Brian and I were knocking around from place to place, up until our mother secured the apartment. Cheryl continued living with Nennie.

My older brother Evans, though still just a teenager, had since seen the birth of his first child, a son whose name is Kerry. Evans had since been living in Princes Town with our father's father and our father's brother, whose name is David Ayres, but visited us most weekends. After himself returning to Point Fortin and training as a draftsman, he secured a job in that field in Port of Spain, and relocated there.

His then girlfriend, whose last name was Fletcher, lived about 4 houses up from us on the opposite side of Adventure Road with her family. Her four brothers, Ralph, Winston, Kurt and Clint and I were close friends, though they were not in the Georgia football fold.

So, after enjoying several years living in relative luxury, sleeping on a fiber-filled mattress bed; tap water with only sporadic interruptions; the uses of an inside toilet and bath; a refrigerator, television and even a telephone at Nennie's, like all of the others that we live in before then, there would also be no such luxuries to be had at our then newest residence.

While there was electricity, it was back to sleeping on a wooden floor on old clothing; an irregular water supply and back to regularly collecting (toting) water in a bucket from an outside stand-pipe to wash clothes and dishes etc.; back to using an outside bathroom and latrine; back to using a Styrofoam container with ice from a neighbor's fridge to store and preserve perishables. And I would no longer have the luxury of enjoying television entertainment and football in particular.

The house in which we then occupied one of 2 apartments it contained, stood on about twelve 7 feet tall iron posts and was built from a combination of mud, cement and wood. It was located at the very top of an extension of Lyle Street named Guadeloupe Street, at the top of which was a dead-end that ended where oil pipelines ran between the residences.

So, after a period of homelessness, the good news was that our mother ensured that we finally had a place that we could call home. Another upside was that our newest residence kept us in Point Fortin, which, after a relatively short separation period, allowed me to reunite with my cousin David, my best friend Junior and the rest of the Georgia boys.

I assumed that someone was lending our mother financial assistance, as in the ongoing domestic chaos, she was unable to do her usual hairdressing work, during what were extremely desperate times. And while I had already been exposed to the world of the Spiritual Baptists, living at the Guadeloupe Street residence would provide me with an understanding of that of the Shango Baptists.

You see, the small one-story house, was in fact owned by one Miss Marion, a well-known high-ranking Shango Baptist within the Point Fortin community. It would be while living at that residence, that I would come to experience some of the rituals of the Shango Baptists firsthand.

But it was just a year earlier, that I had actually witnessed a segment of Miss Marion's Shango / Orisha Feast, which was usually held during the month of August. We were residing at Nennie's at the time of course. As earlier mentioned, Miss Marion's residence was located at the very top of the Lyle Street extension, which was about a 250 meters distance away. There were two streets one would cross between Nennie's and Miss Marion's residence. The first was Baptist Road and second was Kalloo Road.

On the occasion that I witnessed the segment of Miss Marion's Shango / Orisha Feast, I was liming (hanging out) with the boys one night at our usual liming spot, under the street light where the Georgia sign was installed on the lamp post, at the corner of Lyle Street and Baptist Road. It was held in August as per usual, which was during the July to September school holidays.

While liming, we were hearing the drumming from Miss Marion's Shango / Orisha Feast in the distance, as we were used to hearing during the August months in the past, but we never bothered with it. However, on that particular occasion curiosity won out. A few of us decided to take the walk to the top of Guadeloupe Street to see what was actually going on. Upon our arrival there was a crowd of onlookers standing in the yard, as well as on the street. Entering the yard, I went as close to the action as I could.

The activities were taking place under a brightly lit shed, constructed specially for the event with wood and covered with a Tarpaulin, as an extension of part of the front of the house. The Tarpaulin roof covered a square area of about 20 feet x 20 feet. Around the perimeter, wooden benches were also constructed on the dirt yard, with a gap at the front, where I stood, and a smaller gap off to left side corner at the back, that led you down the right side of the house.

The worshippers, including several drummers, sat together on the benches. The drummers were using sticks with curved ends, as together in unison they beat out pulsating, hypnotic rhythms on the drums, which were held tightly between their thighs.

A barefooted woman, wearing an extremely loose white ankle length dress with a matching head tie, was dancing around on the dirt square to the beat of the drums. I seem to remember her holding some object in one of her hands while dancing. She appeared to be possessed by something. She had what I could only describe as a weird facial expression, which led to the following comment from a middle-aged male onlooker standing right next to me. "Like she turnin' intuh ah beast boy?"

We made eye contact, as I anxiously looked up at him then turned to leave upon hearing his comment. Immediately recognizing that his comment had gotten me scared, he stopped me and explained to me that there was no need to be, because what I was witnessing was a part of my African culture and heritage. With his explanation then quelling my fear, I stayed.

The woman danced until whatever might have possessed her seemed to have left her body, upon which she then collapsed into the waiting arms of two similarly dressed fellow female worshippers. She was then led away from the dirt square. Meanwhile, the crowd of onlookers had kept on growing.

Shortly after the woman was taken away, an intoxicated middle-aged male character arrived on the scene, and immediately made his way to the center of the dirt square. While the woman had been taken away, the drumming never stopped, and Mr. Intoxicated began to dance mockingly to it.

At that juncture, the drumming suddenly ceased, upon which one of the drummers, a very robust looking gentleman wearing a red headband, who appeared to be the main man, politely asked the intoxicated individual to remove himself from the dirt square. He did so reluctantly.

The drumming started up again, upon which the intoxicated gentleman reappeared, and continued with his drunken antics on the dirt square. He was then holding a small branch with some leaves on it in one of his hands, which he started to chew on. Almost instantaneously, he began moaning loudly, blurting out in obvious discomfort, "ah feelin' like it hah san' in mih mouth. Ah feelin' like it hah san' in mih mouth."

Unknown to him, the leaves that he was chewing on, he apparently picked off from one of the Stinging Nettle plants that was growing in the yard. The Stinging Nettle plant is known to cause an immediate, highly irritable rash accompanied by pain, on contact with the skin. And Mr. intoxicated was not spared. The drumming then stopped again. Mr. Intoxicated was again asked to remove himself. He did. But on that second occasion, with even more reluctance.

The robust looking drummer was exercising much patience with him. The entire sequence that went twice before was repeated a third time, except on that third occasion when asked to leave, Mr. Intoxicated totally ignored The Robust One. Visibly angry, it was then that The Robust One delivered the following warning to the intoxicated man. "If yuh eh leave here right now! You dead in September!"

His words were expressed with such venom, that it scared the hell out of me. An eerie silence then fell over the entire scene. Mr. Intoxicated most definitely got that particular message, as not only did he immediately leave the dirt square; he also left the scene completely. Those bone chilling words from The Robust One, was enough for me to also immediately disappear from the scene as well.

Having then taken up residence where it all went down; the memory of that night's events was then triggered. It then also occurred to me that a face-to-face encounter with The Robust One might well be on the cards. The mere thought of that moment left me feeling very uncomfortable. And so it came to pass, shortly after we relocated there, when he did indeed return for Miss Marion's feast that August of 1973.

From the very first day we moved in, Miss Marion and her husband David were always nice to me. And while the anticipation of our very first encounter had me nervous, The Robust One was also quite nice to me as well. His very pleasant and inviting personality continued to be on full display throughout his entire stay at Miss Marion's, over the week-long duration of the feast.

But even as my fear of him subsided, with his chilling words of a year earlier then resonating in my mind, it was still very much there to a significant degree. I eventually came to know his full name, which carried the initials IL.

During the actual night-time into early morning feast, accompanied by the drumming, the worshippers chanted specific names, which I understand was to invite the presence of the respective spirits whose names they were chanting. The names and melodies of at least two of the chants in particular, stayed with me even up to today. I guess they always will.

On one occasion during the feast, I witnessed Miss Marion's husband David, bite through the throat of a living white fowl, after which he drained its blood into a bowl made from a Calabash; for subsequent use I imagined. And very early one morning, I also witnessed a goat being killed, by having its head severed.

Experiencing the entire feast firsthand over its week-long duration and witnessing all of the various rituals, took away most of the initial fears I had about the religion a year earlier, which was brought on primarily by those chilling words from The Robust One. A year later, I then had a fairly good idea of what it was all about.

My mother on the other hand, seemed to have already had a fairly good understanding of all of it. She eventually developed close relationships with Miss Marion as well as with The Robust One and his wife, who I learnt were members of the highest rank, and held in very high esteem in the Shango / Orisha world.

I eventually found out that they lived in Fyzabad, which was located on the far outskirts of San Fernando, where Brian and I had actually also spent some time early on with relatives living there. Those relatives, who carry the last name Procope, lived in Pepper Village.

I was also reliably informed that there were quite a number of individuals who held very high offices in Trinidad, including politicians and certain Sports Administrators, who paid visits to The Robust One "to fix deyself" and or "to fix dey business", as the sayings goes in Trinidad.

For the uninitiated, that involves spiritual rituals that are performed on an individual or on individuals, and or on one or more of their personal possessions. The ritual or rituals to be performed, depends on the need. Some are performed to protect the individual or individuals, and in some cases their families, against harm from evil and or evil doers.

Other rituals are performed to achieve financial and other forms of successes, including success in one's chosen career, or in a business pursuit, or in a business one might have already own. My further understanding is that apart from a financial cost to those hiring the services of the High Priest, which could be very significant in some instances, certain other personal sacrifices are also required in some cases, if one wanted to increase their chances of achieving their objective. I was also informed

65

that there are also rituals that are performed to cause harm to others, as well as to get and or keep the relationship with the woman or man of your dreams, as the case may be.

Upon our relocating to Miss Marion's residence, Mr. P from the Spiritual Baptist group became a frequent visitor. I gathered that he may have been instrumental in securing the apartment for my mother, as it became very clear that he knew both Miss Marion and her husband David quite well. The Baptist connection I suppose.

Mr. P was more or less nice to us kids, that is, until the friendship between him and our mother had soured and eventually ended. In the aftermath, he made life even more difficult than it already was for us, when he actually began stalking and harassing our mother.

We had to always keep the doors locked in the event that he showed up. And on those occasions when he did, whomsoever was home at the time knew that they had to stay completely silent and don't respond if he called out to anyone, until he got tired of calling out and left. The harassment and stalking from Mr. P lasted for a couple of months after which it stopped for good. It was a period during which we were living in constant fear of him.

Meanwhile, my cousin David and his family had moved out of Nennie's residence, and relocated to a forested area called Reservoir Hill after they had built a house there. It was about an hour on foot from Miss Marion's. I made the journey fairly often to visit them.

Not long after my cousin David and his family relocated, my best friend Junior and his family left Trinidad to join his father in Canada. They left on May 27th 1974. And not very long thereafter, we relocated one final time in Point Fortin after living at Miss Marion's for just under a year.

Junior would eventually send me a package from Canada containing the very first Adidas track suit I would ever wear, as well as a pair of black platform boots made from genuine leather. Platform shoes with bell-bottom pants was the craze at the time. The track suit was blue with the Adidas stripes in yellow.

And even as we would only see each other on probably just over a half dozen separate occasions over the 49 years since he left Trinidad, at the time of my book being published, Junior without question, is still my best friend in every possible sense of the word. I am certain that we will remain best friends for life. We keep in touch primarily via e-mail.

As indicated in the prologue, the lyrics to some of the songs that I have written over the years but were not recorded, which were inspired by some of my life experiences, are included in my book; with the said lyrics to those songs appearing at the very end of the passages of the chapter, in which I share those respective life experiences.

The following are the first of those lyrics to the song "Shango Feast", which was inspired by actual events.

SONG TITLE: SHANGO FEAST

Written by Alison Ayres © 2003 Alison Ayres All rights Reserved

VERSE 1

Busin' ah lime (lime—hanging out with friends)
We hear de sound of de drums
Yuh know how Trini farse (farse—inquisitive)
Hah tuh see wuh goin' on
So jus' out ah sheer curiosity
Ah make it mih business tuh go an' see
De drummers beatin' out ah haunting riddum
Ah woman in the center dancing aroun'—An' dey chantin'

CHORUS: Hosein de Moliere...de Moliere (Repeat)

VERSE 2

Ah in the midst
Ah Miss Marion Shango feast
Ah geh frighten like hell

Ah man say she turnin' beast

Ah turn around tuh buss' it de Mister said

Young fella there's no need fuh yuh tuh be scared

Instead consider it ah real privilege

Yuh witnessing yuh African heritage—Now dey chantin'

CHORUS: Ah Sharajah Olokun Oh (Repeat)

VERSE 3

Boy then ah drunkard

Find heself in the ring

Geh Shango Leader mad

He jokin' with serious t'ing

Shango Leader warn him not once but trice

Didn't wuh take Shango Leader advice

Geh back he senses when Shango Leader said

If yuh eh leave right now September yuh dead—**END**

OUR FINAL RELOCATION IN POINT FORTIN

Our then latest, which also turned out to be our final relocation in Point Fortin, took us to Warner Road, which was a stone's throw from the village's shopping area. The Kattick family, who lived only one house away from us on Adventure Road, also relocated to Warner Road sometime after we did.

Theirs consisted of six members, including their mother, sons Bobby, Juno and the youngest Filburn, and two daughters Annie and youngest family member Rose Marie. Two of the Kattick's family members, Bobby and Annie, had since gone off on their own before the rest of the family made the move to Warner Road.

Filburn was my younger brother Brian's best friend at the time, but he and I eventually became very close friends as well. His nickname was "Pet". He and I used to do a lot of long distance running together, with the Guapo beach and the Clifton Hill Golf course being a part of the course. Sometimes we would stop and try to catch crabs in the mangrove swamp near the Guapo beach.

Pet and I also played a lot of pool together at Valentine's Pool Hall, which was located right at the corner of our street, just one house away from our residence. Mr. Valentine was the very popular owner of his primary business, the also then very popular Valentine's Photo Studio.

Many Point Fortin residents would have taken photos at Mr. Valentine's Studio. Sadly, the older of his two sons, who we knew very well, committed suicide by hanging himself from a Long Mango tree in the back yard of their residence. I still have a vivid memory of the image of his limp lifeless body hanging from the piece of rope, that he tied around a branch of the tall mango tree.

Our new place of abode was owned by two Church going seniors, Mr. and Mrs. Mc Knight, who had their then two teenage grand-daughters Jean and Dalier living with them. Two even younger grandchildren (I think), Patsy and Hollis King, came to live with the Mc Knights and their two other grandchildren at some point. We occupied one of two small two-bedroom apartments on the ground floor of the two-story house, with the Mc Knights and their four grandchildren children occupying the entire top floor.

Mr. Mc Knight was a butcher, and reared pigs in the backyard just a few meters away from our kitchen window. So, we had to live with the constant stench emanating from the pig pens. Mr. and Mrs. Mc Knight were both extremely "hoggish" (no pun intended; in Trinidad meaning hostile) towards their grandchildren, and was verbally and physically abusive to them.

Our small two-bedroom apartment at Warner Road, which was an upgrade from the usual one-bedroom we previously lived in, except for when we lived at Nennie's, would eventually be occupied by eight of us in total; my mother; my sister Cheryl, her then husband to be and their then infant daughter Keithann; my other sister Sandra and her then infant son Marlon; my younger brother Brian and me. Cheryl, who had lived with Nennie from very early childhood, came to live with us at the Warner Road residence. My older brother Evans, as stated before, had relocated to Port of Spain a couple of years before, while we lived at Nennie's residence.

With our mother occupying one, the other seven of us shared the other bedroom, which had one glass louvre window. It contained 1 double-decker and 1 small single bed. Cheryl, her then husband to be and their infant daughter slept on the bottom of the double decker. Sandra and her infant son slept on the top. And there would be no more sleeping on the floor for Brian and I, as we then shared the single bed.

There was about a 25 to 30 inches passageway between the beds, which were each up against the walls on the opposite sides of the room. There was not enough ground space for anything else. So, we drove lots of long nails into some of the wooden 2 inches x 4 inches beams around the perimeter the room, that formed the frame for the walls to be built, on which we hung our clothes. To protect them, they were covered with long pieces of colored plastic that were installed like curtains against the wall, using the then very popular thin flexible wire curtain rods.

During the time we lived at the Warner Road residence, I distinctly remember our grandfather sending funds from England on a few occasions for my mother and his grandkids. He would eventually pay a visit to Trinidad.

As she continued to struggle to make ends meet, my mother continued doing her hairdressing from a tiny enclosure adjoining our apartment on the outside, that was situated directly beneath the also adjoining stairs leading up to the Mc Knight's top floor residence. We lived about five houses away from one Austin Lyons and his family, who lived on Baptist Road, which ran right into Warner Road, with the Techier Main Road separating both. Warner Road had a dead end.

I remember Austin's mother coming to have her hair done by my mother on many occasions. His younger brother Matthew and I were in the same class at Point Fortin Intermediate RC School. Then there was his sister Karen and an older brother who I knew as Moth, but who was also known as 'Big Zork", because he was tall and well built. Unknown to all at the time, Austin would become very famous.

Life continued to be rough. Once again there was no inside toilet or bath at our newest residence, but thankfully there was running water most times. And while we had electricity, my mother still could not afford a refrigerator. So, like at our Guadeloupe Street residence, our refrigerator was a small Styrofoam container with a bag of ice at the bottom, to store and preserve whatever perishables my mother would buy.

While there were the "grocery making" days off and on, grocery items were usually bought as needed, after my mother had been paid by the respective customer or customers on any given day, for her hairdressing services. I would then be sent to the supermarket to buy one 5lb pack Five Roses flour, 3 or 4lbs rice, 2 or 3lbs brown sugar, 1 or 2lbs split peas etc., as the case may be, as those items used to also be sold loose back then.

It was no different when purchasing canned foods. It was usually, "Ali, go an' buy ah tin ah corn beef, ah tin ah sardine, ah tin ah condensed milk, ah tin a baked-beans", etc. There was no buying of any one food item in quantity back then.

Whenever a tin of Nestle's sweetened condensed milk was bought, opened, and partially used, it also had to be stored in the Styrofoam container. And whomsoever used it last, had to ensure that both the milk and Styrofoam container were properly closed each time they were opened; and especially at night.

If they weren't, the next morning you'd be sure to find at least one large size cockroach stuck on the surface of the thick creamy milk inside the can. And since our ongoing financial struggles did not allow for it to be simply thrown out and purchase another, instead, upon discovery, the cockroach was quickly scooped out and disposed of, and the milk put to use in the pot of steaming hot Fry's Cocoa at breakfast time. When reminiscing sometimes about those days, my mother reminds me that at one time I even wanted to quit school, so that I could have started working to help her out.

Many years later; 1994 to be exact; in his song titled "Poverty Is Hell", one of Trinidad and Tobago's Soca and Calypso music geniuses, legends and icons, Winston Bailey (deceased), who was known in the music entertainment world as Shadow, vividly describes the "cockroach in the condense milk" scenario. Shadow sings;

"Then cockroach gone in the condense milk
Mama get vex for she condensed milk
Who leave the condensed milk open
Come here yuh picky head good fuh nothing
Mama get vex an' she blood get hot
She buss ah lash in dey you know what
Poverty is hell—Poverty is hell"

I assumed that the very poignant message in Shadow's very powerful song, may have merely represented good calypso humor to many in my homeland. I certainly was not one of those laughing, because I lived that reality. With me, Shadow's "Poverty Is Hell" struck a nerve, bringing back very painful memories of the then often unpleasant conditions that we were then forced to live under, as a result of our father's parental neglect. Given the extremely serious theme and lyrics, I doubt very much that Shadow himself meant any of the references made in his song as a joke.

The Mc Knights, our newest landlords, had inside toilet and bath on their top floor residence, but neither of the two ground floor tenants did. For me, using the backyard latrine especially at night, was quite an experience, which at times was a quite frightening one.

The Warner Road latrine adjoined the row of pig pens to its right, which were built directly against the backyard boundary wall, that marked off the back end of the plot of land. Most times, while surveying the inside of the cramped dilapidated wooden structure with a lighted candle in hand before making my full entrance, I would see the candle light reflecting in the eyes of something between the rafters and the galvanize roof. Out of an abundance of caution, I would then postpone the activity until daylight.

And that's because, while it sometimes turned out to be a lizard we knew as a "Wood Slave", there were occasions, having settled on the rough wooden seat relieving myself, the shining eyes I saw of what I thought was one of the said lizards crawling across the said rafters, turned out to be a snake that could have been about 30 inches long.

Instantly, the otherwise relaxing and enjoyable bowel movement activity was forcibly cut short. Some quick wipes with the damp sheet of gazette paper, and I was out of there. With lighting candle in one hand, hot grease spilling all over it, I pulled up my jockey-shorts (underpants) and short pants with the other after I exited.

Our landlords eventually built new double Latrines in front of the pig pens a couple of years into our residency. One was for our family exclusively, and the other for the tenants occupying the other downstairs apartment. That family included 3 children. They were all boys; Leo the eldest who was a few years younger than I was, Angus and Dexter the youngest. We all naturally became friends. The father was Mr. Ifill and the mother Miss Anita.

There was also a really cool, very friendly dude living at the end of the street, who we all knew as "Pessy". He could have been about twice my age at the time. He worked at the nearby gas station. And I can never forget Miss Ida, if only because of her extremely inquisitive nature. She was an old lady who was our next-door neighbor, who had a nephew whose name was Sterling living with her. Her grand-daughter, who lived in Venezuela before then, came over to Trinidad to live with them. Her name was Ingrid.

1975 at Warner Road would be a memorable year for me for two primary reasons. Firstly, it was the year that I would finally come to own my very first pair of football boots (soccer cleats in the U.S.). My older brother Evans bought it for me after I had made a request to him, since my mother could not have afforded to buy me a pair. I received it in early September, just in time for the then upcoming college football season. It was a brand called Gola, which was quite popular back then. It was black with the yellow Gola trademark device on the sides.

Then, out of the blue on Christmas Eve of 1975, almost five years later, and only 6 months before I would have been leaving Vessigny Government Secondary School, my father unexpectedly showed up at our Warner Road residence with the Chopper Bicycle he had promised he would buy me as my reward back in 1971, if I passed the Common Entrance Exam, which I did. It was purple.

I was still quite thrilled to receive it. But for the obvious reason, it was for me a bittersweet moment. And as time passed, I began realizing that having it then did not really erase the memory of the absolutely crushing disappointment and accompanying hurt I felt at the time, when it was not delivered when it was supposed to have been, as promised by my father, especially since I had earned it.

And thereafter, the disappointment and hurt that I had continued to feel with the passing days, weeks, months, and years without him still not delivering on his promise, and moreover, with him not even having the common courtesy or decency to ever offer an explanation during that time.

Still, the Chopper did however serve a significant purpose, as I was then able to take the two minutes ride down Egypt Stretch to Harriman Park every evening, to pick up the much-needed bags of ice from one of my mother's friends. Her name was Miss Louisa.

She and my mother became good friends after they met in Canada. She had since returned to Trinidad and more specifically Point Fortin to live, upon which they reconnected. She made a special batch of ice in her freezer just for my mother, since she knew that my mother didn't own a refrigerator, and couldn't afford to buy ice every day. It ensured that we always had ice in the Styrofoam container to store and preserve those perishables that needed to be at a certain temperature.

Our Warner Road relocation allowed me to still frequent my old "Georgia" block, which was less than a 1-minute ride away, to engage in what for me was then a weekend ritual of small-goal football on the street with the usual crew. I had since graduated to the green field of the Mahaica Oval during the week.

My mother was somehow able to acquire a black and white television, which was the very first television set that we had ever owned. It then allowed me to watch football from Europe once again, which made me extremely happy of course. Eventually, she was also somehow able to obtain a telephone.

I also remember 1975 as the year that one of my all-time favorite recording artistes and performers, Guyanese born Eddy Grant, released one of my all-time favorite songs "Hello Africa". It was a monster hit throughout the Caribbean region and the UK where Eddie was based at the time, and I would imagine other countries as well.

A very simple but powerful song with an infectious melody, extremely potent lyrics, and a wicked, hypnotic bass line, "Hello Africa" served to connect and reconnect many black people throughout the Caribbean region to their African roots to some degree. It most certainly served as such for me personally.

The then upcoming 1976 Trinidad and Tobago Carnival celebration was being held in February that year. On my very own initiative and though unintentionally, I would end up arranging a tune for my beloved Dunlop Tornadoes Steel Orchestra. I was then an established member, and one of the band's younger "Crack Shot" tenor players (a player who can pick up any tune on the instrument quickly and accurately and pass it on to others) along with my then very close friends Tony Dora and Ellis Fredrick.

Some of the older "Crack Shots" tenor players that I can remember by full, last and nicknames include Eric "Breadman" Benjamin, Bendrick "Knocky" Lewis, Figaro, Michael Toussaint, John Davis, Bakeface, Lee Fy and one Austin Lyons.

Other band members I can remember also by full, last or nicknames include Fitzroy Lennon the band's captain and his sister Stella, Julyn and her son Victor, Robert "Dub" Bernard (from the pitching yard), Winston "Pappy" Frederick, Gags my best friend Junior's uncle, Max, Cobham, Black Jack, brothers Dagger and Penknife, Edrick, brothers Gregory and Lay Burns, Seldom and Tony the 2 Drummers, Tano, Kegman and Chris aka Rakehan.

So, what tune did I arrange for the band? It was Hello Africa, which I am revealing for the very first time here in my book. It was Carnival Sunday in February 1976. We were to report to the pan yard that evening to learn what was called the "Bomb Tune". The Bomb Tune was a tune other than a calypso, that the band's arranger would select and arrange, and the band would play for the then "Bomb Competition", during the very early Carnival Monday morning celebration known as J'ouvert Morning, which started at 4:00 a.m.

I loved Hello Africa so much, that I decided to go to the pan yard earlier than the time we were actually scheduled to report, so that I could learn it on my tenor pan for my own self-gratification. I did so, inclusive of my very own musical arrangement.

I then proceeded to learn the song's bass line on the six-bass and four-bass pans, adding to what was on the original track, which was easy pickings really, given the simplicity of it. A six-bass player was one of the first to eventually report to the yard, upon which I taught him the bass line notes on his instrument.

No sooner we two were jammin' Hello Africa; him on the six-bass and I on my tenor. I then moved to the Double Second Pan where I changed the original arrangement of Eddy's guitar track on his original recording. I created a distinctive strum for the musical accompaniment for that particular instrument, while the bass man continued playing the bass line on his bass pan.

Austin Lyons was next to arrive. I showed him the tune playing my tenor, which he quickly picked up on his instrument. I then proceeded to learn and play the cords on the guitar pan, while he played the tune on the tenor and the bass man continued to play the bass line on his six-bass.

Fellow band members eventually started showing up as scheduled. They simply followed our leads and quickly picked up the song on their respective instruments. Austin was then an ambitious steelpan musician with aspirations to be an arranger. So much so, that around that period, he also had his very own four or five-member steel band side called Apple Stars.

By the time the then Dunlop Tornadoes arranger, one Cuthbert "Cutty" Matthews arrived in the pan yard on that Carnival Sunday to arrange the Bomb Tune he had in mind, the band, with its full complement of players was already rehearsing Eddy Grant's Hello Africa. As such, Cutty shelved any idea he may have had in mind to arrange the Bomb Tune of his choice. The following morning at J'ouvert, we won the Bomb Competition.

And like the many bystanders and revelers who chipped along to the tune in front and behind the band that J'ouvert Morning of '76, Cutty and the band members themselves were totally unaware that I was the one responsible for selecting and arranging the piece. Some may have even assumed that it might have been Austin; but it wasn't. It was all my doing. I was 16 years 6 months old at the time. So, perhaps I may have a case for being the youngest person ever to have not only arranged a song for a bona-fide Steel Orchestra, but also to have won an official competition when doing so.

During that then final year at VSS, I remember there was a friendly ongoing competition between my then very close friends Aldwyn Alexander, Carlyle Mc Call and myself, to see who can score the highest mark in art class, as we prepared for our GCE O Level Art Exam. We were trying to outdo each other, which pushed us to excel, resulting in our term marks being in the mid to upper 90's over the course of that final year.

I left Vessigny Antilles Government Secondary School in early July 1976 after taking the University of Cambridge General Certificate of Education Ordinary Level Exams, for which I gained 3 passes, with Art naturally being one of the three. The two others were History and English.

Some of my former class mates that I can remember apart from Aldwyn Alexander and Carlyle McCall include Derrick Nedd, Rene Carabon, Fazal Mohammed, John Rambert, Courtney Griffith, Jeffrey Martinez, Ricardo Duncan, Winston Gooding, Garvin Montoute, Joe Wallace, Maxine Mc Millan, Elaine Charles, Jennifer Alpsonso, Denise Edwards, Donna Samuel, Glenda Gadogan, Margaret Dillon, Kathleen Hackshaw, Marilyn John, Gail Alleyne, Beverly La Fortune, Marlene Mc Cloud, Janice Lewis, Vernice Marshall, Angela Ramlal, Denise Daniel, Adrianna (was it Geoffrey?) and Albertina Sookoo. I had crushes on at least two of my female classmates.

For me, the highlights of my 5-year term at VSS were the friends that I made, art classes and playing football for the school team during that final year. Some of my former football team mates I can remember include my class mates Jeffrey Martinez the team captain, Carlyle McCall, Courtney Griffith, and Ricardo Duncan our goalkeeper, as well as Peter Mc Colman, Mervyn James, Clinton Benjamin, and Herdis Lewis.

After my five-year term at VSS had ended, I returned to Curepe together with my cousin David for what was the third time, at the very end of July of '76 for a short week-long vacation. As mentioned earlier, my older cousin BoPeep had already been spending lots of time there from years before, and had been playing in the community's minor football league competition.

He was known by the nickname "Civic", since he then played with our hometown community team Point Fortin Civic Center in the national league of the day. So, David and I were well aware that there was a football field somewhere in the area, but didn't know exactly where it was located.

Upon our arrival that Saturday evening, having traveled with my then almost 1 year old well cared for Gola boots, we immediately found out where it was located from Nennie. A quick change of clothes and David and I then hustled off to the football field, which was conveniently located only about a 10 minutes walk from the Watts Street residence on a street named Knowles Street.

When we got to the football field, there was a small-goal game in progress right next to the pavilion off to the side of the main playing area, which involved some of the youngsters from the community, who was around our age group. They were being very attentively watched by a young adult male.

I asked him if we could, and David and I was given the okay to joined in. At the end of the game, the young adult male informed us that he was the Coach for what was the community club Curepe Nautico's U-16 team. He then further informed us that the small-goal game, was actually a final practice session in preparation for a real game that was scheduled for the following morning, Sunday.

Recognizing that David and I most definitely "had game", he asked us our names and where we were from. Upon responding and hearing that we were from Point Fortin, which reputation for producing some of the nation's top players preceded it then, he immediately invited us to join the team for the 10:00 a.m. game the following morning. David had no football boots, so he had to decline the invitation.

The game was being played in the Eddie Hart Football League, which was by far the biggest, most prestigious and most popular community football league on the island at the time, especially at the youth level.

As small as I was then for my age, the coach would have quite understandably assumed that I could have been around 13 or 14 years old, so he never even bothered to ask how old I was. I was hungry to play competitive youth football apart from the schools' league, which I had never done up to that point.

So, although already 16, I excitedly accepted the invitation to play for the team, knowing that one solitary game, would have been the only opportunity I would have had to showcase my talent on such a massive stage at that age level. And being that I lived all the way in deep south Trinidad, where there was no youth league at the time, it was indeed a once in a life time opportunity for me. So, I seized it.

The following morning, with David as a spectator on the sideline, I excitedly took the field decked out in Curepe Nautico's red and white team kit. I played in my favorite striker position, and scored what turned out to be the winning goal. It was the very first goal I had ever scored in an official competition game, as I'd never scored when I played for the VSS football team. And it was in the country's then biggest, most prestigious youth football league at that.

I remember it with vivid exactitude. Mid-way into the first half, I ran on to a through-ball from one of my team mates. I controlled it with my stronger right foot just inside the box. I was then one on one with the Goalkeeper who began advancing off his goal line. I could hear David's voice shouting from the sideline, "take yuh time Ali! Take yuh time!" I did.

With the same right foot that I used to control it, with my second touch I passed the ball all along the ground into the net to the Keeper's right. Goooooooaaal!; the first with my Gola boots. I sprinted off in rapture, celebrating first with David on the sideline, then with my new-found teammates. We won the game 1 goal to nil.

Both David and I was supposed to return to Point Fortin the Friday of that week, which would have been the end of the first week of August. But only David did, as I got a request from the coach to play in a second game the following Saturday evening. And of course, I could not turn down his request, and did play in that second game.

Again, I scored the winning goal once again in another 1-0 victory. On that occasion, I was on spot to tap home from close range, after the opposing goalkeeper failed to hang on to a cross from one of my team mates from the right side, a couple of minutes before full time. I had learnt the guile of poaching inside the box to take advantage of mistakes by the opponent, by watching Wilfred "Bound tuh score" Cave in action over the years; and it certainly paid off in that game.

The very next morning Sunday, my exploits over the two games saw arrangement hurriedly made for me and another team mate, with whom I had initially connected during what was then my second visit to Curepe back in 1973, to attend a screening session for the National U-17 team. The session was being held at the Queen's Park Savannah the said Sunday morning.

We hustled down to the savannah as fast as we could. Still, we arrived a bit late because the arrangements had only been made a couple of hours before the session was to begin; and we had to travel from Curepe into downtown Port of Spain, then to the savannah, which was uptown.

The coach conducting the screening session was one Winston "Bee" Phillip, one of my heroes from the Trinidad & Tobago 1973 World Cup team, that was cheated in Haiti that year, out of a possible World Cup Finals place in Germany the following year, 1974. Bee was also a member of the Defense Force football team, which played in the National League of the day. Being a member of the army and thus a strict disciplinarian, he did not really want to hear any excuses about why we were late to the session.

Once we geared up, he immediately made two substitutions from a game that was already in progress when we arrived. But it ended about 5 minutes after we took the field, so we really did not get a chance to show our abilities. He also recognized same, and so left us both on for another game which followed.

In that game we were able to show a bit of our respective abilities. While I did not get an opportunity to, I did set up my Nautico team mate to score during that session, upon which we were then substituted. We were on the field for about 10 minutes. Unfortunately, however, we both failed to make the cut. I returned home to Point Fortin at the end of that week.

After we had initially connected during my second visit to Curepe back in 1973, and then connecting further through verbal engagement and playing together during that most recent visit, I was then developing a closer friendship with that Nautico team mate in particular, during what turned into an almost two weeks Curepe stay that August of 1976.

Our friendship would eventually grow into a very close long-term one, after my eventual permanent relocation to Port of Spain in 1979, whereby over time I would get to know his parents and two siblings, both girls, very well. We became so close over the years, that he made me the Godfather of his first child.

However, my then football buddy cum very close friend, turned out to be the first individual who would provide me with my first real insight, into what I should expect from anyone claiming to be "a friend"; and the reason that I should probably never be too trusting of "so called" friends, when he perpetrated his first transgression against me.

It was a malicious deed that involve a third party who was a female. She revealed his malicious deed to me. Up to today he still doesn't know that she did, because I chose to never say anything to him about it. His transgression was more than enough for me to have ended my friendship with him, but I chose not to. But at least I knew then the type of person he really was.

And although it took a while, perhaps only because he had immigrated to the U.S., not surprisingly, he would eventually give me another reason to end our friendship. And I did so without hesitation that time around, because his then latest transgression confirmed that he was never really a genuine friend in the first place. In contrast, during what was up to that point a 20 plus years "friendship", I had proven myself to be a true friend and had been loyal to a fault. It was indeed my first lesson about "so called friendship". But it would not be the last of course.

MY VERY FIRST JOB

Around mid-1977, I got my very first job in my Point Fortin home-town. It was secured with the help of one of the members of the Singh family, who had a twin brother and who as earlier mentioned, lived diag-onally across from us on Lyle Street. The twin's names were Rudy and Rudal. It was an apprentice position at an auto body shop, and required me to be on the job from 8:00 a.m. to 4:00 p.m. Monday to Friday.

The shop was located in the community of Fanny Village, which was about a 15 to 20 minutes ride on my bicycle. It was owned by a man whom I knew only as "Tantwee". I was supposed to be paid TT$20.00 per week.

It didn't take me very long to realize that Tantwee loved drinking alcohol, after I spent my first week on the job rubbing down an entire car by myself using different grades of water-proof emery paper, in prepa-ration for priming and painting. Meanwhile, Tantwee was at a rum shop drinking.

He simply returned to the shop once or twice during the course of, and almost at the very end of the work day to check on the progress of my work. Being that I was new to that sort of labor, by the end of that first week my hands and fingers were extremely sore and somewhat numb; in addition to which they had several cuts and bruises, because of the nature of the work.

However, "after all dat hard wuk", I was not paid my meager wage at the end of that first week, upon which Tantwee told me that I would be paid at the end of the work day on the Monday. At the end of that Monday's work day, Tantwee was nowhere to be found. I left for home that day without being paid and never returned to the job. Although it was a very short one, I had then experienced my very first stint of appren-ticeship level exploitation.

Not very long thereafter, I got my second job, which was working in the Canteen of the Trinmar Oil Company. Again, it was one of the twins, either Rudy or Rudal who hooked me up. My wage was TT$35.00 weekly. The twin who got me the job also worked in the Canteen at the time.

The Canteen was managed and run by a half Chinese gentleman named George and his East Indian wife Betty. They lived in my birth place of Princes Town, which was about a 1 hour and 45 minutes drive to Point Fortin. A young East Indian male whom they called "Chess", drove them back and forth every day except on Sundays when the Canteen was closed.

It took me about 5 minutes riding my bike to get to and from work. I had to be on the job by 5:00 a.m. Monday to Saturday, since breakfast and lunch meals had to be prepared for the workers who worked off-shore, in time for them to then catch their boats to take them there.

I usually got out of bed just after 4:00 a.m. and left home no later than 4:45 a.m. I had breakfast and lunch on the job. My job entailed assisting in the kitchen, serving those workers who ate breakfast and or lunch meals in-house, cleaning up after them, and sweeping and mopping the Canteen floor. 18 years old at the time, I took great pride in doing my job, through which I was able to earn an income for the very first time in my life, which, as little as it was, then allowed me to assist my mother.

I worked up until 4:00 p.m. during the week after which I headed home, then to the Mahaica Oval to engage in the daily ritual of playing football. We worked up to mid-day on Saturdays, after which I spent a few hours at home, then attended Civic Center matches at the Oval or away during the football season.

While employed at the Trinmar Canteen, I learnt to make Fried Rice and Fried Wontons. I stayed at the Canteen job for almost a year before I left it. During that time, I had sold the purple Chopper bicycle that my father bought me and bought myself a new one, which was red.

During that period, I began being invited and started to train once or twice a week with the Civic Center squad, and given a bit of playing time off and on, on the main field with them. On those occasions, I never wanted to make any mistakes.

So, I found myself always playing it extremely safe, which meant I was always playing short passes, which were usually sideways or backwards. And though having the skill to do so, I hardly ever held on and dribbled the ball. Passing was always my very first thought. So much so, that I distinctly remember Monty Douglas (deceased) always encouraging me to dribble and or play the ball forward.

His brother Mohammed Saleem (deceased; formerly Keith Douglas), who like the others saw that I had some talent, basically took me under his wing. He knew that I aspired to be a goal-scorer. So, he spent time with me separate from the team's training sessions, to assist me in working on my first touch and shooting, which was done against one of the tall sturdy walls that stood several meters behind both goal posts on the Mahaica Oval football field.

Saleem knew that I did not like heading the ball, a skill that he was excellent at. So, he never forced me to. Instead, he would pass the ball to me from different distances at different weights and angles, either all along the ground or at different heights, and I had to either take one touch, trap it on the ground, bring it down off the chest or thighs, or the inside or outside of either feet or instep and shoot, or shoot one time on the half-volley when it drops, or hit it on the full volley before it drops, which is a skill I liked to do; and which Saleem was also excellent at. Saleem taught me to use and shoot with my weaker left foot. He also gifted me a few of his medals from those he had won from competitions he had played in during that time. He usually came to my home riding a bike to deliver them.

During those days, I remember Austin, who would become famously known as the Soca / Calypso Artiste "Blue Boy", would also show up at the Oval. Like myself, and many of the other youths from the community, Austin also aspired to be a footballer, and was also a die-hard Civic Center football team supporter.

I secured what would have eventually been my third job in Point Fortin, as a result of my very own initiative that time around. It was a field of employment that was more in line with what I wanted to do, although not quite. It was an apprentice position; that time with a sign painter whose name was Jeff. He was one of only two in Point Fortin in those days. The name of his business was Jeff Signs.

But he was not only a sign painter. He was also a silk-screen printer. He was excellent at both. So apart from sign painting, I was also going to be learning how to do silkscreen printing. As an apprentice, that time around I was not going to be paid initially.

I was to have started getting paid when I was actually able to do the work on my own. However, a few months into learning the sign painting and silkscreen printing craft, and while I was thoroughly enjoying doing so, a situation arose which caused me to leave before I could become an official full-time employee.

I left because Jeff's wife insisted that I stop wearing my Marvin Gaye hat to work, which I found made no sense, since I was in fact working with paint every day, which I obviously did not want to get in my hair. I mostly wore my hair in braids during those days. And not only did she object to me wearing my hat, she also did not approve of me wearing my hair in braids for work. So, I quit.

Still, despite ongoing hardships, there was much happiness to enjoy during the period that we resided at Warner Road, which involved good times with family, relatives and friends, and included playing sports in the streets of course.

I will however, also remember that time for a horrible incident that took place involving my mother. It was the night when she was physically assaulted by a man on her way to visit a friend. It happened close to the park near Frisco Junction in the heart of Point Fortin, where people often hung out both day and night.

She suffered a severe hip injury as a result of the attack and spent weeks in the hospital. She was able to recognize her attacker during the assault. I also happened to have known the individual from seeing him on the streets. I planned to take revenge.

But as time passed, my thoughts were taking on a more positive and rational trend, with my sights set on pursuing and achieving my dreams. Furthermore, I trusted that through the law of Karma, the individual would have eventually paid for his evil deed.

During that decade of the 70s and beyond, there was another extremely famous international sports figure apart from my then Brazilian football idol Pele, that I would come to absolutely love, look up to and draw inspiration from. And not just for his undeniable extraordinary sporting talent, but also for his fearlessness in standing up, speaking up and most importantly, acting upon what he believed in.

He was the epitome of what would become one of my lifetime aspirations, which was to utilize the powerful platform of sport, to promote and bring about positive personal and social change. That extremely famous international sports figure, cum sports legend and icon, who was also a prominent Civil Rights Activist, and to whom I refer, is the greatest boxer of all time, the one and only Muhammad Ali, who was formerly known as Cassius Clay.

CHAPTER THREE

THE EIGHTIES

COUNTRY BOY GOES TO TOWN: MOVING NORTH TO THE NATION'S CAPITAL IN PURSUIT OF MY DREAMS

I may have been able to pursue and achieve both my football and music related dreams while still residing in Point Fortin. But to have given myself a realistic chance of pursuing and realizing my dream of becoming a bonafide Commercial Artist, I had to leave the tranquil southern country life, for the hustle and bustle of city life in the nation's capital of Port of Spain, in north Trinidad.

I took the initiative. And after weeks of scanning through the classified section in the daily newspapers, followed by countless phone calls, I finally got an interview and landed my very first job in Port of Spain. It was only a messenger position paying a very meager wage, but it was a start. It was at a small business establishment called Provan & Associates, located in the heart of the city. As a matter of fact, the exact location of the business was at the corner of Hart (no pun intended) and Frederick Streets.

Although I knew that I would have been returning to Point Fortin to spend the weekends, it was still a very sad day when I left my family and friends. However, on the other hand, I was also extremely excited at the same time, as I knew that the move marked the beginning of my journey toward the horizon in pursuit of my dreams in earnest. I was therefore looking forward to what lay ahead.

I was 20 years 1½ months old when I arrived in the nation's capital on Sunday September 30th 1979. I started the job the very next day, Monday October 1st 1979. Arrangements had been made for me to stay with my Aunt Eileen, my father's sister, until I was able to stand on my own two feet.

Aunty Eileen resided in a government high-rise building housing project known as "The Plannings", located at St. Francois Valley Road Belmont, a very vibrant community on the north east outskirts of the city. As mentioned in an earlier passage, I had a brief stint with her during my very early childhood when she lived at 11 Baggan Avenue in San Juan.

While I had not really been and wouldn't be around my father's side of the family much during the course of my life, she was actually my favorite Aunt on that side of my family, and I was very happy to be reunited with her.

Like Nennie, Aunty Eileen was an A class seamstress, from which like Nennie, she also earned her living. She lived in her two-bedroom high-rise apartment with her son, my then 7 years old cousin Kendal. I shared Kendal's room with him, which already had two beds.

My salary at Provan & Associates was TT$60.00 per week. I traveled to Point Fortin on Friday evenings after work by bus since it was the affordable mode of transportation for me, and would give my mother what I could afford to help her out. I also gave "ah little something" to my Aunt Eileen, so that I still had enough funds left, to be able to at least feed myself throughout the course of the following work week.

However, my well-intentioned gesture toward my aunt did not go down well with her. I recall that upon handing over the very first bit of cash to her, which I believe was $10.00 from my first week's pay, which was all that I could have afforded, she appeared to have been insulted by the amount. She looked down at it, then at me and asked, "how much is your salary Ali?"

When I told her that my salary was $60.00 per week, she flatly stated that she did not believe me. And unfortunately for me, there was no pay stub or any other evidence to present to her as proof, because I was working off the books and being paid in cash.

Her response to my answer to her question naturally made me feel extremely uncomfortable, especially because I was telling the truth, and created an unnecessary element of distrust and tension between us from that instant. As such, I tried to spend as little time at the apartment as possible thereafter.

To show my further appreciation for what she was doing for me, I did a beautiful oil painting of a pink rose on white canvas, and gave it to her as a gift. She absolutely loved it and proudly hung it on the wall in her living room. I even bought a fish as a pet for her son Kendal, called a 'Fighter", that I was also fond of and had a few myself, among other types I used to mind, while living at Nennie's in Point Fortin.

During my work week at Provan, breakfast was usually 2 or 3 slices of Choeloe's white slice bread with Blue Band butter and on occasions with cheese, with a hot cup of Fry's cocoa before I left for work. Lunch was also 2 or 3 slices of Choeloe's white slice bread with Blue Band butter and on occasions, with cheese. I washed it down with a glass of water. My usual dinner menu at my aunt's was rice or spaghetti with butter or some-times with minced meat (ground beef), all of which was on my weekly grocery shopping list.

My Aunt Eileen sometimes prepared a dinner meal for me, which usually consisted of menu items that I preferred not to eat, or that I simply did not eat at all. I usually politely declined when she offered such meals to me. More so because I did not want to be viewed as a burden, by mak-ing her feel that she needed to provide meals for me.

But refusing my aunt's meals usually made her quite upset. So, there were times when I actually forced myself to eat whatever she was serving at the time just to appease her. I would eventually learn that she used to call certain family members, to complain to them about me not wanting to eat her food etc.

With my meager wage of TT$60.00 per week, from which I had to feed myself, and give both my mother and my aunt something, I could not afford the then $1.00 taxi fare to and or from work on a regular basis. So,

I simply walked to and from work the majority of the time. The journey was over an hour one way from Aunty Eileen's residence.

My workplace was on the second floor of a three to four story concrete building. There was a staff of five. Mr. Provan the boss, who was Caucasian; his personal secretary Sushla who was of East Indian descent; two young adult males, one African descent and the other light-skinned East Indian and me. My work space was a small desk and a chair in a corridor behind a partition wall that separated it from Sushla's and the boss' office in front of it. To this day, I couldn't tell you what business my then boss Mr. Provan was involved in. I simply minded my own business and did whatever I was instructed to do.

The job mostly involved dropping off small packages by hand somewhere around the city for Mr. Provan; or picking up similar packages from somewhere around the city for him, in addition to loading and off-loading stuff contained in mostly regular size boxes from various types of vehicles. I also ran personal errands for Sushla, who had a particular liking for a pastry called Cheese Bread, which I grew fond of myself after she offered one to me one day.

And here is where I give my father the credit he deserves, for the first of two instances that he would make significant contributions, at what was a critical point of my life, as I referred to much earlier. He somehow became aware that I wanted to pursue a career as a Commercial Artist. I figured that it was my Aunt Eileen who would have told him, since I shared it with her.

Just over a month into my Provan stint, he contacted me and advised me to go and see someone at an Advertising Agency called Christiansen & Belgrave (C&B). There I was introduced to someone through a contact that my father had there, with a view to possibly being recruited by the Agency. C&B was located on Ariapita Avenue Woodbrook in the west outskirts of Port of Spain.

I subsequently learnt that Christiansen & Belgrave was the Ad Agency for Southern Sales & Service, the car company that sold Mazda cars exclusively, that my father had been working for as a new car salesman for many years. And thus, the then most recent development.

The person I was introduced to at C&B was one Victor Lewis, who was then the head of the art studio. Upon meeting Victor, and after a formal discussion during which I expressed my unwavering desire to be a Commercial Artist, he gave me an assignment to complete, which I had to present to him the following week for a critique. Based on his instructions, he appeared to have been somewhat of a perfectionist.

The assignment was to redesign an ad that appeared in a daily newspaper, for a fast-food outlet that sold Fried Chicken, Fries and Hamburgers. I believe the name of the business was Chuckwagon. With no computers back then, everything, from the lettering to the products that appeared in the ad, had to be rendered by hand for presentation.

At C&B they were using a combination of fine and medium tip black and colored markers and broad tip gray scale and colored Magic Markers on onion skin layout paper, a combination of which Victor provided me with, after I told him that I could not afford to purchase any of those items.

Victor was very impressed with what I presented a week later, and gave me at least two more assignments to complete, which I continued to take back to him for his critique. After work at my aunt's apartment or any down time at Provan, would have seen me working diligently on the respective assignments.

It was indeed the once in a lifetime opportunity that I was desperately hoping and praying for, in order to get my foot into any door in pursuit of my dream of becoming a bonafide Commercial Artist. It was then being presented to me by Victor Lewis at C&B. So, there was absolutely no way that I was going to allow it to slip from my grasp. I intended to grab and hold on to it with all my might with both hands.

As such, I was executing the assignments that he had been giving me to test my skills, to the absolute best of my artistic ability, employing all that I had learnt under Ronald "Sluggo" John's tutorship years earlier, and which I had been continuing to practice over the years in preparation for that very moment.

MY FIRST ADVERTISING AGENCY EXPERIENCE

However, being that I never expected that any such opportunity would have been presented to me at the time it was, I had already taken my own initiative towards achieving my dream, before I was introduced to Victor Lewis. You see, I already had an interview and had been accepted into the John S. Donaldson Technical Institute Commercial Art Program, which was the only one of its kind in the country at the time.

But thankfully, as I was hoping and praying for and anxiously antic-ipating, at the end of what was about a month-long evaluation, I was also accepted as a Trainee Commercial Artist at C&B. With my lofty dream uppermost in mind, I knew with 100% certainty that there was no other environment that I wanted and needed to be in.

And equally important, at C&B I was going to be acquiring real-world on-the-job experience, in addition to the fact that I was going to be receiving a stipend, which was going to be critical to my survival. Therefore, the decision was a no-brainer.

And so, the very first week in January 1980, I left my messenger job at Provan & Associates after just 3 months and joined Christian & Belgrave Advertising Agency. Normal working hours was supposed to be 8:00 a.m. to 4:00 p.m. But I would quickly learn that normal working hours does not apply in the Advertising business.

As a trainee Artist, the stipend I was being offered was TT$300.00 per month, which was an increase of $60.00 on my Provan wage. And while I would continue to struggle financially, I was only too happy then to finally be where I really wanted to be, and was most definitely not about to complain.

The exciting times continued then, when I joined Starlift, my favorite city steel orchestra, during what was then the 1980 Carnival season. The band was located about a 20 minutes walk from C&B. So, Monday to Friday I worked up until it was time to leave to get to practice, which started at 7:00 p.m.

At the time I joined, the band was about to begin preparations for the upcoming February Steelband Panorama competition, to determine the National Steelband Panorama Champions of that year. Once I joined the band, and since we would also start practicing on Saturday evenings, my weekend trips to Point Fortin came to a halt over the 1-month period I would be engaged with what was then one of my favorite cultural activities.

Starlift had scored a famous "come from behind victory" in the 1979 Panorama competition. They played a song called "DoDo Yeami", sung by the Calypso King of the world, the Mighty Sparrow. Being that they were my favorite city steel orchestra, I was elated over the band's memorable '79 National Panorama victory. Coincidentally, one of my assignments at C&B during my first few months, was to design the Mighty Sparrow's record jacket for what was his then upcoming 1980 25th Anniversary Double Album.

Suffice it to say that it was an absolute honor for me to do so, with the icing on the cake being my design being well received by the man himself. I used silver as the background color for the record jacket, in keeping with the traditional 25 years anniversary theme.

I first visited the Starlift pan yard on a Saturday evening in January, upon which I expressed my interest in joining the band, to one of the gentlemen who I approached when I got there. The individual to whom I spoke, turned out to be the band's Captain. He asked if I could come back the following morning, Sunday. I replied in the affirmative.

Upon returning to the pan yard the following morning, I was introduced to a band member who went by the nickname "Belmont". Quite interesting I thought, given the fact that I had only recently relocated to the said Belmont community from Point Fortin.

That Sunday morning, he put me through my paces, testing my tenor pan playing skills, which included teaching me an entire song to see how quickly I could pick up. I passed the test with flying colors, upon which Belmont then invited me to the band's official practice session the following night, Monday, for which I was most present of course.

I attended practice every night Monday to Friday, and every Saturday evening into night time, as the band prepared for the then upcoming 1980 Panorama competition. And as mentioned prior, I went to the pan yard straight from work during the week, as practice usually started at 7:00 p.m., and usually ended before midnight. However, sessions went passed that time as it got much closer to our preliminary appearance.

Thankfully, with the $60.00 increase on my monthly income, I could then have afforded the $2.00 to take the two taxis necessary to get home after practice during the week, and to and from on Saturdays. I walked to get to work at C&B from the get-go, which took about an hour and a half from my Aunt's Eileen residence.

My lunch menu during the work week basically remained the same as it was while I was at Provan, although there were days when I would buy 1 or 2 Aloo Pies at a shop close by named Hi Hi, which was owned by a Chinese family, just for a change from the usual bread and butter, which had cheese sometimes.

I remember one Miss Hessel, served either Orange Juice, Milo (hot or cold), Green Tea or Coffee to the employees during the course of the work day. Miss Hessel was a very nice older lady and worked as a server at the Agency. She could have been around her mid-50s at the time I joined C&B and lived in Morvant.

She also offered home-cooked meals to employees at an affordable price, which she prepared at home very early every morning before coming to work. I usually ordered based on what was on the menu. Miss Hessel was an excellent cook and was loved and highly respected by all. In fact, she was viewed as more than just the server at the Agency, as to most she was more like a mother or grandmother figure. She also ran a Sou Sou among certain members of the Agency staff.

At Starlift I met one Russell "Teesh" Teshiera, a very famous son of the soil, being that he was an outstanding footballer for his club team Malvern and also his country, as a former captain of our Senior Men's National Team. He was a member of the 1973 team that was cheated in Haiti during the final round of CONCACAF's FIFA World Cup qualifying tournament that year.

I eventually learnt that "Belmont", the band member who tested my tenor playing skills was actually the younger brother of David Rudder, another very famous son of the soil, being one of our Calypso and Soca music legends and icons. Teesh and Belmont were both "Crack Shot" tenor players as were all of the others. Therefore, any new additions to Starlift's tenor section, had to be somewhat of a "Crack Shot" themselves, if they wanted to be in the final selection for the Panorama competition.

For me, the challenge of trying to make the final cut was both exciting and a tad nerve wrecking at the same time; especially the last couple of nights of practice before the Panorama preliminaries. During those particular sessions, certain senior management members of the band, took turns standing right next to me when we rehearsed the tune.

They each stood right next to me to make absolutely sure that I was playing every note of the entire tune. And especially every note in the scale runs that were usually included in the musical arrangement, which meant playing up to 25 notes or more in rapid succession.

There was no room for mistakes or "Shadowing" (meaning at times forgetting which notes to play, and simply pretending to play them on the instrument). But yours truly possessed the required skills, which I learnt and honed during the eight years that I played with Dunlop Tornadoes. I came through with flying colors and made the final cut.

I then had the absolute privilege of playing right next to Russell "Teesh" Teshiera on one of the band's "Floats" at the Panorama preliminaries. That year our Panorama tune was another Mighty Sparrow selection titled "The Robot".

Playing with a big city band in the preliminaries of the National Panorama competition was a most exhilarating experience for me. Back in those days, hundreds and hundreds of supporters and pan lovers alike would be "jumping up" in front, inside, at the sides and behind the bands and in the bleachers, as the bands played their respective Panorama tunes going down what was called "the track", which was the approximately 125 meters of asphalt road that led up to the stage, where the bands would then perform for the judges.

Playing in the prelims was an experience in itself. But playing in my first national semi-final was just UN-BE-LIEVABLE. Standing behind my shiny chrome high-tenor pan that night on the fairly dark Queens Park Savannah stage, I felt the adrenalin flowing through every single member of the band.

My excitement kept mounting with every passing second, and more so when I heard the band being introduced over the powerful sound system by the announcer, upon which the throngs of Starlift supporters that filled the North and Grand stands, erupted into thunderous cheers and applause in unison.

In that instant, the huge stage illuminated as the very bright lights all came on simultaneously, shining down on our large band, which was one hundred members strong. We the players then picked up the arranger Hershel Puckrin's tempo count. Feet start stomping on the wooden stage in time with the tempo; the excitement and anticipation building to a crescendo.

Then came the final count from Puckrin's counting iron. Ting! ting! ting! ting! We burst into the introduction of the piece that then took us on a 10 minutes journey of absolute musical ecstasy! Oooohh! What a feeling! It was most certainly one that I would never, ever, forget.

Sadly though, after all the long nights of intense practice and the subsequent build up and excitement, in the end it all turned into an anti-climactic let down; as while we won the semi-final and were perhaps poised to win it all, disappointingly, the finals of the 1980 National Panorama competition was cancelled.

It was cancelled as a result of the usual, and to use the appropriate Trinidad lingo, "Carnival Bacchanal" that is predictable during the annual festivities. And so, Carnival 1980 which was on Monday the 18th and Tuesday the 19th of February that year, came and went. I continued to live at my Aunt Eileen's, and continued to travel to Point Fortin for the weekends once again.

Meanwhile, although I was being taught and was learning a lot from Victor Lewis at C&B, with whom I developed an extremely good working relationship and friendship, it was one Trevor Cardinal who became my mentor.

Trevor was a Trinidadian who had returned to Trinidad to take up the position of Creative Director at the agency, after working for many years in the United States at Leo Burnett Advertising Agency in Chicago among some other top New York based Ad Agencies. The Assistant Creative Director and Chief Copy Writer then was one Rodlyn Douglas.

Also working in the Art Studio apart from Victor Lewis at the time were Robert O'Brien, Adrian Chandler, and Leslie Ann Sherwood. Robert, Adrian, and Leslie-Ann were all Junior Artists from whom I would also learn a fair amount. While I became very good friends with Adrian and Leslie-Ann, Robert and I would become very close friends. Both Adrian and Leslie-Ann eventually left C&B to pursue their Graphic Arts Degrees at Pratt Institute in New York.

Like Adrian and Leslie-Ann, Robert O'Brien was a very good graphic designer. He also knew and taught me the tricks and short-cuts of the trade. Victor Lewis, who as I mentioned prior, was the Studio Manager, was excellent at executing finished art-work, or past-up as it was known back then. In fact, that was his specialty and he taught me that aspect of the job.

One Clive Belgrave was the then boss at C&B. He was quite easy-going. I would eventually come to learn that Mr. Christiansen, the other partner of the Christiansen & Belgrave partnership, had died sometime before I joined the agency.

During my first few months at C&B and thereafter, I felt most comfortable when I was in the Art Studio. Outside of the studio environment, the attitudes of some of the other employees towards me, especially those in the front offices, all of whom was of the "so called" local upper-class ilk, was as though I was somehow out of place.

I distinctly remember the boss's secretary's attitude in particular. I could tell from day one that she did not like me at all. She was Caucasian, which is also referred to as French Creole locally. She was the first person one would encounter upon entering the building, since she sat at the front desk, which was situated right outside the boss's office. She never responded to my extremely polite daily "good morning" greetings when I arrived to work, and also never made eye contact with me.

She ensured that I did feel totally out of place indeed. She treated me with absolute disdain. I guess I did not qualify for acknowledgment by someone of her ilk. Whatever her reason might have been, my feeling that she did not like me was eventually confirmed by a co-worker who held a senior position at the agency, to whom she had expressed that sentiment.

Though having to see the individual's face upon entering the building every day that I arrived for work, I refused to let it bother me. I simply continued saying good morning to her.

But I was at the agency on a mission. And I was not going to allow her, others like her, or anyone else for that matter, to deter me from accomplishing it. In any event, I identified with, could relate more, and much preferred to engage with the employees at the agency, that did not belong to the so called "upper class ilk" anyway.

So apart from those in the Art Studio at the time, among whom it was always fun to work with, I established very good relationships with fellow employees Carlyle Joseph and Cheryl Woodroffe, who worked in the accounts department. And much later on, with Beryl and Sally-Ann when they eventually joined the Agency. They both worked in the traffic department.

I remember Trevor Cardinal immediately throwing me into the deep end with the very first assignment he gave me, which was a very important one. It was to design the logo for a company named Audio Visual Productions.

After conceptualizing and doing a number of sketches, and finally coming up with an idea that met with his approval, he had me do over the marker execution that was to be presented to the client for approval, until I got it as close as possible to what a final printed version would look like. The height of the bar in terms of Trevor's expectations was then set.

Thereafter, my natural talent and passion for Graphic Art was recognized by Trevor. And so, he took me under his wing. He had extremely high professional standards, and always made learning fun.

Having worked at such a reputable agency like Leo Burnett among others, Trevor was indeed the consummate professional. He was highly creative and had full mastery of all aspects of the Advertising and Graphic Design fields from ideas to executions. He most definitely represented what I aspired to be. I was indeed extremely fortunate to have had him as a mentor.

As stated earlier, fine, and medium tip markers, broad tip Magic Markers and Onion Skin Layout paper was the order of the day. After the layout for a newspaper or magazine ad or an entire Print Ad Campaign or Graphic Design idea was executed utilizing the aforementioned, it was then mounted on a material known as Stag Blank, using a transparent glue called Rubber Cement, which was applied with a brush. The excess Rubber Cement, was cleaned away with a Rubber Cement Pick-Up (eraser).

At C&B, with Trevor as Creative Director and leading the troops, working through an entire night and well into daylight the following morning was very much common place among studio employees. We referred to it as "Making ah dawn". And while "Making Dawns" took its toll both mentally and physically, it was enjoyable work, given that the studio staff was like a family. Then there was always Robert O'Brien, who was the official "Studio Comic" so to speak, to provide the humor that contributed to making the work enjoyable.

Meanwhile, for reasons still unknown to me, about 6 months into my stay at my aunt Eileen's Belmont residence, she decided that she no longer wished for me to continue staying at her apartment. That was at the very beginning of the Easter school holidays in April 1980.

To get me to vacate, she told me that she and her son were going to visit family in the southern part of the country for the entire 3 to 4 weeks of the Easter school holidays, and she did not trust to leave me in her apartment alone, because she felt that I would have been entertaining girls and other undesirables in her absence.

I found her reasoning very strange, since she knew that I didn't even have as much as one friend, much less girlfriends, to invite to the apartment. And even if I did, I never would have disrespected her and her place of abode by doing so, period.

And even further, given the ongoing tension that existed between us since the very first week I had been there, I wouldn't have even entertained the thought, to jeopardize my continuing to enjoy the accommodation that she had afforded me, which was critical as I tried to find my feet in the nation's capital.

But whatever her real reason, I realized that she simply wanted me out, and I did not want to be where I wasn't wanted; so, I left. I then moved in to my older brother Evans' place. At the time he lived in a small self-contained room on French Street Woodbrook, just west of the Port of Spain city center, and a relatively short distance from C&B.

During the first 2 weeks that my aunt said she would have been away visiting family, I called her phone at the apartment from C&B every other day from Monday to Friday. She answered it every time. I simply hung up upon hearing her voice. I was deeply hurt given that as mentioned before, she was my favorite Aunt on my father's side. I always wanted to know her real reason for wanting me out, knowing full well that I didn't do anything to have warranted such treatment from her.

But then again, she really didn't need a reason, given the fact that she knew that our own father, her brother, had neglected us from very early childhood. So, she was well within her rights to not want to assume the responsibility for another one of his children.

You see, she had already done so for my older brother Evans over an extended period, at some point during his childhood. She lived in the Eastern community of Barataria at the time. I remember accompanying my mother on at least one occasion to visit them there.

While relocating to French Street Woodbrook made getting to work at C&B much easier for me, since the distance was then reduced to about a 15 minutes walk, my brother's room was much too small to comfortably accommodate the both of us. I was then also taking away the privacy that he would have been enjoying, while he lived there on his own.

So only a few weeks after I had moved in, we both relocated a bit further west to Fort George Road St. James at the corner of the Western Main Road, which was also another very vibrant community. There we joined two other bachelors who then shared the up-stairs 3-bedroom accommodation of the 2-story concrete dwelling, where the common areas were the living room and dining room, kitchen, toilet, and bath.

One of the two other bachelors was Popeye, who was one of the John brothers, with whom we grew up in Point Fortin, whom I then gathered, would have told my brother about the vacancy at our new place of abode. Popeye had relocated to Port of Spain some years before, and they were then working at the same drafting firm, after my brother had secured a job for him there. The name of the firm was Planning & Associates.

My brother and I shared the bedroom that was available at the time for several months, until Popeye eventually relocated. I then occupied the bedroom Popeye vacated. Both my older brother and I then had our own private space, which also allowed me to feel some sense of personal independence for the very first time in my life.

The individual who occupied the third bedroom, whose name was Knolly, also eventually moved out, upon which my buddy Tony Dora from my Point Fortin home town, who had since also relocated to the nation's capital moved in, and resided with us for some time. Like my older brother Evans and Popeye, he was also employed as a draftsman.

My $300.00 per month stipend from C&B, in addition to income I then began generating from freelance jobs, enabled me to meet my basic living expenses, and continue to help my mother financially as much as I could.

After initially recognizing and thereafter verbally acknowledging my natural talent and passion for not only Graphic Design, but also for Advertising during my first six months at C&B, Trevor Cardinal suggested the idea to me of going abroad to pursue a degree in those fields.

Traveling abroad to study was never a thought that I had entertained, because I knew that realistically, my lack of not only personal finances, but also of outside financial support, would have never enabled me to do so. However, Trevor's idea did in fact give me food for thought.

Trevor further suggested that I approach my father for financial assistance. That was when I more or less figured out that Trevor was my father's contact at the agency, through which my initial evaluation from Victor Lewis came about, since my father's then employers Southern Sales & Service, was on C&B's client list, as mentioned earlier.

I then had to explain to Trevor through a brief history of the relationship between my father and me, why approaching my father for any type of financial assistance wasn't an option that I wished to explore. But on his own accord and unknown to me at the time, Trevor had subsequently approached my father, with a view to my father lending the necessary financial assistance towards the proposed idea.

Trevor then came back with the news that he received a favorable response from my father. I was shocked. I didn't quite know what to make of it. I figured that my father gave a favorable response only because he would have wanted to create a false impression for Trevor and thus, couldn't say no. That was around June / July of 1980.

We then set the September 1982 Fall Semester as my enrollment target, which would have allowed for a full 24 months to put the necessary things in place. While Trevor himself had attended and obtain his degree from The School of Visual Arts in New York, the school that he recommended was Pratt Institute, which was also in New York. I then assumed that he may have also recommended Pratt to both Adrian Chandler and Leslie Ann Sherwood as well.

And again, unknown to me at the time, Trevor went even further than just approaching my father. He was also devising a plan that would enable me to start accumulating my own funds, which would increase my chances of achieving the set goal. Towards that end, after 9 months of intense training at C&B under him, his plan was then put into action.

He secured a job for me in the Art Studio at a label printing company called Cariflex, which was owned and operated by a family whose last name was Sooknarine. Cariflex was located in Kelly Village Caroni, Central Trinidad. Trevor even went so far as to negotiate my salary with the bosses at Cariflex, who were a father and son team. I was going to be paid TT$1,200.00 per month; $900.00 more than the $300.00 stipend amount I was receiving at C&B.

Nennie had since moved out of her sister's Watts Street residence, and moved into an apartment at a house located directly behind her sister's house but on another street. She continued to spend time between Curepe and Point Fortin. Curepe was not very far from where my new job was located. So, I made arrangements to stay at Nennie's new residence during the workweek, while I would continue to spend the weekends at the other residence at Fort George Road in St. James.

And after what was then a 12 months hiatus, football was back on my personal agenda once again; as the move to Curepe then saw me join

Nautico's Senior Men's Team, whereupon I was reunited with some of my old team mates, that I played with on the club's youth team years before.

I started to work at Cariflex the first week in October 1980. The job was basically doing label designs and pre-press art work for a host of different products, from nail polish to a wide variety of food packages and other products. My normal working hours was 8:00 a.m. to 4:00 p.m. Monday to Friday. To get to the football field on time for training, which was at a field on the University of the West Indies Campus at the time, I left work promptly at 4:00 p.m. every day during my first week at Cariflex.

However, I observed that each day that I was preparing to leave, the other two artists who worked in the Art Studio at the time, whose first names were Adel and Willis, would look at me in a sort of strange way. It continued into my second week. At that point in time, I guess Adel felt comfortable enough with me to reveal the reason for their strange looks upon me promptly departing at 4:00 p.m.

Apparently, all employees were expected to work overtime every day. Oh really? I thought to myself; because it was a company policy, which the Cariflex bosses never conveyed to me. So, I simply continued to disregard it. But I was totally unaware that the bosses were themselves also taking note of my prompt daily 4:00 p.m. departure, by observing me through the one-way mirror installed in a partition wall of their office, which all employees had to pass by to exit the building.

I got the feeling that they may have told Adel and Willis to get the message across to me and expected me to comply, when after about 3 weeks to a month, I was called into their office on my way out one evening. The son (initials JS), then revealed to me what I had already became aware of. I told him that I was involved with a football team, and needed to get to the practice field by a certain time; and I was not prepared to forgo training simply to facilitate their overtime policy, because I was never informed about it in the first place.

I told JS that I would rather leave the job, if I was asked to give up football. He seemed stunned by my stated position. Still, in the back of my mind I knew I was at Cariflex for a specific purpose, and would not have wanted to disappoint and or embarrass Trevor by leaving, after all he was doing to open doors for me, whereby I would then have a shot at enjoying a comfortable life in the future.

But I had already proven my worth over the very short time I was employed there, so JS gave in. I felt a deep sense of relief, because if I had been given an ultimatum, I would obviously have had to choose the job over football. Thankfully, it turned out to be a win-win situation in the end.

In addition to Nautico, I also began playing in the then very popular Curepe community minor league competition with the team aptly named Curepe Youths, since it was made up of mostly young players from the area. The league was being conducted on the very same Knowles Street Recreation Ground, where I was discovered by the then Nautico U-16 coach Wayne Ferreira 4 years earlier.

Our extremely talented and skillful squad of players from back to front, as well as our entertaining style of play and most importantly our winning ways, made us a huge fan favorite. We had several goal scorers on the team, myself included. The team Captain was one Dale "Bragger" Hinds, who was himself one of the team's goal scorers. Bragger was our best player and was "Mr. Skillco" himself. He was most definitely one the community's young football stars.

Other former Curepe Youths team mates I remember by first and or last names include Kenneth Thorpe, Wendell Ferguson, Carvel Collins, Greenidge, Claude (one of two goalkeepers), Nanton, Fitzroy and Kenrick and Kenneth Gaskin who were twins. Kenneth Gaskin was the other goalkeeper. Other team mates I remember by nicknames include Cockorn, Bahlay, Pop (who was deaf), Laddy, Bumpy, Ahlose and W.

As skillful, flashy, and highly entertaining as Bragger was, I am sure that most of the players, fans, and supporters within the Curepe community, will agree that the then undisputed king of Curepe football and the absolute star of the Nautico team, was one Victor "Peanuts" Hazel. He was a slightly built creative midfielder who possessed the full repertoire of skills.

Peanuts deservedly went on to represent the Trinidad & Tobago Senior Men's National Team, and was dubbed "The Bionic Boy" by the local media, because of what he was able to do on the football field, given his size. I believe that Peanuts had since joined another team, TECSA, who played in the then top-flight National League, when I rejoined Nautico.

Apart from Peanuts and Bragger, other members of the Nautico team I can remember by full names or nicknames included Glenrick King who was one of the team's goal scorers, Steve Grayson, Wayne Earle and by their nicknames, Groover, Bunny, Gozeh and Mango the goalkeeper. The coach was Leon "Yipper" Grayson. Most of the Curepe Youths players transitioned into the Nautico team.

During that period, the team played in the Trinidad & Tobago Football Association's East Zone competition. I had come to absolutely love the team, and grew close to all those involved. Once again, I made many new football friends. However, my playing days with Nautico was short. It was short because although an extremely important part of my life, I simply couldn't make playing football the priority then.

The first week of October 1981, exactly 1 year after joining Cariflex, I was back at Christiansen & Belgrave Advertising Agency, in a move totally orchestrated by Trevor Cardinal once again. He also negotiated my salary. My C&B salary was then up to $1,500.00 per month, $1,200.00 more than the $300.00 stipend I was receiving when I first arrived at the agency 2 years earlier. It was all Trevor's doing with one goal in mind, which was for me to attend Pratt.

Notwithstanding my ongoing monthly living expenses; assisting my mother, and expenses then attached to courting my first real girlfriend, the sacrifice of saving toward my goal of attending Pratt Institute continued. Additional funds earned from freelance assignments kept it on track. It was then 11 months out from when I was scheduled to be enrolled.

As for my aforementioned first real girlfriend? It was during the last 6 months of the one-year period that I worked at Cariflex, during which I was spending time between the Curepe and St. James residences that I met her, and entered into what evolved into the first of only two totally committed relationships I would have, during the course of my lifetime.

I had noticed her for the very first time at a Nautico football game, which was played at Constantine Park in Tunapuna. I played in that game. It turned out that she was the sister of one of my Nautico team mates. We had our very first face to face encounter on Easter Sunday of '81, when we were simply passing close to each other going in opposite directions. As we passed each other I said a few words to her.

That very brief encounter occurred after an event which I attended, that was held in what was known as the Plannings located along the Southern Main Road Curepe, which consisted of a number of separate Government family housing units. She lived with her family in one of the housing units.

After getting to know each other a bit over a few months, I asked her mother if I could take her out on a date to see a movie. Her mother allowed me to, I guess because by that time her mother would have gotten to know a bit about my background as well. On that first date, I took her to see the movie at the Palladium cinema in Tunapuna. I'll refer to her as "my then girlfriend", from this point on.

So, with love then very much in the air between me and my then girlfriend, my ties to Curepe was becoming even stronger. It also meant that my weekend visits to Point Fortin became less frequent. As such, my mother then traveled to Port of Spain to visit me on the job at C&B.

For the then obvious reason, I was making night visits to Curepe once or twice during the workweek and spending most weekends from Friday night to Sunday evening at Nennie's apartment, from where I would go visit my then girlfriend, which was only about a 15 minutes walk to her home.

I began to play competitive football once again in the Curepe community minor league, whereby I just had to show up for games, generally once a week during the workweek or on the weekends. But that time around I played with a team called Spartans, led by one Glenford Daly. I eventually stopped playing in the Curepe minor league completely.

But I must say that my days playing football in Curepe were some of the most enjoyable times I had, especially with the many players I had the pleasure of playing with, most of whom became my friends.

I had come to accept that my dream of playing the game at the highest local level was not going to be realized. I then wanted to at least have the experience of playing the local club game at its second highest level. So, I joined Malvern Football Club, which was competing at that said level at the time, in the Trinidad & Tobago Football Association's North Zone competition.

The Woodbrook Port of Spain based club was then in preparations for their '82 season. Malvern was one of Trinidad's top football clubs during the 60s and 70s, when they were then known as the "Woodbrook Glamour Boys". They had a very talented squad of players when I joined the club.

At Malvern I first trained under Coach Hannibal Najar. He was a former national player, who years after he retired from the game, became the coach of the Trinidad and Tobago Senior Men's National Team. I never appeared in a competitive match for Malvern under Coach Najar.

Najar was eventually replaced by one Kelvin Nancoo. But I was also never given the opportunity to play in a competitive game under Coach Nancoo. I felt that I did well in training under both coaches, and was extremely disappointed that I did not get the chance to play. But I did not give up.

I so badly wanted to be playing on the team when I joined the club, that I was training twice daily on most training days. It was a work ethic that Warren Archibald and some of my other Point Fortin idols adopted back in the day, which I had witnessed on a few occasions, so I decided to apply it to my then current situation.

My first session began at 4:15 a.m. each morning. After some intense stretching, I would leave the house promptly at 4:30 a.m. With boots and ball in my relatively small traveling bag, which strap was hung over my right shoulder and across my back and chest and held at my side with my left hand, I then took the 15 to 20 minutes warm-up jog from the corner of Fort George Road and the Western Main Road in St. James to the Queen's Park savannah.

There I did my own physical and ball skills training for about an hour, after which I then jogged back to my St. James residence, had breakfast, and readied myself for work. It took only about 15 minutes for me to get to work by taxi in those days, including a 10 minutes walk after being dropped off on Tragarete Road by the taxi. Each evening after work at C&B, I then attended the official training session with the Malvern team, which included running the sand track where the race horses trained.

I finally got my opportunity with the Malvern team under our third coach, after another coaching change. He was then a member of the Trinidad & Tobago Coast Guard. I only knew him by his nickname "Smiley". I played in three successive games; the first as a sub, and starting in the other two. I had worked extremely hard and had finally made the team. But by that time, tertiary education abroad was then coming quickly into focus, so I had to abort the rest of the season thereafter.

And even as I never played under either of Coach Najar or Coach Nancoo, the upside was that apart from thoroughly enjoying and benefitting from the training sessions, I certainly gained some new football friends, which I would not have if I had simply given up and left.

Those by first or last, or full names or nicknames that I can remember include, Eldon Kujufi, Ruskin Mark, Willis, Boxhill (Boxo), Hustler, Chris (the defender), X, another Chris (a then very young speedy forward from San Juan), Tom, and Smokey and Flyman, who were both Goalkeepers.

After leaving Malvern, and since I did not have to dedicate any time to training and just simply show up for games, on invitation from Robert O'Brien, my then work colleague at C&B who had since become a very close friend, I began playing in another community minor league in the village of Bourg Mulatresse San Juan.

I played with a team called "Bran United", which was formed by a group of brothers from the community, spearheaded by the youngest Ralph Harewood, aka "Lux". Bran was managed by no other than Robert O'Brien himself. I totally enjoyed my time playing with Bran United, during which I once again made many new football friends.

LEAVING MY HOMELAND: MY FIRST EVER TRIP TO THE UNITED STATES AND THE BIG APPLE

I had applied to Pratt sometime in early 1982, with a view to enrolling in the institution's Manhattan Associate Degree Program in September that year. In response to my application, I was invited to either submit my portfolio by mail, or bring it in to Pratt for a review.

After contacting the Dean of Admissions via telephone, I decided that I would travel to New York for the Portfolio review, as I felt that a face-to-face meeting would have increased my chances of being accepted. I informed my mother, who was equally excited about the prospect as I was.

I intended to live on the Brooklyn Campus while attending school in Manhattan. But anticipating that I would have been attending Pratt from that September of '82, my mother then decided that she wanted to travel to New York ahead of me to work, so she could secure an apartment, so that I would have a place to live comfortably while I was attending school. I felt it was a sensible idea. And so, I facilitated my mother's timely departure from Trinidad. My younger brother Brian also left Trinidad for the U.S. shortly thereafter, but resided in New Jersey.

In addition to a favorable portfolio review, to gain admission into Pratt, I was also required to provide proof that I was going to be able to pay the tuition fees for the first year of study. I had to do so by way of submitting official paperwork from my sponsor, who was going to be my father, after he gave that assurance to Trevor. When the time drew near my portfolio was ready. The only thing then left for me to do personally, was to purchase my plane ticket for my trip to New York.

Then the time came for my father to provide the documents required to confirm his sponsorship. I really wanted Trevor to, but instead, Trevor urged me to call him. I did. "Boy listen nah. Yuh go hah tuh put off going to Pratt until next year yes," he bluntly stated to me over the telephone. He did not give the reason. And so, after 2 long years of planning, preparation, and high anticipation, I simply had to accept that I would not have been attending Pratt come September.

I was totally devastated and felt really bad for Trevor after all his efforts. But at the same time, I also felt that it would have then given him an idea of the kind of person my father was, in case he may have had doubts after I had alerted him prior.

It was a colossal let down indeed. And not for the first time, I was extremely angry at my father, as my dream of becoming a full-fledged commercial artist, was then very much a dream deferred. I then also had to give my mother the bad news. Utterly deflated, and while it was an extremely difficult thing to do, I somehow managed to refocus, and so continued to further develop my Advertising and Graphic Design skills under Trevor's tutelage.

Songwriting then began to play a more significant role in my life, as I sought a way to deal with another bout of pain, that came with another major disappointment by my father. And so, I also continued to keep developing my skills as an aspiring tunesmith. As a part of the process, I bought myself a keyboard and started to learn playing it self-taught. I eventually composed two original musical pieces on the keyboard.

Continuing to play minor league football, that time around in a Sunday morning league that was conducted on a ground in the community of St. Joseph, with a team called Savannah Boys, which was comprised of some of Nautico's former older players, and continuing to build my then one-year old relationship with my then girlfriend, also helped to ease the pain of the Pratt disappointment.

I naturally became overly anxious about the prospects for entering Pratt the following year, with my thinking then being that my father was simply going to continue his lifetime trend of disappointing me, which was also continuing to further diminish any chance of us ever cultivating any type of solid father / son relationship.

I was then willing to make even more sacrifices and go it alone if I had to. I was prepared to work even harder by way of increasing the number of private jobs I was doing in order to save more, towards realizing my dream.

1983 arrived. I reapplied that said January month for enrollment at Pratt to begin classes that September. I was once again given the option to either submit my portfolio by mail or bring it in to the school for a review. I stayed with the second option. My trip was tentatively planned for April.

Expecting disappointment from my father, I was very cautious about being too optimistic over the prospect of him delivering that time around. So, one can only imagine the initial high anxiety, then the absolute relief I felt when the time came once again, and my father actually provided the paperwork that I needed, which included a letter of intent towards my first year's tuition of US$6,045.00, which TT equivalent was $14,645.15. The exchange rate was then TT$2.421.00 to 1 USD.

I would be totally responsible for all of my other expenses, including living, school related, clothing and other miscellaneous expenses, towards which I had already been saving. And by then, I had in fact saved enough funds to cover my expenses through almost my entire first year of school.

I traveled to the U.S. for the very first time with New York as my destination on Friday April 29th 1983, on British West Indian Airways

(BWIA) Flight 420. We departed Piarco International Airport at 9:30 a.m. and arrived at John F. Kennedy (JFK) International Airport at around 4:50 p.m.

My mother met me at JFK accompanied by a male friend, who was the owner of the car that would take us to our final destination. I was extremely happy to see my mother, not having seen her for almost a year at the time. As expected, the weather was quite chilly, as it was the Spring season. So, I made sure that I wore a couple of long-sleeved jerseys, together with a track top. I enjoyed the journey from JFK to our Brooklyn destination; totally absorbing the new environment.

At the time my mother was living with her Aunt Louise (Nennie's sister and the owner of the Watts Street Curepe house) and her husband at their Lincoln Road residence, just off the famous Nostrand Avenue that I had heard so much about while back in Trinidad. I stayed with them the entire 3 weeks of my visit.

Upon our arrival at the apartment, we all chatted for a while. I then headed back outside to get the vibes of the Brooklyn streets. I was also anxious to window-shop to see all the inexpensive stuff that I had also heard about. I took a casual stroll up Nostrand in the direction of the even more famous Eastern Parkway, where the annual West Indian Labor Day Carnival parade is held.

The sight of huge Boom-Boxes in show-windows as I walked by for as little as $50.00USD (just over TT $100.00 at the time) was enough to get me very excited. Why ah didn't walk with some keyash (American Express Travelers Cheques) boy? I thought to myself. I was ready to buy without even first shopping around, like most first time Trini visitors to New York that I knew who had the experience, which they admitted was a mistake.

My Portfolio review was scheduled for Monday May 2nd. Not knowing how to get to the Pratt Manhattan location, my mother asked one of our relatives, Jenny Hercules, if she would accompany us. Jenny was happy to oblige.

It was at Jenny's mother, Cynthia Hercules, who was Nennie's other sister, that we sometimes also use to spend bits of time with during the very early years. They lived in Prizgar Lands Laventille as indicated in an earlier passage. Their entire family had already been living in New York for many years.

My very first ride on the New York subway was thrilling, but at the same time it also gave me a bit of an uneasy feeling. Fellow passengers' faces all seemed to have had the same deadpan look. Some were sitting with eyes closed or fixated on some type of reading material. Others were staring downwards or upwards. At what? I couldn't tell you.

Without warning, the lights inside the car of the train would go out unexpectedly, leaving the car in total darkness for a few seconds on each occasion. The first few times it happened I was like, "what de hell!" until I realized during the course of the journey that it was normal.

Pratt Institute Manhattan Center was located at Lexington Avenue and East 30th Street. The then Dean of Admissions was very impressed with my Portfolio. And based on what he was seeing, felt that I chose the right program.

He even jokingly commented that he didn't even think that I needed to attend school; a comment that was a direct reflection of Trevor Cardinal's mentorship. After reviewing the sponsorship paperwork that I submitted, he gave me the assurance that I would definitely be accepted as a student at the institute. I was ecstatic. So too were my mother and Jenny.

Having then taken care of the official business at Pratt, the rest of my time in New York was spent doing some shopping and visiting relatives. My mother and I also took the opportunity to visit my younger brother Brian in New Jersey, who like my mother, I was also very happy to see.

My mother said she intended to get her own apartment before I returned to start school in September, so that I could be totally comfortable. I had in fact heard stories about some of my countrymen and women having some extremely unpleasant experiences, while living with their very own families or relatives in Uncle Sam's country. I guess my mother did not want me going through such experiences. I know that I most certainly didn't.

So, after what was a very successful and enjoyable first ever trip to the U.S. and New York in particular, I returned to Trinidad on Friday May 20th 1983. Upon my return to work, I found out that while I was abroad, Trevor had unexpectedly left both Christiansen & Belgrave and Trinidad to return to Leo Burnett in Chicago. For obvious reasons, I was extremely saddened by the news.

He was my mentor and did a lot for my career and for me as a person. Most significantly, he put me on the path towards achieving my dream of becoming a full-fledged Commercial Artist / Graphic Designer. More than anyone else, including my father, I truly owe Trevor Cardinal an eternal debt of gratitude. So, Trevor, wheresoever you are; I say thank you for recognizing, acknowledging and most of all, believing in me and my artistic talent. Thank you, thank you, thank you most sincerely, for completely changing the course of my life.

The three months between returning to Trinidad and having to leave for the U.S. once again seemed to have flown by. It was spent focusing on continuing to build on the then two years old relationship with my then girlfriend and replenishing my savings.

During that time, I received a formal letter confirming that I had been accepted as a student at Pratt Manhattan School of Design. After a bit of the then expected uncertainty from my father, all the final paperwork was eventually done, my Student Visa was secured, I received my first semester tuition cheque, and I was readying myself to take on the "Big Apple", to fulfill the first of my three childhood dreams.

But something very interesting occurred during the final weeks leading up to my departure. There appeared to have been a changing of attitudes towards me, from those who were generally snobbish towards me during my time at the agency, when those particular co-workers from C&B's front offices, found out that I was leaving to go to the U.S. to study.

When the time finally came, I received a grand send-off with a gift of a brown genuine leather shoulder bag, in a ceremony held in the Agency's Boardroom in the presence of the Staff. And to my astonishment, it was presented to me with a kiss on the cheek, by one of the female front office co-workers who was usually one of the snobs.

Meanwhile, my then girlfriend was also going to be leaving Trinidad for New York for summer vacation, a few weeks before I would myself have been departing for school. She had since graduated from the Secondary School she attended, after which she had then attended a Secretarial School, both of which were known to be institutions of prestige. She subsequently landed a job at a top financial institution.

The week before she left for New York, we sat down and we discussed plans for a future together. She was extremely excited about the idea of us settling down together by way of marriage sometime after I graduated, as was I.

So much so, that we went as far as to even select a name for our would be first child, during our discussion. The name was a combination of both our first names, should it be a girl, which is what she wanted. I was most definitely looking forward to a future together, until death do us part.

However, after my then girlfriend left for New York, I received some very disturbing information, for which I will admit I was very thankful, from a female who was then one of her closest friends, and with whom I had just a casual friendship at the time.

And maybe it was because I was still so very naive and ignorant, but not for the life of me, could I have quite understood why her then very close female friend would have seen it fit to volunteer the information she did, and moreover, at the time she did, which was after my then girlfriend left for New York.

The information I received was certainly disturbing enough for me to have addressed the issue with my then girlfriend sooner rather than later, since we had only very recently sat down and discussed plans for a future together. But for some reason, I never brought it up with her then, or at any other time during the course of our entire relationship.

Maybe it was because I was suffering from a serious case of "first love syndrome", and feared that bringing up the issue would have jeopardized the relationship. However, I most certainly kept the information I had received at the forefront of my mind.

I arrived in New York on the U.S. Labor Day weekend Friday September 2nd 1983, excited, and eagerly looking forward to what promised to be a life changing experience. My mother had secured her own apartment as she intended, earlier in that very same week in anticipation of my arrival.

I took a taxi into Brooklyn from the JFK airport, not certain as to where my final destination was going to be. I was supposed to meet my mother at the residence of the Thomas family, who we knew from Trinidad since back in the 70s. They were originally from Arima, in the north eastern part of Trinidad before they immigrated to the U.S.

Patricia (or simply Pat), a member of the said family, actually had a daughter, Jolene, with my older brother Evans, during a longstanding relationship while the Thomas' were living in Arima. Jolene was my older brother's second child, with Kerry his son, as I mentioned earlier, being his first.

I arrived at the Thomas' residence just before nightfall. They lived on Madison Street between Throop and Thompkins Avenues in Bed-Stuy, which unknown to me at the time, had a well-established reputation for being one of the very toughest neighborhoods in Brooklyn.

My younger brother Brian came up from New Jersey and was at the Thomas' waiting to take me to our mother's apartment. After exchanging pleasantries and engaging in "ah lil bit ah Trini ole talk", I left my luggage at the Thomas' and accompanied Brian to check out the apartment where our mother lived. It was a relatively short distance from the Thomas'.

As we got near, Brian pointed out the building. It was located at the corner of Gates and Thompkins Avenues, a couple of blocks north of

Madison Street. To me it looked like one of several abandoned buildings that littered the general area. There was a Chinese Fast-Food Restaurant on the ground floor. Still, looking from the outside, I honestly didn't think that any of the other floors above it was habitable to anyone, let alone my mother.

Brian led me up the fairly dark wooden staircase to our mother's 2nd floor apartment. He opened the door. We stepped inside, closing the door behind us. The very first thing that I noticed was that candles lit up the apartment. It immediately conjured up memories of years gone by.

I stood still for a few moments and looked around from where I was standing a few steps into the living room. My mother hurriedly approached and greeted me with a big smile, a hug and a kiss. But I was speechless. There was absolutely no way that I was going to stay there. Not even for one night; much less actually live there.

My sister Cheryl was also in New York on vacation at the time with her three daughters, Keithann, Keisha and Kellyann, my nephew Marlon, all under the age of ten, and one of her sisters-in-law who was in her mid-teens. They were all at the apartment when I arrived.

Like the actual building itself, the apartment, which was a 1 bedroom, was run-down. There was no electricity, thus the use of candles to light up the apartment. There was also no water in the taps, no gas, and no heat, when it was already Fall, heading into the Winter.

They actually had to go over to the Thomas' to take showers. There was a very old refrigerator that was useless anyway without electricity, and a similarly very old stove, which was also useless with no gas in the apartment. So, they were buying meals every day since they occupied the apartment.

The living room furnishings included a single used couch, a small table, and a few dining room type chairs, all of which were not in very good condition. I did not even bother to venture into the bedroom or bathroom areas.

It was revealed to me that it was someone else who found my mother the apartment and not my mother herself. I knew then that she took it out of desperation; and I knew that because of time and financial constraints, it was the best that my mother could have done in the circumstances, in her effort to provide accommodation for me; and I deeply appreciated it.

But I also knew right there and then that I had a major decision to make, as I simply could not myself, let alone have my mother live under such deplorable conditions. There was absolutely no way that I would have been able to function, considering that I was in New York for the sole purpose of studying.

I immediately began thinking that I would then have to resort back to my original plan, which was to live on the Brooklyn Campus, whereby my mother would have then been able to return to Trinidad if she wished to with my sister Cheryl and her kids, when they were returning.

I left the apartment and returned to the Thomas'. I explained my predicament. Immediately recognizing the dire situation, Pat's younger sister Ann informed me that there was an apartment available in a house across the street from their residence, which was owned by a fellow Trinidadian whose name was Moses. Ann knew Moses, and offered to speak to him on my behalf the following morning, with a view to him possibly renting the apartment to me and my mother.

I asked if I could, and the Thomas' granted my request to allow me to stay at their apartment for the night. With Ann's help, I was hopeful of sorting out what was an extremely desperate situation the following morning. I was so anxious, that as comfortable as their living room couch was, I did not sleep a wink that night.

School was scheduled to commence the week after the Labor Day week. Ann kept her word and spoke to Moses the following morning Saturday, after which she took me to meet and speak with him personally. Immediately sensing my desperation, Moses agreed to rent the apartment to us. And while I had already done so way back then, again I say to you Ann "Lucy" Thomas wherever you may be, thank you.

His house was 2 floors plus the basement, which Moses himself occupied with his wife and then very young son. We rented the 1st floor, which was the one that was available. The 2nd floor was occupied by a mother and daughter who were originally from Barbados. The apartment was a fairly large one bedroom and was in very good condition, and had all the necessary utilities.

The rent would be $400.00 per month. With the additional one month's security deposit, $800.00 would have been required as upfront payment in order to secure the apartment, which presented my first major New York headache.

You see, the only cash that was available was the cash that I had traveled with. I had always intended to contribute to the rent, utility bills and food etc., at any apartment that my mother and I lived in.

But the cash that I had was also supposed to cover other expenses like transportation, meals while at school, school supplies and seasonal attire etc., during my first school year, which would be 8 months long from September to May, with Christmas holidays and Spring break in between.

But in the given circumstances, I had no other choice but to promptly pay the $800.00 to Moses to secure the apartment the very Saturday morning.

Then there was the matter of furnishing the apartment so that we could have lived comfortably, which represented my second major New York headache, keeping in mind that I had only arrived for school less than 24 hours before.

Again, I really had no choice in the matter. Thankfully, a stove and refrigerator came with the rental of the apartment. Both items were in good condition. Later on, that Saturday morning, accompanied by Ann's brother Don, we headed to a furniture store that he was familiar with, located just off Fulton Street in the vicinity of Bedford Avenue.

There I purchased furnishings for the entire apartment, including carpet to cover the fairly large living room area. The items were delivered by the store that Saturday afternoon. From that day on, Don and I became good buddies.

I made sure that my mother moved into the apartment that same afternoon. We then had a much better than decent place in which we both could live comfortably over the long haul, wherein I could have then been totally focused on school. 401 Madison Street, Brooklyn New York 11221 would be my first official address in the U.S. The residence was between Thompkins and Throop Avenues.

After taking care of registration at the main campus in Brooklyn on the Tuesday following Labor Day, which included payment of tuition fees for my first semester, I was then officially enrolled in the Pratt Institute School of Art and Design / Associate Degree Program. My student number was 999-20-2230. Then began mental and other preparations, as I was about to embark on my New York mission.

As mentioned earlier, my then girlfriend would have already been in New York prior to my eventual arrival. She had paid us a visit at the new apartment on the Sunday, just two days after I had arrived.

I spared her all the drama that I had already experienced since my arrival less than 48 hours before, by not telling her anything about it, and never did tell her about it at any time thereafter. My mother for her part, having heard much about her, was extremely happy to have finally met her, having only seen her in photos before then.

My then girlfriend and I hung out and had fun on several occasions thereafter. But the truth is that what was revealed to me about her by her then very close female friend before I left Trinidad for New York only a few weeks before, was still very fresh on my mind.

It was during one of the occasions when we were hanging out, that I decided to find out if she was really committed to our relationship or not. We were sitting in her then favorite fast-food restaurant, close to where she was staying with relatives.

While enjoying our respective favorite fast-food meals and having a deep conversation, I asked her what she thought about us getting engaged in the not-too-distant future. Her response was immediate. "I eh ready fuh dat now nah." Her immediate, negative response, certainly sent the message that it was not in the cards for her anytime soon.

I really didn't know what to make of it at the time, especially after we sat with each other and had discussed it only weeks before, on the heels of what I considered to have been going on three really good years together up to that point, and for which she had left absolutely no doubt that she was 100% on board with the idea. I then thought to myself that something must have happened within that time to have seen such a drastic change in her attitude towards our future.

And while it may have been the perfect opportunity to do so as disturbed as I was about it at the time, I still decided not to address what was revealed to me by her then very close female friend before I left Trinidad. I decided not to delve into it since my objective was simply to find out if she was in fact as committed as I was to our relationship, to which she had responded accordingly.

I took it in stride, and simply made the best of our time together during the rest of her New York vacation, up until she returned to Trinidad. But naturally, after she left New York, I did a lot of thinking about the future of the relationship.

At the then young age of 24 years, and it being my very first serious relationship, I was only just really starting to learn about women in general and my then girlfriend in particular, while our relationship was still evolving. And I was most definitely absorbing the lessons being taught.

We kept our long-distance relationship going through communicating the old fashion way, via hand written letters that we mailed to each other, since we could not afford a phone for some time, given what had transpired upon my arrival in New York.

My mother assumed that she would have been working constantly, which would have helped to alleviate any financial challenges we would have then been expecting to face going forward, after I had no other choice but to expend the substantial amount of funds that I did, immediately upon my New York arrival. The road ahead then promised to be a very rough one. But neither I nor my mother could have ever imagined what was in store.

I eventually reconnected with Leslie-Ann Sherwood, one of my former colleagues from C&B, who was already attending Pratt at its main campus in Brooklyn. During that time, I was using a pay phone. We spoke fairly often and continued to do so when we were eventually able to obtain our own house phone from Ma Bell. Leslie-Ann and I also hung out every now and again.

Being that I was an ardent music lover with aspirations to be a song-writer, I treated myself to a large collapsible Boom-Box, on which I listened to all different genres, including of course, Soca and Calypso, the music of my beloved homeland. A music called Rap was then beginning to emerge into the mainstream. I instantly fell in love with the genre.

Kurtis Blow was my favorite Rapper then. I remember I always pumped up the volume whenever I heard his then monster hit single called "The Breaks". I also listened to a lot of Reggae music on a reggae program that was hosted by the then well-known Jamaican DJ Gil Bailey. I also became a regular listener to Frankie Crocker on WBLS.

Listening to music would serve to get me through some of the extremely challenging times while attending Pratt. I would sometimes also turn to songwriting when I sought solace, and wrote a few songs of different genres.

My mother and I also became huge New York Knicks fans. We would watch their games together on the old-fashioned black and white television set that someone gave to her.

The goal I set for myself as a student at Pratt was not to simply successfully complete my chosen course of study, but to excel by achieving and maintaining the maximum 4.0 Grade Point Average (GPA) throughout.

I also felt that attaining and maintaining the maximum GPA, would have also served to ensure that my academic record would not be the reason that my father would eventually withdraw his tuition support, as I had it in the back of my mind that he might do so at some point, before I completed my entire course of study.

I remember the fairly short walk to get to school, after exiting the East 28th Street and Park Avenue subway station on the very first day. I couldn't resist looking up and around.

What immediately struck me about Manhattan, with its tall high-rise buildings towering over me on both sides of the streets, was that it seemed as if the physical environment was itself compelling you to "THINK BIG"; "DREAM BIG".

What I was about to experience in New York in general, and at Pratt Manhattan in particular over the course of the next few years, that very "THINK BIG"; "DREAM BIG" concept would eventually become deeply embedded in my mind.

The first thing that I noticed on my very first day of classes was that I was one of only two blacks. The other black student was a guy named Kirk; an African American. He was an exceptionally talented comic book illustrator. However, he dropped out sometime during the first semester, so I ended up being the only black student attending the school. There was also one Latino student, a female whose name was Angela Pelaez.

My other classmates included Wayne Scot Lukas, Melissa Urban, Rosemary E. Lavin, Deborah Anne Kelly, Nancy Gospodinoff, Donna Gershon, Lisa Elliot, Asude Barlas, Greg Agnello, Glenn Cohen, Michael Dellis, Margret Dressel, Cornelia Campbell-Graham, Grace Paradise, Karin Strong and Sarah Wunsch.

I had to take a total of seven mandatory classes my first semester. Namely, Art History, Light Color & Design, Drawing and Composition, Comprehensive (Comp) Rendering, Letter Forms, Advertising and Graphic Design and Life Drawing.

I found the life drawing class to be particularly interesting, because it was the very first time, I would have the experience of having a completely nude female model posing standing, sitting or lying mere feet in front of me. And she was indeed very attractive from head to toe. I eventually got used to the sight.

Some of the instructors I remember include a Mr. Elliot, Mary-Jane Mazuchowski, Rudy Battenfeld, Jack Schecterson, Karl Steinbrenner, Jacqui Morgan, a Mr. Goldblatt and last but certainly not least, Rose Wasserman.

Rose Wasserman was our Graphic Design instructor, and was most definitely a hard taskmaster. I remember her stating at her very first class, that in the beginning and perhaps for the many months that would follow, we students would probably hate her; but at the end we will all come to love her.

I was always respectful to my class mates and they were to me. I got along fairly well with all of them, but was quite reserved generally speaking. I developed friendships with both the Assistant to the Dean whose name was Chandra who was Guyanese, as well as the Librarian who actually had Trinidadian roots. Her name was Sharon Lewis. I would eventually meet her then husband Derek who also had Trinidadian roots. He was then the Manager of Audio-Visual Services at Pratt.

So then, with medium to longer term financial uncertainty hanging heavily over it, having already expended a huge junk of the cash I had saved for school and for domestic needs etc. over my first year, I put my head down and began the work towards realizing the first one of my dreams. I was totally focused on the mission. As such, there would be absolutely no social life for me.

I quickly found out that Art supplies for school weren't cheap. But thankfully, I still had enough funds for supplies during my first semester. Throughout the course of that first semester, my stress level kept increasing as a result of the very heavy school work load, and the extremely high expectations I had for myself, coupled with the domestic challenges we were facing.

It was all compounded by thoughts of the information I had received back in Trinidad, about my then girlfriend from her then close friend before I left for school, which was still weighing very heavily on my mind.

You see, according to her then close friend, my then girlfriend had still been hooking up with a supposed ex behind my back, over the then almost 3 years that we were supposedly in a monogamous relationship.

She had never mentioned anything to me about him upfront, but did share a bit about him later on in the relationship, and had told me that she had totally broken it off with him once we became a couple.

I believed her; only to find out the truth about the status of their relationship from her then very close friend, a couple of weeks before I left Trinidad to attend school.

But I had naturally became emotionally attached to her over the almost 3 years we had been together at the time, during which I fell deeply in love with her, which made it extremely hard for me to just suddenly break it off.

So, then already also being faced with mounting challenges during that first semester at Pratt, I was in desperate need of an outlet for my stress. And since I was never one who indulged in drugs, including alcohol and or clubbing or partying etc., neither offered a stress relieving option for me.

And while playing football would have definitely served the purpose, because my focus was totally on school, it was not on my agenda at the time. So, I just had to suck it all up and get on with it; which is what I did.

During that first semester I was getting an average of about 5 hours sleep each night during the school week. That should be each morning actually, as I usually worked on my respective homework assignments from around 7:00 p.m., through the nights into the wee hours of the mornings. I got up at around 7:00 a.m. to have breakfast and get ready for school, which started at 9:00 a.m.

My mother worked. But without a Green Card or Social Security number then, it was the much lower than minimum wage domestic job cleaning white people's apartments and or taking care of their kids, for which payment was "off the books". And to get that sort of job, she had to go to an employment agency that dealt with those specific types of jobs. They then sent her out to a location to work for the day. Most times it would be for less than 8 hours.

Generally, there were times when my mother worked four or five days a week, then there were times she would only work two or three days per week, usually for about 5 or 6 hours each day. Consequently, there were times when the refrigerator and kitchen cupboards were almost full. Then there were times when they were almost empty.

Lunch for me at school from Monday to Friday was usually a slice of Pizza, which cost less than a dollar then. Sometimes I had it with a beverage but most times not. For dinner I usually ate whatever my mother prepared when I got home from school, or whatever was left over from the day before.

If she didn't cook or there was no left-overs, then dinner would simply be bread and butter with cheese, fried or boiled eggs or chicken bologna, with a cup of hot chocolate or a glass of Soda. By December, the last month of my first semester, accumulating the cash to pay the full rent and other bills was starting to become a challenge.

But in spite of those faced, I managed to survive the Big Apple and my first semester at Pratt. I received three A's, three B's and one C from my 7 classes and a 3.33 GPA for my efforts, which saw me make the Dean's List. And while the three A's were great, the three B's and the C were not what I was aiming for. I had not achieved my goal of obtaining a 4.0 GPA.

I was not in the least satisfied, since I had not met my own expectations. And as hard as I had worked during that first semester toward that goal, I knew then that I would have needed to work even harder to achieve it the following semester. I was prepared to do just that.

While I did not originally plan to, I felt it necessary to return to Trinidad for the Christmas break, because I simply did not trust my father to send my tuition cheque to me in New York for my second semester. I was able to afford my plane ticket with funds I received for some freelance graphic design assignments I did, with some of it also going towards the payments of our bills.

Once back in Trinidad, I was happy to be reunited with my older brother. But interestingly, while he was doing very well for himself then and seemed to be living his life to the fullest, he never enquired about how my mother and I was doing back in U.S. Not even just simply out of curiosity.

And especially since I knew that my sister Cheryl, who was on vacation in New York with her 3 very young daughters at the time, would have told the rest of the family what had transpired, when I arrived in New York to start school. But since I was never really one to complain about or burden others with any of my personal issues, I did not mention anything to him.

Meanwhile, although I had totally trusted her prior to, my then girlfriend had begun to lose my trust since it was revealed to me that she had been still seeing her ex behind my back, during the almost 3 years we had been together. I had been totally faithful to her during that time. I'll say it again. I had been totally faithful to her during that time.

And as if continuing to hook up with her ex wasn't enough, my then girlfriend directly served me the ultimate dose of relationship humiliation, hurt, and disrespect, while I was in Trinidad during that said '83 school Christmas break. And she did so without care or conscience.

About a month before, she told me she had joined a modelling school, after being encouraged to do so by another female friend who was already a student at the school, which was located in Chaguanas, a well know community in Central Trinidad.

Her friend also lived in the said community. What my then girl-friend didn't tell me, was that she had gotten involved with a male model, who was attached to the modelling school.

Here's how it all played out that night just before Christmas of '83. The female owner of the modelling school was throwing a Christmas party for the students at her residence, which my then girlfriend informed me that I wasn't allowed to attend. I was driving a vehicle that I rented from my father. So, I agreed to drop her and her girlfriend off to the party.

On the way there we passed a dude on the road. He was walking in the same direction we were heading. The friend recognized him and excitedly exclaimed, "Stop, stop, stop! That is (name called)!" "No, no, no! Doh stop!" My then girlfriend responded nervously, so I kept on driving. It immediately got me thinking, why wouldn't my then girlfriend want me to stop, when it was obvious that they both knew the dude.

Anyway, upon arriving at the location, which was a relatively short distance from where we had passed the dude on the road, my then girl-friend invited me inside for a quick introduction to the owner of the modelling school, after which I left to return to pick them back up later that night.

On my return trip to pick them up several hours later, I saw her girl-friend standing alone at the corner of the street, which was some distance from the residence where the party was being held, which I found to be very strange. I asked her for my then girlfriend. She told me that she was still at the residence where the party was being held.

I then continued to the residence, but parked a few meters away. I got out of the vehicle and went in. The party had actually ended, so there were only a few people left in the living room area, including the owner of the residence and modelling school.

It was obvious that she was caught by surprise, because she seemed very uneasy by my sudden appearance. My then girlfriend was nowhere to be found, which really aroused my suspicion, especially given that her girlfriend had actually left the scene of the party for some reason.

I asked the modelling school owner where my then girlfriend was, but she didn't answer. She just stood there looking at me nervously. But as fate would have it, I was right on spot to see my then girlfriend and a dude emerge from a bedroom moments later.

I could not believe my eyes. There was nothing to be said between us, because it was then clearly obvious that something very improper went down between my then girlfriend and the dude in the privacy of the bedroom.

I then figured out that my then girlfriend's girlfriend was much too embarrassed to stay at the scene, knowing what was taking place between my then girlfriend and the dude back at the residence. She therefore decided to removed herself from the situation to send a clear message to me, that she was not a party to my then girlfriend's actions on the night.

The dude my then girlfriend was with in the room, was the same dude we passed on the street. Having already eroded my trust to a significant degree with her involvement with her ex, the events of that night most definitely saw me totally change my attitude towards our relationship.

I worked at C&B, in addition to undertaking some freelance assignments during that '83 school Christmas break, which provided me with enough funds for my plane ticket back to New York, to assist with the rent, and take me through the first couple of months of my second semester. I returned to the Big Apple, tuition cheque in hand, the last week in January of '84 for the early February start of the new semester.

Once again, I had to take a mandatory seven classes during my second semester. Those included Light Color & Design, Drawing & Composition, Photography, Advertising & Graphic Design, Directed Studies, History of Communication Design, and Illustration Techniques, which was my personal choice. I intended to work much harder than before to achieve my academic goal of obtaining all A's; and along with it a 4.0 GPA for that second semester.

Not very long after I had returned to New York, I got involved with another female. It was the "friends with benefits" type of scenario, and lasted for a while during the very cold Winter months of '84.

It was the first time that I had been unfaithful to my then girlfriend, since we entered into what as I mentioned before, was then an almost three-year-old relationship. That first time turned out to be my initiation into becoming a serial cheater myself.

By the time the '84 April Spring Break rolled around, it was becoming more of a challenge to pay the bills. And while my mother's income and funds that I was generating from freelance assignments was keeping us going, the really tough times was beginning to bear down upon us. Rent was then being only partially paid and thereafter started to back up. My stress level just kept rising.

Through it all, I willed myself to remain focused on my academic mission, summoning every ounce of physical, mental and other energy. During the school week throughout that second semester, I was getting an average of about 4 hours sleep each morning as I was usually going to bed at around 3:00 a.m. And even when I went to bed it was very difficult for me to actually fall asleep.

As a result, I was forced to start taking sleeping aid pills, to ensure that I did in fact get some deep sleep during the few hours that were available. It usually took about 45 minutes for me to get to school by subway. My mother did the job of waking me up in time for me to get to classes by 9:00 a.m.

Almost every night and into the wee hours of the morning, while working on my various class assignments she would plead with me, "Ali. Come inside an' get some rest. Yuh goin' tuh get yuhself sick." But it appeared that she herself wasn't getting much sleep, as a result of me being up all night and into the wee morning hours.

Her advice, as sound and sensible as it was, simply fell on deaf ears, because I then had a monomaniacal focus on achieving the academic goal of a 4.0 GPA that I had set for myself. I usually tried to make up for the sleep that I was losing during the course of the school week on the weekends, when the task of completing my school assignments continued.

Don Thomas, as he did during the course of my first semester, came over sometimes during the early part of the night and hung out with me for a couple of hours, while I worked on my school assignments. His sister Ann also paid us visits.

Pat usually visited with my niece Jolene mostly on weekends when she was off work. But she also visited on some weekdays to pick up Jolene my niece, when my mother did not work and filled the role as Jolene's baby-sitter. The Thomas' were basically the only company we kept.

To deal with the situation that was then becoming somewhat overwhelming during that second semester, upon coaxing from Don during the Spring break, I decided to try out for a Semi-Professional football team of which he was a member.

The team, which name I can't quite recall, was owned and or sponsored by a white gentleman named Mike who lived in Bay Ridge Brooklyn. He owned a video games arcade chain.

I remember making the journey with Don on the subway to his flagship business location in Bay Ridge, so that he could have met me personally, being that I was a new member of the team. He seemed to be a quite nice individual.

The team was coached by former Trinidad and Tobago men's national team goalkeeper Kelvin Barclay. Also playing with the team was one of my childhood Point Fortin hometown idols, and former Trinidad and Tobago men's national team player, Leo "Twinkle Toes" Brewster, who like Barclay, had immigrated to the U.S. many years before. They were both members of the 1973 Trinidad & Tobago World Cup team that was cheated in Haiti that year.

I remember Richard Chinapoo, another former Trinidad and Tobago men's national team player, who played with the New York Cosmos during 1982-1983, dropping in on a training session one evening. Training sessions were conducted at Prospect Park. After about two weeks of intense training, I was included in the squad for a then upcoming game.

Mike, the teams' owner / sponsor, actually bought me a brand-new pair of football boots, since the one I had traveled with from Trinidad had served out its time during the 2 weeks of training, and I could not afford to buy a new pair. He presented it to me at the football field before the game.

I went on for about the last 10 to 15 minutes. I was back playing the game I love, only that time around it was at a Semi-Professional level. It is something that I would have never even imagined, given the fact that I had totally given up playing the game at all competitive levels, and football was nowhere on my agenda then.

I was introduced with our opponents leading 2-0, and had the absolute privilege of playing alongside "Twinkle Toes". He scored a beautiful glancing header from a corner after making a darting run from his starting position at the middle of the goal just inside the 6 yards box to the front post to make the score 2-1. Unfortunately, we lost the game by that same score line.

While it was most definitely serving its purpose of relieving my then mounting stress, joining the football team was taking critical time away from my school work; time that I needed to stay on top of what continued to be an overwhelming workload. I therefore decided to quit the team after making just that one appearance.

At the end of the second semester in June of '84, there was great and not so great news. The great news was that all my hard work had paid off, as I did in fact achieve my goal of getting all A's in each of my classes, which saw me make the President's List. I was extremely proud of that achievement.

The not-so-great news was that the mental and physical energy that had been expended to achieve it, took its toll. The then sometimes overwhelming stress attached to school was compounded by having to also deal with our ongoing financial challenges. Fortunately for us, Moses our landlord was very understanding of our situation. Another landlord may have chosen to evict us since having fallen behind on the rent.

And there was additional good news. Being that I was then on the President's List, the school, through my Graphic Design Instructor Rose Wasserman, arranged for me to begin a Summer Internship at Fox Television Channel 5 in the Graphics department.

It was arranged with a view to me eventually securing a job with the organization. I did present myself and was given a walk-through of the graphics studio by a staff member to get an idea of the operation. Unfortunately, it was not going to be a paid internship; and we needed money desperately.

I therefore had to pass up the opportunity, and instead return to Trinidad once again to continue working at C&B during those June to August summer months. Together with additional income from more freelance work, I would have then been able to address the issue of the back rent. And equally important, I also had to collect my third semester tuition cheque from my father.

I was extremely worried that I would have been leaving my mother in such a precarious situation. But I really had no other choice but to hop on that BWIA aircraft and head to sweet T&T (well...it still was at that time).

Before I left New York, I gave Moses the assurance that I would set-tle our outstanding rent debt upon my return. Moses in turn, requested that I deliver the outstanding rent amount in TT currency to one of his relatives who then lived in Vistabella south Trinidad. I gave him my word that I would.

I arrived in Trinidad in mid-June of '84, with long term plans for my ongoing relationship with my then girlfriend then out the window. Neither of us would ever speak about it again; with good reason I suppose.

It was as if we had both already accepted what then appeared to be inevitable, and were both then just simply going along for the ride, however long it lasted. As such, during that summer, while we continued seeing each other as normal, I also enjoyed the company of a couple of other females as well.

September of '84 had arrived; and after a summer of working and playing hard, and with my third semester cheque in hand, it once again became time to return to the U.S. I was frugal with my almost 3 months salary from C&B and funds generated from the customary freelance assignments.

I kept my word to our landlord Moses, by honoring our arrangement to settle our outstanding rent debt, and delivered the TT cash equivalent to his relatives in Vistabella. And after purchasing my plane ticket to return to New York, I was left once again with limited funds for living expenses and school supplies etc. My third semester would turn out to be my toughest.

For that new Fall semester there were two new first year students. They were both black. One was a female whose name was Yolanda Cunningham, but she much preferred to be called "Coco". She was African American and lived in Harlem.

The other was a male foreign student like myself. His name was Christopher Mosieni. He was from South Africa. He claimed that the U.S. Government of the day had agents keeping an eye on him while he was on U.S. soil, which for obvious reasons, was not inconceivable at the time.

Coco and I became very good friends. I remember on one of our jaunts through midtown Manhattan one evening after classes, we happened to pass by Radio City Music Hall.

Coco, being a born and bred New Yorker, immediately knew something major was happening when we saw trailers, barriers and a crowd gathering on the street outside the building. It turned out that a host of A list celebrities, were arriving for a rehearsal for an event called "The Night of 100 Stars".

The occasion presented me with my very first close up encounter with a few of those A list U.S. celebrities, since I came to New York. They included the stunningly beautiful Debbie Allen and Brooke Shields, and Mr. Tap Dance himself, Gregory Hines, among others.

I had to take 8 different classes for my third semester. Namely, Graphic Design; Advertising Design; Story Board; Publication Design; Package Design; Directed Studies; Professional Communication and Illustration. The illustration class was by choice once again.

My mother's work situation remained the same, more or less. She was doing all within her power to improve it so as to improve our financial situation. I continued to enjoy some freelance work, which funds, together with that of my mother from her income, was just barely keeping our heads above water.

Some of that freelance work came through a friend and former business associate Wilford Harewood, who put me on to some of his friends who needed Graphic Design services. I originally met Wilford back in Trinidad during my earlier days at C&B. He was a photographer who did work for the agency.

I actually designed the logo for his business, Wilford Harewood Photography. Now based in Atlanta, he still operates his photography business and has the very same logo I had designed for his business. We still keep in touch with each other.

Given our ongoing financial difficulties, I had no other choice but to get a part-time job. I did and started working with a company based in SoHo, lower Manhattan called Stadri. There I designed custom embroidery patches and labels for all different types of clothing.

I went straight to the job after classes, at which I spent 3 or 4 hours, three or four days a week depending on my then employer's need. Although paying less than minimum wage, the Stadri job was serving its purpose somewhat. But like when I joined the football team, it was also taking away from the time that I usually dedicated to attending to my school assignments, which I was then starting later at nights.

Having less time to work on my assignments, the quality was being affected. So, not wanting to see a regression of my GPA after getting it to where I wanted, I eventually made the decision to leave the job. I continued to function on about 4 hours rest most mornings during the school week. My insomnia also continued during those hours, because I had since ceased using the little red sleeping aid pills.

My stress was constant as a result of our ongoing financial struggles, and was compounded by the high levels of mental and physical energy and the time that was being demanded and expended on my assignments during the course of the semester. And with not the greatest of diets, I could feel myself gradually breaking down both mentally and physically.

Then one morning on my way to school I had a most frightening experience. I was walking from the apartment with my portfolio case in hand as usual, to catch the C train at the Fulton Street, Kingston and Throop station as I had done for over a year. About halfway into the journey, I suddenly began to feel a bit disoriented, and as if I was losing control of my thoughts.

My focus was appearing to be somewhat erratic. It felt as if I was then functioning purely on visual memory. I managed to make it to the train station and onto the train. It was the morning rush-hour, so it was jam-packed. While I did not seem to have total thought control, I was still very much aware of the physical surroundings.

Strangely, the presence of people all around me on the train that particular morning seemed to irritate me. At that point I started to feel a deep sense of anxiety and imbalance in my head, and as if things were spinning slowly all around me. I felt like I was losing my equilibrium, which led to me leaning my head to one side and then the other in an effort to regain it. I kept closing and opening my eyes over and over during the absolutely harrowing episode. It felt like if I was losing my mind.

Looking around almost aimlessly, my eyes then fell on a very familiar face. It was Pat Thomas. The sight of her somehow jolted me back to full conscious awareness. A profound sense of relief came over me. I was then very anxious to start a conversation with Pat to find out if I was in fact ok; if my mental faculties were still in place.

I eased myself around until I stood right next to her. I explained to her that I was not feeling well, as I was getting this weird feeling in my head. She suggested that I go back home. But all I could think about then was my assignments that were due for both my morning and afternoon classes; assignments that I had worked extremely hard on.

With those thoughts in my head, I decided against returning home, although maybe I really should have. Pat and I continued talking until we eventually arrived at our stop at Broadway Nassau in Manhattan. Pat headed for the exit. I had to transfer to either of the 4 or 5 train to 14th street, then transfer to the 6 to my final stop at East 28th street on Park Avenue. The conversation with Pat seemed to have somehow stimulated me back into a feeling of normalcy.

By the time I got to class I was feeling much better and totally normal again. I got to class early as usual but I did not want to "push my luck". So, I immediately went to the back of the classroom and created a bed from about 4 desks that I brought together to take a nap.

While napping, I heard when each of my classmates came into the classroom. Out of concern they were asking each other what was wrong with me. Then I finally heard the voice of the Professor Schecterson, who taught the Package Design class I had that morning.

"What's wrong with Mr. Ayres today?" He enquired. "Apparently he's not feeling well," my classmate Angela Pelaez offered in reply. That was good enough for Professor Schecterson, who knew that I was always 100% present, attentive and engaged in all of his classes, as I was for all of my other classes as well.

I eventually got up from my nap, which turned out to be about half an hour into Professor Schecterson's class. I immediately approached him at the front of the class and offered my explanation for the nap I was taking, which he accepted.

I then presented my assignment, after which I participated in the rest of his class, whereby each student's assignment was being critiqued not only by him, but by fellow students as well. I participated fully in my afternoon class, which was Graphic Design, taught by none other than Rose Wasserman.

On my walk from the train station back to the apartment after class that evening, as a precaution, I decided to pay a visit to the hospital, which was only about a 100 meters distance from where we lived. After describing the frightening episode that I had that morning to the doctor, he inquired about my life situation leading up to it.

I decided not to get into the issues with my then girlfriend, which quite naturally had also been affecting me. After relating the other aspects of my life situation at the time to the doctor, that is, my school regimen and lack of sleep, my having to deal with ongoing financial challenges, my diet, and no social life, his diagnosis was that it was a case of extreme mental fatigue, related to my overwhelmingly stressful life situation.

He told me that it was a very wise decision on my part to visit the hospital when I did, as I was on a path to possibly having an actual mental breakdown. He strongly recommended an immediate change in my life-style including getting lots of rest, an improved diet, and getting out and socializing and having fun with friends.

So, as desperate as I was to maintain my 4.0 GPA, I then needed to take things easy for the balance of the semester, for which there was then about 6 weeks left before it ended. But with our ongoing financial situation, there was no refusing freelance work that came my way, funds from which had to be used very wisely, which took going out and having fun with friends out of the equation.

If I would have ever needed a reason to return to Trinidad before that fall semester ended, the doctor most definitely gave me one. And as justifiable as it would have been to do so, it was a thought that I could not even entertain, given the mission I was on. But another reason emerged, that would then actually force me to return to Trinidad before the said semester ended.

We had gotten news that something was wrong with my older brother Evans, which left him unable to speak. In fact, he had not spoken a word for close to a month, up to the time we eventually received the phone call. Upon relaying the news to her, my mother immediately went into panic mode.

Totally disregarding the fact that I still had 2 weeks of school left, and that we had the rent and other bills to pay, she insisted that I use the funds that we had on hand at the time, to go down to Trinidad immediately to see what was going on with my older sibling, since no one could tell us anything except that he couldn't speak. And apparently, he hadn't been working for a while, so his financial situation at the time, did not allow him to go to a medical professional to address his issue.

So, having been raised with and thus believed in the ideal of "family first above all else", and also never being one to ever go against my mother's wishes, I complied. We pooled our funds together, and I rushed down to Trinidad within days of receiving the news about my older brother. It was about a week and a half before the scheduled end of the semester in December of '84.

Once in Trinidad, I took my older brother to two medical specialists to get two opinions regarding the diagnosis and treatment for his issue. The first diagnosed it as laryngitis. But interestingly, the second of the two, who was of East Indian descent, seemed certain that my older brother's issue was not medically related.

He somehow knew something that my older sibling apparently also knew, and chose not to reveal it to anyone, including me. It would be years before I would come to fully understand what actually caused my older brother's issue. But what I can say is that the East Indian specialist was right. It was not a medical one.

During my time in Trinidad, which included the time that I would have been there for the school Christmas break, I continued to dedicate time to my then girlfriend. I also continued to enjoy the company of other females as well, since I no longer considered our relationship to be exclusive.

I worked at C&B as per usual, to obtain the much-needed funds that would help to cover some of the back rent, and other living expenses and school supplies etc., when I got back to New York. I also collected my last tuition cheque from my father, for what would be my final semester at Pratt.

But true to form, upon informing me that the usual arrangement had been made for me to collect it at his bankers, he remarked, "Boy leh mih tell yuh something nah. If yuh had one more term after this one, yuh woulda hah tuh drop out ah school inno." His remark implied that he would not have continued his tuition support if I had one semester left after the then upcoming one. I was not at all surprised.

I was forced to reschedule my usual end of January return to New York. I extended my Trinidad stay by a week and a half into February of '85, to ensure that my older brother was back to normal before I left, so that I could have reported that he was to my mother, without having to lie to her otherwise. He was only back to normal at the end of my extended period.

As a result, I started classes almost 2 weeks late for what would be my fourth and final semester. Upon my return to school, I received my third semester grades. I received 3 A's, 3 B's, 1 C and 1 D, and with that, out the window went my 4.0 GPA. But given the many challenges faced during the course of that semester, they were then more than acceptable to me.

My final semester was somewhat different from the other three, apart from the fact that it represented the final months of my two-year New York mission. There were still lots of homework assignments, but the focus was on creating a portfolio. Our respective individual portfolios, were then going to be reviewed and evaluated by members of the Art Directors Club (ADC) of New York at the end of the semester.

The members of the ADC were New York's top Art Directors in the fields of Advertising and Graphic Design. My understanding was that they would give you a very good indication as to whether you were on your way to a successful career in either field or not.

For me personally, the pressure was intense. Having returned to New York almost two weeks late because of my older brother's situation, I had to put in extra hours of work to catch up on all my class assignments, in addition to redoing some that I had already done to improve the quality, in order to attain the highest professional standards of the day.

I desperately needed to impress the members of the ADC, because if they were impressed with your portfolio, it could mean landing a very good job after graduation, which was then my post Pratt objective.

I had to take 8 different classes that final semester. Namely, Advance Graphic Design; Advance Advertising Design; Typography Design; Advance Package Design; Marketing & Copy; Publication Workshop; Portfolio Development; and Advance Illustration. I also had to do a Senior Project of choice, for which I chose to do an illustration assignment, since I was also excelling in the illustration program, and had been thoroughly enjoying the illustration classes just as much as the others.

The illustration instructor was one Jacqui Morgan, who was one of the top illustrators in New York at the time. I remember she did the illustration for the poster for the Broadway Show "Tap Dance Kid", which headliner was one Alfonso Ribeiro. He would come to be more famously known as "Carlton" on the sitcom Fresh Prince of Bel Air, which stars one Will Smith. Miss Morgan gifted me a postcard copy of the original illustration, which I still have in my possession today.

Upon eventually catching up, and on completion of his Marketing & Copy course work, the instructor, one Robert Moulthrop, presented me with a type written note, commending me for the effort that I put in. At the end of his course, he took the students to the World Trade Center to a restaurant on the 90 something floor in one of the Twin Towers, where he treated us to Caviar and Sushi, which I was having for the very first time.

143

After a grueling 3 months of work, the day for our portfolio review and evaluation arrived. It was sometime in mid-May of '85. It was conducted at a location in mid-town Manhattan. I remember there being at least 4 or 5 Art Directors who were seated at separate tables around the large room.

We students sat in a certain area waiting to be called to a specific table by an Art Director. I happened to be one of the first students to be called. I sat before that Art Director with my portfolio case already opened on the first page.

Upon viewing the first few pieces of the absolutely best 15 pieces of a combination of Advertising and Graphic Design work in my portfolio, he made an announcement to the other Art Directors in the room, who were also reviewing and evaluating other student's work; and I quote "Hey guys. You'd better hold on to your seats for this one." End of quote.

At the end of that most significant event, I received the Art Directors vote for the most outstanding portfolio. I was also deemed to be the student most likely to achieve a very high level of success in which ever of the fields I chose, whether it be Advertising or Graphic Design.

Receiving such accolades from some of the professionals who were considered the very best in the business at the time, was indeed validation of my artistic gifts, which had been bestowed upon me by "The Higher Power". It was without doubt a highly emotional and at the same time, a most gratifying and humbling experience for me. And so, my two years course of study was then almost at an end.

I reflected on our Graphic Design instructor Rose Wasserman's statement during her introduction speech at the very first class, which was to the effect that we may not be exactly fond of her during the months that would follow, but would come to love her in the end. I most certainly respected her from the very beginning. And I most definitely loved her at the end.

The advice she gave at the very end stuck with me. That advice was to always try to maintain the highest professional standards in the execution of your duties, and of decorum throughout your career, even when being treated unjustly and or with disrespect by future employers, clients, work colleagues or business associates, which she warned was likely to happen. And if you had to end any of those relationships, always try to do so with your professional integrity intact.

That May month of 1985, brought with it some of the happiest moments and days of my New York adventure, and of my entire life. After the portfolio review and evaluation came the student exhibition, which was held at the school's art gallery. I ensured that my mother was most present of course.

Everyone, from the Dean to my instructors were showering her with praise. And she was most deservedly absorbing all the pride of mother-hood, which made her feel extremely happy. Seeing my mother happy, made me feel equally happy as well.

The grand event, the graduation ceremony, was scheduled to take place on May 31st on the Brooklyn Campus grounds. I extended an invitation to my father for him to attend. Not surprisingly, he declined the invitation. I also extended an invitation to my then girlfriend for her to attend. She accepted and traveled to New York for the event.

Being that she was in New York upon my invite and on my account, specifically for my "Big Day", I assumed that she would have been staying with my mother and me at our apartment. But she instead chose to stay with a relative, even as our residence was much closer to the graduation venue than where she was staying at her relative. I felt slighted. And although very much bothered by it, I decided to say nothing to her, as usual.

Graduation day for Pratt Institute's class of '85 had finally arrived. Billionaire Malcolm Forbes of Forbes Magazine was a speaker on the day. I was overcome with emotion to see my mother so extremely happy. Words cannot fully describe the feeling I felt. I only knew that I was feeling the way I did because I could see that I was making her extremely proud, which was a step towards the fulfillment of my ultimate life ambition.

My sister Carol, who lived in Queens, also received an invite and was also in attendance. We were meeting each other for the very first time at the event. We were all in high spirits on the day. That is, all except my then girlfriend, who was noticeably very sour from very early on in the proceedings, and had separated herself from my mother and my sister, for reasons unknown to me at the time.

After the ceremony was over, I asked my sister how come my then girlfriend stood so far away from them the entire time. According to my sister, my mother, upon seeing other family members moving in much closer to their graduating subjects to take photos, told my then girlfriend, who I gave my camera to take photos of me, to also get closer to take the photos, since she was quite far away at the time.

Apparently, my mother spoke a bit loud, which could have been understandable, being that she is deaf. I also knew that my mother was overly excited. So, apart from speaking a bit loud, her excitement may have also been reflected in her tone of speech. And on such a momentous occasion, also understandably so.

After all, it was one of my mother's proudest life moments. But my then girlfriend did not see it that way, and had instead taken offense to how my mother spoke to her. That happened very early on in the proceedings. Thereafter, she refused to interact with my mother and my sister, totally separating herself from them for the entire ceremony.

When I asked her about it, my then girlfriend confirmed that my mother's tone of speech was in fact the reason for her being angry. Ok; fair enough. However, although I personally did absolutely nothing to her, for some reason she was also displaying a very hostile attitude towards me. So, I simply got her a taxi to take her back to wherever she was staying.

As much as I wanted my then girlfriend to be present to share that very special moment with me, thus my reason for extending an invitation for her to attend, I simply could not allow her to "Rain on Our Parade", by denying my mother and myself our moment, which was the culmination of an extremely difficult life journey, that had continued even up to that point.

With my Diploma that I had worked so extremely hard for and had earned in hand, confirming that my New York mission had been accomplished, I was then in fact a legitimate full-fledged Commercial Artist cum Graphic Designer. The first of my three childhood dreams had been realized.

My then girlfriend was also supposed to attend my graduation celebration get-together at the apartment that night. But after what transpired earlier in the day, that was definitely not going to happen. I then invited another female with whom I had been hanging out off and on, who my mother had since come to know and like. The relatively small group of specially invited guests together with the hosts, all had an enjoyable time.

The following day I contacted my then girlfriend so that we could meet, so that I could have a talk with her. I took her back to Pratt's Brooklyn Campus, where the graduation ceremony took place the day before. We sat together on one of the benches. As hurt as I was, I got right to it and told her that I no longer wanted to be in the relationship. I didn't think that any explanation was necessary.

There was absolutely no doubt in my mind that she would have been more than happy to see the back of me, and so be then totally free to do whatsoever she pleased, with whomsoever she pleased. It was all the more reason that I was left totally flabbergasted by her response.

With tears rolling down her cheeks, she was extremely apologetic and assured me that she was still in love with me and did not want our relationship to end. She was adamant about it to the point where it seemed like I had no say whatsoever in the matter. And I will admit that I still had feelings for her.

So, since she was so adamant about wanting the relationship to continue, I decided that I would continue with it. But I knew fully well then, that I would have been no longer fully committed, which, as young as we both were at the time, would have allowed for both of us to continue to explore other possibilities behind each other's backs, without guilt or regret, until we both eventually found Miss and Mr. Right respectively. She returned to Trinidad not too long thereafter. I stayed in New York.

It was extremely difficult for me to know that my mother had been working so hard over the years through winter, spring, summer and fall but still struggling financially. I distinctly remember one occasion during the heights of the winter of '85 during my final semester, when she went out to the city to perform her usual domestic work.

After working all day cleaning the woman's Manhattan apartment, she totally insulted and disrespected my mother by only giving her reimbursement for transportation. Upon her return to the apartment my mother broke down in tears relating the story to me.

Always knowing my mother to be an extremely proud and strong woman, seeing her break down in tears over that particular situation instantly filled me with rage. It was heartbreaking to see my mother having to subject herself to such treatment, which was tantamount to slavery. I myself also did some good crying over what transpired, but only after my mother went to bed.

I stayed up most of that night bearing my mother's cross, thinking about how this individual, whoever she might be, was at that very moment enjoying her clean surroundings as a result of my mother's hard labor, for which my mother was not paid; and the individual was getting away with it.

The thought was driving me absolutely crazy. Very unpleasant ones were entering my head. I felt so helpless that all I could have done at the time was stand at the living-room window and cry my eyes out to release my rage, while staring aimlessly at the snow that was falling outside. But as hurtful as it was, we just simply had to let it be.

And of course, I also experienced my fair share of racial discrimination. One such occasion was when Rose Wasserman had instructed us to purchase a particular book for our Graphic Design class. She gave the location of the book store where she knew the book was available. The bookstore was on Park Avenue in mid-town Manhattan, in the vicinity of East 42nd Street. I made the trip to the bookstore to purchase the book, which was being sold from behind the counter.

It was in full view of myself and all the other customers standing in front of the counter at the time. I asked for the book by its title. "We don't have it," stated the sales attendant, who was a white lady in her late 40's early 50's, in a very dismissive tone. Thinking that she was just making an honest mistake in not realizing that the book was in fact right there on the shelf, I pointed to it to let her know that the book was in my full view.

She repeated her initial response, only that time in a louder tone of voice. "I said we don't have it." Looking around quite puzzled at the people standing at the counter together with me, all of whom also happened to be white, they in turn were all then looking at each other and at me as if to say, "Don't you get it." I did. She was simply refusing to serve me because I was black.

Another such occasion was when I went to apply for a work permit at the Immigration Department after I graduated. The white attending officer simply looked me straight in the eyes and said very bluntly, "Why don't you just go back to your country." I wasn't in the least bothered by his attempt to ridicule me and advised that he just do his job, which was to provide me with the information that I needed to complete the process.

While awaiting the decision on my work permit application, I continued freelancing to continue to assist with paying the bills. At the same time, I was trying to make up my mind as to whether I should stay in the U.S. to continue my career, or return to Trinidad to do so.

Meanwhile, my best friend Junior, who I had kept in touch with over the years was going to get married and asked me to be his Best Man. At the time, we were struggling financially more than ever. But I managed to accumulate enough cash to purchase the return bus ticket to Canada, as there was no way that I was ever going to disappoint him.

Since I could not afford it, Junior paid for the rental of my Tuxedo. He also contributed the majority towards the purchase of the new pair of shoes that I would wear to the wedding, as I had none back in New York that was suitable for such an occasion, and also couldn't afford to buy a new pair. As embarrassing as it was, that was simply my reality at the time.

The wedding ceremony took place on September 14th 1985. Financial woes aside, the visit in general was an absolute blast from the day I arrived to the day I departed.

That week that I spent in Canada, as timely as it was, given the sometimes overwhelmingly stressful circumstances I had been facing during my Pratt years and was still facing at the time, remains one of the most enjoyable and memorable weeks that I spent anywhere, during the course of my entire lifetime. I just had to memorialize that visit in song, which I did. It was a rap song.

After returning to the U.S., the decision about whether to stay in New York or return to Trinidad, was then back in focus but still up in the air. But there was a couple of things I then knew with absolute certainty; which was, if ever I had questions about my mental, psychological, emotional and spiritual strengths, my New York and Pratt experiences in general, having tested them to the fullest, definitely provided me with all the answers.

And if I had any doubts about my artistic and creative talents and abilities, which were bestowed upon me by "The Higher Power", and initially validated by Trevor Cardinal, my experiences at Pratt in particular, together with the final outcome, which included further validation from the members of the New York Art Director's Club, totally erased them all. As a result, my self-efficacy and self-worth were elevated to new levels.

Unfortunately, my work permit was denied. And since I would not have wanted to risk getting on the wrong side of U.S. immigration law, and in so doing jeopardize the possibility of returning to the U.S. in the future, by being denied a work permit, the decision I was mulling over was then made for me. I was then going to be returning home to Trinidad, though not by choice. My mother however, decided that she would stay in New York.

It bothered me tremendously that I would have been leaving her to basically fend for herself in a land where it was extremely tough to survive and most times was unforgiving; a land where life could be brutally unkind, especially to undocumented immigrants, which my mother was at the time.

RETURNING TO MY HOMELAND: PROMISES; DISENCHANTMENT; AND DISCRIMINATION

I returned to Trinidad in late February of '86. With my newly acquired Advertising and Graphic Design knowledge and skill set, validation from some of the very best in the business at the time, New York freelance experience, and literally bursting with ideas, confidence, and enthusiasm, I was eagerly looking forward to the new phase of my career.

My then newly acquired professional status, would have allowed me to join any of the top local Advertising Agencies. But I wanted to show my gratitude to the one that gave me my big break. Coupled with the fact that there was familiarity with the staff, with Victor Lewis and a few other familiar friendly faces still being there, I chose to return to C&B. I formally rejoined the Agency on March 3rd of '86.

Most sadly, just over a month later, on April 8th, my grandmother Monica Theodorine Bowen, the matriarch of the family whom I had called Nennie all of my life, who had been ailing with Cancer for some time, succumbed to the disease. Thankfully I was able to see her and actually have a conversation with her before she passed on.

Once I returned to Trinidad, playing football was back on my agenda. I was then playing my favorite sport strictly for the love of doing so, exercise, and fun. Then 26 going on 27 years old, I was done with any competitive version of the game. My primary focus then was on the new phase of my Advertising / Graphic Design career and by extension, professional and personal growth and advancement.

Based solely on merit then, inclusive of my almost four years of work experience, which I gained at the very Agency, together with my unquestionable loyalty to the company, I thought, just like anyone else in my situation would, that I would have gained a significant promotion upon my return, which I further felt would have been well earned, having certainly paid my dues.

I assumed that it would have been the natural trajectory my career would have taken upon my return to the Agency. And while I did receive a promotion, it was not what I expected. Therefore, I felt like Mr. Belgrave the boss, was telling me that my degree was completely worthless, except for when it came to me doing the actual work, which I was then executing to the highest professional standards. I was also doing the presentations of the assignments I had worked on to the respective clients.

The only really significant change I would experience upon my return to C&B, was a dramatic increase in my work load and more job responsibilities. I did receive the expected salary increase, but it still was not what it should have been. Not having gained the expected level of promotion, and a salary commensurate with the position as anticipated upon my return to the Agency, most definitely served as my wake-up call. However, I would remain patient.

Meanwhile, my worst fear came to past a few months after I left New York, when my mother had to give up the Madison Street apartment. Thereafter, she moved from one place of abode to another for one reason or the other. During those times, I made trips to New York to continue to assist her.

On those occasions, I was not satisfied with the conditions under which she lived, which was far removed from that of the Madison Street accommodation. Thereupon I made another promise to myself. That promise was that should we both live long enough, at the very least, I would ensure that my mother would one day enjoy a life of domestic stability, and do so in relative comfort.

During that third stint at C&B, I experienced my first blatant incident of racism in my homeland. It involved the only Caucasian who worked in the art studio at the time. It occurred on one of those Friday evenings, when the studio staff stayed back for a while after the end of the work week, to unwind with some "ole talk" and laughter over a couple of beers.

I drank any non-alcoholic beverage that was available, since I never consumed alcohol, which is something that I committed to throughout my whole life. On those occasions, I sometimes treated the studio staff to some impromptu acapella performances of one of the Calypsos that I had written.

On that particular Friday evening, we were cracking jokes and giving each other "fatigue" as usual. While I cannot recall it, ah buss ah really good one on the individual, which had everyone absolutely cracking up. But more than just feeling the fleeting moment of embarrassment that one usually felt in such situations, the individual, who had no come back "fatigue" to offer, got angry. Wanting to get back at me, the individual then did so with a vengeance. "Yuh stupid nigger!" the individual exclaimed.

A few seconds of complete silence and aimless stares followed, with body language and facial expressions clearly indicating that the individual's unquestionable racist response absolutely shocked everyone. That is, everyone but me. Everyone but me because although subtly most times, I had been experiencing incidents of racism from those of a similar ilk at the Agency, since I joined as a trainee back in 1980.

I knew exactly what was intended by the individual's highly offensive response; especially since having experienced my fair share of racism, during my time in the country known to be racist to its core. But while at the time I chose not to; I should have absolutely responded. And not only to call out the individual, but more importantly, to dispel the myth that racism does not exist in the land of my birth. That particular Friday evening lime ended abruptly after the individual's racist remark to me.

The individual offered a verbal apology, in addition to one in the form of a postcard immediately upon their arrival at work on the Monday morning following that weekend. But interestingly, they chose to do so privately. I felt it would have been more appropriate, for the individual to have offered their apology in the presence of the other black studio staff members who were present when the remark was made, since it would have also offended them as well.

So, clearly, the individual did not want the others to know that they were offering an apology. Thus, to me it seemed insincere. Therefore I "quarter-heartedly" accepted the verbal apology and post card with reservations. The individual's racist remark in the given situation, was indeed a defining moment for me personally. Because if ever I had any doubt, the individual's response to a simple joke that day confirmed what I had already known, because of my personal experiences at the very Agency.

And while I do believe that there are always exceptions to the rule, that day I had also gotten confirmation of exactly what the individual's kind, and others who looked somewhat like them, truthfully thought of me and others who looked like me in my beloved homeland. I had been put on official notice.

At years end of '86, I received a Christmas bonus representing about 1/3 of my monthly salary. We then entered the first, then the second month of the new year. Still there was no change with respects to my career growth at the Agency. It was then that I decided to have my very first discussion with my then boss to address my issues of concern.

During our session, I presented my case for career advancement at the Agency, all of which he was already aware of and so, agreed with. He assured me that my situation was definitely going to change for the better in the not-too-distant future, upon which he revealed that there were plans to restructure the company, with the institution of the new plans to begin in six months, at which time my issues would be resolved. I took my then boss at his word, and so continued to remain patient.

A few months after my meeting with my then boss, the Agency hired a new Graphic Artist. He was a young Caucasian Englishman. By his very own admission, he was just an ordinary British citizen who had been trying to survive as an average Graphic Designer back in England. His portfolio attested to his admission, with his skill set limited specifically to Graphic Design.

He therefore would have been absolutely "Gobsmacked" at the reception and adulation he was receiving upon his arrival at C&B, especially among the "highfalutin" female employees. He would be treated as "royalty".

As he did with me back when I was a trainee, Robert O'Brien showed him the ropes, so to speak, after he arrived at the agency. In appreciation, Robert was rewarded with numerous gifts. They both eventually became close friends.

The English chap and I just became acquaintances and developed a good working relationship, whereby we treated each other with mutual respect. As part of his "Royal Treatment", he did not work out of the Art Studio as all the other Artists did; he obtained a brand-new car through the agency; and was being paid a hefty enough salary, that allowed him to live in an upper-middle class neighborhood.

In contrast, while my salary was covering my monthly living expenses, I still had to continue to take on freelance assignments to supplement it. And even so, I still couldn't afford to buy my own car. So, I had to settle for the use of what was the company car on some weekends, although it was just usually parked on the premises with no one using it.

And for me, getting to use the company car, even when it was only sporadic, was not "a walk in the park". You see, I initially had to go through the boss' Caucasian secretary, who as stated much earlier, never liked me from day one. I eventually found out that she did not approve of my use of the vehicle, which was a Mazda RX2. With that knowledge, I then used to go directly to the boss, who allowed me to use the vehicle, but my use of it remained sporadic.

Meanwhile, the six months timeline for the Agency's restructuring came and went without any word from my then boss, with respects to resolving my career advancement issue as promised. I stayed silent and patient. Then another six months came and went, during which time Robert O'Brien left for the U.S. to study. I was back at the Agency for two years. At that juncture, I met with and reminded my then boss of our then year-old discussion, and the promise he had made to me then.

Once again, he simply comforted the fool, but there was no action on his part thereafter. So, with seemingly no action on my situation forthcoming, even after my reminder to my then boss, and considering that I had then been at the Agency for six years all told, to my mind the message could not have been much clearer.

What was more disconcerting was the fact that I had been delivering big time, since I returned to the Agency. I was producing outstanding work consistently, and had continued to make lots of dawns in the process. I knew that my contribution to the Agency's bottom line was significant, because I was on the Agency's biggest accounts, which consisted of some of Trinidad and Tobago's largest companies.

Namely, the ANSA Mc AL Group of Companies, under which the Carib Brewery Limited and the Trinidad Broadcasting Company Radio Network fell; Lever Brothers West Indies Limited; West Indian Tobacco Company Limited (WITCO); LJ Williams Ltd; Angostura; Southern Sales & Service Limited the agents for Mazda, my father's then former employers; and Republic Bank Limited among others. The 1987 Republic Bank Annual Report which I designed cover to cover, received a write up in the Trinidad Guardian daily newspapers for its outstanding design.

I also remember directing a Du Maurier Cigarette (WITCO) television commercial that focused on our local culture, that received rave reviews. In addition, I was also feeding the then Creative Director ideas, and was also passing on my acquired knowledge and skills to the other Studio Artists, as well as mentoring Trainee Artists as Trevor Cardinal did with me.

Against that backdrop, and given all that had transpired since I returned, I felt that I had enough reasons to believe that the reason I was being denied opportunities for career advancement at the Agency, was simply because I was being discriminated against.

It was then that the rebellious trait in my character started to fully emerged. And even as I never view myself as being better than anyone else, I then made yet another vow to myself. That vow was that I will also never view anyone else as being better than me, and as such, be made to feel inferior by anyone or to anyone ever again in my lifetime; and especially in the land of my birth. I would hold steadfast to that vow.

Thereafter, and throughout the remainder of my career in the Trinidad Advertising / Graphic Design industry, and in my personal opinion with justification, I became a rebel with my very own cause. As a part of my personal rebellion while at C&B, and as a way of then unequivocally displaying my African heritage and pride, I started to keep my hair unkempt, which I knew would not have been in keeping with the image that the Agency would have wanted to project to their respective clients, and with whom I was interacting. But at the point I was at, that did not matter to me in the least. I simply did not care.

After residing at Fort George Road St. James for almost 7 years, I relocated to a new residence nearby in January 1988, which was a much bigger place, because I needed more space. More space was needed for two specific reasons. One was because I had plans to start my own Advertising & Graphic Design business. Additionally, my older brother also had plans to start his own business, and wanted me to facilitate him with the space that he needed to do so. He was unemployed by choice at the time. The other reason was that I was going to be hosting my best friend Junior and his wife that February. So, more space was necessary.

Meanwhile, my ongoing non-committed relationship with my then girlfriend had continued. She was still continuing to see other people behind my back, but was totally unaware that I had knowledge of that fact. I also continued to see other people, without any feeling of guilt. I had multiple female "friends with benefits" since returning to Trinidad from New York in February of '86.

One of those "friends with benefits" was my then girlfriend's very close female friend who volunteered the disturbing piece of information to me about her, before I left for Pratt back in 1983. We continued to be "friends with benefits" for many years.

But there would be fulfillment and joy beyond compare, that most experience during the course of their respective lifetimes, that would come from one of the uncommitted relationships I was engaged in. That particular relationship was indeed the most fulfilling and equally, the most valued, because it produced my beautiful daughter. She was born on December 26th 1988. She also turned out to be my one and only child.

And while it never developed into anything serious, my daughter's mother and I would enjoy an extremely close friendship that believe it or not, was without any type of conflict up until the time she passed away in 2010. She turned out to be one of only two genuine (and I mean that in every sense of the word) female friends that I would have during the course of my lifetime.

Around mid-1988 I had decided that I was going to resign from C&B that year. It was then just a matter of exactly when I would do so. Another company vehicle, a Mazda 626, which had since replaced the Mazda RX2, and which I had never used, was then up for sale. So, having already decided that I was going to resign, and knowing that owning a vehicle would have made life a bit easier for me then, I told my boss that I wanted to purchase it.

I eventually did by taking full advantage of the company perk that was being enjoyed by certain employees, and entered into a payment agreement with a finance company through C&B. It was a company perk that was never revealed or offered to me until then, even as I qualified for it upon my return to the Agency in February '86.

As it turned out, it would not be until early the following year that I would actually resign from my job at C&B. I will always remember the words from my then boss that day in February of '89, upon informing him of my decision to resign, with intentions of returning to the U.S.

"Well Alison, the door here will always remain open to you. So, you'll always have the option of being ah big fish in ah small pond, or you can choose to return to the States an' be ah small fish in ah big pond," he stated with his usual pleasant laid-back demeanor. But oh...the irony of his words. I left Christiansen & Belgrave Advertising Agency after 3 years for the third and final time in March 1989.

THE VISIT FROM MY BEST FRIEND

In February 1988 I played host to my best friend Junior, his then wife Yvette and their then close friend Terrence, whom I then also considered to be somewhat of a friend, since we all hung out together during my first trip to Canada. I was still working at C&B at the time of course, but had since relocated from Fort George Road as indicated earlier.

My new address was Coronation Street St. James, which was less than 10 minutes away, walking from my old address. My older brother relocated with me as planned. Minus the living room, I had to furnish the entire residence, which contained 3 bedrooms.

They were invited to Trinidad for the Carnival celebrations, which was scheduled to take place on the 15th and 16th of February that year, after they had shown me such a great time on the two occasions that I visited Canada as their guest. My first visit was for the purpose of attending Junior's wedding in September of '85. The second visit was in August of '86, when, believe it or not, I took my then girlfriend to meet them. Junior and his then wife had also shown us a really great time during our visit.

According to the plan, my then girlfriend was supposed to have taken her vacation from her job as I did, to coincide with their visit. She was supposed to have been staying with us at my new residence until our guests returned to Canada, so that we could have hosted them together as they hosted us during our trip to Canada.

However, my then girlfriend decided to withdraw herself from the plan at the very last moment, and left me to host our guests by myself. I could not have been more embarrassed, especially since they were so hospitable and had shown us both such a fantastic time during our visit to Canada. They must have felt embarrassed for me as well.

Thankfully, my friends were fully understanding of the situation. And so, we made the very best of the time we spent together during their visit. I remained apologetic to them almost throughout the entirety of their 2 weeks stay. My best friend Junior, his then wife Yvette and their friend Terrence returned to Canada a few days after the Carnival celebrations, with some fond memories of their visit I hoped.

It was then time to turn my attention to my then girlfriend, and the matter of the latest episode, in the series of major embarrassments that she had caused me during the course of our relationship. She would have been well aware of what she did on that latest occasion and the embarrassment that it did cause.

With our relationship being what it was for quite some time before that then most recent situation, I was then ready to end it once and for all and move on, and communicated such to her. But once again, she still wanted to continue with the relationship. And once again, I could not understand why; especially since she knew that she was seeing other people at the time. Maybe it was because she still had no clue, that I knew she was.

Adding to the mystery of her decision, was the fact that she knew then that I was also seeing other people at the time. I had already told her about one of them in particular, who my then girlfriend actually met on one occasion at my Coronation Street residence, during that said '88 Carnival season.

With the notion that the end with my then girlfriend was only a matter of time, then 28 going on 29 years old, I remained very open to continuing to meet new females, in my quest to find Miss "Right for Me". I then met another new female (initials BCA) that same February of '88, shortly after my friends returned to Canada. At the time, she was employed at a business establishment across the street from my then new Coronation Street residence. I was open and honest with her about my relationship situation with my then girlfriend.

She informed me that she had a very young daughter from a previous relationship, which had since ended. She made no mention of being involved with anyone at the time. I therefore assumed that she was single. Her having a child was not an issue for me at all, because the truth is that I had really taken a special liking to her from jump.

We really clicked on many levels, including when I discussed my business ideas with her, which was extremely important since I had business ownership ambitions. She was being very supportive of those ambitions, which was also going to be extremely important to me, relative to any future committed relationship that I would eventually have been considering, because I never had any such support from my then girlfriend.

But as I mentioned previously, it was all a learning process for me, and continued to be, towards my goal of finding the person that was right for me. So, I decided that I would take as much time as was necessary to really get to know BCA, before even thinking of committing. She and my then girlfriend would eventually have a face-to-face encounter and a brief conversation at my then work place at C&B, that made my then girlfriend also aware of that particular situation.

By the third quarter of '88, construction work began to transform the large living room area of the new Coronation Street residence into my Advertising and Graphic Design studio space. With an eye then on resigning from my job at C&B, I had also started to entertain a few clients.

Around that same time, I reconnected with a female that I became acquainted with a couple of years earlier. Her name was Alicia. She lived in Woodbrook with relatives. We had gone out on just one date in the past, which was one of those "getting to know you" kind of dates. Thereafter we had remained casual friends. But after reconnecting, we became good friends.

With construction work progressing as planned, out of the blue, my older brother abruptly dropped his plans for starting what was going to be a security business venture, and decided that he wanted to immigrate to the United States instead.

But having been unemployed by choice for quite some time up to that point, except for when he took on a few freelance assignments as a draughtsman, he did not have the financial means to do so, and was therefore relying on me for assistance. He wanted to leave Trinidad as soon as possible.

I had been bearing most of the financial burden for us for a while. Having been also investing heavily in transforming the new residence into my studio space and office, I was short on cash when he made his impromptu decision. Still wanting to assist him, I sold all of my still fairly new major household appliances and some of my bedroom furniture, to raise the funds to facilitate his immigration to the United States.

As a result of his decision, I was then forced to shelve my Advertising / Graphic Design business idea, because I would not have been in a position to bear the entire financial burden alone, relative to paying the household expenses, i.e., rent etc., since I would have also been incurring start-up business expenses.

But as it had been since childhood, our sibling relationship had continued to be very tight. He was then experiencing some really challenging times, so naturally I had his back 100%. I was therefore making the sacrifices for him that I was, without any reservations whatsoever. I was doing so purely out of the genuine, unconditional love that I had for my family.

As a matter of fact, whatever their respective requests or needs, which were mostly financial, I never ever said no to any of my siblings in general, and my mother and older brother in particular, even when it was detrimental to my own professional and personal progress, as it was in this case.

After my older brother left for New York, having then been forced to shelve my business ownership plans, I relocated once again. I then moved into a more affordable one-bedroom annex in Westmoorings, which was further west of St James, in January of '89.

But I was then left absolutely confounded, when my brother returned to Trinidad just weeks after he had left. He never gave me the reason for his highly unexpected return and I never asked. Unaware that he had permanent alternative living accommodation, I invited him to move into my Westmoorings apartment. But he declined my invitation. He instead opted to stay with a friend in Belmont.

I continued to be involved with multiple women, including BCA, apart from the relationship I was having with my then girlfriend, which was then more or less only physical, as I had detached myself emotionally, which I never ever envisioned when it began.

By then, I had totally accepted the fact that I was then just as guilty as she was; and as painful as it could be for all involved, was just another one of those harsh realities that we all had to deal with, at some point during the course of our respective lives.

Still, as enjoyable and ego boosting as it was, my hope was that I would come out of the protracted multiple women phases sooner rather than later, and do so with enough education, so that I would have then been able to choose, and eventually commit to the person that was right for me; until death do us part.

RESIDING IN "UPSCALE" WESTMOORINGS: THE VERY FIRST TIME I HELD A GUN

With my January '89 relocation to Westmoorings, I was then about to experience living amongst some of the so called "upper class" folks. My landlady was a really cool individual, who was always very nice to me. Her then very young daughter lived with her.

I would resign from C&B only 2 months later. Apart from having my domestic financial responsibilities; my rent, food, phone, etc., I was still paying the finance company for the car that I had bought from C&B several months earlier. So, to generate an income, I was then about to embark on a career as a full-time freelance Graphic Designer.

1989 would also be the year that my music career as a songwriter would be launched, by having the first of several Soca songs that I had in my writer's catalog, recorded by the then new Soca artiste Rikki Jai, who was launching his recording / performing career that year. The name of the song was "Gettin' On", for which I also designed Rikki's record jacket. I actually wrote that particular song while in New York during one of my usual trips there.

The song was released for the Carnival season that year, together with another song Rikki also recorded titled Sumintra. But it was Sumintra that turned out to be the monster hit for him, instantly establishing Rikki as a new Soca music star. Sumintra was written by the then prolific Soca and Calypso writer Gregory "GB" Ballantine.

A music video was produced for Sumintra, in which I appeared. I would also design the record jackets for two of Rikki's subsequent Carnival releases the following years, namely "Pumpin" and "Wild And Rough".

With the freelance Graphic Design work flow starting off slowly and with bills to pay, I took up a part-time teaching position at the then newly established Academy of Media Arts, which was housed in the GTM Life Insurance Building on Dundonald Street, Port of Spain. The school was the brainchild of one Theo Alfred.

I felt it was a great idea, since there was a definite need for such a school. My teaching stint, although not as long as I wished it would have been, was a very enjoyable and successful one, as one of my students, one Quentin Questel, won a prestigious Caribbean-Wide logo design competition under my tutelage.

Another student, Simone Brown, who I mentored, went on to become the owner of Brown & Partners, an Advertising & Graphic

Design Firm located in Port of Spain. During my tenure as a part-time Graphic Design instructor, I continued to freelance.

Early 1989 was also a period during which our Senior Men's National Football Team, that would adopt the nicknamed "The Strike Squad", was engaged in full preparations for participation in the final round of the CONCACAF qualifying tournament, in our quest to qualify for our first ever FIFA World Cup Finals, which was being hosted by Italy from June 8th to July 8th 1990.

The home and away round-robin tournament was scheduled to start in March of '89. The Strike Squad's first game was scheduled for May 13th, away against the USA. With a songwriting career also being very much in focus then, I saw an opportunity to make my contribution towards our country's qualification through that medium. With that objective uppermost in mind, in preparation for the Strike Squad's first home game, which was going to be against Costa Rica on May 28th at our National Stadium, I decided to put pen to paper.

Qualifying for a FIFA World Cup Finals was a feat that had always eluded us as a small football loving country, and we as a nation absolutely yearned for that success. The song that I would write and compose, appropriately titled "Road To Italy", would become the National Football Anthem during the qualifying campaign. My 1989 Road To Italy FIFA World Cup Qualifying Campaign experience, will be shared in detail in the succeeding passage.

Apart from that of The Road To Italy, there are three other experiences that stand out in my mind, during the time I resided in Westmoorings. The first was the time I got a visit from a friend from Point Fortin. His name is Joe. It was the first time he was visiting me at that new address.

I was totally unaware that he had arrived, because he did so earlier than expected. So, he had simply parked in front of the house as against calling out my name or honking his car horn, which would certainly have been viewed as him creating a nuisance by those in my "upper class" neighborhood, none of whom I ever really saw from any sort of close distance or spoke with.

But apparently, Joe was being observed by one of the residents, who decided to call the Police on him. It was only when an officer came around to my apartment at the back of the main building and brought me out front, that I realized that my friend was there.

There were two Police officers who were both black (I have never seen any white, Syrian or Chinese Police officers on the Trinidad and Tobago Police Force), who responded to the call, and had been actually interrogating Joe about why he was there etc. They did not believe the reason he gave, which was that he came to visit a friend (me) who lived there. They also did not believe that I was living at the residence. I had to return to the apartment to get my Drivers Permit which contained my address, to prove to the Police that I was.

It became quite obvious that the resident who called them thought that something fishy was going on; maybe they thought that a burglary was in progress, as did the two Policemen themselves, and Joe's one of a kind, bright orange customized Mitsubishi Lancer sports car was the getaway vehicle.

I suppose the resident who contacted the Police, would have claimed that they were just looking out for a fellow resident. Fair enough. But I know for a fact that had it been a person of Caucasian, Syrian or the like descent parked in front of the residence that day, the scenario would not have played out as it did.

Why? Simply because the resident, whomsoever they were, would never have chosen to call the Police in the first place, because it is known to all and sundry, including the said Caucasians and Syrians and the like, that they are the privileged elite in my homeland, and are basically untouchable.

The second event that stands out in my mind, while I was a resident of Westmoorings was my terrifying near-death experience. A friend who had immigrated to England had returned to Trinidad for a visit. I knew him through my old C&B colleague Robert O'Brien, and only by his nickname "Scraps". Scraps had brought two parasailing parachutes with him to Trinidad for sale.

Having become aware that my landlady's husband at the time, who did not live with her, was the owner of a boat, I suggested to Scraps that he might be interested. I inquired and as it turned out he was. Arrangements were then made for a live demonstration. On the day of the demonstration, another friend, Gregory McCalpin, whom I also knew through Robert, and who was also a friend of Scraps, accompanied him.

After meeting me at my residence, Scraps, Gregory, and I left from there, and headed down to a 25 meters long jetty a short distance away at the end of the street that I lived on, to meet my landlady's husband on his boat. He was accompanied by a female companion of Caucasian descent as he was.

However, there was one small problem. A volunteer was needed to go up in the parachute to give the demonstration to ensure that it worked. No one else apart from Scraps had done parasailing before, and he could not do it because he needed to be in the boat to direct the driver. He informed that knowing how to drive the boat was critical to the activity, especially with regards to the take-off and landing.

With Gregory declining; I then had no other choice but to be first up. Being a very capable and confident swimmer, I was ok with that. With no life vest available, I got into the harness and buckled up. I was then ready for take-off. But although being instructed by Scraps, with the driver being inexperienced, my take-off from the jetty was a bit rough.

Soaring through the air surveying both land and sea from very high above was an extremely thrilling experience. It gave me quite an adrenaline rush. I stayed up for quite some time. Then came the landing. Whatever the driver of the boat was being instructed to do he certainly didn't; because I was dumped in the water where it was still very deep and went under. The water was very dark.

Then there was a sudden acceleration as if the driver was attempting to somehow pull me back up to the surface, which spun me around. I became a bit disoriented. Because of the speed of the boat, there was very strong tension on the two straps attached to the harness clips that connected them to the two straps on the parachute.

There was no give that would allow me to open the two harness clips and release myself from the parachute, which was connected to the boat by the long length of rope. I was being dragged by the boat while underwater. And although it was for less than 30 seconds, to me it seemed like an eternity.

I was holding on to the harness clips for the first sign of the release of tension on the straps, to open them to free myself from the parachute. I was opening and closing my eyes repeatedly while I was underwater. Then with my eyes continuously shut for a bit, I suddenly started to see a few past events that occurred during my life, as well as the images of the faces of my loved ones flashing before me while submerged in the darkness.

I did not panic and remained calm and held my breath throughout the terrifying ordeal. Then came the moment I was desperately hoping and praying for, when I felt the sudden release of the tension on the straps. I instantly freed myself from the parachute.

With my eyes totally shut, and still in the harness, I started kicking desperately for the surface while taking in gulps of water, which each time felt like my very last breath as I ascended. I kept on kicking like crazy; kicking for dear life. Then there was a feeling that no words could ever possibly describe, "the oh so sweet breath of life"; having been lucky not to have surfaced inside the parachute.

As my head broke through the surface of the water, I heard cheering and applause in the distance. It was coming from another jetty where Scraps and the others were all then standing. They cheered and applauded simply because they were all so extremely relieved to have seen me finally surfaced alive.

And with almost zero energy left, I still had a 15 meters swim to the jetty where they were standing, presumedly very nervously before I surfaced. I continued to maintain my calm while just allowing myself to float in the water for a while. After finally catching my breath, I took my time swimming to the jetty. While it was a pretty close call indeed, apparently it was not yet my time.

I had no idea why, but Gregory still felt confident enough to take a turn with the second of the two parachutes. Thankfully all went smoothly for him, I guess as a result of the experience gained by the driver of the boat from my misfortune. In the end the objective was achieved, as both parachutes were bought by the boat owner.

The third and final experience of the three that stands out in my mind, during the time I lived in Westmoorings, came in the form of a visitor from a Western European country. And for me it was indeed a real eye-opener. My landlady was out of the country at the time.

Before she left, she had informed me that she was expecting the male guest from Europe. The country and first name of the guest were given. He arrived as scheduled. After a couple of days and a few conversations between us, I guess he then felt comfortable enough with me, whereupon he told me that he wanted to show me something. He invited me inside the main residence where he was staying.

We both sat at the large table situated in the very spacious dining area of the house. Lying in front of him on the table was a set of silver metal objects. With his strong accent from that particular Western European country, he asked me if I knew what they were. Because of the shapes, I quickly figured it out, but said I didn't. He began fitting the parts together, and in record time had completely assembled a firearm.

Then with a broad smile he handed it over to me. I inspected it while holding it for a bit. It was the very first time in my life that I held a firearm. Never would I have ever imagined holding one, let alone imagined having that first experience in one of the neighborhoods, where the general local perception is that "there liveth the saints, but not the sinners".

Immediately lots of questions entered my mind. The uppermost of which was, "who the hell is this individual boy?" He took back the firearm, upon which he then gave me a demonstration of how to load and unload and use it. He then offered it to me as a gift. Without a second thought, I politely declined his offer. He then proceeded to tell me a bit about himself, which most definitely answered the question that was uppermost in my mind.

He also divulged other information than I would have much preferred he kept to himself. The experience most definitely opened my eyes as wide as they could possibly have been, to the goings-on in that particular "upper-class residential area" in my beloved country, which I imagined were also going on in others as well. I most certainly appreciated the education.

Some of his revelations left me with a sense of uneasiness during the remainder of the time he spent at the residence, and for quite some time after he had left. I never mentioned any of what transpired with her guest to my landlady when she returned. I felt it best to have left that Pandora's Box very tightly shut.

MY HOMELAND'S 1989 ROAD TO ITALY
FIFA WORLD CUP QUALIFYING CAMPAIGN:
THE MAKING OF A FOOTBALL ANTHEM:

As established in a much earlier passage, I had known Austin Lyons since we were growing up in Point Fortin during the 60s and 70s, during which period we both played tenor pan with the Dunlop Tornadoes Steel Orchestra.

At the beginning of the next decade, 1980 to be precise, and surprising to most in the community, Austin would launch what would be a highly successful music career as a Soca and Calypso writer / recording and performing Artiste with a really big bang. He would become more popularly known by his then stage name "Blue Boy". He absolutely took Trinidad and Tobago by storm, as his very first release titled "Soca Baptist" was a massive hit.

Austin's piercing well-toned voice, original and infectious melodies, creative lyrics and unique way of story-telling in song, and unique and hypnotic ad-libs accentuated with deep spiritual undertones and the style of his execution, was topped off by his absolutely magical live stage performance, which included dance maneuvers and tricks with the old fashion cord microphone, that were never seen anywhere before he came on the scene.

Dark-skinned and good looking with a good physique, a captivating dimpled smile, a warm engaging personality and a solid spiritual foundation, he was the total package indeed. Together, all of those attributes saw Austin instantly propelled into the Trinidad and Tobago entertainment limelight and the "Big Times".

He became an inspiration to all aspiring Soca and Calypso writers, recording Artistes and performers from Point Fortin, including myself. That said year, Soca Baptist won Austin his first of many of Trinidad and Tobago's highest and most prestigious musical accolades, which is the Road March title, as he began to blaze the Soca music trail.

Trinbagonian Soca and Calypso music lovers from all different walks of life instantly fell in love with him and his music. He also gained throngs of fans throughout the Caribbean, North America and Europe. He ascended to great heights in the Soca and Calypso music world over the first 4 years of his career. Austin was most definitely my local music idol.

Then the spotlight that once shone oh so brightly on him suddenly went dim. It was blamed on an alleged drug habit. And while still continuing to write, record and release new music, the spotlight that initially went dim, eventually went totally out on his music career.

Having had most of his vinyl record releases in my personal record collection back then, there was one song in particular that he recorded during those extremely rough years, which absolutely struck a nerve within me and stuck in my mind, because of its poignant heartfelt message.

The title of that song is "Jingay", which Austin released for the 1987 Carnival season without the usual pomp and circumstance, which surrounded his releases when he was at the peak of his musical powers earlier in the 80s. In fact, during that dark time, with his usual undeniable dominating musical presence not being felt, one newspaper headline actually asked the question, "Where's Blue Boy?"

In his song "Jingay", Austin was unequivocally expressing his yearning to get back to the very top of the Soca music world; desperately pleading in song to "The Preacher-man", whom he believed possessed the "Jingay" powers (Supernatural powers) to grant him his wish. More specifically, to help him to make a song that will instantly propel him back to where he once was, and where he did in fact truly belong.

Whenever I listened to Jingay, I could actually hear and feel my then local music idol's dire misery and pain. There were 8 absolutely heart-wrenching lines in particular in his song, that kept eating away at me ever since I first heard the song.

And it would in fact be those 8 heart-wrenching lines in "Jingay", that would provide the impetus that would see us have a musical reunion, which process actually began several months prior to us actually collaborating on what was then the unknown project.

It was sometime in late '88 when "ah bounce up" (I encountered) Austin in town, after not seeing him for a very long while. I was driving through the nation's capital one evening when I saw him standing on the side walk at the corner of Park and Henry Streets on the northwestern side. He was wearing a combination of blue and white cowboy style attire, and was holding an acoustic guitar. It was about an hour or so before nightfall.

"Whey yuh goin?" I stopped and asked. Bending and peering through the car window, he looked pleasantly surprised when he realized it was me, "ah old hometown boy". "Ah reaching Belmont," he replied excitedly. Being that I was in the vicinity, I offered him a drop (lift), which he gladly accepted.

The seemingly coincidental encounter that day, ushered in the start of fairly regular visits to check him at calypsonian Struggler's Belmont apartment, where he then regularly hung out, as I wanted to get his opinion on some of the songs that I had written.

He took a special liking to a song titled "YinWan", which was inspired by a true story of a co-worker at C&B. She was Chinese and once revealed to me that YinWan was her given Chinese name. She gave me her consent to write the song, wherein she was going to be the subject.

Upon hearing the demo, which I recorded with back-up music I played on a small Casio-Tone keyboard that I had since bought, Austin suggested that I record that particular song myself. Regretfully, I never did. After a few months, I could no longer locate Austin in Belmont, and we lost touch with each other.

As mentioned earlier, from early '89, our Senior Men's National Football Team was engaged in full preparations for participation in the final round of the CONCACAF qualifying tournament, in our quest to qualify for our first ever FIFA World Cup Finals, which was being hosted by Italy from June 8th to July 8th 1990. If successful, it would see my tiny twin island nation of just over one million people, represented at the greatest sporting spectacle on the planet.

It would also be an historic feat, being that we would have then been the smallest English-speaking Caribbean country ever to do so. For the uninitiated, qualifying for a FIFA World Cup Finals, is the moment that every football fanatic who ardently supports his or her respective national team, absolutely live for; yours truly included.

That final qualifying round involved a group comprising of 5 teams. Namely, Trinidad & Tobago, USA, Costa Rica, Guatemala and El Salvador. The top two teams at the end of the home and away series, would go on to represent the CONCACAF region in Italy. Our first game would be away to the USA on Sunday May 13th 1989.

I had an overwhelming desire to contribute to the realization of what was a longstanding, collective national dream, which had eluded us time and time again. And so, I was highly motivated to utilize my song-writing gift to make my contribution. The song I would write, would be inspired by the events that occurred in HAITI 16 years ago then, when we were robbed of a possible place at the 1974 FIFA World Cup Finals in Germany.

My vision was to write and compose a song that would be recorded and played on the airwaves, that would serve to stimulate the entire nation of 1.3 million citizens, to rally behind the team; and at the same time, also serve to motivate and inspire each player individually and collectively the team, to play every single game with "Pride, Passion, Purpose and Patriotism upper most in mind", in its efforts to achieve the ultimate goal of qualifying for the Italia '90 FIFA World Cup Finals.

Sitting on a gray steel folding chair underneath a mango tree in the backyard of my then Westmoorings abode, I started the process of writing the song appropriately titled "Road To Italy" in early April, just about one month after I had resigned from my advertising job at Christiansen & Belgrave.

As is usually the process for me, the melody of the verse came first, with the initial lyrics also coming into my head simultaneously. I then wrote those lyrics to the first verse down on paper. Singing the first verse over and over to myself, the melody and initial lyrics to the chorus then came into my head, upon which I also wrote those lyrics down. The writing process was then continued indoors, when I then also wrote the first draft of 2 of the other 3 verses over the course of the next few days, while sitting at my dining room table.

Once the first draft of 3 of the 4 verses and the chorus were completed, I subsequently went over them again and again, making changes to the lyrics and switching around lines to create clearer images in the minds of the listener, to evoke the feelings and the emotional response to the story I was telling, towards the ultimate objective that I was trying to achieve.

Throughout the entire process of writing the song, there were two things constantly resonating in my head; one was Austin's voice singing those 8 heart-wrenching lines in "Jingay", and the other was hearing his voice singing my Road To Italy song.

While the emotional dimension of the song was captured through the melody and lyrics in the verses and chorus, after singing it over and over and over again in my head mimicking Austin's voice, and at times outwardly with my own voice, being that it was inspired by the events of 1973 in Haiti, I felt that establishing that connection in the song was extremely important to reinforce the emotional dimension.

In that moment, with the yellow-colored lyric sheets lying on the dining room table directly in front of me, and focusing my mind on the events that occurred in HAITI, I just sat in complete silence at the table with my eyes closed, willing divine intervention. Then it happened.

Both the melody and lyrics to the introduction of the song came to me simultaneously, along with the idea for the tempo to be much slower than the tempo of the rest of the song. It was perfect. It took the emotional dimension of the song to a whole other level. I knew then that the song was almost complete. I say almost complete because I would wait until we played the first game away against the USA, before writing a 4th verse of the song.

When we eventually played that game on Saturday May 13th, we drew 1-1, with an unforgettable 88th minute equalizer from midfielder Hudson "Barber" Charles, on a magnificent headed assist by team mate Marlon Morris. It was an excellent result to kick off our qualifying campaign. I then wrote the 4th verse of the song the following day, Sunday May 14th.

The next day Monday May 15th I was at Kenny Phillips' Music Lab Recording Studio recording the demo. I had first met Kenny through one

Percy Parker Williams, who was a former colleague at C&B, who actually took me to Kenny's studio on that occasion.

I kept the cassette of my Road To Italy demo with me in my car. The day after recording it, I was pulling into a parking spot at the Long Circular Mall St. James, when I saw former national player and friend in football, Ron LaForest, who, in his prime, was a deadly striker for both the national team and his then club team the Defense Force.

I invited Ron to sit in my vehicle to listen to the demo. He absolutely loved it. I then told him that the singer I had in mind to record it was Blue Boy (Austin), but I needed a sponsor to pay for the recording. Ron told me to take it to one Tansley Thompson. "Tell him I sen' yuh," Ron said with an air of optimism and expectancy.

Though I had never met him personally, I knew Tansley from his days playing with a team named Essex in the top-flight local football league back in the 70s, and later as one of the then owners of WOT (Wilson O'Brien & Thompson) Sports, which was a fairly expansive sporting goods outlet, located at the Roxy round-a-bout Woodbrook Port of Spain.

I immediately followed through on Ron's suggestion and took the demo to Tansley, who was then running his own sporting goods store on Ariapita Avenue, Woodbrook. After listening to my demo, Tansley invited me to sit down for a while, as he wanted to make some phone calls.

The phone calls he was making was to solicit the financial sponsorship that I needed for the final recording of the song. He was unable to attract any sponsorship interest before I had to leave, but indicated that he would pay for the final recording himself, if he couldn't secure a sponsor in a timely manner.

Tansley assumed that I was also going to do the final recording, until I informed him that in my head, I was hearing Austin's voice singing the song. But Tansley felt that I should record it myself, and tried his utmost to convince me to do so. He eventually conceded after I insisted that I wanted to first propose the idea to Austin for him to record the song, since his was the voice, I was hearing singing it, during the entire process of writing it.

Uppermost in my mind at the time was Austin's desperate, heart-wrenching pleas in Jingay. And given that his career was nonexistent then, I felt that it could possibly have given my then local music idol a new lease on his music and by extension personal life. And the song did in fact match his style perfectly. I was therefore hopeful that he would buy into the idea, given its greater purpose as well.

My demo was subsequently played over the sound system at a warm up game that I attended at the National Stadium that very same week, which was before we would play our first home game against Costa Rica on May 28th at the very same venue, where all of our home games would be played. A few thousands attended that warm up game, and the general response to my song was very positive, and left me feeling extremely excited about its potential to achieve its intended objective.

But to present my proposal to Austin for him to record the song, I first had to find him. And finding him turned out to be much more of a challenge than I expected. I first went to Belmont where I last met with him. I was informed that he was back somewhere in Malabar Arima, where he actually owned a house. With his friends in Belmont not knowing exactly where in Malabar he lived, I was given Calypsonian Explainer's address, and was told he would be able to provide me with Austin's exact location.

The very next day I made the drive up to Explainer's residence, which was about an hour from my Westmoorings residence. Following his directions, I ended up at what was supposed to be Austin's residence at Melodians Crescent Malabar, Arima.

Like all the others in that particular government housing development, it was a flat house, which not surprisingly, was painted blue. There were just the gaping spaces where louvre windows should have been. One just simply had to step over the window sills and you were inside the house. He could hardly have felt any sense of security living there, I thought to myself.

After parking and exiting my car, with noticeably no one at the front, I then walked around to the back of the house while calling out Austin's name. Arriving at the back, I discovered that his house was one of several bordering a football ground, which I found quite interesting, given the reason I was there. The football ground was more or less grassless, thus my referring to it as a football ground and not a field.

At the back of the house, I saw another gaping window space at a back bedroom. Not really expecting anyone to be inside since there was no response to my shouts, I peeked inside. To my utter surprise, there was a female sleeping on her stomach on a bed. I immediately stepped away and began saying good afternoon to get her attention.

She was definitely a sound sleeper, because it took repeated good afternoon shouts, before she finally responded. "Come," she said in her sleepy voice. With both arm clutching the pillow she was sleeping on, she was then looking up in the direction of the gaping window space, while still lying on her stomach.

I introduced myself using my nickname, which is Ali, and told her that I was looking for Austin. She told me that she did not know where he was, but that I could check at a certain house across the street from the football ground. I asked and was informed by the female that Austin did not have a telephone.

I thanked her then left and got back into my vehicle and drove over to the location. There I met a couple who told me that I should check by Ethel, upon which they informed me that it was the same "Ethel", who was the subject of Austin's 1981 Carnival hit of the same name, that won him his second Road March title that year. They gave me directions to Ethel's residence, which was not very far away.

When I got to the destination, the house where Ethel lived was still under construction. After calling out and honking my car horn several times without response, I returned to the couple's house. There I left a message for Austin that I had visited to see him, and that I would return the following day.

I decided to return the following night instead. I took my older brother Evans along for the ride on that occasion. I remember I drove straight into Austin's empty garage space on the right side of his house and parked.

The house was very dimly lit. I called out his name. "Austin!" His response was immediate. "Ah comin'," he replied. No lights came on, either inside the house or in the garage, so I assumed that he had no electricity. And I was right. I then turned on the inside lights in my car. When he came out my brother moved to the back seat and I invited Austin to sit in the passenger seat. After quickly getting the usual pleasantries out of the way I got right down to business.

"Listen tuh dis," I said, loading my "Road To Italy" demo into my car's cassette deck, while handing him a copy of the lyrics, which were written on three yellow sheets from my writing pad. I distinctly remember him playing with a small penknife he was holding, while listening most attentively to my demo from beginning to end. He then asked for it to be played again. I rewinded the cassette and played it again.

After he listened to my demo for the second time, I then explained the project and its core purpose to Austin, and asked whether he would be interested in recording the song. I told him that I needed an answer right then because time was of the essence, since it was then just over a week before our first home game against Costa Rica on Sunday May 28th; and I wanted to get the song released with ample time before then to drum up public support.

He asked which studio I would be using to record the song. "Kenny Phillips," I replied. After thinking in silence for a bit, Austin said, "Ali ah go do it. Ah go do it." I left both my demo tape and lyrics sheet with him so that he could learn and rehearse the song. My older brother and I then left his Malabar Arima residence and headed back into Port of Spain. The following day I informed Tansley Thompson that Austin had agreed to record the song. The news was well received.

During a subsequent visit to his residence a day or so later, Austin wanted to talk about the business side of the project. I had no knowledge or experience about that aspect, and thus, really hadn't given it any thought at the time. So then, to ensure that money issues didn't get in the way of and distract from the core purpose of the project, I proposed the fairest deal that I knew existed, which was that we split any revenue generated from the project, including live performances 50-50, after subtracting out-of-pocket expenses. He accepted my proposal, upon which we shook hands on what was a verbal agreement.

The day after, I was contacted by Tansley Thompson, who through his own efforts, had gotten a verbal commitment from the Carib Brewery, brewers of the island's most popular Lager Beer, through its then Marketing Manager Colin Murray, that they were going to sponsor the final recording of the song.

I entered into an agreement with them worth $12,325.00 TTD, of which $4,000.00 would go to Austin for his services for recording the song, which he wasn't expecting but I negotiated; $2,500.00 would go to the arranger for musical arrangement; $400.00 would go to the back ground singers; $1,200.00 would go towards the design and artwork for the record jacket; $1,725.00 would go toward the cost of a stamper to press records; and $2,500.00 would go towards pressing an initial quantity of 500, which because of time constraints, would initially be in plain record jackets.

In exchange, Carib would get the rights to use the song in anyway whatsoever, without paying for or requesting copyright permission or approval for said use. I signed the official sponsorship agreement with Carib Brewery Limited on June 5th.

Tansley indicated that he had just one request, which was for his sports store to get some advertising and promotional mileage on the record jacket. His request was more than fair, and he would most deservedly get even more than he expected, as his name would feature prominently in the introduction of the song as well.

It was then a race against time to record and release the song on the airwaves before our first home game against Costa Rica, which was then just days away. I contacted Kenny Phillips to do the musical arrangement.

The day after contacting him, we headed down south to his Music Lab studio located at Flamingo Drive Philippines San Fernando in two vehicles. Making the trip to the studio was Tansley, with Austin and his then girlfriend Singing Sonia in his vehicle, and my brother Evans and I in my vehicle. The Martung sisters Arlene and Beverly, who Kenny hired to do background vocals, was already at the studio when we got there.

We arrived at the studio sometime between 10:00 and 11:00 a.m. on the day. With no time to waste, the work in the studio started shortly after our arrival, with Kenny working out the key, cord patterns and tempo of the song, on his acoustic guitar, with Austin.

Once those things were sorted out, Kenny then proceeded to start working on the rhythm track together with Austin, after which he then put down a track with his electric guitar. Austin eventually put down his guide vocals. The Martung sisters then had the mic, as it then became time to start laying down the background vocals.

Upon hearing the original background vocals line, which was "On de road, de road to Italy", Tansley then suggested that it be changed to, "On de road, we going Italy". There was no need to have any sort of debate about Tansley's suggestion. It was a simple but quite potent change indeed; and so, it was immediately instituted.

I remember Tansley was actually shouting the phrase and using vigorous hand gestures with his index finger pointing upwards and outwards to make his point of "we goin' Italy". The change most definitely reinforced the song's positive, uplifting, motivational and inspirational message.

The Martung sisters, who were used to working together as a team, were absolutely amazing. They were nailing the harmonies with consummate ease. Or I should say, they made it look easy. Such was their chemistry.

Austin and Sonia had exited the studio once the process of laying down the tracks for the background vocals began. That left Kenny, the Martung sisters, Tansley, my brother Evans and me in the studio. I joined Austin and Sonia outside not to long after.

They were sitting underneath Kenny's Julie mango tree in the yard. I remember Austin having the lyrics sheets in his hand, changing lyrics here and there in the song with a pen. I found it quite interesting that he was doing so while sitting underneath a mango tree, given the fact that I myself was sitting underneath a mango tree when I began writing the song.

During that time, a phone call came in for me from Colin Murray from the Carib Brewery. He wanted to know if Austin would be up to performing the song live at the Costa Rica game; and if so, what would his fee be.

I put Colin on hold and exited the studio with the cordless phone and asked Austin if he would be in fact up to it, and if so, what would be his fee for the performance. He thought about it for a few seconds, then he replied. "Tell him fifteen hundred nah." I felt that my then local music idol was selling himself very short.

I knew immediately that he was simply pricing himself based on what he felt his market value was at the time, given what his professional and personal state of affairs had been for years at that juncture, which, being human, would have certainly taken a toll on him and his self-esteem; and I also knew that.

For me personally, with those eight lines in his song Jingay resonating in my head, it was all about contributing to my then local music idol's ultimate goal of getting back to the top. And so, I took over the negotiations. "Colin. Five thousand. An' he'll wear a Carib Beer T-Shirt for the performance," which I threw in as part of the deal, as I responded confidently to Colin's inquiry.

"Five thousand boy?" Colin responded. "An' he go wear ah Carib T-Shirt to perform," I reiterated, knowing that the offer would be hard to resist for obvious reasons. "Dat sounding kinda steep, but awright," Colin ended. "Cool," I replied, then quickly hung up so as to not give him the opportunity to continue the negotiations. The total amount of revenue already generated then was TT$9,000.00.

Sometime between 1:00 and 2:00 p.m., Austin, Sonia, my brother Evans and I headed to Gulf City Mall to have lunch. Tansley decided that he would remain at the studio, while Kenny continued working. Austin continued tweaking some of the lyrics of the song while we were having lunch.

We returned to the studio just over an hour later. By that time, the Martungs had completed the background vocals. Kenny continued to work on laying down the rhythm and most of the other musical tracks over Austin's guide voice well into the night.

At that point, I began to feel a bit tired and sleepy. So, having to drive back to Port of Spain and not wanting to fall asleep behind the wheel on the road, while the others stayed in the studio, I decided to take a nap on Kenny's couch in his living room, which was just through a door that separated it from the studio. I eventually dozed off.

After about half an hour to 45 minutes, I awoke to the sound of Austin's voice and the accompanying music emanating from Kenny's then very small studio, as he played what was the second verse of the song through the studio sound system. It was then just before midnight, and Austin was putting down his final vocals.

He was at the end of the second of the four verses of the song when I awoke. His piercing vocal tone and hypnotic execution of the song then kept me wide awake. I decided that I would absorb a bit of the vibes while lying on Kenny's living room couch, before heading back into the studio to witness what was the main event of the recording session.

I was doing just that, when I heard a particular line at the very end of that second verse, that was proving to be quite a challenge for Austin to execute, while still maintaining the melodic flow. The lyrics he was executing was, "Spann an' Maurice is blows!"

After listening to a few unsuccessful attempts while still lying on Kenny's couch, I recognized the problem. The word "is", in the line was making it six syllables long, which was one too many. I intervened. I told Austin to drop the word "is". He did. The line then became "Spann an' Maurice blows", which then allowed him to execute the line, while maintaining the flow of the melody.

Witnessing Austin executing the song behind the mic in the booth was an experience in itself. The atmosphere in the studio was highly charged, with the positive spiritual energy that Austin was exuding and invoking. Everyone present could feel that something extraordinary was unfolding.

Austin was in his zone, as he belted out the song's lyrics with the utmost emotional and spiritual conviction and passion. What an experience it was. Once his vocals and ad-libs were all laid down, it was felt that another hook could be placed inside the band chorus.

He began verbalizing several ideas utilizing the word dribble, then singing along to see if it worked with the band chorus, which was being repeated over and over on the sound system. Then out flew "Dribble Dong Dey!" from Austin's mouth. Immediately upon hearing that hook, my brother Evans seemed to have then lost all sense of self.

He started jumping up and down inside the studio like a madman, while vehemently voicing his uncompromising endorsement, shouting repeatedly, "Allyuh dyse it! Dyse it!" "Allyuh dyse it! Dyse it!" He was so adamant, that we did not even dare consider another.

My brother Evans was absolutely right. "Dribble Dong Dey" was indeed it. The complete lead vocal track was down. The Martung sisters then added background vocals to the Dribble Dong Dey hook. Kenny then played what was the very rough mix of the entire song from the top down. It was impossible for anyone to have remained sitting down; such was its stimulative power.

It was then just before 1:00 a.m. After the 14 hours session, the Port of Spain crew, comprising of Austin, Sonia, Tansley, the Martung sisters, my brother Evans and yours truly, all left the studio quite tired but in very high spirits nonetheless. We then headed back to the city, leaving Kenny to complete his work on what we all knew by then, was definitely going to be an extremely special song.

I was so excited, I hardly slept. I could not wait to hear the final mix. Just after 12 noon I got a phone call from Kenny. He played it for me over the telephone. I got goose bumps upon hearing just the first 15 to 20 seconds of the highly spiritually and emotionally charged introduction, which I purposely did in a very slow tempo when I was writing it, to maximize the effects of those dimensions. It worked perfectly.

I listened to about two verses of the song over the telephone. After a quick shower and throwing on some clothes, my foot was very heavy on the gas pedal, as I flew down to Kenny's studio to pick up cassette copies of the final product.

When I actually heard the entire song played on Kenny's studio system, I was completely blown away. I got even more goose bumps then. Kenny did an outstanding job with the musical arrangement. With 3 cassette copies of the final mix in hand, Tansley and I then met with Colin Murray at his office. He was equally impressed with the finished product, and especially with the way the name of his Carib beer product was integrated into the song, which was Austin's doing, which was a huge bonus for the Carib Brewery, since there was no cost attached to same.

Records were then hurriedly pressed at HEWCO's record pressing plant, and distributed to the various radio stations in plain record jackets. The song immediately began enjoying extensive air play, especially as our first home game against Costa Rica was then only a few days away.

While most of the radio DJs of the day had it on heavy rotation, Ian "The Goose" Eligon and Phillip "Phil the Thrill from Laventille" Simmons in particular, literally played it "like ah road march". Without any shadow of a doubt, Carib was getting much more than their sponsorship money's worth, by receiving massive brand exposure through said extensive air play.

My first of several newspaper interviews, followed close on the heels of Road To Italy being released on the airwaves. It was conducted by one Rolph Warner. I believe it was the Saturday night before the Costa Rica game on Sunday May 28th. At the time he was an entertainment journalist with the Sunday Punch newspaper, which was a weekly publication.

While I knew of him and had seen him at various entertainment events that I had attended, I was meeting him for the very first time. His was going to be my very first interview I was having, in my capacity as a songwriter. I found him to be very affable and down to earth. I got really good vibes from him. The interview was conducted in the back seat, while I was moving around in Tansley's vehicle, with Tansley himself driving.

Rolph revealed that he was an ardent longstanding supporter and friend of Austin, who he referred to as Blue, as against Blue Boy. I remember him first asking me for the correct spelling of my name, after which he posed his very first question, which was how did the collaboration between Blue and myself come about. My answer was, "Through Spiritual Orchestration"; a concept and term I created to explain such occurrences in my life.

Judging by his facial expression, it was clear that it was not the response that Rolph expected. It most certainly got his attention, and seemed to then spike his curiosity beyond the purpose for which he was conducting the interview.

He seemed quite intrigued, and asked about the meaning of the term. I define Spiritual Orchestration as, "the process through which positive spiritual manifestation brings all the necessary elements together, to make a desired outcome a reality".

And given how the events unfolded that lead up to the collaboration, I truly believed that it was not as a result of happenstance. I sincerely believed that it came about as a result of "Spiritual Orchestration". I remain steadfast to my belief in the concept. I always will.

The interview lasted for about an hour, during which Rolph got all the necessary details for his article. Rolph had the notion that all and sundry would have naturally assumed that Austin wrote and composed the song himself. It would in fact be the only time during his illustrious career, which would span several decades, that someone else had written and composed an original song for Austin, which he recorded.

The article was published the weekend following the Costa Rica game, by which time most of the population would have heard the song, and so would have become aware of it. The headline read, "The Man Behind Road To Italy". Rolph told me he chose that headline because he wanted the public at large to know who was actually responsible for writing and composing the song, to ensure that I received the credit I deserved. But unfortunately, that still did not happen. More on that particular issue later.

The then Trinidad and Tobago Men's National Football team had adopted the "Strike Squad" as its nickname after it was referred to as such, in another then very popular world cup campaign rally song, written and recorded by Rapso legend and icon, Lancelot Lane. "The Strike Squad" became the team's official nickname and was referred to by such by everyone.

Like the first game away to the USA, our home game against Costa Rica ended in an exciting 1-1 tie. But there was other big news that day that was most certainly welcomed. The Trinidad and Tobago public had also witnessed the return of their beloved local music icon. Blue Boy was finally back.

That day at the national stadium, in front a crowd of about 15,000 to 20,000, he performed Road to Italy live for the very first time. He wore a blue track suit sponsored by Tansley's Sports Store, and of course the T-Shirt displaying the Carib logo on the front. He put on a very entertaining performance, incorporating a bit of ball juggling and all.

He was visibly ecstatic to be finally back in his element and in the spotlight once again, after years of being totally out of it. The thousands of fans who turned up at the stadium, were also visibly excited to have witnessed the return of one of their all-time favorite musical sons of the soil.

Having since become privy to Austin's then living conditions, and while I was also in dire financial need at the time, in addition to the TT$4,000.00 he collected for recording the song, I made the decision to also let him have all of the TT$5,000.00, which was the fee I negotiated for his live performance.

So, while our verbal agreement called for a 50-50 split after out-of-pocket expenses, the entire TT$9,000.00 in revenue generated up to that point was given to Austin, and which apart from food and clothes, we agreed that he would use for home improvements, since it was desperately needed.

But I too needed to eat and I had bills to pay. So, in the months that followed, it was all about distribution of the single to record stores local and foreign to generate much needed income. Kenny had indicated that he would have delivered the master tape to one "Charlo", a Trinidadian business associate of his, who was a U.S. based record distributor, to press and distribute the product there.

But I remember one New York based Trinidadian Radio DJ, Eric St. Bernard, still having to travel to Trinidad to obtain copies of the record, as it was not available for purchase in the U.S. and New York in particular. There was also a published newspaper article about the demand for the record in New York.

So, both Tansley and I traveled to New York at different times with product that was manufactured in Trinidad to distribute ourselves, focusing on Brooklyn based record Stores like Charlie's on Fulton Street, which was the most popular. Had I known better then, I would have done a deal with Charlie himself, to press and distribute the record in north America. Knowing that I was new to the business, Austin could have advised me relative to that aspect, but he never offered any.

I was also invited and did an extended interview on Eric St. Bernard's New York radio program. Eric also linked me up with then top Jamaican

Radio DJ Jeff Barnes at New York's WBLS sister station WLIB, who also played and promoted the record on his program.

My older brother Evans, who had since returned to New York sometime during the qualifying campaign, actually had a verbal confrontation with the Charlo distributor over the phone, after I asked Evans to retrieve the master tape from him, since the Charlo distributor had been simply sitting on it. He never returned it to my brother when my brother made the request for him to do so, in order for us to hand it over to another distributor, to have then enable us to generate the revenue we might have.

Meanwhile, Austin and I was developing a very close friendship as the campaign progressed. I was gaining his trust, which was something that he told me he had lost in some of the people who used to be involved with his career in the past.

As such, he revealed a lot of personal experiences about his life in the music business to me, including an experience at a certain hotel, where he was betrayed by someone who was then in his inner circle. That particular experience seemed to have left him with an emotional scar.

It was actually during one of our many talk sessions, that time while sitting on a bench around the Queen's Park Savannah, close to the St. Anns round-a-bout and the Belmont Circular Road one evening, that the decision to change his stage name was made.

It also became quite obvious where the inspiration for doing so was coming from. "Ali, ah want ah name dat go bring out de Superness (his exact word) in mih. Yuh know, like Superman," he stated excitedly. "Wuh yuh think?" He asked.

Having already likened himself to the American movie superhero in his song of the same title years before, logic then determined his new stage name. That day, while sitting on a bench around the Queen's Park Savannah with dusk descending upon us, Blue Boy became SuperBlue. The Trinidad and Tobago Soca music superhero was born.

THE GRAVE INJUSTICE DONE TO ME BY
MY THEN EMPLOYERS McCANN ERICKSON
ADVERTISING AGENCY: THE TRUTH WELL TOLD

By August of '89, just about at the midway point of our Road To Italy World Cup Qualifying Campaign, I was becoming quite popular because of the song, but struggling to pay my bills. So, after being offered, out of necessity I accepted a job at McCann Erickson Advertising Agency.

Adrian Chandler, my former colleague from my early days at C&B, who was then employed at McCann, recommended me to the bosses there. I laid all my cards on the table when I met one on one with the then McCann CEO Ronnie Lee, because I had absolutely no intention of being subjected to any more exploitation, discrimination, and office politics etc., as was the case when I was employed at C&B.

For me, that dive back into the Trinidad Advertising / Graphic Design industry, was simply about earning a high steady income, that would have then allowed me to pay my bills and enjoy my chosen recreational activities etc., without having to struggle to do so, as I had in the past. As such, I asked for the salary that I felt I was worth at the time.

I also made it my business to inform the CEO that I was directly involved with our Road To Italy World Cup Qualifying campaign, with which by then, the majority of the country had become totally engrossed.

I got the salary I asked for; and the then McCann CEO did not view my involvement with our Road To Italy campaign as a problem. Had he viewed it as such, as desperate as I was for a steady income at the time, I would have definitely turned down their job offer.

I took up the position of Junior Art Director at McCann Erickson on Tuesday August 15th 1989, one day after my 30th birthday. And not that having a job title mattered to me then, but for some strange reason a particular Director of the company told me, that detail of my official position should be kept confidential. I immediately thought, "Red Flag", because I couldn't understand why it should be.

At McCann, I had the pleasure of meeting and working with some really cool individuals, including Carlyle Mason, Rory Loregnard, Mark White, Caryl Welch, and Darren "Cheese" Che Wah. Another very cool individual I would also have the pleasure of meeting and working with was actually a client.

That was one Dennis Ramdeen. He was then the Brand Manager for Stag Beer, which was on the Agency's account list at the time. I found him to be extremely "down to earth", which was fairly rare, given his professional and social status. He and I would collaborate on a Stag Beer World Cup promotion, which theme "Bound for Italy. Bound To Be Stag," I conceptualized. The promotion was an overwhelming success.

Meanwhile, there was a home game against Guatemala upcoming on Sunday September 3rd. On Thursday August 24th, just over a week before that game, another article about me being the writer of what was then becoming the official World Cup Qualifying anthem, appeared in one of the daily newspapers.

That article, together with the song's ever-increasing amounts of daily radio air play, and my name being mentioned as its writer, would in due course be used by my new employers, to perpetrate a grave professional injustice against me.

By the end of August, only 2 weeks after I joined the company, I had chalked up my first "Ad of The Month" award at McCann. It was for a full-page newspaper ad, celebrating our nation's 27th Independence Anniversary. We won what was the penultimate game of our World Cup Qualifying Campaign at home against Guatemala on Sunday September 3rd 2-1, which then put us in an excellent position to qualify for the 1990 FIFA World Cup in Italy.

On October 23rd, I signed an expansion to the original sponsorship agreement I had with the Carib Brewery. The additional fee paid by Carib was $12,710.00, of which $7,080.00 would go towards printing 1000 record jackets, and $5,630.00 going towards pressing 1000 additional records, which would then bring the total of records pressed to 1500.

In exchange, the Carib crown cork logo would be displayed on both the front and at the back of the record jacket. In addition, a Carib distribution truck displaying the said logo would also appear at the back of the record jacket. The color scheme of the record jacket was blue and gold, which reflected the brand identities of both the Carib beer product and Austin, who wore coordinated ensembles of blue on stage.

But to my total dismay, Colin Murray wanted me to repay Carib $10,710.00 of their $12,710.00 sponsorship expansion fee, and had me sign an agreement to the effect. The repayment would have been after Carib had in fact enjoyed the additional brand exposure, and promotional mileage from its logo appearing 3 times on the record jacket, that the said $12,710.00 fee would have paid for in the first place.

Thus, Colin was suggesting that $10,710.00 of the $12,710.00 sponsorship expansion fee, that was paid for said additional brand exposure and promotional mileage it would have been receiving, was actually a loan, making the actual value of the sponsorship then $2,000.00.

So clearly, Colin, like most of the population, was anticipating that we would have qualified for the World Cup, whereby the record would then have been such a huge seller, that the $10,710.00 would have been easy to repay. It did not work out that way. But even if it did, I had absolutely no intention of giving back any monies to Carib.

At the very end of that said October month, SuperBlue was officially introduced to the Trinidad and Tobago public and the world, at the official record jacket reveal event for the Road To Italy single. The event took place at the Mas Camp Pub, which was located at the corner of French Street and Ariapita Avenue, Woodbrook.

The very first time Austin's new SuperBlue stage name appeared anywhere, was on the Road To Italy record jacket, which was designed by yours truly. Its design elements included an original illustration of the FIFA World Cup Trophy on the front, done by me, as well as the autographs of all the members of the Strike Squad and technical staff at the back, which was also my idea.

That same October month, I had chalked up my second "Ad of The Month" award at McCann. It was for another full-page newspaper ad, which was in support of the Trinidad & Tobago Strike Squad, for the then huge upcoming final game of the CONCACAF qualifying tournament on November 19th, at home against the USA. That game would determine who would be the final team between the two to qualify for the 1990 FIFA World Cup Finals in Italy.

November arrived, and our World Cup Qualifying Campaign was at fever pitch, with my Road To Italy song reaching the heights of its popularity on the local airwaves. But my involvement with our campaign went beyond writing the then football anthem. On my very own initiative, I was also re-assembling my beloved 1973 Trinidad and Tobago team that was cheated out of a place at the 1974 Finals in Germany, to be a part of the huge November 19th event.

And here I must first point out that none of my off the job activities, were interfering with or affecting my ability to perform on the job, which was evidenced by my winning the two Ad of the Month Awards, in addition to the written commendations I was receiving from my bosses for other assignments I had worked on.

But on Friday the 17th, exactly 48 hours before the huge Sunday November 19th Game against the USA, in a move I viewed purely as a "Massa Day Power Play", I was called into the office of one of the company's Directors just before the lunch time interval, upon which he invited me to have a seat. We both then sat down; he behind his desk and I on one of two chairs in front of it.

After a brief opening remark about some company policy, he stated that I had to choose between continuing to work at McCann or continuing to be involved with my country's World Cup Qualifying Campaign, and that I had to decide right there and right then. "Mr. Ayres," he stated authoritatively, "so is either the Road To McCann or The Road To Italy," he then sarcastically declared, with an equally sarcastic chuckle.

Quickly analyzing the situation while sitting at the goodly Director's desk, McCann's "Massa Day Power Play" appeared to have been born out of the assumption that if we did qualify for the World Cup, then like the Strike Squad players themselves, I may then perhaps have been elevated to international level celebrity status myself. And as such, attention may have then been brought to the Agency, for what they clearly felt would have been the wrong reason, since they may have also been assuming that I would have continued my employment there.

So, I asked myself right there and right then; what the hell dis man expect mih to do at that point, just 48 hours before the big game? Everything that was going on at the time, was in fervent, unbridled, prideful support of one of our national sports teams, which was then involved in what up to that time was the biggest single sporting event ever to take place in my homeland; an event of historic proportions that was capturing the attention of the global football world.

The fact is, I did inform the CEO of my involvement upfront, and he said that he did not have a problem with it. Furthermore, the Director and his cohorts would have been well aware of my involvement since back in August with the publication of the Newspaper Article, in addition to the regular air play that the song was receiving and the mentioning of my name as its writer. So, if not a "Massa Day Power Play", as was my rational, then why else would they have waited until just 2 days before the "Big Game", to hand down such an unjustified ultimatum?

To even think that he and his fellow Directors, all native Trinbagonians I presumed, had the audacity to demand that I choose between continuing to serve their private business interests, through my continued employment at their advertising agency, and continuing to serve my beloved country at such a pivotal point in its sporting history, was beyond me.

Moreover, having since made a vow to myself to never be subjected or subject myself to such injustices ever again, the decision was one of the easiest that I ever had to make in my entire life. So, while he demanded that I decide right there and then, I instead offered no response to the Director's stated ultimatum. I just simply got to my feet and immediately headed for the exit.

I returned to the agency after the lunchtime interval and handed in my resignation to the said Director. I then proceeded to my work station and gathered my belongings. Most of my co-workers in the studio were wondering what was going on.

I believe that I might have offered a quick explanation to one or two of them. After gathering my things, I said some quick goodbyes and headed for the exit again, for what would be my final time. I had worked at McCann Erickson for exactly 3 months and 2 days.

While I had already made arrangements for someone else to do so, I then immediately headed to the Airport to personally pick up Warren "Archie" Archibald, who was flying in from the U.S. that day. We then headed into Port of Spain and straight to the Fatima College football field, where the 1973 team I reassembled, engaged another team in a friendly game.

That Friday evening November 17th 1989, I had the absolute honor of playing alongside some of the legends and icons of the local game as a guest player of the '73 team, many of whom were my local childhood football idols. It was only a 10 minutes appearance; but it was indeed one of the most memorable 10 minutes that I ever spent on a football field.

To honor and pay homage to them, which was the purpose of reassembling the team, they were paraded before the huge crowd inside the stadium before the start of the game as part of the pre-match activities. They received a rousing reception, as was to be expected.

On the day the atmosphere was electrifying. Thirty thousand plus, anxious but excited fans and supporters painted the national stadium totally red, figuratively speaking of course, wearing their red outfits to display their allegiance to what was then "their Strike Squad".

There was much pre-match fanfare with local music and culture on display. Then came game time. A loud blast from the referee's whistle and the "Big Game" was on. The eyes of the entire football world were on little Trinidad and Tobago. We only needed a draw to qualify.

But on that fateful day, Sunday November 19th 1989, achieving our historic feat of qualifying for our first ever FIFA World Cup Finals was not to be. A 31st minute Paul Caliguri goal, which stood as the eventual game winner, gave the United States the victory, and the final spot at the Italy '90 FIFA World Cup Finals.

Most of the citizenry of the twin island republic was left in absolute shock and in tears. The entire nation went into immediate mourning, literally speaking. It was a day that I would never ever forget for as long as I live.

I sat in what is referred to as the covered stands with the then Coach's daughter Renee Cummings to watch the game. She sat on my right. Warren "Archie" Archibald sat in the seat to my left behind me.

And believe it or not, Archie was predicting a shot from distance at goal before it actually happened. Anytime the ball was about 10 meters out from on the top of the 18 yards box whenever the U.S. was in attack, he would tap me with rapid motion on my left shoulder saying, "watch eh, watch eh, he go hit it in he arse from dey eh, watch eh."

In the 31st minute Paul Caligiuri did just that. He hit a left footed volley that floated and dipped past Strike Squad goalkeeper Michael Maurices' desperate dive to his left, and into the far corner of the net from about 30 yards out. Goal!

Throughout almost the entire game, Renee was biting her finger nails with anxiety and nervousness, which I am sure the entire population also felt that day. I most certainly did. I was left with a feeling of total numbness, when the referee blew the final whistle to signal the end of the game. I was totally devastated and was left in a sort of a trance.

Our World Cup dream had eluded us once again. Oh, so very close, but yet so very far. It was not to be. The following day, extremely depressed and in bed, I received a phone call informing me that members of the U.S. team wanted to obtain copies of the Road To Italy record.

With a very heavy heart, I drove to the Hilton to deliver the records, more so as a deed of goodwill on behalf of the people of Trinidad and Tobago than anything else, which I conveyed upon delivery.

Still, I was offered a handsome amount in USD as payment for the records, which I politely refused. The players, whom I met at poolside, did their best to try to console me, be it genuine or not. John Harkes was one of the players who were at poolside. His sister, who was also present, sent me a thank you card from New Jersey after they had returned to the U.S.

In the aftermath of that absolutely devastating loss, I became so depressed that except to oblige the U.S. team with respects to delivering the records, I did not venture out of my Westmoorings apartment for almost a full week. I simply slept, and slept, and slept some more.

At those intervals when I managed to drag myself out of bed, I just moped around, showered, and with absolutely no appetite then, just nibbled on some dry food-stuff, sipped some whatever, moped around some more, then it was back to bed. My landlady, who was fully aware of my very deep involvement in the campaign, kept checking on me on a daily basis to ensure that I was okay. I let her know how much I really appreciated her for that, because the truth is, I was not okay at all.

It took me a very long time to get over that November 19th 1989 loss to the U.S. I could not even begin to tell you how many times in my mind I imagined Leonson Lewis, Russell Latapy, or Dwight Yorke, scoring the equalizer that would have taken us to Italy.

Hell! I even dreamt on more than one occasion that I was on the team, and actually scored the equalizer myself. Talk about a "World Cup Football Tabanca"? Ah had it bad; really, really bad. The memory of that day will continue to live with me until the day I die.

THE PHONE CALL FROM ALWIN CHOW:
THE THEN MANAGING DIRECTOR OF
THE GUARDIAN NEWSPAPER

About a week and a half to two weeks after the devastating 1-0 loss, I received a phone call. The male voice on the other end of the line identified himself as Alwin Chow from the Guardian, meaning the Trinidad Guardian daily newspapers. I really did not know who he was at the time.

He indicated that he was calling with regards to the circumstances surrounding my McCann Erickson resignation. I therefore assumed that he probably wanted to expose the grave injustice that was done to me through a newspaper article.

I sincerely appreciated his interest in wanting to take up the matter, and did express that sentiment to him. I however, very politely declined to offer any comment at the time, but indicated that I would be more than willing to address the matter at some future time. Yours truly was then dealing with "de November 19th Football Tabanca". So, I guess that future time to which I referred way back then is now.

Upon further investigation, I learnt that the Alwin Chow who had called, was actually the then Managing Director of the Guardian. The fact that he personally made the phone call, given his status at the company, told me that he was taking the matter very seriously. It was then obvious that one of my then former colleagues at McCann, acting on principle I suppose, contacted Mr. Chow on my behalf, as most of them would have come to find out that a very serious injustice had been done to me.

And apparently the McCann bosses knew that as well, because I received another phone call from my buddy Adrian Chandler, informing me that they asked him to reach out to me once again; that time, to let me know that they were offering me my job back. What professional hypocrisy, I thought.

To me it sounded very much like an admission of the wrong they had done to me. In response, I flatly turned down their offer. While I desperately needed a job, and while my former colleagues wanted me to return, in the final analysis they totally understood my reason for deciding not to accept the agency's offer. As Malcolm X once said and I quote, "A man who stands for nothing, will fall for anything". And I stand firmly against injustice.

So, for me there was absolutely no room for compromise, given the grave injustice that was done to me in the first place. I took absolute pleasure in turning down McCann's offer to rejoin the Agency, fully aware of the consequences.

And there were very serious consequences indeed, the primary one of which was financial hardship thereafter, which resulted in me having to sell my vehicle. It was bought by one Dereck "OC" Blackman, songwriter / recording artiste / performer and famous son of local music legend and icon, Ras Shorty I, formally known as Garfield Blackman.

Still, I had absolutely no regrets whatsoever, when sacrificing my own personal welfare for the purpose of making a statement that I felt needed to be made, to those at McCann Erickson who were responsible for perpetrating and supporting the injustice against me.

It is my understanding that as a result of the stance I had taken not to rejoin the Agency, there were other resignations that followed in solidarity. Even with the dire consequences thereafter, I never ever regretted either of my two decisions, which was to resign in the first instance, and to flatly turn down the offer to return in the second.

THE ROAD TO ITALY SONGWRITER CREDIT ISSUE

Unknown to all else but myself, Tansley Thompson, Rolph Warner, Austin "SuperBlue" Lyons and probably his then manager, while all the Road To Italy World Cup qualifying excitement was gripping the entire nation, behind the scenes there was an extremely contentious issue that was being stirred up by Austin, and threatening to explode into the public domain.

You see, for his own reasons, Austin was refusing to publicly admit that I wrote the vast majority of the lyrics, created the entire melody and composed the Road To Italy song, with himself making a lyrical contribution for which he was duly credited.

Whenever the issue came up during interviews about who wrote and composed the song, he either avoided addressing it, or he would always say that I brought a rough sketch of the song on paper to him and he took it from there; which was not only extremely baffling, but also extremely hurtful to me.

The first such occasion he did so, was at our first home game against Costa Rica at the National Stadium, in the presence of Rolph Warner and myself, while being interviewed by the Costa Rican Television Media down on the athletic track, close to the stadium's tunnel entrance.

When the question was posed about the origin of the song, Austin quickly jumped in. I was standing on his right with Rolph standing on my right. Pointing sideways at me he responded, "well, he come up with the idea an' bring ah rough sketch ah some ah de lyrics on paper..."

Upon hearing just those opening words of his response, Rolph and I looked at each other in utter disbelief. Without saying a word, we left the scene, leaving Austin to do the interview by himself.

Rolph wanted to do another story addressing that specific issue, but the then naive me said "nah". Why Austin did not want to give me the credit that I fully deserved remains a mystery to me. Perhaps his ego did not allow him to accept the fact that someone other than himself, the musical genius that he is, was actually going to be credited with reviving his career, which was then non-existent.

I say here and now, that Austin's contribution to the overwhelming success of the song is undeniable. Never did I even entertain the thought of taking anything away from him with respects to his contribution. Why would I? I respected, admired and idolized him too much to do that.

Austin's displeasure, which he eventually voiced to a journalist (not Rolph Warner), was that while he was credited as the co-writer of the song on the record jacket, he was not given that credit on the actual circular shaped label on the vinyl record itself, since his name did not appear there. Neither I nor Tansley thought it was that big of a deal. But to Austin it was a huge deal indeed.

I only became aware of how major the issue of his name not being on the vinyl label was to him, a few days before the "BIG GAME" on November 19th, when both Austin and I were supposed to have done an interview together with one Angela Fox, at the Sunday Punch Newspaper office in Barataria.

When I got there (and I was on time as always), Angela Fox informed me that Austin had already done the interview and left. I was totally confused. Angela further informed me that during her interview with him, Austin expressed that he was quite upset about not getting enough credit as co-writer of the song.

I simply could not believe what I was hearing. I was in total shock. The Angela Fox story, which would have certainly exposed the issue publicly, was never published because we lost the game against the USA, and I guess the story then also lost its significance.

It spoke volumes to me at least, that while he was upset about his name not appearing on a label as the co-writer, Austin, even to this day, never even once saw it fit to express any semblance of gratitude to me, either through words or deeds, for bringing the song to him. The song that would give him what was then his second lease on his musical career, which he pleaded for so desperately in his song Jingay.

And as the then Sunday Punch editor Anthony Alexis put it in his article of April 1989, "after being in a musical coma for the longest while". Yet, there Austin was, waging war against me because his name didn't appear as co-writer on the vinyl label. I was really hurt, but as per usual, I said nothing; that is, until now.

Following are the lyrics to "Road To Italy". Austin's lyrical contribution appears in underlined type. I now invite you to come to your own respective conclusions.

SONG TITLE: ROAD TO ITALY

INTRO:

Sixteen years ago in Haiti

<u>We were denied</u> fame and glory—Changed from: "they deny we"

On de road, de road to Germany

Ah new breed similar journey

Trying to erase that memory

On de road, de road to Italy

On de road, on de road

On de road, we going Italy

On de road, on de road

On de road, we going Italy

VERSE 1

Mama World Cup fever in town

Bacchanal in the stadium

On de road, we going Italy

Calypso football at its best

T &T versus the rest

On de road, we going Italy

Captain Morris and Earl "Spiderman"

Francis, Faustin and Williams

Lawrence, Allen, York and Latapy

All ah dem on the journey

Charles, Alibey, Morris, Jamerson

Chinnas, Skeen and Lewis
On de road (3) we going Italy

CHORUS:

Shouting Goal!—Changed from: Score ah
Is ah Goal!—Changed from: In de hole!
In de hole is goal for T&T—Changed from: On de road, we going Italy
Shouting Goal!—Changed from: Score it now!
Is ah Goal!—Changed From: Anyhow!
In de hole is goal for T&T—Changed from: On de road, we going Italy

Dribble down dey (4 times)

VERSE 2

De back four like de Berlin wall
Cyar hit spiderman web at all
On the road, we going Italy
Skill in midfield an' speed up front
T&T on ah treasure hunt
On de road, we going Italy
Sir Everard Gally Cummings
Coach for coach is king of kings
With players like Jones and Dexter Lee
Yes we going Italy
Nakhid, Nelson, Lovell, Fonrose
Spann an' Maurice, blows
On de road (3) we going Italy

VERSE 3

So is licks for Costa Rica
An' is licks for Guatemala
On de road, we goin' Italy

Well doh talk for El Salvador

Dem cyar get nothing less than four

On the road, we goin' Italy

<u>De streets like ah festival</u>

<u>People making bacchanal</u>

<u>East west north and south lord hear dey mouth</u>

Lord we going Italy

<u>People jumpin' half naked</u>

<u>And sippin' dey Carib</u>

On the road (3) we going Italy

VERSE 4

Journey started up in LA

When we draw with the USA

On de road, we goin' Italy

But tell Steve Trittschuh an' his men

We have ah score tuh settle with dem

On de road, we goin' Italy

When we ketch dem in de stadium

We'll beat dem like bongo drum

We go show dem yankee who is gnats

<u>Soca tempo tit fuh tat</u>—Changed from: "we go make dem pay for dat"

To our final destiny

<u>We flying Bee Wee</u>—Changed from: "De whole ah T&T"

On the road (3) we going Italy

When T&T (2)

When T&T go on to Rome

I would like to be in dat number

When T&T go on to Rome—**End**

But as massive a hit that Road To Italy was, receiving tons of airplay across most local radio stations over a 6 months period, the royalty payment from the Copyright Organization of Trinidad and Tobago was only $1,916.00. And as per our verbal agreement, Austin received 50% of that royalty payment. So, I guess that after all that was said and done, he did in fact receive the credit where it mattered most.

Still...for all the obvious reasons, the "Road to Italy" project will always remain one of the most memorable, significant and special of all such football projects (10 in total), that I have had the pleasure to have been personally involved with as the songwriter, with one of the ten as the songwriter and singer.

From the motivation and inspiration that stimulated the initial process of writing and composing the song and producing the demo; to the hook up with Tansley Thompson; to the search for Austin; to the recording session; to the absolutely phenomenal response from the players, technical staff, fans, radio DJs, the media and the public in general, the entire experience was one I can only describe as "ABSOLUTELY UNFORGETTABLE".

I felt a profound sense of pride and humility and truly blessed; steeped in the knowledge that "The Higher Power" had chosen me as the instrument, through which my then local music idol desperate pleas and prayers in his song "Jingay" would be answered, at a time and I quote a Bee Wee Beat magazine article, "when he was at Rock Bottom".

The following are the 8 heart-wrenching lines that always hit me hard back in the day, whenever I listened to Austin's JINGAY, from the time it was released for the Carnival season of 1987 up to early 1989, when "Spiritual Orchestration" took over.

4 lines are in the first verse, and the other 4 lines are in the last verse of the song, which music was arranged by top Trinidad and Tobago music arrangers Leston Paul, Carl "Beaver" Henderson and Errol Ince. If you really listen carefully to the song for yourself (YouTube), maybe then you'll

fully understand the way I felt at the time. The 4 lines from the first verse appears first; My one-time Soca music idol sings:

"Well ah want ah Jingay to make ah song
Ah want ah Jingay tuh wake up town
Ah want ah Jingay in pain I cry
Jingay Jingay most spiritually high"

"Well ah want ah Jingay to rise and shine
Ah want ah Jingay tuh blow dey mind
Ah want ah Jingay Lord I'm in tears,
Jingay Jingay oh pleeease answer my prayers"

My siblings and I; from left to right standing behind me are my sisters Sandra and Cheryl and brother Evans.

My late grandfather Samuel Andrews, with my late aunt Daphne (right) and a friend back in England.

My late grandmother Monica Bowen's Point Fortin residence that often served as our house of refuge.

Lyle Street Point Fortin, where I first learnt to play football and where I honed my skills.

My mother (center) with two friends in Canada in the 70s.

My cousin David and I, with whom I grew up and consider as a brother.

My best friend Junior Nelson left, his sister Ann Marie and brother Ricky back when they were very young.

The Guadalope Street Point Fortin home where we lived that was owned by Shango Baptist leader Ms. Marion and here husband David (standing on stairs), which I revisited in 1995.

In the saddle of my chopper bicycle.

The 60's (top) and 70's (below) versions of my then beloved Point Fortin Civic Center football team; back row center (below) is my cousin Michael aka "BoPeep".

The downstairs apartment where we lived at Warner Road, Point Fortin.

The kitchen of the Warner Road apartment, occupied by Irvin Belfon (deceased), a friend of the family, In the background is the latrine (out house).

In my tailor made ensemble sponsored by my brother Evans for my sister Cheryl's wedding, which my father refused to provide.

Posing back row left with team mates of Santa Cruz minor league football team Bran United.

Posing in my bedroom next to posters of
my childhood football idol "Pele".

In grey hat playing with Starlift Steel Orchestra
at Panorama preliminaries on the float next to
the late Russell Tesheira on my left.

Nursing a broken collar bone
after being hit by a car.

At my desk creating at my then employers Christiansen & Belgrave Advertising.

Above: Trevor Cardinal my mentor during the early part of my Graphic Design / Advertising career, who also worked at Leo Burnett Chicago.

A farewell gift from the Christiansen & Belgrave staff prior to my departure for PRATT NY.

With some of my studio colleagues during my time at Christiansen & Belgrave; at centre is the late Victor Lewis studio manager.

Exiting the New York City subway with my mother on the way to my entrance interview at PRATT Manhattan.

PRATT Manhattan, then located at E30th Street and Lexington Avenue New York NY.

Yolanda "Coco" Cunningham who became my closest friend while I attended PRATT.

My classmates and I (the only black student at the time) at PRATT Manhattan.

At my PRATT graduation with some of my classmates.

With my extremely proud mother on graduation day.

Proudly wrapped up in my national flag.

Posing a few questions to the engineer during a tour, upon the opening of Robert Amar's recording studio, which launched the Kiskidee Karavan. Top American producer Dr Dre did do some work out of this studio.

Bestman at my best friend's Junior wedding in Canada September 1985.

On Atlantic City's boardwalk on the way to witness Trinidad and Tobago's then world light-heavyweight boxing champion Leslie Stewart's first title defence against Virgil Hill.

Fun time at Niagara Falls with my best friend and his then wife and some relatives of hers.

The mango tree in the backyard in Westmoorings where I resided at the time, under which I started the process of composing the song "Road to Italy", sung by SuperBlue during T&T's Italy 1990 FIFA World Cup Qualifying Campaign.

SuperBlue juggling at a T&T World Cup '90 Qualifying game at home with yours truly in the background just off to his right.

With Jeff Barnes at WLIB/WBLS New York, during the U.S. promotion of the "Road to Italy" record.

With the 1973 Trinidad & Tobago National Team, which I reassembled to witness the November 19th 1989 World Cup Qualifying game between T&T and the U.S.

With SuperBlue (left) and world famous song writer / recording artiste Eddy Grant (center).

My Parasailing adventure while living in Westmoorings.

CHAPTER FOUR

THE NINETIES

A RETURN TO MY POINT FORTIN ROOTS

BCA and I had then been seeing each other for almost 2 years. As such, I was then finally seriously considering having an exclusive relationship with her. As I mentioned in an earlier passage, we had really clicked and I had taken a special liking to her since we met in early 1988. She is the female who had a very young daughter, and was then employed at a business establishment across the street from my then Coronation Street residence, when we first met.

As I had stated when introducing her in that earlier passage, I had decided that I would take things very slow to get to know her much better before entering that stage, having already been bitten. During that time, I had met and also got to know her mother and only brother, to some extent.

We had a date on Old Years night of '89, when I planned to let her know that I wanted to have an exclusive relationship with her, with a further view towards a long-term commitment. She also had something that she wanted to tell me that night, and beat me to it.

She revealed to me for the very first time, that there was another male in the picture, and she was torn between the two of us. But having experienced and endured many years of relationship stress because of similar situations, courtesy of my then soon to be ex-girlfriend and learnt lessons therefrom, I decided to spare myself more of it.

So, as much as we clicked and had progressed, I told BCA that I would make it easy for her and remove myself from the situation from that night. "So yuh wouldn't fight fuh me?" She asked. I offered no response, since that was definitely not an option for me, for the aforementioned reason. So, I then dropped her off at her mother's residence where she lived at the time, with a kiss on her cheeks and my very best wishes. It would be almost a decade, before we would communicate with each other again.

Once we entered the first week of the new year, I decided that I would officially end what had then been for years, a non-exclusive relationship with my then girlfriend. And so, that very week, I finally ended it after 9 years. I did so in a very respectful manner, since her entire family had always been very hospitable to me over the course of those 9 years. We then went our separate ways thereafter. And so, the 90s began with me being a totally free and single 30-year-old.

Having been so deeply involved and emotionally invested with our Road To Italy World Cup Qualifying Campaign, at the time I was still going through "de November 19th football Tabanca". But I still had to eat and had bills to pay.

So, with no plans of returning to employee status, I then secured an office space at a building located at the corner of Dundonald Street and Tragarete Road Port of Spain, with the intention of starting up my own Advertising and Graphic design business once again, which I hadn't given up on. I had even moved in some office furnishings.

Around that same time, I received a phone call from my sister Cheryl. It was a phone call that would result in me immediately shelving my business ownership plans once again, and that time around, giving up the city life and relocating to my old home town of Point Fortin.

As it were, a few years earlier, my sister Cheryl's husband who was an off-shore worker, had immigrated to the U.S., with plans to send for his family once he got settled. Her husband needed to leave Trinidad in a rush at the time he did, for some reason. It was most definitely a spur of the moment decision. However, they did not have the financial means to facilitate his travel abroad. So, my sister also made a phone call to me back then on her husband's behalf, to request my assistance as a matter of urgency.

Coincidentally, the very day that my sister called on her husband's behalf, I had planned to go in to a travel agency to purchase the plane ticket, which I was then sponsoring my younger brother Brian for him to travel to the U.S., as he too had also decided he wanted to immigrate.

But because of the urgency indicated, and without asking any questions, the plane ticket that was supposed to have gone to my younger brother, then went to my sister Cheryl's husband. I was more than happy to assist, based on the premise that he intended to send for his family. Disappointingly however, my then brother-in-law never sent for his family as promised.

Over the time that her husband was in the U.S., my sister was left to shoulder the responsibility of taking care of and providing for their three then very young daughters on her own. During that period, she was receiving significant financial assistance from the U.S. from our ever and forever generous and dependable mother. So, being unemployed with three young daughters to provide for, my sister finally decided that she could no longer sit around, and hope that her husband would eventually deliver on his promise.

During her then latest phone call, she communicated to me that she was herself then very desperate to immigrate to the U.S., to try to make a better life for herself and her three daughters, given the fact that her husband had reneged on his promise. She wanted to leave as soon as she was able to secure the funds that would have enabled her to do so. She planned to then send for her three daughters sometime in the not-too-distant future, once she got settled herself.

But there was going to be another major obstacle standing in her way, because she had no one to look after her three then very young daughters if she left. They were ages 7, 12 and 13 years old at the time. Understanding her dire situation, I decided to step up to the family plate once again. I volunteered to take on the huge responsibility of looking after my three nieces in her absence, for as long as was necessary.

And so, in late January 1990 in anticipation of her departure, having left just over a decade before, I returned to my roots, relocating to my sister's residence, which was located in the residential neighborhood of Harriman Park, in my old hometown of Point Fortin.

After a few weeks had passed with no word from her about any progress being made on that front, it then became pretty obvious that securing the funds that would have then enable her to immigrate, was proving to be a challenge for my sister. So, I decided to step up even further. Within a matter of days after I realized that having no funds was the reason that she hadn't left, she was heading to the U.S. and the Big Apple in particular, to embark on her mission.

And there was more good news before she left, as she was able to get one of her female friends from the area to assist me with looking after her three daughters. Her friend's name was Jasmin Rouse. I found her to be an extremely nice person. We got along very well.

So, my sister departed for New York, secure in the knowledge that her daughters were in extremely good and safe hands. My time would then be devoted to caring for my three nieces together with Jasmin, songwriting and freelancing, which provided two sources of income.

My move back to Point saw me reunite with my cousin David. He was then also an aspiring songwriter. He paid me regular visits, during which we would work on songs together. Barnett Henry, aka "Preacher", the then up and coming Point Fortin Soca / Calypso writer / recording Artiste and performer, joined us on a few occasions.

Using the success of my Road To Italy World Cup qualifying campaign theme song as the springboard, and though not giving up freelancing for the obvious reason, I decided then that I would give music and songwriting in particular more focus, with the goal of establishing myself as a bonafide local songwriter.

As such, for Carnival 1990, I had three of my original songs recorded by two Artistes. Two of them, namely, "The Pledge", a patriotic nation building song and "'94 Fuh Sure", which was the second song I had then written on the football theme, were recorded by Preacher. Tansley Thompson and Kenny Phillips were the Executive Producers. The third song, titled "Carnival Again", was recorded by a new female Artiste Agie Sealy, who paid a fee for the rights to record it. Agie was the sister of the then lead female vocalist of the then top Jamaican Soca Band, Byron Lee and The Dragonairs.

During that 1990 Carnival season, world-renowned Guyanese born Eddy Grant, who as I mentioned much earlier is one of my all-time favorite songwriters, recording artistes and performers, confirmed his interest in signing me to his Ice record label as a songwriter.

We actually had a meeting at the Knights Bridge, Cascade, Port of Spain residence where he was staying. He wanted me to sign on there and then, since he was returning to his adopted homeland of Barbados the following day. As such, there would not have been enough time for me to consult a legal professional about the contract he was offering.

And while I was really tempted to, because it was a huge opportunity to get to work with such a huge international entertainer, I certainly did not want to sign before I fully understood what I was signing on to. So, unfortunately, the then prevailing circumstances did not allow me to take up his contract offer.

Eddy subsequently re-recorded a song titled "One for De Road", which was another song I wrote that was originally also recorded by Preacher. Eddy re-recorded it with then top Barbadian band Square One on his Ice record label, with lead vocals by none other than Alison Hinds. The music video can be viewed on YouTube.

It was a deal that was done by Kenny Phillips, who did the musical arrangement for the original version of song that was recorded by Preacher. As the songwriter I received US$50.00, but I was never privy to any of the details of the deal.

1990 would also turn out to be a year that my beautiful twin island nation would make world headlines once again, following those related to 100 meters Olympic goal medal winner Hasely Crawford in Montreal in1976, Miss Universe winner Janelle "Penny" Commissiong in 1977, and Miss World winner Giselle Laronde in 1986. The 1990 headlines however, was not for any such overwhelmingly joyful reasons mentioned.

For on the evening of Friday July 27th that year, the local organization known as the Jamaat Al Muslimeen, attempted to overthrow the government of the day. I was at the National Stadium at a big football game between Trinidad and Tobago and Jamaica during the Shell Caribbean Cup Finals tournament, when it all went down.

Well-armed members of the Jamaat Al Muslimeen organization, held the then Prime Minister as well as Cabinet members hostage at the Parliament building (or Red House) for several days. It turned into a violent event, which resulted in total social chaos and a number of deaths, causing the authorities to declare a state of emergency.

I subsequently learnt from a local high-ranking law enforcement officer who was also a close friend, that a U.S. battleship was off-shore just awaiting the order for its crew to intervene. He was in charge of the operation, and was on the ship mapping out a plan of attack.

Thankfully, no U.S. intervention was necessary as the overthrow attempt was eventually averted, with those responsible being arrested. My beloved Trinidad and Tobago was then experiencing its very darkest period in its history.

With a dust to dawn curfew then in effect, and knowing that my three nieces would be in very good hands with Jasmin, I left Trinidad for New York not long after the coup attempt occurred to visit my mother and siblings, and most importantly my daughter. She was then 1 year and 7 months old.

She had immigrated there with her mother, stepfather and her two brothers months before. They resided in New York, but not in Brooklyn. Sadly, a then ongoing domestic situation, prevented me from seeing her. I was however, able to at least hear her voice over the telephone whenever possible, while I was in New York or back home in Trinidad. It was a very complicated situation, which lasted for several years, during which time I was able to see her on at least one occasion.

I was finally able to start spending time and bonding with my daughter, and start making memories whenever I would visit New York, when they relocated to a new residence in Manhattan, after the domestic situation was finally resolved. It was then just her mother, her and one of her brothers residing there. Their residence was just over an hour by subway from my mother's Brooklyn apartment.

Whenever I was in New York, apart from time spent with her at their apartment, I would take her to school and pick her up at the end of the school day. During one winter season that I was in New York, I also used to take her to her ice-skating lessons. She was usually treated to her then favorite fast-food afterwards.

While in New York during that then latest trip in the aftermath of the attempted coup, I would once again be thrusted back into the national music spotlight back home in Trinidad. "The Pledge", one of the songs that I had written that was recorded by Preacher, which as mentioned before was a patriotic, nation-building song, began being used through extensive radio air play, to help provide the healing that my beloved nation desperately needed at the time.

I received a phone call from Trinidad informing me that the record was in high demand back home, but was unavailable for purchase in record stores. So, I was forced to cut my New York visit short, and headed back to Trinidad to have records pressed and distributed to supply the demand.

With Road To Italy being the first, and while definitely not in the preferred circumstance, The Pledge provided me with my second local number one song. It also saw Preacher himself gaining high-profile public recognition and acknowledgement as a recording Artiste.

With the popularity of the song, a re-recording of The Pledge was then also produced by Kenny Phillips, its original producer, featuring a number of top local Soca Artistes and Calypsonians, from which came the absolute honor of having the voice of Ras Shorty I himself, the inventor of the Soca Music genre, on that re-recording of my song. That was definitely one of the highlights of my career as a songwriter in the Trinidad music industry.

A music video for the re-recorded version of the song was also produced for and on behalf of the Trinidad and Tobago Government. It aired extensively from that time onwards, on a particular government owned television station. It continued to be aired up to 2008, eighteen years after the re-recorded song and music video were released. I can personally attest to that fact, having viewed it myself on many occasions during that time.

At the end of the music video, all the various Artistes and contributors to the project were credited by way of their respective names and or photographs being prominently displayed on the television screen. But my name and photograph did not appear to credit me as the writer of the song.

I was extremely displeased about that, especially since the song and accompanying music video was being used for such a meaningful purpose. Kenny Phillips had entered into an arrangement with the government representative, who I understand was one Judith Laird.

I, as the writer of the song, was never furnished with any of the details of the arrangement entered into with the government of the day for its use. I most certainly never signed any document granting the government or its representative(s) permission to use my song. Therefore, I have absolutely no idea what the deal was, even up to today.

Thus, I have always wondered if anyone benefitted financially from what was a government undertaking, wherein my song was used. While that question still remains unanswered, my gut feeling is that whosoever was hired by the government to do the project, may have received financial compensation.

THE PHONE CALL FROM THE
PRIME MINISTER'S OFFICE

In late 1990 my three nieces, Keithann, Keisha and Kellyann left Trinidad to join their mother in New York. I also intended to immigrate sometime during the course of the coming New Year. A few weeks after my nieces left, I received a telephone call at the house that left me totally flabbergasted.

The caller addressed me by my full name, identified himself as (initials HB) and stated that he was calling from the then Prime Minister's Office. "Sir, before you go on, do you mind if I ask how did you find me?" I questioned politely. He gave a chuckle then stated, "Mr. Ayres, this is the government yuh know. We could find anybody we want." A very interesting assertion I thought to myself.

He then went on to explain that he was calling because the government of the day was interested in my services. More specifically, he said they wanted me to write a theme song for their political party for the upcoming General Elections the following year, and that he would like to meet with me for further discussions.

I assumed that a huge pay day would be involved. So, I agreed to meet with the gentleman on the date that he already had in mind. I immediately contacted Tansley Thompson whom I came to trust, and informed him of the development. Having forged a very close friendship during the Road To Italy World Cup Qualifying campaign, he had since become somewhat of my business confidant.

We were both quite excited about the prospect, and the financial benefit that could be derived from such a major assignment. I invited Tansley, and he accompanied me to the meeting. It took place at one of the two Financial Complex buildings, at the Eric Williams Plaza located on Independence Square Port of Spain, which then housed the office of the then Prime Minister as well as HB's.

At the meeting, HB informed me that they were extremely impressed with my Road To Italy song, particularly the way that the song had managed to stimulate the entire population to rally behind the national football team, during our Road To Italy World Cup qualifying campaign. As such, I was being commissioned by the then government, to write a song that would do a similar job for the then ruling political party, in the aforementioned upcoming general elections.

During the meeting, HB asked me about my professional background and what I was doing to earn a living at the time, to which I provided the answers. He even enquired about my family, which I found to have been a bit odd. He then proceeded to lay out what my compensation package would look like.

The package he laid out included a cash payment, as well as the possibility of setting up my own Advertising business, with support from the then government, with a view to receiving advertising and related work assignments from the said government.

He assured me that there would be additional perks, should the party gain re-election. He gave a few examples of the additional perks. Given what had transpired, Tansley and I left the meeting even more excited than we were initially. I then headed back to Point Fortin ready to start working on the commissioned assignment.

While writing the song, I also had time to really think hard about the arrangement. The more I thought about it, the more I began to have second thoughts about undertaking the assignment.

I reflected on the fact that it would most probably be viewed as a direct political affiliation on my part. And further, as me pledging allegiance to the particular political party, which could possibly be very detrimental to my future livelihood and career, if the party did not win re-election.

There were more than enough examples for me of individuals, and more specifically local entertainers, who suffered consequences by an opposing party as a result of their political affiliation, where there seems to be a very strong element of vindictiveness in those circles. I certainly had no wish to be on the end of the aforementioned. Thus, my reason for having second thoughts.

While such songs that were written and recorded by other local entertainers was usually up-tempo, and sought to capture a celebratory, party-like mood, being the very serious minded individual that I am, and with General Elections being the single most serious and significant socio-political event in any country, it was natural for me to take that approach to writing the song.

I therefore wrote lyrics, created a melody, and used a slow tempo to capture an equally serious tone, to maximize the emotional and psychological effect of the message. The lyrics that I wrote for the song was reflective of what was at stake, and was intended to have relevance far beyond just the impending General Elections.

When the song was completed, Preacher obliged me and voiced the rough demo accompanied by an acoustic guitar. My cousin David, Jasmin and I provided background vocals. After discussing my concerns with Tansley, the demo was subsequently presented to HB at a second meeting.

He absolutely loved it, and gave it his verbal stamp of approval. He then instructed me to deliver it to one Tony Deyal at the Ministry of information, which office was in St Claire at the time. I complied. But as is usually the case with most local government agencies, and thankfully so in that instance, the Information Ministry procrastinated on moving the project forward.

That then left me with even more time to further ponder my involvement, upon which I came to a final decision. Without even informing Tansley beforehand, and as badly as I needed the cash at the time, after weighing the pros and the cons, I decided that I no longer wanted to be involved.

I subsequently contacted Mr. Deyal and communicated my decision to him, and made arrangements to retrieve the demo tape, which I still have in my possession today. The General Elections was held in

December 1991, and as it turned out, the then ruling political party was not re-elected.

Would my song have made any difference with respects to that result? All I would say is this; like the unwavering belief that I have in the power of sports to inspire and bring about positive personal and social change; I also do have the same unwavering belief in the power of music to do the same.

And so, with the musical blessings that were bestowed upon me by "The Higher Power", I continued on my raft, braving the ever-treacherous stormy seas, as I continued on my journey towards the horizon, in relentless pursuit of the second of my three childhood dreams, which up to that point, had only been partially achieved.

LAUNCHING MY RECORDING / PERFORMING CAREER: SHARING THE STAGE WITH LEGENDS AND ICONS OF CALYPSO AND SOCA MUSIC

With music then becoming more of the focus for me, and with Tansley Thompson then filling the role as my part-time manager, I decided that I would launch my recording / performing career for that '91 Carnival season, and see where my gift of music takes me. The annual Carnival celebrations were being held on Monday the 11th and Tuesday the 12th of February that year.

After completing my first ever recording in late 1990, a single titled "Party", I subsequently traveled to New York and signed a distribution deal for the single with Straker's Records on November 7th that year.

It was during that visit to Straker's Record Store on Utica Avenue in Brooklyn, that I had a chance encounter with Montserrat's highly successful Soca Superstar Alphonsus Cassell, better known in the Soca and Calypso music world as "Arrow".

He was making a hasty exit when I arrived. So, I quickly took the initiative and introduced myself to him and politely asked, "Do you have any advice for someone who is new to the industry?" As busy as he appeared to be at the time, he was gracious enough to offer a response.

Arrow's advice to me was straight to the point. "Youngster, learn about the business behind the music," he replied. He didn't need to say more. I thanked him for his advice and he continued with his hasty departure.

Once I got back to my mother's New York apartment, I told my older brother Evans about my encounter, and the advice I had just received from Arrow. With the anticipation of his involvement in my music career, I presumed, my older brother already had an idea for an entertainment management company, which he called Caribbean Entertainment Enterprises (CEE).

So, we decided that we would manage my career together through CEE. He also had an idea for a logo for the company, but it needed some work to bring it up to a professional standard, so I took his idea and transformed it into a logo that met that standard. We then got down to the work of learning about the business behind the music as advised by Arrow.

Since he was unemployed, I provided him with the funds for him to purchase books related to the subject and to keep him going. I also began dedicating lots of time to learn about the music business, with my focus on the marketing aspect.

Several weeks later, I returned to Trinidad and launched my "Party" single in front of a huge crowd at a launch event at the then King George the 5th Park (now the Nelson Mandela Park) in Woodbrook Port of Spain, together with the then top Soca band Taxi, who was also launching their new recordings for that year's Carnival celebrations.

Had it not been for quick thinking on my part, my very first live public performance and entry into the Soca and Calypso performing arena might have been a total disaster. You see, vinyl records were still the order of the day back then.

As I began to sing and perform using the instrumental version of the record, which was being played by the DJ who was also on the stage, I started to dance and jump around on the wooden stage construction, causing the needle to jump, and the record to skip. Immediately recognizing the problem, I jumped off the stage unto the grass turf ground, and immediately pick the music back up, and continued and finished my performance from there.

I remember being highly commended for my quick thinking and not losing my composure, by the MC Eric St Bernard who was a radio DJ at the time, given that it was my very first time performing live, and the fact that I was performing in front of a massive crowd.

Eric had since relocated from New York to Trinidad, and worked at the then local radio station Radio Tempo. Renee Cummings, who was then a journalist, did a post-performance newspaper article a few days later. The headline read "He's Coming From Behind The Scenes". I guess I was.

But after that very first live performance, while I didn't mind writing such songs for other Artistes to sing, I knew right then and there, that the party song and circuit was most definitely not the path that I wanted to follow as a recording Artiste and performer.

As much as I thoroughly enjoyed it in that moment, the truth is, that really isn't me. Even as mine is a culture that is defined by it, as mentioned before, partying, clubbing and the night life etc., was never ever my thing; not even during my younger years. And it would stay that way my entire life.

I also believed that I had the ability to write songs on any theme in some of the other music genres, since I had in fact already been doing so for many years. Still, being Trinbagonian, Calypso and Soca music was naturally in my blood.

But admittedly a rebel in disguise, writing, recording and performing songs that addressed and or exposed social and political ills and injustices, as well as real-life experiences, was the preferred musical path that I wanted to take. However, I do also like to write songs with uplifting messages.

It was indeed one such Calypso, an unrecorded social commentary titled "Race Hate", that won me accolades during my very first year as a performer. The song addressed race relations in my homeland, juxtaposed against race relations in South Africa, and encouraged locals not to follow South Africa's example. In Race Hate, I also pronounced my personal feelings towards those who wished to display such attitudes towards me.

During that '91 Carnival season, I performed Race Hate at the Mas Camp Calypso Tent. For the uninitiated, Calypso Tents are entertainment venues in which Calypsonians and Soca Artistes perform during the Carnival season to earn income. The Mas Camp Tent was operated at the Roxy Cinema, (thereafter Pizza Hut), located at the Roxy round-a-bout St. James.

At the tent I had the great honor of sharing the stage with some of the legends and icons of Calypso and Soca music, including the undisputed king of Calypso himself the "Mighty Sparrow", the late Lord Pretender, Shadow and SuperBlue, among others.

My song Race Hate saw me qualify for the Finals of the "Young Kings" calypso competition that year, for which I won the special award for "Most Promising Calypso Artiste" by the organization that produced the event. Back then, the Young Kings competition was a huge event that attracted huge crowds at the Skinner Park venue in San Fernando. All in all, my debut into the local performing arena was a quite successful one.

MY RETURN TO THE NATION'S CAPITAL: GOING PLACES: MY ADVERTISING AGENCY SWAN SONG

The 1991 Carnival season had then come and gone. And after being back in and enjoying my beautiful old country home town of Point Fortin for just over a year and a half, and with most of my immediate family members having immigrated to the U.S., I decided that it was time to follow suit. I intended to continue to pursue a music career as a writer, where I would delve into other genres, while also exploring other career paths while residing in the United States.

However, that plan would change unexpectedly with a business trip to the city in early September that year. Upon visiting one of my former C&B colleagues, one Robert Brathwaite, who was then employed with another Advertising Agency, Lonsdale Saatchi & Saatchi, he informed me that the agency was at that very time, actively looking for someone of my caliber to work on a launch campaign for a new client, and thereafter service what was the really huge account.

The account to which he was referring, was that of the Telecommunications Services of Trinidad and Tobago, better known as TSTT. However, because of my experiences at both Christian & Belgrave and McCann Erickson, I informed my former colleague that I really had no interest in returning to the local advertising industry, apart from the fact that I was about to immigrate to the United States. But he persisted. And after his verbal prodding, I agreed to at least meet with one of the agency's Directors (initials MC) in a hastily arranged informal session.

The work itself was not of concern to me, because I knew that I could handle any assignment that came my way. I was at the point where I could be persuaded to return to the local advertising set-up if the compensation package was attractive enough. The Lonsdale Director's initial offer wasn't; and I communicated that fact to him. He then invited me to call my price. I did. After thinking about it for a bit, he agreed to meet it.

Our meeting lasted about 10 minutes, during which I was up-front once again about my active involvement in the music industry, so as to avoid a reoccurrence of what transpired while I was at McCann Erickson. I expressed my intention to continue to be actively involved in the music industry while I was an employee at Lonsdale. The Director did not express any reservations or concerns over the issue.

And so, I left my old home town of Point Fortin once again, and returned to the capital city of Port of Spain. I join the staff at Lonsdale Saatchi & Saatchi on Monday September 23rd 1991. They gave me the title of Senior Art Director.

And while I would carry out all the duties and responsibilities that came with it, the job title meant nothing to me professionally and personally then. It was then simply a matter of getting the job done to the very best of my ability, and getting paid what I felt I was worth at the time. I was unexpectedly back in the local Advertising / Graphic Design industry; but that third time around, it would be on my very own terms.

For the first few weeks after moving back to Port of Spain, I shared living accommodation with Tony Dora (real name Antonio Lewis), my childhood buddy from Point Fortin. He had become an A class Draughtsman and worked with one Alvin Dorsett. He lived on Dundonald Street Port of Spain at the time. Knowing that it was only a temporary arrangement, I slept on the floor on a mattress in one of the two bedrooms in his apartment during those weeks.

I then found permanent accommodation at 42 Luis Street, Woodbrook, which I would share with two former McCann Erickson colleagues, Carlyle Mason and Rory Loregnard. Carlyle was then also a Lonsdale Saatchi & Saatchi employee. It was a large 4-bedroom house.

Since she lived fairly close to my new residence in Woodbrook, an on the street encounter, which was more or less inevitable, saw me reconnect with Alicia once again. Being that I was still single at the time, over the ensuing weeks and months, we were talking regularly over the phone, until she eventually started visiting me quite frequently at my residence. We gradually began going steady. It all happen very naturally.

For me, my Lonsdale Saatchi & Saatchi stay was supposed to have been a short term one. Perhaps a year or a year and a half at the most, which would have allowed me to save a lot of cash, towards my eventual move to the U.S.

However, because of my family's needs, more so those of my mother and two of my three older siblings in particular, that year and a half turned into three and a half years. Nevertheless, I continued to put my best foot forward during my employment at the Agency.

My first two to three weeks at Lonsdale was intense with an extremely heavy workload. I worked exclusively on the TSTT account, as the agency prepared an expansive campaign for a formal presentation to the new client. The campaign was to launch TSTT's new Cellular phone and Info-Zone Services, as well as their Phone-Card product. I worked on all three.

I insisted on being a part of the agency's team at the presentation, to present what I had worked on to the client myself; firstly, to ensure that it got approved as is, and secondly, because I did not want anyone getting or taking the credit for my work. And so, I was given the opportunity to present what I worked on by the Lonsdale boss.

At the end of my presentation, I was highly commended by the then TSTT boss. "We were waiting for someone like you to come along." I quoted his exact words, which I actually wrote down after I presented on the day, and kept in my personal commendation file. He was obviously extremely impressed with my work and presentation.

But apparently not so the Lonsdale boss, who convened a special staff meeting a couple of days after the agency's presentation was made. He called the meeting to announce that the agency had officially landed the TSTT account, and how extremely happy the client was with what the agency presented.

The meeting was actually held at a Lodge located just across the street from the agency, which I came to learn that at least one of the

Lonsdale Directors was a member. I could not quite understand why the meeting was held there in the first place, when there was adequate accommodation at the agency's premises. That definitely aroused my suspicions.

Unfortunately, mere weeks into my unexpected return to the local advertising industry, at what was a relatively short staff meeting, I was rudely reminded of one of the reasons I left in the first place. There was the agency's boss, who was of Syrian descent, singling out all the individuals who were involved with the campaign; verbally commending and heaping praise on them.

That is, all except me, the new employee who was specifically employed to work on the launch campaign, and thereafter, service the said TSTT account. For his own intents and purposes, I suppose, a certain female account executive, who I understood was very new to the agency and the advertising business, received special praise.

You would have sworn she conceptualized, wrote the copy, and did the layouts for the print ads; or conceptualized and wrote the scripts for the television and radio ads; or designed the logos that were required etc. I simply could not believe it when the man simply chose to totally ignore me and my contribution, which was a very significant one at that.

I knew that there was no way in Heaven or Hell that he could have simply forgotten, since he was at the client meeting when I made my presentation. Oh Hell! I was also standing right there in front of the man with the rest of the staff while he was making his speech. But I really should have come to expect such.

Above all else, I felt totally disrespected, but elected to say nothing then. But I swear, if not for the needs of certain members of my family at the time, I would have simply walked off the job that said day and never returned.

During my employment with Lonsdale, there were occasions when the said boss would totally shut down my ideas without justification, and without them first even being presented to the respective clients. I will give just one example here.

I recall my idea being shot down by the boss for a name change I was proposing for a large insurance company, that was one of the agency's clients. Its name at the time was Caribbean Insurance Company Limited, which had a beacon as its symbol. I was charged with the responsibility of designing the company's 1994 Annual Report.

Before starting on the assignment, I proposed in-house that we propose that the company consider changing its name to The Beacon Insurance Company Limited. Logical and sensible I thought, especially given what a beacon represents, which I felt would have lend itself to a focused marketing message and strategy for the company.

But my idea was flatly shot down by the boss, who did not support or approve of my proposal. So, I simply went on to design the Annual Report, which was produced utilizing the company's then existing name. I still have a copy of the printed Annual Report in my possession today.

I then convinced the Account Executive to present my name change proposal to the client anyway, which he did. Then sometime in 1996, after I would have resigned from the agency, in April 1995, I saw the name of the company officially appearing as The Beacon Insurance Company Limited. So, to the current hierarchy at The Beacon Insurance Company Limited, please know that your name change was exclusively the idea of Alison Ayres. I can be easily contacted on social media, if you wish to compensate me now.

Like at C&B and at McCann, I met some really cool individuals during my time at Lonsdale, that is, apart from those with whom I had actually reunited from my time at McCann, and who was then at Lonsdale.

Those cool individuals to whom I refer include, Steven Wong Kang, Keith Lancaster, Wayne, Ken Henry, Arlene Babb, Sharon Veronique, Mary Joseph, Lea King, Susan Salandy, John Ruiz, Moe, Gregory, Dave Williams, Joseph Renee (de biggest Tiger Woods fan I knew before I knew anything about Tiger Woods), Kathleen Maynard, "and ah cyar forget Stephen Jacob."

Otherwise, the Lonsdale advertising agency experience would be for me just more of what I had then come to expect but not accept. One particular incident was very similar to the one I experienced at Mc Cann Erickson, that caused me to resign from that particular agency.

As already established, I was actively pursuing and deeply involved in my music career prior to taking up the job at Lonsdale, and had clearly communicated that fact to the Director with whom I initially met before accepting the job, so as to avoid a McCann repeat. But I guess I just could not avoid it.

Here's the scenario. As a result of an anti-drugs music project that I had initiated through a song that I wrote and recorded targeting youths, I was bestowed with the absolute honor of being chosen as a United Nations Environment Programme Goodwill Ambassador in September 1992. I kept it to myself.

Then the first of several newspaper articles announcing that major development in my music career subsequently appeared in one of the daily newspapers. I guess it took the Lonsdale hierarchy and the rest of the agency's staff by surprise. Before I even had a chance to see the article myself, a co-worker saw it, cut it out and stuck it on the inside of the door leading into the agency's kitchen facility, which was frequented by all and sundry during the work day. I was not aware that my co-worker had done what he had done.

One of the agency's Directors who was Caucasian, was one of the first to see it. He apparently assumed that I stuck it on the kitchen door for all to view, in what he may have perceived as an obvious display of arrogance and or conceitedness on my part. It was a perception that most certainly rubbed that particular Director the wrong way.

I was told by the co-worker who actually stuck it on the kitchen door, that the said Director (initials DM), upon seeing the article, blurted out angrily, "who stick dis here?" And in a rage, he proceeded to rip the article off the door, ripped it up further, then threw it in the trash exclaiming, "we doh want no prima donnas working in Lonsdale."

Upon witnessing what had just occurred first hand, the co-worker who actually taped the article on the kitchen door, had rushed over to the Art department and related the episode to me. The said company Director came over to the Art department shortly thereafter, where he reiterated the comments that he had made earlier.

But while he did not do so directly to me or in my direct presence, which most certainly saved him from what would have been my equally disrespectful response, he made certain that he said it very loud. It was obvious that he wanted to make sure that I heard his message. Not only did I hear it, but more importantly, I saw his racist message as well.

Then there was the day I received a call over the intercom from the same Caribbean Insurance cum Beacon Insurance Account Executive, with a request to come to his office. He wasn't Caucasian or even Syrian / Lebanese as far as I could tell.

But it was obvious that he saw himself as belonging to those local so-called upper-class groups, as a result of having their skin tone, and to a lesser extent their hair texture. Such is the significance in my homeland, especially if you are well off financially.

Upon arrival in his office, I expected him to enter into a discussion about one or more of several assignments I would have been working on for him, in his capacity as the Account Executive. But he didn't. He instead verbalized a notion about my salary as compared to his, which he obviously wasn't pleased about. "So ah hear you working for more money than me," he stated resentfully.

He was implying that regardless of my professional status, work experience etc., because I was black, and he was whoever he perceived himself to be, that was enough to see him earning a higher salary than I was. It was a statement that could only have been made on the basis of the privilege that the color of his skin, and social status would have afforded him, because it most certainly was not based on merit.

Having immediately understood what he was implying, and given the other experiences I had with a similarly demeaning objective since I joined the Agency, I automatically switched into rebel mode. And as was the case in the other incidents, I had an equally demeaning response to offer. But with great restraint, I managed to hold my tongue once again while maintaining my professional decorum, during what I turned into a very brief visit.

Another incident involving the very same AE confirmed what I had since come to believe. One day a male co-worker who was black, and who had probably also suspected what I had since come to believe, posed the following question to the AE in my direct presence.

AE's full name called, "ah still wuh know wuh yuh really think about black people inno. So wuh yuh really think about black people?" my black colleague questioned. "You come back with dat again boy", the AE responded, suggesting that they had been on the issue for a while.

The AE then continued. "Okay. Yuh want tuh know wuh ah really think about black people? Ah think dat everybody like me should own one. Ha ha ha ha ha!!!!" he busted out in laughter. I expected an equally dehumanizing, condescending, rapid-fire response from my black co-worker. But he didn't deliver it. He instead seemed confused and oblivious to the AE's racist response. I was itching to engage with the individual in like manner, but I thought better of it, and decided once again to hold my tongue.

Still, I had good working relationships cum fairly close acquaintanceships with at least two individuals of the Caucasian ilk, while I was employed at Lonsdale. Those developed out of the mutual respect we had, displayed and maintained for each other, both professionally and personally.

Then there was the situation that finally led to me resigning from Lonsdale in April of 1995. Long story short. I was working on an Annual Report assignment for the National Gas Company (NGC) at the time. Now keep in mind that during those days in my homeland, all the elements that were contained in the mock-ups for such assignments were not computer generated. It all had to be done manually, by cutting and pasting etc.

I had first worked on a number of thumbnail sketches, and then finally on the 36-to-48-page full-size mock-up over a period of about 2½ weeks, including late nights and weekends, into and over that year's Carnival days. It took 2½ weeks only because I actually did the assignment over cover to cover at least 3 times, just to please the Creative Director.

I even took the risk of flying on a helicopter to an off-shore platform somewhere in the middle of the ocean with no land in sight, to get the photos that were to be included in the Annual Report done. When I had finally completed the 3rd and final version of the mock-up, which was early on Ash Wednesday morning of that year, the Creative Director wanted me to do it over again, which like both times before then, were unwarranted and without merit, but was done simply to please the individual.

So then, the rebel in me resurfaced once again. I flat-out refused to do it over. The individual reported me to the boss, who supported the individual without even hearing my side of the story. Given all the extremely unpleasant experiences I had at the agency up to that point, for me, that was indeed the last straw.

That Friday after Ash Wednesday I had my resignation typed up by a co-worker (initials NB), after which I immediately handed it in, and by so doing, giving them the 1-month advance notice in adherence to the company's policy.

With my older brother in the U.S. having been dependent on my ongoing financial support over the years, I subsequently contacted him via telephone to inform him that I had resigned from the Lonsdale job, with plans to then start my own sports marketing business.

"Oh God Ali. We cyar afford dat now nah," he responded, with an obvious sense of anxiety in his voice. Explaining further, he gave me the impression that by me resigning from my job, which meant that the funds that was flowing to him would stop, I would be curtailing his ability to advance our Caribbean Entertainment Enterprise (CEE) management

240

agenda, and by extension my music career, which, truth be told, I had in fact been advancing totally on my own.

Not once during our phone conversation did my older brother offer, and or express any semblance of "brotherly support", moral or otherwise, for my just stated decision, and or the sports marketing business venture that I had also indicated that I was going to pursue, as I was expecting him to do.

So, while in the past there may have been signs, which my naivety did not allow me to recognize, his response during that particular phone conversation, was the very first time there was a clear indication that my older brother might have been simply using me over the years, to fulfill some hidden personal agenda. I took note.

On Friday April 7th 1995, I walked out of the Lonsdale Saatchi & Saatchi door, and away from the local advertising agency establishment for the final time. Interestingly, as happened when I left McCann Erickson, my resignation from Lonsdale, and once again more so the reason I resigned, also caused a mini exodus; as subsequent to handing in my own resignation, several of my studio colleagues also handed in their resignations as well.

So maybe, while I became an Ad Agency rebel and thought that I was simply fighting my own cause, not with words but with action, it appeared that I may have also been unknowingly fighting the cause of others as well.

Still, I have retained some very fond memories of my time in the Trinidad Advertising / Graphic Design industry, which are made up of my interactions and experiences, professional and otherwise, with those really cool individuals that I met, and with whom those memories were created.

But my reality is that those fond memories will always be overshadowed by those that are made up of the discrimination and racism I experienced, and those who perpetrated those acts against me; whose sole intention was to devalue my worth, in an attempt to impose their unfounded notion of superiority, in their efforts to make me feel inferior, both as a professional and as a human being.

But I refused to let them. The rebel in me emerged every time, and I resigned from their respective advertising companies. I came to realize that I was a rebel; and perhaps always was; only that I was a rebel in disguise.

BEING A UNITED NATIONS ENVIRONMENT PROGRAMME GOODWILL AMBASSADOR: THE PHILIPPINES EXPERIENCE: RECEIVING THE KEY TO QUEZON CITY

That part of my journey came about as a result of action taken on my behalf in June of 1992 by one Abigail Loregnard, about 9 months into my employment at Lonsdale Saatchi & Saatchi. Abigail was the sister of Rory Loregnard, with whom I then shared the residence at 42 Luis Street Woodbrook together with Carlyle Mason, both my former work colleagues from my days back at McCann Erickson. Carlyle was then also a Lonsdale employee.

Rory's family paid him fairly regular visits at our Luis Street residence. On those occasions, we all usually engaged in some good Trini "ole talk" and fun, which sometimes included me playing demos of songs that I had written and recorded. Abigail worked at the United Nations Information Centre in Trinidad at the time. It was on one of those occasions, that I played a song titled "Ah Not On Dat", which was actually a finished recording.

It is an anti-drugs song, that addresses the extremely serious social issue of youths and drug abuse. The musical arrangement was done by Pelham Goddard, another of Trinidad and Tobago's music icons, with background vocals by Sandra Dopson and Sonia Francis. Ace guitarist Tony Voisin also played on the record. The song was played on a certain radio station by one radio announcer/DJ in particular, the then extremely popular Dave Elcock.

When Abigail heard the song she liked it a lot, and proposed the idea of talking to her boss, the then Director of the United Nations Information Centre, one Janet Badjan Young, with a view to me performing it at a then upcoming event, that the center was hosting to mark the United Nations International Day Against Drug Abuse and Illicit Trafficking.

I totally embraced Abigail's idea, since as I stated before, I much preferred writing, recording and performing music that addressed socio-political and real-life issues. I therefore saw Abigail's idea as one that could have possibly presented an opportunity for me to play a role in bringing further attention and public focus to that particular issue through my music, as some other local entertainers before me had also been doing.

More specifically, the song described a scenario where I was having a chat with a teenage male about the issue of drugs. During our chat I asked and he assured me that he was not involved with illegal drugs of any kind on any level, and was instead focused on his education, which for him was priority number one.

In the chorus of the song he asserts, "No cocaine! Ah not on dat. No smokin'! Ah not on dat. No drinkin'! Ah not on dat. Distort my thinkin', ah not on dat," at the end of which he says, "Ali my education. Is! Priority number one." It was actually the life that I lived, so quite naturally I had a very strong conviction to the song's message.

Abigail had arranged for me to meet with Ms. Badjan-Young. At that meeting, Ms. Badjan-Young extended a formal invitation for me to perform the song, at the then upcoming event marking the United Nations International Day Against Drug Abuse and Illicit Trafficking, and asked about my fee. I told her that her invitation was most definitely being accepted, and that I would perform free of charge.

The event was being held that same month on Friday June 26th, at the auditorium of the Eric Williams Financial Complex in Port of Spain.

I invited journalist Rolph Warner, who had since become a friend. He accepted, and was in attendance to cover the event.

I felt I gave an impressive performance the night of the event before a very appreciative audience, which included a few VIPs. Rolph himself confirmed that it was, and highly commended me. Ms. Badjan-Young was herself very impressed with the said performance, and expressed that sentiment in a formal letter after the event.

Unknown to me at the time, as a result of my performance, she had recommended me to a Ms. Dulcie De Montagnac, the then director of the United Nations Environment Programme, at the United Nations New York headquarters. Ms. Badjan-Young's recommendation further led to a New York meeting with Ms. De Montagnac that September of '92. I took time off work from Lonsdale, without pay of course, to attend the meeting.

Being that we were supposed to be managing my music career together under the Caribbean Entertainment Enterprises (CEE) banner, I invited and was accompanied by my older brother Evans to the New York meeting. He had been residing there for about 3 years at the time. Journalist and friend Rolph Warner, who was also in New York at the time, was also invited to cover the proceedings.

Ms. De Montagnac was extremely impressed with not only my music, but also with my well-rounded background. She felt that I would be perfect for a role in her organization. And so, she made the decision to bestow upon me the official designation of United Nations Environment Programme (UNEP) Goodwill Ambassador, which I was most proud and honored to receive. In fact, it was actually Rolph Warner's story announcing my designation, which subsequently appeared in the Trinidad Guardian newspapers, that created the uproar from the Caucasian Director at Lonsdale.

At the time, I shared the honor of being a UNEP Goodwill Ambassador with the likes of Ziggy Marley, son of the late reggae legend and icon Bob Marley, Kenny Loggins and Olivia Newton John, among other world-famous entertainers. I was the very first entertainer from Trinidad and Tobago to have received the honor.

Also visiting Ms. De Montagnac at her New York office at the time I was there was a Mrs. Cecelia Alvarez, the wife of a senator of the then Philippines government. She had traveled from the Philippines to the UN as a representative of her government to also meet with Ms. De Montagnac for discussions, as the Philippines was going to be hosting the 1993 Global Youth Earth Saving Summit from April 12th to April 19th.

Mrs. Alvarez was also very impressed with my music and background, and my genuine concern for and interest in the youths, which was reflected through my anti-drug song. Together with Ms. De Montagnac, we then held an impromptu meeting, upon which Mrs. Alvarez then extended an official invitation to me through Ms. De Montagnac and her office, for me to travel to the Philippines to attend the Summit as a specially invited guest performer. I naturally accepted the invitation.

It was then that I would get my most significant and challenging musical assignment up to that point. Mrs. Alvarez had in her possession, a one-page document from a Philippines based organization called The Earth Savers, with which world-renowned French explorer Jacques Cousteau was involved. I immediately recalled watching his television documentary series, "The Undersea World of Jacques Cousteau" as a teenager.

The Earth Savers document was based on the organization's "Ten Commandments of Earth Saving". Mrs. Alvarez commissioned me to write and record a song on the "Ten Commandments of Earth Saving", which she wanted me to perform during the summit in the Philippines.

I was more than happy to undertake such an important assignment. I subsequently wrote, recorded, and produced the song titled "The Earth Savers Commandments", which musical arrangement I did myself. It was recorded at one Tony "Woody" Woodroffe's Diego Martin home studio, with background vocals by Juslyn Jones and Betty McCrea.

April 1993 had arrived, and once again I took a leave of absence without pay from my job at Lonsdale Saatchi & Saatchi. I was then off to the Asian continent for the very first time on a one week mission, traveling for the first time in my official capacity as a United Nations Environment Programme Goodwill Ambassador. The local United Nations office handled all the travel arrangements.

The VIP treatment began upon my arrival at the Los Angeles Airport (LAX) in transit to the Philippines. Upon arrival, I was met by a young male, dapperly dressed in a well-tailored suit. He politely introduced himself and requested my passport. He was attached to the Philippines Consulate General's Office in LA. For me there would be no standing in line, or being subjected to any of the other usual airport hassles.

My two pieces of luggage, one piece being a steelpan, my country's national musical instrument, which was in a specially made travel case, was being automatically transferred to my connecting flight. So, I just had my carry-on with me. My Filipino chaperone instructed me to please follow him, upon which he escorted me to a VIP lounge, where I would await my flight to my final destination.

While waiting in the lounge, I had the pleasure of meeting Guatemalan Noble Prize winner Rigoberta Menchu. She is a political activist who dedicated her life to publicizing the rights of Guatemala's indigenous feminists during the Guatemalan war (1980 to 1996), in addition to promoting indigenous rights in her country. She was a UNESCO Goodwill Ambassador, and was also on her way to the Philippines for the Summit.

The flight was called after a short wait. I was then escorted right up to the door of the aircraft by my Filipino chaperone. After a stopover in Hawaii where we disembarked, we eventually re-boarded and continued on to the Philippines. The journey took approximately 24 hours from Trinidad. I arrived at my final destination around mid-afternoon on April 11th.

The VIP treatment continued upon landing in the Philippines. I was met by a welcoming party after disembarking from the aircraft. A Lei was placed around my neck and I was being videotaped as I was being escorted out to a waiting SUV, which took me to the hotel in Quezon City.

The hotel was a two-story structure located in what appeared to be an upscale area. Other foreign delegates were already there when I checked in. There were delegates from all the continents of the world. One delegate, who was from Africa and whose name was Moses, would turn out to be the life of the party so to speak.

Once I had settled in, I received a phone call from Mrs. Alvarez who extended an official welcome. She informed me that there would be chaperones assigned to the delegates who were staying at my hotel. The hotel meals were quite healthy. It consisted mainly of fish and vegetables, and there were always lots of fresh fruits to be had.

All of the events related to the Summit were being held in Quezon City. Mrs. Alvarez informed me that the first official event will be the following evening April 12th. It was a cultural event held outdoors at a fairly huge park. All the foreign delegates were in attendance. At that event I met Francis Magalona, the then top Filipino Hip Hop Artiste. He wanted us to do a track together before I left the Philippines, but unfortunately time constraints did not allow it to happen.

The following day we attended a second event, which was held at an indoor venue. Then on the morning of April 14th at 10:00 a.m., we attended the opening ceremony of the Summit at the Plenary Hall at the House of Representatives. The interior of the Hall was spectacular.

Later that same day at 6:30 p.m., we attended a welcoming dinner hosted by the then mayor of Quezon City, Mayor Ismael A. Mathay Jr. at the Quezon Memorial Circle, which is a monument and national shrine dedicated to former Philippines President Manuel Quezon.

Attending those events together as a group, made it possible for the delegates, about 15 all toll, who were staying at my hotel to become quickly acquainted with each other. I also became quickly acquainted with the young, highly intelligent Filipino chaperones.

I had three performances while in the Philippines. The first was on the night of April 15th at an Amphitheater in a park, with a lake as the backdrop. It was an absolutely breathtaking sight. And what a memorable night and performance it turned out to be, as I was actually joined on stage by one Jo Ramos, which was totally unplanned. I just saw some drums set up on the stage, and was told just before my performance that she would be joining me on stage. Jo Ramos was the daughter of the then Philippines President Fidel Ramos.

Unknown to me at the time, Jo Ramos was a top entertainer in the Philippines. That night, I performed "The Earth Savers Commandments" for the very first time; the song that I was commissioned to write and record by Mrs. Cecilia Alvarez.

I sang over the pre-recorded music track. Jo Ramos further backed me up playing the drums that were set up on the stage, which were similar to those that top American entertainer Sheila E plays. And like Sheila E, Joe Ramos was fantastic. There was lots of interaction between us on stage. It was a totally enjoyable and memorable performance.

After that first performance, I gained quite a number of Filipino fans, both young and mature adults alike. And I was also quickly falling in love with the Filipino people. I also became very popular among the other delegates, as well as our chaperones. I guess my Trini persona was in full effect.

The following day, April 16th, all the delegates staying at my hotel were taken sightseeing. On the tour we saw the Araneta Coliseum, the venue where the famous Muhammed Ali vs Joe Frazier "Thrilla in Manila" boxing match took place. The Araneta Coliseum is located in Cubao, Quezon City, Metro Manila, Philippines.

That day we also visited the Malacanyang Palace, which is the official residence and principal work place of the Philippines President. It was majestic, with its red and gold themed carpet and handrail entrance from the ground level, all the way up the very wide flight of stairs, where two palace guards stood guard at the very bottom, leading up to the main floor.

During the Malacanyang tour, we actually stood in the bedroom that was once occupied by former President Ferdinand Marcos and his wife Imelda. It had since been transformed into a tourist attraction. They both made many international news headlines during President Marcos' reign.

Stacked around the bottom half of the bed in the bedroom was a large portion of the countless pairs of the very expensive designer shoes Imelda was reported to have owned, reflecting the extravagance that she had become notoriously famous for, and for which she had made some of those aforementioned headlines. Several of her also very expensive designer dresses were also on display.

Adjoining the bedroom was another room, that we were told only a very select few were allowed to enter. It was said that the interior design of that particular mystery room included several pyramid structures.

We were also told that former President Marcos would retreat to that mysterious room, whenever he was ill, or whenever his Presidency was experiencing turmoil. The visit to the Malacanyang was a quite revealing and enlightening experience.

Being then quite acquainted with each other, the chaperones and some of us delegates spent time together learning about each other's countries and cultures before retiring to bed at night. Those times were usually spent in the room of one of the delegates. On one occasion we went outdoors around the hotel swimming pool, where I entertained them playing my tenor pan, which had a collapsible stand.

My second performance was on April 17th back at the House of Representatives Plenary Hall, where an official session was convened to discuss local, as well as global environmental concerns. That performance however, was an impromptu one, as while I was not actually scheduled to perform, a special request was made for me to do so on the day. And of course, I was more than happy to oblige.

At the end of that day's proceedings, special honors and awards were given out to a select group of individuals. I was chosen as one of those individuals. Thus, it was a great honor indeed and at the same time very humbling, when, in the direct presence of President Ramos, I received the key to Quezon City from the then Mayor Ismael A. Mathay Jr.

Back at the hotel that night, during another of our chat sessions in the room of one of the delegates, I was deeply touched by the plight of one of our chaperones. It came in the form of a letter that she wrote and wanted me to deliver to the President's daughter Jo Ramos, seeking her urgent assistance in an extremely critical personal matter.

And once again, I was more than happy to oblige, as it was obvious that I represented the best chance of her getting her letter to the President's daughter. I delivered her letter to Jo Ramos, reiterating its importance to the young lady who had asked me to deliver it.

And apparently action was immediately taken to address her situation outlined in her letter, because the young lady subsequently wrote me a very touching thank you letter, which I still have in my possession today.

April 19th, the last day of the Summit was then upon us. It was also the day I would give my third and final performance. That performance would be outdoors at the Quezon Memorial Circle venue, where the stage would be the actual platform upon which the memorial was built. I was then aware of what the Memorial Circle symbolized, so to me that meant that my final performance should be a really special one.

So, I decided that on the night I would not sing, but instead play a song on my country's National Musical Instrument. I learnt a new song on my Tenor Pan especially for that occasion. That song was "Can't Help Falling In Love", one of my all-time favorite songs. Given my experiences over the relatively short period I had been there, to me it was a most fitting tribute to the Filipino people.

I had all the foreign delegates join me on the Memorial Circle stage, for what turned out to be a very special and emotional performance indeed. The audience were fascinated by the sound of the steelpan. So much so that after my performance, a fair number of them actually lined-up just to get the opportunity to play a note or two on the instrument, which absolutely filled me with pride.

The following day April 20th, most of the delegates including myself, were scheduled to leave the Philippines to return to our respective homelands. So that night of April 19th at the hotel, the delegates who roomed there, together with the chaperones, all assembled in one room for the very last time for our final farewell.

We chatted among ourselves and exchanged addresses. I also presented the chaperones with specially designed Air-brushed T-Shirts that I had traveled with as tokens of appreciation, after which I said my final goodbyes and retired to my room.

However, there was a slight mix up with arrangements for my flight out of the Philippines. So, I had to stay put for an extra day, which I really didn't mind at all. The President's daughter Jo Ramos intervened on my behalf, and arrangements were made for me to depart the following day. That day, Wednesday April 21st, a few hours before my departure time, I received a phone call, and was informed that someone would be picking me up in about an hour.

I naturally assumed it was to take me to the airport. But when I was picked up, I was actually taken directly to the President's official residence. There I was met by and was the guest of the President's daughter Jo Ramos. She apologized for my flight mix up, and assured me that I would definitely be on a flight later on that evening.

We sat and chatted, during which she presented me with a gift. It was a book about her father President Ramos, which she autographed with a message that she ended with the word "Mabuhay", meaning "long may you live" in the Filipino language.

Then the time came for me to leave for the airport. I thought that the same chauffeur who picked me up from the hotel would have taken me there. But I was about to receive next level VIP treatment.

The vehicle that picked me up at the hotel, was one of three SUVs that awaited us outside the President's residence. The driver was joined by another individual who sat in the passenger seat. That vehicle was in front. Jo Ramos and I occupied the SUV in the middle, which also had two individuals including the driver. The SUV at the back was also occupied by two individuals. It was obvious that they were Jo Ramos' security detail. And so, we headed off to the airport.

During the journey as we continued chatting, Jo pointed out several landmarks to me. And by mere coincidence, and by some distance, we just happened to cross paths with her father's motorcade, which was headed in the direction from which we came. "There goes daddy," Jo said with a deep sense of pride and excitement in her voice.

When we got to the airport, accompanied by two of her security personnel, I was escorted into an office of a senior airport official by Jo Ramos. There she ensured that I was confirmed on the next flight out and ticketed. There was no wait before boarding. It was obviously planned that way.

Jo Ramos and I then exchanged hugs and pecks on the cheeks. I expressed a sincere thank you to her, after which we said our final goodbye, then I was off. My first mission in my capacity as a United Nations Environment Programme Goodwill Ambassador was completed. And for a variety of reasons, it was a most memorable one indeed.

My second mission as a UNEP Goodwill Ambassador was a performance in Boulder Colorado at the University of Colorado a few months later. A no-pay leave of absence from my Lonsdale job was in order once again. That performance was indoors in what appeared to be a huge performing arts theatre.

I invited all the foreign delegates, who were of a much younger generation, on stage for my performance as I did in the Philippines. However, the Russians, and perhaps not surprisingly, declined. Still, I did the United Nations Environment Programme, myself and my country proud once again.

The day following my performance, an invitation was extended for me to appear on a Los Angeles kids television show several days later called the Drip Dudes, a show which was affiliated to the Earthsavers movement. But I was forced to decline the invitation because I had to get back to "the security" of my Lonsdale job, because of the ongoing financial needs of my family.

Had it not been for that ongoing situation, I certainly would have accepted the invitation. I would have then followed where ever the music took me; especially since it was already taking me on the very music career path that I wanted to follow, and also to places that I never thought I would have been.

I really wasn't exactly sure what was in store with respects to my UNEP overseas missions the following year, 1994. However, the FIFA World Cup Finals was also going to be hosted by the USA from June 17th to July 17th that year, for which I had already began working on a special tribute song.

So, I then found myself in a bit of a dilemma. On the one hand, UNEP was allowing me the opportunity to follow my desired music career path. On the other hand, football, and more specifically the USA '94 World Cup, was then also going to be presenting another once in a lifetime opportunity, that would still also involve me doing music; one that I also did not want to pass up.

In the end, it turned out that my next major overseas music mission, would not be one as a UNEP Goodwill Ambassador. Instead, it would be one related to the greatest sporting event and spectacle on planet earth. Thus, and I hasten to add, regretfully so, my Boulder Colorado performance turned out to be my final mission, as a United Nations Environment Programme Goodwill Ambassador.

INITIALLY MEETING AND EVENTUALLY WORKING FOR DISGRACED FORMER CONCACAF PRESIDENT AND FIFA VICE PRESIDENT JACK WARNER

And now, for readers who may not have any idea of exactly who he was; allow me to introduce you to the subject who would feature prominently in the next three passages. He happens to be a quite unusual character.

So maybe it was no coincidence, that for many years in his capacity as a top football official, one of his offices was housed in a Tower located on 5th Avenue in New York City, which is owned by another very unusual character; a character who would become the leader of the free world, much to the disdain of most people throughout the aforementioned free world.

In my birth place of Trinidad and Tobago, which is both our homeland, the subject used to be worshipped by some and equally despised by others. The subject to whom I refer is one Jack Austin Warner; a man who at the very peak of his powers, might have possibly been the single most powerful and influential sports administrator on the planet. And that is definitely not overstated.

His power and influence stemmed from the position he then held in the hierarchy of the then administration of the world's most popular sport, football (soccer). And that power and influence stemmed from the two other positions he then held simultaneously as President of the Confederation of North, Central American and Caribbean Association Football (CONCACAF), and President of the Caribbean Football Union (CFU).

I met Jack Warner, the former FIFA Vice President and CONCACAF and Caribbean Football Union President for the very first time in person in very early 1994, by what I thought at the time was just by happenstance. I had since concluded that our initial encounter did not happen just by chance, but was in fact one of those events that occurred through what I refer to as "Spiritual Orchestration".

That spiritually orchestrated encounter between Jack Warner and I, occurred in very early January that year, and would result in me fulfilling the third of my three childhood dreams. The encounter took place on the compound of my then employers Lonsdale Saatchi & Saatchi Advertising, located at 10 Herbert Street St. Clair, Port of Spain, Trinidad.

Jack Warner had just come out of a business meeting with my then boss. As he was walking through the front yard to get to his waiting vehicle, which was parked on the street directly in front of the building, I was arriving at my work place at that precise moment.

Having been involved with local football all of my life, I knew about him. His then status, power, and influence at the highest levels of the game locally, regionally and internationally in his administrative capacities, was well known in our homeland. So, upon recognizing him, I calmly approached and introduced myself. We shook hands and I informed him that I worked at Lonsdale. He was quite pleasant and I got a good first impression.

At the time, I was already in possession of the demo I had recorded for the USA '94 World Cup tribute song I had been working on. The finals event, which was scheduled to take place from June 17th to July 17th, was then only five months away.

With his then status and direct involvement with the event in his capacity as a FIFA VP, I assumed that he would not mind, and took the opportunity to share my project idea with him. The song was titled "Soccer Fever USA". Aware that our time would have been very limited, I quickly explained to him that I had plans to record the song myself and release it on the local air waves.

I then quickly followed up with an inquiry as to whether he would be willing to present the final recording to the relevant USA '94 World Cup authority, with a view to it being used at the tournament, and about whether there might be any possibility of me actually performing the song in person at some of the world cup entertainment events.

To my surprise, he was very receptive to my ideas, and suggested that I first let him hear the demo of the song. We ended our relatively short conversation, with him further suggesting that I call his office to set up an appointment to meet for him to do so. I went away feeling extremely excited about the possibilities that might then lie ahead.

At the meeting, after twice listening very attentively to the demo, he offered a suggestion, which he felt would make the final product that much more appealing to the members of the USA '94 World Cup Organizing Committee.

His suggestion was for me to somehow find a way to include the names of three specific members of the said organizing committee in the song. The names he provided were Alan Rothenburg, Scott Le Tellier, and Dr. Henry Kissinger. Dr. Kissinger was the only name and physical image I was familiar with, since he held some very high-profile positions in U.S. administrations and was usually in the news.

I acknowledged Warner's suggestion as a brilliant idea, and agreed to find a way to fit the three names that he provided into the final record-ing of song. We then confirmed a date for a second meeting, at which time I would present not just another version of the demo, but the fin-ished product. Our meeting ended on that note.

I explored several creative possibilities wanting to make sure that the fit was perfect, and did not feel or sound out of place in the song. I finally came up with the idea of creating a special introduction, where I would mention the respective names. I also felt that mentioning their names in the very opening of the song, would have made the individuals themselves feel that real sense of importance, as indeed they were.

Then as my personal tribute, I decided to also include one other name, since I knew that he would have also been at the World Cup. The name that I decided to also include was that of my childhood idol, Edson Arantes do Nascimento, "King Pele" himself.

The body of the song included the name of each of the states that were staging World Cup games. Once the introduction was completed, off I went once again to Kenny Phillips' Music Lab Recording Studio. I was totally satisfied with the final recording. I personally thought it was excellent.

The only question then left to be answered was whether Jack Warner would agree with my opinion. Not that he was a qualified music critic or anything of the sort. But the reality was that for my project to have moved forward according to the vision I had; his opinion would be the one that counted.

The question was finally answered when the final product was presented to him at his CONCACAF Office, at the previously arranged meeting date. He once again listened very attentively to the entire song from beginning to end. He then shared his opinion.

"Mr. Ayres. I must say that I am very impressed." Slight pause. "Your final product is fantastic and the introduction is extraordinary." He ended by commending me for as he put it, "an exceptional piece of work". He then advised that I get a copy to him as soon as possible, so that he could forward it personally to the relevant party at the USA '94 World Cup Organizing Committee. I complied. He kept his word.

I subsequently received a formal letter dated February 24th 1994, which confirmed that the USA '94 Organizing Committee was interested in using my song at official world cup entertainment events. I was ecstatic at that news. I then reminded Jack Warner of my willingness to travel to Los Angeles to perform the song live at any world cup event.

On that front, more great news subsequently arrived, when I was informed by him by way of a faxed letter to his Trinidad CONCACAF office from one Sunil Gulati, that the second part of my proposal to perform live at any USA '94 World Cup event got the okay. More specifically, it was confirmed that I would be booked to performed at a huge event in Los Angeles. Full details about my USA '94 World Cup experience would be shared in the next passage.

As a result of being impressed with my USA '94 World Cup tribute song, as well as with my very professional conduct, Jack Warner then commissioned me to do what would be the very first official work assignment that I would undertake for the Caribbean Football Union. That assignment was to write and record a theme song for the then upcoming Shell sponsored Caribbean Cup Finals Football Tournament, which Trinidad was hosting.

The tournament final was scheduled to take place at the Queens Park Oval Port of Spain in April, just about two months before the June FIFA World Cup Finals would begin. The Caribbean Cup Finals Tournament was the showpiece of Caribbean football, and involved the top senior men's national teams from throughout the Caribbean region.

Although I would have been paid a substantial fee; after writing the song I decided that I would not record it myself, but instead give another Artiste the opportunity to do so. That Artiste would then have been paid that fee. My first-choice to record the song was Preacher, since we had worked well together on previous projects without any problems. Unfortunately, it did not work out that time around.

And so, believe it or not, although unexpectedly, I would collaborate for a second time with Austin, who was then more popularly known as "SuperBlue". After submitting the demo of the song to him, which Preacher had already voiced, he decided on his own to use the ideas from my song, and adapt it and write a totally new song.

I had no problem with that arrangement, once he agreed that we would share the credit equally, which he did. He recorded the song at Pelham Goddard's Agra 9 studio in St James. Austin did a good job as was to be expected, and we were all happy with the final product. He was paid a substantial fee for his services.

I formally presented the Official Shell Caribbean Cup theme song to representatives of the title sponsor Shell, and co-sponsor Pepsi, at a meeting which was held to discuss the tournament. Both got mileage in the song as their brands were mentioned. The song would receive a fair amount of radio airplay, which served to help promote the then upcoming event.

Upon my invitation, Rolph Warner was present as ever to cover the meeting, during which Jack Warner decided to reveal the news about me, relative to the USA '94 World Cup developments, upon which he suggested that the deal could turn me into a millionaire.

Warner's revelation took me by complete surprise, since the details of the deal were still to be worked out. So, his suggestion was all speculation. And I can assure you that the deal that was eventually struck, was as far from the millionaire dollars that Jack Warner suggested, as Trinidad was from Los Angeles. But that was not an issue for me personally, because as was the case when I received the UNEP Goodwill Ambassador designation, I was not in it for money in the first place.

Recognizing that he had just gotten a major scoop, though misleading, and which story he would have eventually gotten from me anyway, I had no other choice but to furnish Rolph with the full details right there and then, minus the millionaire bit of course, which was a gross exaggeration on Jack Warner's part.

That weekend, the story appeared in a front-page article in a Trinidad & Tobago weekly newspaper. The headline read, "SOCA FOR WORLD CUP "94; Composer Alison Ayres is likely to be turned into an instant Millionaire". Jack Warner's pronouncement was very misleading for sure. But Rolph was a journalist, and he had heard it from "The Man" himself so to speak, so he naturally ran with it.

However, that newspaper headline immediately invited a period where I was bombarded with financial requests from various quarters. From the very next work day, I started receiving phone calls at my workplace at Lonsdale from people, including relatives on my father's side, that I hadn't seen or even spoken to in many years. Some, who were merely acquaintances, just showed up at my job. They all had varying financial requests. They did not even bother to ask whether the millionaire part in the newspaper article was true.

One relative called me over the phone with a request for me to sponsor her and her son an all-expenses paid summer-long vacation to New York. A cousin, who just showed up at my work place, came with a request from his mother for a substantial amount of cash. I hadn't seen or even spoken to that particular Aunt and cousin for many years. I was never even close to them. Even an acquaintance who was also involved in the music business, showed up unexpectedly at my job with a substantial cash request as well. And those are just a few examples.

My explanation to each of them that the instant millionaire headline in the newspaper article was not true, was met with varying responses of resentment, I guess because they all felt that it had to be true, since it appeared as headline news in a newspaper. Such is the power of the news media, I guess.

Meanwhile, as an extension of the initial assignment to write and produce the theme song, Jack Warner then also hired me to produce a half-time show for the final of the Shell Caribbean Cup tournament. It would be my very first official football event production and management assignment.

And what an occasion it would be for my first. And that's because Jack Warner revealed to me that there was going to be two very important and very special guests in attendance on the day. Those two guests were Joao Havelange, the then FIFA President, and none other than Edson Arantes do Nascimento; "KING PELE" himself, who would have then been making his third visit to our shores.

After the first with Santos of Brazil in 1972, his second was with the New York Cosmos in 1979 for another friendly football game, which I was not allowed to attend, because of the serious injury I suffered during his first visit with the Santos team.

Suffice it to say, that I was extremely surprised at the amount of trust and confidence that Jack Warner was placing in me at the time, which I sincerely appreciated. I also appreciated the opportunity, which came with a huge responsibility, and verbally expressed those sentiments to him.

After his revelation, I immediately asked him if he could arrange for me to meet "The Man Himself", at some point during the course of the event. He replied in the affirmative. I simply could not believe it. I was then asking my Point Fortin self, where the dream was born, "Was I actually going to be meeting the King? And, was the third of my three childhood dreams really and truly about to come through?"

The big day of the 1994 Shell Caribbean Cup Final arrived. That massive final game would see my home country Trinidad & Tobago come up against Martinique. At my own expense, I had designed and had a printer print a quantity of T-Shirts for the very special event, displaying an image of Pele juggling a football, for the players of the Trinidad & Tobago Team, and the half-time performers to wear on the day. It was my way of paying homage to my football hero and idol.

Then came game time. There was a massive crowd on hand. Both Pele and the then FIFA President Joao Havelange accompanied by Jack Warner of course, met the players of both teams before the game started. With both special guests seated in the VIP section of the stands behind the goal post at the Tragarete Road end of the football field, an uneventful first half ended 0-0. It was a first half performance from the home team in the presence of "The King", that was very disappointing from the home fans point of view, I'm sure. Their beloved Trinidad & Tobago team had performed well below its capabilities, which was a fact. But there was a reason for the sub-par first half performance, which I was aware of.

The half-time entertainment show, which was produced and managed by yours truly as commissioned by Jack Warner, featured a live performance by SuperBlue performing the tournament's theme song. In addition to being paid a substantial amount of cash for recording the song, he was also paid equally handsomely for his live performance.

He performed inside the center circle on the field, surrounded by a bevy of beautiful female dancers. The choreography, which was done by the then extremely talented and popular local choreographer and dancer Debra Bernard, was specific to the song.

Except for SuperBlue, they were all decked out in soccer gear, including the specially produced Pele T-Shirts emblazoned with the words "KING PELE", superimposed against a famous image of him juggling a football wearing Puma football boots and warm-up suit.

The half time event also featured a mesmerizing skills exhibition by the Dion La Focade Youth Football Academy. The entire half time show went off without a hitch. And given that it was my very first time undertaking such an assignment, it was an accomplishment for which I felt extremely proud. And being that it was actually witnessed by Edson Arantes do Nascimento, my childhood soccer idol and all-time favorite player, made it so much more special.

Because I was aware of what was going on behind the scenes, it was no surprise to me when the home team came out in the second half with all guns blazing. From the first blast of the whistle, they started putting on a show in front of "The King", scoring almost immediately after the kick-off.

Then came "THE MOMENT" about 10 to 15 minutes into the second half. Pele had to leave for the airport to catch a flight. On cue from Jack Warner, I began the short walk toward "The King", from where I had been anxiously waiting.

Upon reaching him he greeted me with his usual engaging smile. We reached out and shook each other's hand. "I am Alison. I am honored to meet you in person. Meeting you is a childhood dream come through for me," I said. "I am so happy for that," he replied. We then warmly embraced each other.

The King and I then posed for the media and my personal photographer, whom I had hired to ensure that unforgettable moment was captured, and would be preserved for the rest of my life. "I hope to see you again at the World Cup," was my parting words. "Sure," he ended.

I then departed; my heart and soul filled with overwhelming joy. It was, and remains one of the happiest days of my entire life.

He then took several more photos with some local dignitaries, then left the venue for the airport immediately thereafter. In that second half, Trinidad & Tobago annihilated Martinique, coming out 7-2 winners at the end, and raising the Shell Caribbean Cup Trophy for what was then the third time.

The day was Sunday April 17th 1994. It was another one of those extraordinary days of my life; one that will be forever etched in my memory. It was just four months shy of my 35th birthday. And as impossible as it may have originally seemed, it marked the day that I realized the third of my three childhood dreams. If that isn't considered being truly blessed, then I don't know what is.

MY USA '94 FIFA WORLD CUP FINALS EXPERIENCE

With my proposal to perform live at any USA '94 World Cup event approved, I then made another request to the Lonsdale Saatchi & Saatchi boss, for a one month no pay leave of absence. My request was granted. However, I was prepared to resign if it wasn't.

I had to be in Los Angeles by July 8th. So, I traveled to New York in late June to first visit my mother and other family members, in-route to LA. After spending a week in New York, there was still about five days left before my first performance. That presented me with the opportunity to fulfill one of my U.S. adventures that was on my bucket list. That adventure was to travel from the east coast to the west coast and back by land.

So, after spending some time with my family, I was off to LA via Amtrak. The journey took four days, but it was a most memorable experience. There were some spectacular sights during the journey. The absolutely breathtaking views of the Grand Canyon, as we traveled through that part of Arizona stands out in my mind.

Then there was the retired couple that I met, while the train snaked through the Colorado Mountains. We got quite acquainted. So much so, that by the time they had reached their destination, on account of me being in the entertainment business, they wanted me to meet their daughter, and extended an invitation for me to visit their home. I believe they lived somewhere in Santa Monica, if my memory serves me right.

And why did they want me to meet their daughter? Well, it so happened that she was then a casting agent for Janet Jackson. Yes; that Janet Jackson. They further informed me that Janet sometime paid visits to their daughter at their residence, and could possibly do so during the time I would be in LA. So, if I did in fact visit, I might just be lucky enough to meet the legendary Miss Jackson. Did I accept their invitation? Hell Yeah!

The husband left me with his business card with his contact number. To my deepest regret however, due to unforeseen circumstances, I never managed to make it up to Santa Monica. But the Jackson story actually got better; much better.

I finally reached my destination after the very long but extremely enjoyable journey at around 5:00 p.m., on Friday July 8th. I hopped into a cab which took me to the Hilton on Figueroa in downtown LA, which was booked by the USA '94 World Cup Organizing Committee's Entertainment Events Department. The hotel was pretty close to the Los Angeles Convention Center where I would be performing at an event called "USA '94 SoccerFest", which started on that very day.

I could have actually seen the venue while standing at the window of my hotel room. After settling in and taking a much-welcomed shower, I walked over to the Convention Center to check out the venue. And just in case you're wondering; while on the train, I was actually taking what in my native land of Trinidad we call "ah Cowboy bath", at least once daily.

The huge 500,000 square-foot venue, in the center of which there was the huge stage set up for the Artistes to perform, also contained everything that one could possibly associate with football, including displays and information about the history of the World Cup. There were lots of football related activities to experience and enjoy.

I remember witnessing some workers from Pakistan sitting on the ground at a booth, where they were constructing footballs by hand from scratch. That image stayed with me. During that venue check, I had the privilege of meeting Peruvian football legend Teofilo "NeNe" Cubillas, who was on a break from a clinic he was conducting at the time.

I performed at the "SoccerFest" from Saturday July 9th to Tuesday July 12th. I did two performances on two of those four days, at what was an all-day into night event. I made certain that I enjoyed it to the fullest. One Art Arrelanes was the producer of the live entertainment that was taking place on center stage.

But unknown to me, he was much more than just the producer of the live entertainment at the USA '94 SoccerFest. It was not until after one of my performances, when he extended a personal invitation for me to attend the 1994 MTV Video Music Awards as his special guest, that I got an insight into who he was.

He told me that as his special guest, I would have backstage access, whereby directly through him, I would have the opportunity to meet the King of Pop himself, the one and only Michael Jackson, who was appearing at the event. I told you that the Jackson story got much better; didn't I? So, whoever Art Arrelanes was, it was then obvious that his status was such, that it was something that he would have been able to arrange. So, without asking any questions, I gleefully accepted his invitation.

Then there were the other invitations related to the World Cup; one of which was to perform at an event where the then President of the United States, Bill Clinton, would have been in attendance. Unfortunately, I was unable to attend that event, which I deeply regretted.

Hollywood's KABC Television also used my song for a World Cup Television Special called "Vista LA". Our Caribbean Entertainment Enterprises (CEE) Artiste Management Company, received high profile brand exposure in the closing credits of the program. It was truly an exciting time, with respects to my music career. I was keeping my older brother back in New York abreast of all the exciting developments through nightly phone calls.

Jack Warner had provided me with a VIP ticket to the World Cup Semi-final game between Brazil and Sweden, which I picked up from him at the Beverly Wilshire Hotel where he was staying. I had hired the same driver who brought me to my hotel from the train station. His name was Tatchi.

After I picked up the ticket, he took me on a sightseeing tour, which started with a cruise along Rodeo Drive, and included visiting an area where some of Hollywood's Rich and Famous lived. Among the residences I saw on the tour was that of mega film producer Steven Spielberg. I absorbed it all.

But the absolute highpoint of my week-long LA trip, was attending the World Cup Semi-final game between Brazil and Sweden, at the Rose Bowl Stadium in Pasadena on Wednesday July 13th. And what an experience, being that it was my very first time witnessing a World Cup Finals game in person. What made it extra special, was the fact that I was actually seeing my beloved Brazil men's national team play at a FIFA World Cup Finals, which was another item on my bucket list; Brazil being the homeland of my beloved childhood idol Pele.

The atmosphere inside the stadium was like nothing I had ever experienced at any event before in my life. The Brazilian team wore their then also famous blue kits for that game. Hearing the beat of the Samba drums echoing around the stadium in person, and seeing the "Samba Boys" playing in the flesh was simply unbelievable.

The ticket that Jack Warner provided me with, allowed me to sit among some of the elites and celebrities at the half-line, not too distant from the touchline. Among the celebrities was the then Cameroon football superstar Roger Milla, who at age 38 was the star of the Italia '90 World Cup Finals where he scored four goals.

He came on as a substitute at the USA '94 World Cup in the Russia vs Cameroon game, and scored a goal that saw him go down in the World Cup history books as the oldest player to score a goal at a FIFA World Cup Finals. He was then 42 years old. I sat very close to him at the game, and did not miss the photo opportunity.

Though lacking many goals, the game was still an exhilarating, exciting, tension filled affair. And after several missed opportunities up to that point, the goal that turned out to be the match winner, finally came in the 80th minute from a cross from the right side from Brazilian defender Jorginho.

Romario, one of the shortest players, if not the shortest player on the pitch at 5' 6", rose high between two much taller Swedish defenders just on top of the 6 yards box at the last post, and executed the perfect downward header just inside the post past Swedish goalkeeper Thomas Ravelli.

Brazilian supporters inside the Rose Bowl, including yours truly of course, went into total delirium. Final score, Brazil 1 Sweden 0. We had then reached the final, which we won 3-2 on penalty kicks playing against Italy, after the game ended up 0-0 at full time. Brazil, a team that I had been supporting since childhood, had then won its fourth FIFA World Cup.

I did not manage to fulfill my personal "on field" football dream and aspirations, which was to follow in the footsteps of some of my Trinidad and Tobago and more specifically, Point Fortin childhood idols that were mentioned much earlier in my book.

But being right there among a fanatical football audience of 91,856 inside the Rose Bowl Stadium in Pasadena California that day, witnessing my long-adopted Brazil Senior Men's National Football Team play on the world's grandest football stage, was before then, unimaginable.

The title of the official theme song of the USA '94 World Cup Finals was "Glory Land". And I was indeed in "Glory Land". But even more than being in Glory Land, I was in football's "Dream Land". As an absolute football fanatic, myself; what more could I have possibly asked for? I even got to see Pele briefly once again, and got an added bonus when I got to meet French football legend Michel Platini after the game. And there again the photo op was taken full advantage of.

The following day, Thursday July 14th, I left Los Angeles and headed back to New York via Amtrak again, thereby scratching that item to travel from East Coast to West Coast and back by land, off my bucket list. After spending another week in New York with my family, I returned to Trinidad, with my head filled with everlasting USA '94 World Cup memories.

And it all came about as a result of the "Spiritually Orchestrated" encounter I had with Jack Warner that day back in January that year; and for whose major contribution to the experience, I subsequently expressed my sincerest gratitude. But I'll say it here once more; Thank you Jack Austin Warner.

STARTING MY OWN SPORTS MARKETING BUSINESS: THE BIRTH OF MY NOSILA SPORTS BRAND

My experiences during the USA '94 World Cup Finals really inspired me and sparked several business ideas. And while I had attempted to start my own business first in 1988, and then again in 1990, both times with my Advertising & Graphic Design Studio, the third time would be the charm indeed.

For my new business venture, I decided that I would combine my passion for football, song writing and advertising and graphic design. And so, my company SoccerMarketing was conceived in my Los Angeles hotel room, over the course of the week I spent there during the World Cup Finals.

Witnessing the group of Pakistani craftsmen sitting with legs crossed constructing footballs on the spot at the SoccerFest event, also inspired another business idea that would fall under the SoccerMarketing umbrella.

Once Jack Warner returned to Trinidad after the World Cup, he and I eventually met. During our conversation, I revealed my intention to start my own company, which would offer specialized marketing services initially to local football related entities, with a view to eventually offering said services to the CFU and CONCACAF; he then being at the helm of those respective organizations.

He felt it was a great idea, upon which he pledged his full support. However, he was not sold on the word soccer in my company's name. His reason was that he did not like the idea of football being called soccer. I did not volunteer any explanation for naming my company SoccerMarketing.

But I wasn't going to change it either, because I knew that there was a strong possibility that I would have been conducting business in the United States under my company's name sometime in the foreseeable future. And the game in the United States is known as soccer of course.

Meanwhile, remember the invitation that was extended to me by one Art Arellanes to attend the MTV Video Music Awards as his guest? Well, once again I had a big decision to make. That decision was Lonsdale Saatchi & Saatchi or the MTV Awards.

It was then mid-August, and the MTV Awards was scheduled for Thursday September 8th at the Radio City Music Hall in New York, which was then only 3 weeks away. I would have needed to take that entire week off to travel and properly prepare for such an event, inclusive of shopping for appropriate garb to wear on the night.

But having been granted leave for one month as recent as June / July to attend the World Cup, I felt that I needed to be fair to my employers, so I decided not to request more time off to attend the MTV Awards. I would subsequently come to regret that decision. Consequently, the clos-est that I would actually ever get to the "King of Pop", was touching his star on the Hollywood Walk of Fame during my site-seeing tour, during the World Cup.

It was during that post '94 World Cup period, while still a Lonsdale Saatchi & Saatchi employee, that I began developing name ideas for the other business idea I had, which was inspired by witnessing those Pakistani craftsmen constructing those footballs at the SoccerFest event.

That other business idea was to develop and produce my very own sports brand, with the focus on football apparel and equipment. Several name options were explored. Not absolutely sold on any of them, I reflected on a question that arose in similar situations, while I was a student at Pratt.

That question was "What's in a name?" At Pratt we were taught the significance of creating "the right name" as it related to a specific product or service. We were taught that the name, together with the logo design, was of utmost importance in establishing the right image for said product or service.

We were taught that creating a name and or logo design for any business, would be one of the most important assignments we would be entrusted with as professionals, since both aspects contribute significantly to the success of the business, and should never ever be overlooked.

With those thoughts uppermost in my mind, and while there was some substance in the names that I initially conceived, for me personally there still wasn't enough. I wanted a name that was based on what I was attempting to achieve through the brand.

My objective was to use the brand and the power of sport, to inspire positive personal and on a wider scale, social change, especially amongst and through the youths in our society, as I had been personally inspired during my youth. Being a proud product of sports in general and football in particular, in essence, I wanted a name for the brand that represented me. And so, I asked myself, "What's in my name?"

Adopting an approach that I also learnt while a student at Pratt, I decided to spell my name backwards and "BINGO!" The NOSILA brand name was born. My name spelt backwards turned out to be the perfect acronym for the innate substance I sought for the brand name, which was translated to "NO OTHER SPORTSWEAR INSPIRES LIVING ATTITUDE". "INSPIRING LIVING ATTITUDE" would be the NOSILA brand ideal, which means "Stimulating The Pursuit Of A Purposeful And Satisfying Existence".

So, after actually considering changing it at one point earlier on in my life, and apart from it since becoming a part of my well-established professional identity, I came to discover that I could create something positive from my name, which personally, had a very negative connotation to me before then.

While continuing to assume my job responsibilities at Lonsdale, any down time was spent working on designing the logo, as well as developing designs for product items under my NOSILA brand. The prospects excited me to the point where I actually contemplated resigning from my job in late '94, just a few months after I had returned from the World Cup. But again, I had to think about my family's needs at the time.

BAD NEWS FROM NEW YORK

1995 started off terribly, when I received a phone call on my job from my sister Cheryl in New York. She had bad news. Our mother had apparently suffered what was suspected to be a stroke. Cheryl then lived with her 3 daughters on the 3rd floor of the 4-story building. My mother lived on the 4th floor.

After informing my then boss, I took 2 weeks off from work without pay as usual, and immediately began preparations to travel to New York. I knew that my mother had no medical insurance at the time. So, in anticipation of the potential costs that would be attached to her medical bills, I converted all of the cash I had access to at the time into U.S. currency.

I could have only hoped that it would be enough to cover whatever medical and other expenses that would arise, relative to our mother's then dire situation. I was in New York 48 hours after receiving the bad news.

I arrived at the apartment sometime in the evening on the day. Not knowing what to expect, I walked anxiously up the narrow corridor, passing the back bedroom then the toilet and bath and the kitchen on my right, as I made my way into the living room that adjoined our mother's front bedroom on the right.

There was no one else in the apartment at the time other than my older brother, who lived with our mother. After we greeted each other, there was no further dialog between my older brother and myself. I was totally focused on our mother.

In anticipation of my imminent arrival, the heavy curtains installed for her privacy, that separated her bedroom from the living room had already been drawn open. As I approached and she saw me from where she was lying on her bed, she immediately started crying as she got off the bed.

With her left foot barely leaving the ground, and with her left hand held involuntarily at an almost 90-degree angle, she limped towards me for a few steps as I met her in motion. We hugged each other. "Son. Yuh come tuh take care ah yuh mudder," she stated tearfully as we kept hugging for a while. We then sat on the living room couch.

She couldn't explain exactly what occurred during the night almost a week ago then, except to say that she went to bed as usual and was awoken by the episode very early the following morning, whereupon she felt a strange sensation on the left side of her body, that left her with limited mobility in both of her left limbs, and more so her leg.

I naturally assumed that she had already been to the hospital, but my assumption was wrong. When I asked my older brother why she hadn't been, he told me that she refused to go. "What yuh mean she refused to go," I asked, upon which he then told me that she told him that her condition was as a result of a "spirit blow" she had received, so she didn't want to go to the hospital. My older brother accepted her rational and simply left it at that.

And apparently our mother and my sister Cheryl were not on very good terms for whatever reason or reasons, so I understand that they weren't communicating much with each other at the time.

Now; I was in no way shape or form qualified to make any kind of medical diagnosis whatsoever. But one didn't need to be a "medical any-thing" to realize that our mother's condition was extremely serious and warranted urgent medical attention.

And it certainly would not have helped her cause that almost a week had already passed since the initial episode, and she was yet to receive said medical attention. I was absolutely astonished to say the least, that my older brother simply accepted our mother's "spirit blow" rational as the cause of her medical crisis, without seeking medical attention for her, to allow the medical professionals to make a determination. I was never able to wrap my mind around that.

I found his defense to be indefensible, especially since none among her five children and other close relatives, were oblivious to the fact that our mother has always been an extremely stubborn individual, which often made it extremely challenging to deal with or reason with her, which her deafness further compounded.

In such instances the initiative must simply be taken, and or deci-sions had to be made in her best interest on her behalf. Her recent med-ical episode was without doubt one of those instances. And my older brother of all people, would have known that.

In fact, it would be more than fair to say that while none of her five children inherited her hearing impairment, we all inherited the stubborn trait that is synonymous with her character. And trust me when I say that our mother is indeed an extremely stubborn individual.

Still, to me personally, regardless of how resistant or stubborn she might have been in refusing to go to the hospital, the fact is that she needed urgent medical attention. And my older brother should have ensured that she received it. It was our mother we were talking about here; who, since immigrating to the U.S., had provided food, clothing, and shelter and more, to all of my adult siblings and some other relatives who had also immigrated over the years, until they were able to provide for themselves.

My older brother in particular, enjoyed some of those luxuries at no financial cost since he himself immigrated to the U.S. back in 1989, and was still doing so at the time she had that medical episode. The entire situation made me extremely furious. I really wanted to explode on him, especially since I had been assisting him financially over the years as well. But I managed to keep my cool, as I usually did in such situations.

Our mother provided a phone number for a specialist, and the very next morning after my arrival we paid him a visit. According to the specialist, with the week that had passed without her receiving medical attention, the damage had already been done and was irreversible at that point. She would have then needed physical therapy to improve her mobility. She and I would pay several visits to the specialist over the two weeks that I would spend in New York.

Upon the specialist advising that she was more or less "out of the woods" so to speak, I returned to Trinidad and my job as scheduled; a job that I then needed more than ever. But in the then prevailing circumstances, I just had to leave it anyway.

But given what had transpired in her moment of dire medical need, and though not living in the U.S. at the time, I knew then that I would have had to assume the responsibility for our mother's wellbeing and welfare going forward. I committed myself to doing so, being very mindful as I had always been and will always continue to be, that she had always been there for all her children from birth into adulthood, and was actually still continuing to do so at the time. After that experience, I saw my older brother in a whole different light.

But our mother, though very small in physical stature, is extraordinarily tough both physically and mentally, and was not about to let her medical challenges keep her down. And even at the then ripe age of 63 going on 64, and like most other human beings, she had her very own dream that she wanted to fulfill.

Being a devout Spiritual Baptist for a significant part of her life, her dream was to become an Ordained Minister. She had fully supported my pursuit of one of my dreams with respect to my Pratt mission of becoming a bonafide commercial artist years before. So, I was more than willing to reciprocate, after she had revealed it to me during a telephone call to me a few weeks before I resigned from Lonsdale.

Towards that end, almost immediately upon my resignation the first week of April '95, I made all the necessary arrangements, travel and otherwise for her. My mother traveled to Trinidad at the end of the last week of that same month for a two weeks visit. She stayed with me at my then Luis Street Woodbrook residence.

A couple of days after her arrival, I accompanied my mother to Riley Terrace East Dry River at the very beginning of May. I visited her every day, and simply sat close by in silence for a period of time, as she went through a week-long ritual of fasting and praying while lying on the "Moaning Ground", dressed in different ankle length gowns as the days went by.

Her ability to undergo and endure such a ritual on the heels of her extremely serious medical episode only months before, was a prime example of the innate physical and mental strength and determination she had demonstrated throughout her entire life. She successfully completed her days of moaning, thereby fulfilling her dream of becoming an Ordained Minister.

On the day that she was returning to New York, she had another medical episode that gave me quite a scare. Just minutes before we were supposed to have left for the airport, my mother said that she needed to use the toilet. About a minute or so after she went in, I heard her crying out my name. I immediately rushed out of my bedroom and opened the door to the toilet.

There I found my mother falling off sideways on the toilet seat with one hand against the wall bracing herself. She was cold sweating. The problem? She couldn't get her bowels to move. She was experiencing a bout of severe constipation and was in extreme pain.

Standing directly in front of her, she was then holding on tightly to both of my arms crying out over and over again, "oh God help meh," while she tried to force her bowels to move, but without success. I immediately started thinking, hospital.

But apparently the pain she was experience was so unbearable, that she didn't even want to move. It appeared as if she was going to pass out. To me it seemed to be an extremely dire situation. So, without thinking about it, I jumped into action.

While keeping her from toppling off the toilet seat with my left hand and arm, which she was then holding on to, I then took my bare right hand and began extracting what was extremely hard stool from my mother's rectum. I continued the manual extraction until it eventually brought about the total relief that she was so desperate to obtain.

I felt an indescribable sense of relief myself once the entire episode was over. When she herself felt totally comfortable and gave me the assurance that she was okay, I cleaned up thoroughly then we headed off to the airport.

We still got there with time to spare. My mother was then on her return flight back to New York. Until that episode, I never knew that she suffered from chronic constipation. And while that was the very first, it would not be the last time I would perform such a procedure on my mother.

Only a couple of months later, our mother was facing another crisis. There was a fire at her apartment that caused major damage. As a result, both she and my older brother had to seek alternative living accommodation. He found such at a friend who lived on Nostrand Avenue, a couple of blocks south of Eastern Parkway.

In my mother's case, she first lived with my younger brother Brian for a while in East New York, then with my sister Cheryl and her kids at their 3th floor apartment, which suffered no damage from the fire. Our mother eventually ended up living with her aunt.

My portfolio containing my very best advertising and graphic design work up to that time, which I had traveled with on one occasion and left at the apartment during one of my visits in anticipation of my eventual immigration, was lost in the aftermath of the whole fire chaos.

Meanwhile, I had then been working diligently to quickly establish my SoccerMarketing business, having since left Lonsdale Saatchi & Saatchi. I had initially began working towards introducing a line of football apparel under my NOSILA sports brand, to the Trinidad market. But I then decided against it when it was proving too much of a challenge at the time, to have the items produced locally.

However, the process of trying to source a local manufacturer, would provide me with yet another experience that would continue to educate me, with regards to the particular social issues of race and class in my homeland.

That experience unfolded when I met with a local manufacturer and retailer who owned a very popular chain of sporting goods stores. He was of Syrian descent. During one of my visits to his office located in east Trinidad, I was given a tour of his factory to check out the operations. By that time, he had already been informed about my professional background. Then to my surprise, at the end of that particular visit, he offered me the job to run the operations.

And while I would not have taken him up on his job offer in any event, since I had no intentions of ever going back to my days of having "a boss", I was so highly offended by the reason he gave for offering the job to me, that I did not even entertain the thought of considering his offer.

And why would I have done so, when the reason he gave was that he was totally fed-up of having to deal daily with and I quote, "dem stupid illiterate people working in the factory". All of the "stupid illiterate people" to whom he was referring were black as am I, and I presumed, employed by he who was "highly intelligent and literate".

But they were obviously not to "stupid and illiterate" to do his work, which took skill that he himself, as intelligent and literate as he may have perceived himself to be, didn't possess, I'm sure. I quickly realized that he basically wanted to use me as his "slave driver".

He even found it necessary to further illustrate his point. Referring then to the majority of local black people in general terms he stated, "Yuh know, if dey hungry and dey gone tuh buy something tuh eat with de only money dey have; an' dey see ah van selling clothes in front de restaurant, yuh know dey go forget about buying food and buy clothes instead. Dah is how stupid dey is". I just sat facing him at his desk emotionless.

He tried to entice me to take the job by offering me a quantity of sports merchandise, including pairs of football boots; and further indicated that if I ever needed any future tire replacements and or mechanical repairs etc. to my vehicle, which was a Suzuki Jeep at the time, I would not have to pay for them since he had those connections.

And I am sure he did, given his business and social status locally. He even tried to get one of his employees (initials KR), with whom I was already acquainted, and who was also black and held a senior position at the company, to try to convince me to take the job. He too was unsuccessful of course. I instead simply agreed to, and supplied the company with some sports apparel designs, for which I ensured that I was well paid.

I relocated from the Luis Street Woodbrook residence to Brunton Road St. James sometime during the third quarter of '95. My two Luis Street room-mates, Carlyle Mason and Rory Loregnard also relocated elsewhere. I had introduced them to football during the time we lived together, which saw them make positive lifestyle changes. I was happy to have been a positive influence in both of their lives.

As is normal for any new business endeavor, the initial period for my company turned out to be challenging. I was however, still sending funds abroad to my older brother during those times. Thankfully, I had a very understanding girlfriend in Alicia, who was gainfully employed and was not dependent on me financially. We had been going steady for 4 years at the time, and had been living together for most of those years.

Things began to really take off for my SoccerMarketing business with the advent of the New Year. Within the first couple of months of '96, my company was commissioned by Jack Warner to develop and implement an initial marketing program for the new Trinidad & Tobago Semi-Professional Football League (SPFL) that was being introduced that year.

The initial phase of the program involved a Visual and Verbal Identity Program, for which I coined the SPFL acronym and designed the logo, in addition to writing and producing an official SPFL promotional theme song.

The theme song was recorded and produced by none other than Machel Montano at his then Siparia home studio in the Deep South of Trinidad. It was then I learnt that like me, Machel was also a perfectionist. He did an outstanding job.

Years before, I had sort of struck up an initial relationship with Machel and his mother Liz who was his manager. At that time, as a favor to a then close acquaintance, I had made a request to Liz for Machel to attend the birthday party of a little girl named Kafi Matthews.

Sadly Kafi, who was then going to be celebrating her 5th birthday, was terminally ill. She lived with her mother on Redwood Road Morvant in north Trinidad. My request was granted. Machel was just a very young teenager at the time and was Kafi's favorite Soca Artiste.

While he had a performance back in south Trinidad that same evening, Liz drove her son all the way from Siparia to Morvant to surprise Kafi. It absolutely made her day. He also sang her favorite Machel song "Indian Massive" to her, and presented her with a gift of his album. Journalist Rolph Warner, who had since become a very close friend of mine, was ever present as always to cover what was a very touching event. Most sadly, little Kafi passed away only a few months later in New York.

The official SPFL logo and Theme Song were unveiled and released respectively, at a special event held for that specific purpose at the Queen's Park Oval on Sunday March 17th 1996. My company was subsequently officially appointed Marketing Agents for the new Trinidad & Tobago Semi-Professional Football League on April 30th by Jack Warner.

Warner then also hired me to work together with two of Trinidad and Tobago's cultural icons, one Norvan Fullerton and the late Pat Bishop, on the official opening ceremony to launch the SPFL. The Japanese U-23 football team was coming to our shores to play against a local selection in the day's feature event. As the feature of my segment of the day's proceedings, I booked Machel and his band Xtatic, to perform the SPFL theme song live at the event. The inaugural '96 SPFL season officially kicked off on April 3rd.

With the local production of my NOSILA football apparel, which would have included team uniforms, not possible at the time, I then shifted my focus back to the marketing services aspect of my SoccerMarketing business, where I would utilize the full repertoire of my professional skillset, from ideas to execution.

In mid to late '96, which was about a year after I had relocated to Brunton Road St. James, I learnt that my previous residence was available for rent. So, for the second time, I relocated to 42 Luis Street Woodbrook, with Alicia accompanying me of course. We had then been living together for 5 years.

My vision then was to eventually transform the front portion of the residence into a sports store, from which I would sell my NOSILA brand of football apparel and equipment exclusively. The sports store was to be called "The Dressing Room". Both SoccerMarketing, under which the NOSILA brand fell, and the Dressing Room were legitimate registered sole proprietorships.

Jack Warner had continued to employ the services of my company during the course of that first SPFL season. All in all, 1996 was a fairly successful year for my then newly established SoccerMarketing business.

1997 started off well enough; as around mid-February, I received a phone call from Warner's office inviting me to another of the then customary meetings, that I had become used to having with him, during the course of our doing business, over the then almost 4 years up to that point.

At that then most recent meeting, on the basis of my company's performance relative to the SPFL's marketing, I received an offer from Warner to be the Marketing Director of his Joe Public Football Club. But since I wanted to continue to be my own boss, I expressed my preference to being a private contractor instead, to which he agreed.

I subsequently received a formal letter dated Friday February 28th 1997 from Warner, whereby my company SoccerMarketing was appointed as the Official Marketing Agents for his Joe Public Football Club.

We then entered into a verbal short-term agreement, that would last over the duration of the 1997 Semi-Professional Football League season, which would be, as he put it, "the trial period" to prove that my company could deliver. He then immediately used his "trial period" strategy as leverage to then persuade me to keep the costs of my company's services to a minimum, which I noted.

Right there and then, I initiated the discussion and we entered into another verbal agreement. That agreement was that if my company delivered, it would then receive guaranteed two or three-year contracts, to be the Exclusive Marketing Agents for both his Joe Public Football Club as well as the SPFL, before the start of the '98 SPFL season. That verbal agreement also stipulated that my company would be paid the full value for the services it would provide, during the two or three-year term of both contracts.

Under the initial '97 verbal short-term SPFL marketing agreement, I would maintain the copyrights to specific creative works I would produce, which we also verbally agreed would have been addressed and settled during our '98 contract negotiations.

Interestingly; and much to my bewilderment, during the said meeting Jack Warner also declared that Joe Public would be his new national football team, since he was fed-up with the failings of the bona-fide Trinidad & Tobago Senior Men's National Team over the years.

At that meeting, Warner commissioned my company's next marketing assignment, which was for a pre-season tournament involving two local SPFL teams; namely, Joe Public FC, Jack Warner's team; and United Petrotrin along with two other club teams from two other Caribbean islands. The '97 SPFL season was due to start not too long thereafter.

For that particular assignment, my company was required to produce specific components for a short-term Joe Public marketing program. Those components included a Joe Public FC Team Jingle, a 30 secs television commercial, a Joe Public FC Mascot and a Joe Public FC Bulletin for which 1,000 had to be printed. A photographer would also be hired to cover the tournament.

I submitted a cost of TT$23,680.00, which was a minimum charge, as he requested, and received a cheque in the amount of TT$11,840.00 from Warner, representing a 50% upfront payment. There is a reason that I am specifying those figures, which will be revealed later on in this passage.

My company would subsequently be commissioned to also produce cassettes of the jingle, and stickers displaying "JP" the mascot, for sale at the tournament. I proposed producing a promotional music video featuring Machel performing the SPFL theme song, which was titled "Shake De Onion Bag", for the purpose of promoting the league. Warner accepted my proposal.

I then conceptualized and directed the SPFL's promotional music video, which was shot by one Anthony Salandy, the country's top sports videographer / cameraman. After it was edited, for which I provided directions, the music video was released before the start of the '97 SPFL season and aired regularly on the CCN TV6 station, with which Warner had an ongoing business relationship. I was not paid for producing the music video.

It was then mid-March of '97. And in New York meanwhile, my mother, whose apartment had been badly damaged by fire in 1995, was not allowed to reoccupy it after it had been refurbished. So, she had been without her own permanent living accommodation for well over a year.

As stubborn as our mother was, which also meant having things her own way, I knew that staying with others as she had to do, would not have been an ideal situation for her, or for those accommodating her during that period. In the circumstances, she was desperate to regain the independence that she had since lost as a result of the fire.

As such, since he was unemployed, I advised my older brother to look around for an apartment that was affordable, where they both could live comfortably and was suitable for our mother, given that she was then physically impaired for life. I made a commitment to assist financially on an ongoing basis once the apartment was found.

I had already started work on the production of the Joe Public FC marketing components for the pre-season football tournament, when I received a telephone call from my older brother. He informed me that the friend he had been staying with since the fire, was relocating to Florida permanently at the end of that very March month, which was then about two weeks away.

As such, my older brother was being given first option to sub-lease the apartment, but he needed to commit to doing so immediately by paying the first month's rent, plus the customary 1-month security deposit.

My brother assured me that it was an excellent deal as it was a really decent 3-bedroom. And our mother would only have to climb two very short flight of stairs. I told him to confirm our interest, since I did not want them to lose the opportunity. I got on it right away.

In addition to the cash that I had at the time, I decided to also sell my vehicle to ensure that I had enough after the conversion to U.S. currency, to secure the apartment for them for at least 6 months. I called a prospective buyer immediately, who was the individual from Point Fortin who had paid me that visit when I lived in Westmoorings, when the Police appeared on the scene thinking that he was up to no good. While he was a very good friend of mine, he was a very close friend of my older brother in particular. He was a friend of our entire family really.

After explaining to him why I was selling my vehicle, he immediately agreed to purchase it. Being that he understood that I was only selling it out of absolute necessity, we both also agreed that once I accumulated the funds at any time thereafter, I would re-purchase the vehicle from him for the same price, to which he also agreed.

I then had enough cash after the TT to U.S. conversion to execute the plan, which also included funds to cover 6 months utility bills and food, and to give them some cash in hand. I intended to continue to forward funds after the 6 months period, which would have been nothing new as I had been doing so over the years. Within a matter of days, I was in New York to take care of business.

With Jack Warner out of the country at the time, I left the New York telephone number where I could have been contacted, with one of the female employees who worked in his Trinidad CONCACAF office at the time. Her name was Sharon.

I arrived in New York and at the apartment where my older brother found refuge after the fire, on Saturday afternoon March 22nd. Our mother was staying with her daughter Cheryl at the time. But to my surprise, the situation had changed.

The apartment would then be available in late April or early May. I could not understand why my brother did not see it fit to call me to inform me of that development, which would have saved me the trip at what was a critical time work wise. However, it was in fact a very decent 3-bedroom apartment, so I had no problem with the new arrangement.

That Saturday evening, I received a phone call from Jack Warner. "Ayres. Wuh yuh doin' in New York when there is work here in Trinidad to be done?" He questioned. His tone of voice suggested that he was very displeased about my impromptu trip.

I informed him that I was there to address an urgent family matter, and would be returning to Trinidad in a few days. I offered no details. "Awright Mr. Ayres," he ended, in a tone that further suggested that there might be consequences for me to pay upon my return.

Being that I was already in New York, and with the apartment rental arrangement deferred, I then decided that I would use the time constructively, by using some of the funds I had travelled with, to produce the Joe Public jingle while I was there.

So, I contacted Machel Montano and booked time at his then Brooklyn apartment home studio for the following night. My older brother, who I had invited accompanied me, but he seemed to have had an ulterior motive for doing so.

Apart from Machel, Shel Shok, his producer was also there when I arrived. Shok had a music track that he had recently completed, which he played for me. I decided it could work for the jingle, so there was no need to build a new one from scratch.

Having already written the lyrics, the services of the hugely talented Flex, who worked on music together with Machel back then, was employed to do the lead vocals. However, after only a few minutes into laying down his vocals, an apparent ongoing feud between Flex and Shok flared up. And that was the end of that, as the session ended abruptly.

Once we got back to the apartment, I then immediately contacted Tony "Woody" Woodroffe, who had since immigrated to the U.S., and with whom I had established a super working relationship, and fairly tight friendship from since back in Trinidad.

He was working out of a Manhattan studio at the time, and fitted me in for the very next day, so that I could do the Joe Public FC jingle there myself. My older brother decided that he wanted to also accompany me to the session at Woody's Manhattan studio. Once again it appeared that he had an ulterior motive, and like at Machel's the night before, saw a visit to Woody's studio as yet another opportunity to pursue it.

At Woody's, it then became clear that he was trying to make whatever musical connections he could, towards pursuing and fulfilling his agenda, and was using me to do so. And I had absolutely no problem with that, except for the fact that he chose to pursue that objective through deception, which wasn't at all necessary, because I would have been more than happy to link him up with whoever.

As such, while I intended to do the entire vocal track myself, I decided that I would give my older brother the opportunity to record his first ever vocals, by letting him do the introduction to the Joe Public FC jingle. He did a very commendable job. I then executed the rest of the vocals. A few hours later the jingle was completed and we were off.

That very night while back at the apartment with my own thoughts, I was then able to connect the dots after reflecting on the Caribbean Entertainment Enterprises (CEE) Artiste Management master plan he presented to me, and which I had bought into some years before.

It appeared that all along, after I had done so with success, my older brother had been charting a course, laying the foundation, and planning out his own music ambitions, in the form of a songwriting / recording and performing career that he was hoping to launch.

My older brother had simply been manipulating and using me over the years in his own self-interest. And he was doing so under the guise of us supposedly working together towards advancing a supposed CEE artiste management business partnership and agenda, and by extension my own music career. I was then on to him, but decided to continue to support him since he was my brother.

Then it became time for me to return to Trinidad. I made the request before I left, and the lease holder of the apartment furnished me with a letter of intent to sub-lease it to us. I returned to Trinidad on the night of Thursday March 27th. I made a phone call to Jack Warner's residence that very night to let him know that I had returned. He was not at home when I called, so I asked the female who answered the phone to relay that message to him.

Leaving nothing to chance, I followed up and got in contact with him the following morning, upon which he immediately summoned me to a meeting with him, at the Eastern Football Association offices in Arouca, north east Trinidad. I intended to explain the reason for my impromptu New York trip, and present the letter of intent from the New York landlord as proof when I arrived.

But I opted not to do so, because right from the jump, it was clear that he had already come to his own conclusion. In the presence of the then Joe Public FC coach, Warner suggested that there was the notion that I took off with his money with no plans of returning to Trinidad.

The money that he was referring to was the TT$11,840.00 up front payment on the pre-season assignment he had commissioned my company to do, and with which it was then engaged, before I had to make my impromptu New York trip.

Yep folks; the man assumed that I took off with the whopping TT$11,840.00 Jack-Pot (pun intended) on which, when converted to US dollars, I would have been able to live comfortably in the United States for the rest of my life. And therefore, would have had no need to ever return to Trinidad.

I thought to myself that he could not have been serious. Therefore, I chose to simply dismiss his absolutely ludicrous notion as just that. I then informed him that I had called his residence when I came in from New York the night before, and had left the message with the female who had answered the phone.

He told me that he did not receive any message, upon which he proceeded to hurl derogatory remarks at me in the presence of the then Joe Public FC coach, who stood there with a smirk on his face, clearly enjoying his boss' ego boosting tirade against me. I too stood there absorbing it all, while staying cool, calm and collected as usual.

Once Warner's attempt at belittling me to feel better about himself ended, I maintained my professional decorum and turned his attention to what should have been the first order of business, which was the status of the then current assignment. I informed him that I had in fact worked on the Joe Public FC jingle while I was in New York, and just needed to add the finishing touches, which I subsequently did at the then widely popular radio DJ Ian "The Goose" Eligon's Petit Valley home Studio.

Being totally focused on the job of delivering the highly professional marketing services that my company was being very much underpaid to provide, I then verbally proposed two other marketing ideas that I had for his Joe Public Football Club. The first was for the club to adopt "The Eastern Lions" as its nickname. I gave the rationale behind the nickname.

Warner and his audience of one took an instant liking to the idea and expressed their immediate approval. I then proposed the "Lions Den" as the nickname for the home ground of the team, which was at the CONCACAF Center of Excellence in Tunapuna, east Trinidad. No rationale was needed. Warner and his smirking sidekick also gave that idea the thumbs up. I left that session as I entered it; with my head held high.

And I didn't realize that Warner did not believe that I had called his home and left a message when I flew in from New York, until I received a call from him later on that same day after we had met. He simply confirmed what I had already known to be fact.

With my own means of transportation being a necessity, within a few days of my return to Trinidad, I contacted the friend to whom I had sold my vehicle, for the purpose of re-purchasing it. He honored our agreement and willingly sold it back to me. When all was said and done, I delivered on the commissioned pre-season assignment. The tournament came and went. And I guess it served Jack Warner's purpose.

To kick-off the new 1997 Semi-Professional Football League (SPFL) season, I was commissioned to and launched separate aggressive short-term marketing campaigns, for both Joe Public FC and the SPFL. The campaigns involved press, radio and television advertising, as well as the airing of the music video featuring Machel Montano, which was re-edited to freshen it up.

Both campaigns created immediate buzz, capturing national attention. But more importantly, by the end of the first round of competition, most clubs and members of the local administration including Warner himself, were reporting gates receipts that had not been realized in local football before then. Those reports were confirmed and well documented in several newspaper articles.

In one article, Jack Warner himself revealed that an $11,000.00 total in gate receipts at a match involving his Joe Public team, represented the highest ever amount collected at a game involving local teams. He further boasted and I quote, "the take came despite the game being televised live, and showed that once teams marketed their product properly, there was money to be made." End of quote.

I was extremely happy and proud that my full-service company's work was producing immediate results, ushering in a new era, and most importantly, seeing a revival of local club football. But to me personally, Warner's public boast and his celebrating $11,000.00 in gate receipts as the highest ever amount collected at a game involving local teams, simply told the story of the sorry state the local game had been in, and continued to be in under his watch.

After approval by Warner, during the break between the first and second rounds of competition, and after much planning during the first round, my company introduced and staged an SPFL All Star game, the first ever such event. The game was being staged at the Queen's Park Oval Port of Spain venue, and would involve all the stars of the league; those already established as well as those up and coming.

However, the then TTFA President Oliver Camps was strongly against the event. But I wasn't having it, because it was about promoting the SPFL. So, the rebel in me kicked in. Not only did I flatly rebuff his opposition, I personally selected the players for both All Star teams, since

I knew who the SPFL's star players were. I selected the coaches for both teams as well.

The then TTFA President also tried to put a damper on things on the day of the All-Star game itself. I had secured a $500.00 sponsorship as an incentive, which was nothing really, to be awarded to the "Player of the match", and made it known before the start of the game.

I subsequently got a message from the then TTFA President that "he" did not want any monetary awards as part of the event. That was not a surprise to me, given the administration's history when it came to rewarding players financially. I totally ignored the man of course, and his objection to awarding the "Player of the match" with what was just a meager sum.

To the disappointment of the then "TTFA President" I suppose, the event was well organized, fairly well attended, with the game being a quite entertaining affair, as the players from both teams showcased their respective skills and talents on the day, in front of the very appreciative crowd on hand.

The TT$500.00 "Player of the match" award was won by the then extremely talented local star Ricardo Aleong. I actually had to present it to him in his team's dressing room after the game, to avoid any confrontation with the then "TTFA President". All things considered; it was a very successful event.

During the said break between the first and second rounds of the SPFL league competition, I had also submitted a Joe Public FC mid-season marketing report to Jack Warner. In the report I outlined all the marketing activities my company had undertaken, the expenditure and results with relevant figures and statistics, at the end of which I made recommendations.

One of my recommendations was with respects to him considering a possible reduction of the price of admission to his Joe Public FC home games, which came about after conducting a survey on location during a match, and listening to the feedback from a significant number of game attendees.

My thinking being to capitalize on the then growing public support during the first round of matches, by continuing to increase attendance during the second-round games, through a slight reduction of the admission price.

By growing the attendance, I would then have had those figures to present to prospective on-site advertisers, wherefrom additional revenue could have been generated for the club. And even further, the high attendance figures would have eventually seen me pursuing the sale of television and radio broadcast rights for home games.

In his written response, while commending me on the document and my recommendations, Jack Warner stated emphatically that he would not reduce the admission price and I quote, "even if no one was to attend the games." End of quote.

His pronouncement clearly implied that he genuinely really did not give two hoots about the local game. So, maybe to him it was just the means to an end. His statement spoke volumes and gave me much food for thought. Still, I remained optimistic, because the local football business was then looking so very promising after just the first round of the 1997 SPFL competition.

The second annual "Big 4" tournament was then staged at the Public Services Association (PSA) Ground in St. James before the start of the second round. It was a tournament that was being sponsored by Mt 'Dor, one of the local cigarettes that was on the market, which fell under the West Indian Tobacco Company (WITCO) umbrella. My company was commissioned to, and did the marketing for the inaugural "Mt 'Dor Big 4" tournament.

While I was not aware of the amount given, the sponsor and their advertising company (my former employers Lonsdale Saatchi & Saatchi) were so extremely happy with the promotional mileage received through my company's marketing for the inaugural '96 tournament, that they raised the figure for the '97 edition from whatever it was for the inaugural year for marketing to $50,000.00 TTD.

The then Lonsdale boss had himself revealed to me directly how happy both agency and client was, which resulted in the increased figure for the '97 tournament. He did so in the presence of one Neville Ferguson, one of Warner's associates, at the media launch for the '97 tournament, which took place at the Kapok hotel.

But it became clear that like for the inaugural '96 tournament, I also was not supposed to know what the figure for the marketing for the '97 tournament was, because not long after the said media launch, before I could start engaging myself in the marketing spend, I first received a phone call from the said Neville Ferguson, instructing me to and I quote, "leave something in de kitty fuh mih eh".

I then received another phone call from Warner himself almost immediately thereafter, instructing me more specifically to spend only half of the $50,000.00. That meant that $25,000.00 was not going to be used for the purpose for which it was given by the sponsor. I leave you to come to your very own respective conclusions, as to where that other $25,000.00 may have ended up, based on the two phone calls.

Still, even with only half of the marketing budget made available to my company, the tournament was an overwhelming success. Many in the local football hierarchy were commending me once again for the job that I was doing, including Jack Warner himself.

Meanwhile, I had not heard anything from my older brother since I left New York in late March. It was then August, and the second round of the '97 SPFL competition had begun. It was during that time that I received a phone call from him. My first thought was that the apartment was finally available to be rented. But that was not it.

For some reason, which he never gave, the apartment was no longer going to be available for us to rent. And so, after living in New York for 8 years, he decided that he wanted to return to Trinidad. Strangely enough, he wanted to do so within just a matter of a few days, but offered no explanation for the urgency. He however, did not have the financial means to do so and asked me once again to facilitate him. Without asking any questions I told him I would.

But on that occasion, I guess his conscience led him to make a promise that he would pay me back. And so, I stepped up to the "family plate" once again. But that time around, since he made the promise, I did so with the clear understanding that he would pay me back.

And I was most definitely going to hold him to it, given all that had transpired between us in more recent times, during which, for reasons unknown to me, I noticed that his attitude towards me began to change, and not for the better.

I was on the job when I picked him up from the Airport when he came in, a few days after we had spoken on the phone. So, we then headed straight to the CONCACAF Center of Excellence football venue or the preferred Lions Den, where an SPFL game involving Joe Public "The Eastern Lions" was in progress. After the game we headed to my Luis Street Woodbrook residence. While living with me, our then unpleasant ongoing issues and discourse continued.

With the New York sub-lease arrangement not working out, unfortunately, my mother was left in her same situation where she had no permanent address. I naturally continued to worry a lot about her, and was continuing to work diligently towards changing her situation.

And it was in fact that diligent approach, that had since seen my company earn a then well-established reputation of being a highly professional entity, that always got the job done by producing results, no matter the circumstances.

That process included many meetings with Jack Warner, for which on a few occasions he would have woken me up from sleep between 4:00 and 4:30 a.m. with a phone call. Upon answering my phone, he would say, "Ayres. Yuh still sleeping? Meet me at my office in an hour."

Fortunately, his office was only a 5 minutes drive from where I then lived at the Luis Street Woodbrook residence. Unfortunately, those calls usually came when I would have left the TV6 editing suite only 2 or 3 hours before on those particular mornings, after working on television ads.

At TV6 I usually worked with one Phillip Martin all through the night, into those wee hours of the morning. On a few occasions I also worked with one Roger Baron and one Kerry Gibbons. They were all very cool individuals, who were excellent at what they did.

Apart from those mentioned above, at TV6 I would also have the pleasure of working with and developing acquaintanceships with some other very cool individuals, including Curtis St Hill, Richard Purcell, Kid, Tracy Hutchinson, Lesley Ann Charlerie, Rhonda and Jacki.

Warner and I also had a couple of meetings back at his CONCACAF office in Port of Spain, after night time football double-headers at the Center of Excellence in Tunapuna east Trinidad. Those double-header matches would have ended around 11:00 p.m.

Since I had already developed the habit of doing so during my advertising days, from the get-go I always took notes to document the items of our discussions, and any interesting comments or remarks Jack Warner would have made during our meetings.

At meetings involving certain members of his administrative staff, I remember him being almost always frustrated with one specific individual, who often failed to carry out their responsibilities. I also never once witnessed any opposition or challenge to Warner's ideas and or remarks. He usually did most of the talking during the course of those meetings, and they would all simply agree. I was getting to witness firsthand, how he conducted the business of football, locally and otherwise.

During the course of executing my company's marketing duties during the '97 SPFL season, I found myself being subjected to verbal abuse from a few of the local football fans who absolutely despised Warner, and almost anyone who was associated with him.

But those fans were not the only ones who verbally abused me. Taking a page out of their boss' book I suppose, since they may have also been victims of such from him, I was also verbally abused by a few of Jack Warner's close associates as well.

Apparently, there was another ill-conceived notion among some of Warner's toadies, that I was making loads of money off the man. And even if that was so, I would have most definitely earned and deserved every last penny, given the quantity, quality and value of my company's work; but most importantly, the results said work was producing. But that did not matter to them, as their aforementioned ill-conceived notion made me a verbal abuse target.

I had absolutely no idea what might have created the perception that I was making a lot of money while working for Jack Warner. Perhaps it was because they knew that he could have afforded to pay me a lot, as well as knowing that the work that I was doing was actually worth a lot of money. But the reality was, upon accepting the challenge of "selling the local game", I entered into a verbal agreement with him, whereby the '97 season would be "a trial period" to prove that my company could deliver.

That agreement gave Jack Warner all the leverage he needed, to manipulate me into charging much less than the true value for the highly professional services that my company would provide. Upon proving that it could in fact deliver, my company would have then secured two guaranteed 2 or 3-year marketing contracts, from Warner's Joe Public FC and the SPFL respectively. During the term of the agreement, it would have then been paid the full value for the services it would then have continued to provide, from the '98 SPFL season onwards.

I agreed to that deal because I knew the local football landscape and market inside out, and was confident that my company would deliver; not only over the '97 trial period but well beyond. So, while the financial reward therefrom was definitely an important factor, since I obviously had financial obligations that needed to be met, I also agreed to the deal because of the undying love and passion I have for the sport and my homeland.

I knew that I had much to offer to both, in the capacity in which I was then being asked to serve. I genuinely wanted to serve, and was then being given an opportunity to do so in a major way, and in the capacity, I felt that I could make my most significant contribution to the local game, for which I had my own vision.

That vision was to fully utilize my entire professional and personal skill-sets, to embark on a mission to finally transform the local game into a thriving, profitable industry over time, by working together with all the stakeholders, i.e., the players; fans and supporters; the corporate sector, both public and private; the media, the administration et al.

With that vision in mind, I was therefore willing to take all the hits, in the form of being under paid and verbally abused by Warner and some of his cohorts for the cause, towards what I sincerely believed was an achievable ultimate goal.

So, whatever the perception may have been, I knew that I was involved for one reason and one reason only. And that reason was not to serve Jack Warner himself as they were, but to serve the local game and the local game only, to the very best of my ability, in my then capacity as a marketing professional for the sport.

In the final analysis, the records showed that at the end of the '97 SPFL season, without any shadow of a doubt, my company did in fact deliver, as both 1997 short-term season long Joe Public FC and SPFL marketing initiatives not only produced the desired results, but did so beyond expectations.

Suffice it to say that I was extremely proud of what my company was able to achieve for our local football in such a short period of time. However, I hasten to add that the task was a monumental one, and was not easy by any stretch of the imagination. It required extreme amounts of physical and mental energy, as I was always on the go.

Apart from doing all of the Graphic and Advertising Design work, hours upon hours were spent within the confines of my home office viewing 90 plus minutes recordings of games. I insisted that said recordings be done by Anthony Salandy, in an effort to have the highest quality and most exciting pieces of footage at my disposal for use in television ads, that I would produce to establish and promote the images of both the SPFL and the Joe Public Football Club respectively.

As a matter of policy, and in keeping with my own high professional standards, when required, I employed the services of those who were regarded as the very best in their respective fields locally.

And as mentioned earlier, many long hours were also spent in the CCN TV6 editing suites where all the television ads were produced. Many more hours were spent at the Maraval recording studio facility called the Engine Room, where all of the radio ads were produced. I wrote the scripts for all the TV and radio ads. Top local radio DJ Just Jase, was my go-to professional for voice overs for all of the said ads.

Through my company's season long marketing efforts, gate receipts were reported as being the best they had ever been. The profile and images of both the SPFL and the Joe Public Football Club rose to lofty heights. The respective foundations for future SPFL and Joe Public FC success were being laid.

Without a doubt, my company had passed Jack Warner's "trial period test" with flying colors as the saying goes. I was then in high anticipation of, and looking forward to the two forthcoming contracts and further progress the following season.

Enter 1998. On Monday January 19th, Warner held his Joe Public Football Club's '97 awards ceremony at the CONCACAF Center of Excellence, with all the pomp and circumstance one would have expected. The guest of honor was English football legend, Sir Bobby Charlton.

There were also several local politicians in attendance, including the would-be first female Prime Minister of the Republic of Trinidad and Tobago Kamla Persad-Bessessar, as well as local high-profile businessman Ish Galbaransingh. As insignificant as that assembly would have appeared then, in retrospect, it may have actually been the prelude to forming a future government.

Since the night was all about celebrating the players, I wanted to make it special for them. So, as part of the evening's program, as a surprise, I presented a video with highlights of Joe Public FC's '97 SPFL season, which I edited and produced at TV6 as per usual. No one expected it; not the players or even Warner himself. I had to review the VHS tapes of every Joe Public FC SPFL game to select the very best highlights.

The starting spots of the footage that I wanted to use were then documented by noting the precise times in the respective games, so they could have been easily located once I got to the editing suite. It was then edited together in sequence, starting with highlights from the very first game to the last.

But I also had another big surprise up my sleeve. I had also compiled footage from tapes I had in my personal archive, and produced a short video of Sir Bobby Charlton's in his playing days, which was also presented on the night. Sir Bobby was extremely surprised as was Jack Warner himself, who was bursting with pride at my initiative to actually honor his Guest of Honor, in a way that Sir Bobby would have certainly appreciated.

I subsequently received a written commendation from Jack for my company's contribution to the event, wherein he urged me to "continue the good work, in our continuous striving for excellence". But notably, there was no mention of the two contracts that were supposed to be forthcoming.

The new '98 SPFL season was due to kick off the first week in May. My company started rendering its professional services for that season without the contracts, starting with another pre-season tournament the last week of March.

The tournament, which believe it or not Jack Warner called, wait for it, wait for it, wait for it, "The Champions League", involved 4 SPFL teams including Warner's Joe Public Football Club of course. The tournament came and went, and I guess once again it served Warner's purpose.

After I had delivered a letter dated January 28th reminding him of our verbal agreement relative to the Joe Public and SPFL contracts, at the beginning of April, I got a phone call inviting me to a meeting with Warner at his CONCACAF office. With my company already being the official marketing agents for his Joe Public Football Club and the SPFL, at that meeting, I was then verbally offered the position to be the exclusive marketing consultant for two other local football entities.

They were the Trinidad & Tobago Football Association (TTFA) and the Eastern Football Association respectively. I viewed his offer as an opportunity for me to gain an even more in-depth understanding of the operations of the local football administration from the inside. So, I accepted his offer.

In a letter dated 6th April '98, with a c.c. to me, he formally advised a Ms Cyntra Achong, the then General Manager of TV6, that I was appointed to the two respective positions. In the letter he also advised that I was also the exclusive marketing consultant for his Joe Public Football Club; but most notably, that my appointment was "at the discretion" of those organizations. To me that seemed to be a clear indication that the two contracts may not have been forthcoming after all.

So, after a few verbal reminders, a meeting was eventually set up to discuss the SPFL contract. It was convened at his CONCACAF office as had become the norm. Present at that meeting was the then Trinidad & Tobago Football Association President Oliver Camps, the then General Secretary Richard Groden, Warner, and me.

At the end of the meeting, I was instructed by Warner to prepare the draft of the contract, detailing the proposed terms and conditions, which I was to then forward to the then TTFA General Secretary for his review. I complied.

I followed up with the General Secretary about a week later, upon which he informed me that it had been reviewed and met with his approval, and he would arrange for us to meet soon. With that news, my company then commenced its marketing duties for the new '98 SPFL season, since by all indications, the SPFL contract then seemed to be forthcoming.

My brain then went into overdrive, as I then began thinking even further ahead, because Jack Warner was going to be introducing a full professional league from the '99 season. In anticipation, I decided that I would introduce 24 Karat gold championship rings as part of the prize award for the champions, and as a component of my marketing strategy for the inaugural 1999 Professional Football League (PFL) season and beyond.

I felt that introducing the rings as a part of the championship prize award, would have then also given the players themselves of the teams winning the league over the respective seasons, individual pride of ownership of an item of value, that would memorialize their championship victory or victories as the case may be, over the course of their respective lifetimes.

Warner loved the idea, which got his approval. At my very own expense, I then had a prototype of the ring made by a jeweler, which featured the SPFL Star Player logo symbol. But unexpectedly, those plans would quickly change.

Being the then naive, trusting individual I was back then, and even as his reputation preceded him, I foolishly believed that Jack Warner would have honored our verbal agreement based on the merit of my company's performance, as it had proven that it could in fact deliver. But trusting him turned out to be a big mistake, because it only served to open the door for him to deceive, manipulate and exploit me. I then had to accept that reality, because I allowed it to happen.

During the first round of league competition of that '98 SPFL season, timely payments for professional services rendered by my company, started to become a problem. So, it really came as no surprise when Warner started to cut back on the marketing for both the SPFL and his Joe Public Football Club. The first round of the SPFL competition ended in June, just before the 1998 France FIFA World Cup Finals began on June 10th. The league was then on a one-month break for the World Cup.

By that time, the transformation of the entire front portion of my Luis Street residence into my Dressing Room sports store space had been almost completed. It was a substantial financial investment.

I was then approached by one Ramesh Ramdhan, a then local high-profile referee, who actually officiated at the said World Cup, and decided to enter into an agreement with a local distributor to sell official France '98 World Cup merchandise from my store space, which generated a substantial amount of revenue for my company as well as for the local distributor.

But even with the SPFL and Joe Public FC marketing cut back during the first round of competition, the highest single game intake was $20,000.00 by Warner's Joe Public club, in a game against Caledonia AIA (Athletes In Action). That was up from $11,000.00 for the corresponding fixture of the '97 season. And even with the cut back, overall SPFL gate receipts after the said first round of competition were similar to those of the '97 season.

I thought then that in recognition of those facts, the powers that be would have then seen it fit to award my company the two contracts, whereby the marketing program would then kick back into high gear, with the aim of seeing further increased attendances at games during the second round, by capitalizing on the momentum from the World Cup. But I guess it was just wishful thinking on my part, because I so desperately wanted to see the local league and by extension the local game, finally flourish, after many years of stagnation.

During the break for the World Cup, I was contacted by my mother. She and I had been keeping in touch of course. She informed me that she had finally managed to find an apartment. It had then been over a year since I had made my last New York trip. With some time to spare before the second round of the SPFL started, I immediately headed to New York to sort things out for her.

I did not find the original studio apartment that she wanted to occupy to be quite suitable. So, I instead chose a 1 bedroom on the same 2nd floor of the 4-story building. She would have to climb one flight of stairs to get to the apartment. But it was conveniently located just a half block away from where she originally resided, where the fire took place, and my sister Cheryl still lived in that building. So, she was close to family.

The 1-bedroom apartment was still quite small and still far from being ideal. But I did my utmost to make it as habitable and comfortable as I possibly could for my mother. I ensured that it was repainted etc. by the landlord, and purchased all the furnishing that would fit in it.

The France '98 World Cup had begun during the time I was in New York, so naturally I watched the televised games. It took a full week of extremely hard work to make the apartment habitable for my mother. Still, the fact that she was going to be living alone then became my concern; especially since she was deaf.

And while writing letters was her primary means of communication, a phone was a necessity for her to be able to make calls whenever she wanted or needed to, so I also made sure that one was installed and was in working order before I left. I returned to Trinidad after the one-week period, and resumed my company's marketing duties to Jack Warner's football businesses.

THE MOTHER OF ALL MEETINGS

Then came what I will appropriately describe as "The Mother of All Meetings". The said meeting was convened as a matter of extreme urgency in mid-to-late July of '98, after the World Cup had ended, by who else but Jack Austin Warner himself of course.

That extremely urgent session was being convened by the then FIFA Vice President, CONCACAF President, Caribbean Football Union President, and Trinidad & Tobago Football Association Special Advisor, for one reason and one reason only. It is a meeting that I will never ever forget, if only for "my one reason".

It all unfolded while I was hard at work producing a commercial in the editing suite at CCN TV6 as usual, for an upcoming football event. That day, around mid-afternoon, a phone call came in for me from Warner's CONCACAF office. It was his personal secretary. "Alison. The boss want yuh tuh come to his office right now," she stated in a most serious tone.

I informed her that I was in the middle of an editing session, and could not just drop it at that point, as it was in fact Warner's work I was doing. "Alison. Take mih advice. Leave whatever it is yuh doing an' come now; because something to do with you hah Mr. Warner real vex. I eh see Mr. Warner so vex in ah long, long time," she warned.

So, I immediately dropped what I was doing as she had strongly advised. I then promptly left the editing suite, got into my vehicle, and headed up to his office, which was then located on Edward Street Port of Spain. The drive to get to his office was less than 10 minutes.

On my way there, I was racking my brain trying to figure out what this "small fry" from the little country side village of Point Fortin could have possibly done, that could have gotten this "huge world figure" so mad. But try as I did, I could not put my finger on anything.

Upon arriving and entering the CONCACAF office building, I immediately felt the tension in the air. None of his employees greeted or acknowledged me that day as was customary. It was as if they were saying, "Jack vex with yuh, so all ah we hah tuh be vex with yuh too", without actually saying it. It seemed like they all already knew exactly what was about to go down.

I made my way up to the boardroom on the 2nd floor of the two-story building. His cohorts, the four or five who were present, were already seated when I arrived. I met the very same atmosphere in the boardroom when I entered, as I had met upon entering the building.

Absolutely no one greeted or acknowledged me. Not even eye contact was made. I took the seat which had been reserved especially for me, which was directly facing Warner's on the opposite side of the boardroom table.

Then the moment arrived. The man himself appeared, dressed to the hilt in suit and tie as usual. Upon entering the boardroom, he did not utter a word. He made no eye contact with anyone. It was obvious that he wanted to send a very clear message to me that he was really, really livid.

He took his seat. He then put his both elbows on the table, and clasped his hands together in front of his chest. Looking down at the table as if to gather himself, he then shook his head from side to side; my eyes glued to him all the while.

He finally looked up directly at me; and with a piercing stare, stated in a tone that reflected the degree of his anger. "Mister Ayres. I have never been so angry in my 25 years in football, as I am at this moment. But I will assure you of one thing. Somebody gettin' fired here today!" After a slight pause he continued, "we jus' waitin' for Earl John to return from the Express with some information," he ended.

The room maintained its deafening silence after his venomous opening. It was obvious that the "somebody" to whom he was referring was me. It was then crystal clear why the "extremely urgent" meeting was called. We all continued to sit in extremely uncomfortable silence as we waited for the said Earl John, who also worked for Warner, to return.

As if on cue, Earl John entered the "Firing Room" shortly after Warner's threatening opening declaration. Earl John was supposedly bringing proof of some colossal mess-up, for which Warner felt I was at fault; and thereafter, together with the rest of Warner's disciples, also bear witness to my humiliation.

However, there was one little problem. For all his worldly stature, perceived acumen, and experience, the then FIFA Vice President, CONCACAF President, Caribbean Football Union President, and Trinidad & Tobago Football Association Special Advisor, in his haste to wield his famous axe to chop off the head of yet another ill-fated victim, he made the most fundamental of errors. He failed to get the facts.

You see, as much as Warner wanted it to be me, whatever his reason, the information that Earl John received and brought back to the "Firing Room", actually provided proof that it was one of his long serving sycophants, who actually messed up big time.

It all had to do with a project that my company was assigned to at the time, for the '98 Shell Caribbean Cup Finals Tournament, which was taking place about 2 weeks after the World Cup. The tournament was being hosted by Trinidad and Jamaica, with the semi-finals, 3rd place play-off and final, taking place in Trinidad. I had been appointed a member of the Organizing Committee for the Trinidad leg of the tournament by Jack Warner.

The Trinidad Express newspapers and that certain member of Warner's administration were involved with the project. Earl John, had been sent on the fact-finding mission by Warner, apparently, after he had called the meeting. Upon his return, Earl John reported to the meeting that I had in fact visited the Express more than a week before, and had completed my company's part of the assignment.

Thereafter, the Express newspaper awaited the appearance of Warner's representative, to follow up to do his part on behalf of the administration to complete it. He never presented himself to do so, and thus, messed up the project big time.

There was most certainly "somebody" to be fired as he angrily stated; and clearly, Warner was hoping that "somebody" was me. But since it was not "Mister Ayres" to be fired as he had hoped it would be, no one was.

In the circumstances, one would have thought that an apology would have been in order and forthcoming from Warner right there and then. And given the then "stature" of the man, I really thought he would have risen to the occasion. But I suppose that his ego, as badly bruised as it was at the time, did not permit him to offer one.

I had been working diligently from day one in the execution of my company's marketing duties and responsibilities, over which time it was delivering results. My company's performance up the point of the meeting was beyond reproach; evidenced by my receiving several new appointments and commendations from Warner himself, both written and verbal during that time.

The meeting was supposed to have been another one of those days, when yet another undeniably committed servant of the local game, was supposed to have been totally stripped of his professional and personal dignity, by the man who was then perceived to be the "Local Football Messiah".

But as it turned out, in his haste to unleash his wrath on yet another unsuspecting victim, and in the process, totally humiliate the said victim, he instead ended up totally embarrassing his then "FIFA Vice President self". And he did so in the presence of his extremely loyal bunch of disciples, whom I suspected had never experienced their boss being in such a position. I could only assume that they too must have felt embarrassed for him and by him in that moment.

It was quite clear that the long serving member of his administration, who was most present at the meeting, must have told Warner a huge lie to cover up his own huge mess up. But in the end, while the culprit certainly deserved to be fired, he was not; neither was I. I was subsequently informed that the particular individual had always been messing up a lot over the years. Yet he continued to serve in the then local administration. No wonder it had been a football administration that was akin to a circus, with Warner himself as the ringmaster.

One thing was abundantly clear. Jack Warner wanted me out, for whatever reason, and he obviously thought that he found a legitimate one to do so then; one that he had apparently been looking for, which he felt would have served to justify his action. But it backfired. So, for me, it was indeed an unforgettable meeting that day in late July 1998, when

"The Higher Power" served the then "Almighty Jack Warner", a piece of humble pie.

Throughout the entire episode, I remained calm, cool, and collected as usual, without uttering as much as one word. I left "The Mother of all Jack Warner's Meetings" with my head held the highest that it could have possibly been held, reassured that my professional pride and integrity and personal dignity continued to be fully intact.

THE BEGINNING OF THE END

After the Shell Caribbean Cup had ended on July 31st, I received a formal letter from Warner dated August 5th, thanking me "wholeheartedly" for my hard work and dedication etc., etc., relative to the tournament. But it meant absolutely nothing to me. It was viewed simply as empty rhetoric at that point. My company performed its duties to its then well-established high professional standard, and was paid for its services, which was all that mattered to me then.

Once the second round of the SPFL competition began after the break for the France '98 FIFA World Cup Finals and the Shell Caribbean Cup Finals, Warner's decision to cut back on the marketing for the competition and for his Joe Public Football Club, took effect. The positive newspapers headlines and reports quickly changed.

Only weeks into the said second round, one headline then read, "CLUBS LOSING MONEY"; sub-head, "POOR CROWD TURN OUT IN SPFL". The sudden dramatic drop in game attendances was no coincidence.

I took absolutely no satisfaction from reading that particular headline and article, given the tremendous amounts of hard work that had been put in over the almost 2 years period at that point, in beginning to lay the foundation towards eventually seeing not only my vision, but what I knew was also the vision of all the stakeholders, of a thriving local football industry being achieved. But apparently, Jack Warner did not share that collective vision. I thought to myself; what a total waste of time and effort. My company continued to render its professional services as needed.

Given all that had transpired, one can imagine my bewilderment when I was informed by way of another formal letter dated September 4th, from one of Warner's subordinates from the Caribbean Football Union's (CFU) Office, that he had been "directed by Warner", to advise me that I had been nominated to serve on the Organizing Committee of the 1999 Caribbean Nations Cup, a new tournament that was going to be introduced.

So, in a matter of weeks, I went from my head being on Warner's chopping block, to being integrated into his football fold at the regional level. I attended the first meeting of the Committee, which was held on Friday October 9th of '98 at Warner's CONCACAF office, just as a formality; because by then, I had absolutely no interest in continuing to serve "the beautiful game" under Warner's leadership.

I thereafter withdrew the professional services that my company had been providing to his various football entities. Those football entities included, his Joe Public Football Club, the then Semi-Professional Football League (SPFL), the Trinidad & Tobago Football Association (TTFA), the Caribbean Football Union (CFU), and the Confederation of North, Central America, and Caribbean Association Football (CONCACAF).

Because of my bold decision and his well-established reputation, I was certain that I would have been blacklisted by Warner thereafter. And I was; which was told to me by local football coach Jamaal Shabazz who was in the meeting when Warner confirmed it, when Jamaal himself had recommended me for a marketing assignment that was to be undertaken at the time. I would not have taken on the assignment anyway. My feeling was, so be it, because I knew that I didn't need Jack Warner and or his football business in order to survive.

I wish to make mention however, of three of his employees that comes to mind, who were always very courteous towards me, during the time my company rendered professional marketing services to Warner's football businesses. They were Warner's personal secretary (initials PM), one Rolf Doyle and one Boris Punch.

So, having withdrawn my company's services from Jack Warner's football businesses, and with absolutely no interest in continuing to serve the local game with him at the helm, I then left Trinidad for the U.S. on December 21st that year of '98, accompanied by Alicia. Our relationship was then almost 8 years old and going very strong. I left my older brother and our childhood friend Popeye, who had since been also sub-letting from me at the time, in my Luis Street residence.

FIFA BUSINESS

I left behind three outstanding matters that were yet to be settled, after totally withdrawing my company's services from Warner's football businesses and heading to the U.S. They were all copyright matters.

The most significant being one related to the use of a logo, which I had designed and proposed in September of '98 for the 2001 FIFA U-17 World Cup Finals tournament, which Trinidad and Tobago was going to be hosting.

My logo design had been subsequently approved by Warner, in his capacity as a FIFA Vice President and Honorary Chairman of the Local Organizing Committee (LOC). The then CEO of the LOC, initials RJ, was thereafter engaged in ongoing communications with me to settle that particular matter. I had contacted him from New York with a view to doing so. He responded to me on two subsequent occasions; the first via telephone. His other response was sent via a faxed letter dated December 29th 1998.

That letter indicated and I quote, "All intellectual property rights with respects to the mark (design) will be secured in the name of the FIFA and the development of the design is predicated on the early assignment of the rights. I would be grateful for your point of view regarding the issue of copyright as this must be cleared up before any further work or any decision is made on the use of your submission. I would like to hear from you by January 6th 1999." End of quote.

I responded via a telephone call to the then CEO of the LOC, and suggested that they make me a reasonable financial offer for the use of my logo, which, if I agreed to the offer, I would have then provided an invoice to be paid, which would have then cleared the way for the assignment of the rights they needed for FIFA.

I did not hear from the then CEO of the LOC for a while thereafter. I assumed that since financial compensation was required for the assignment of the rights, they were no longer interested in using my logo.

Then on March 10th 1999, I received another faxed letter dated February 1st 1999 from the then CEO of the LOC. Referring to the fax letter dated December 29th 1998, the then most recent faxed letter dated February 1st 1999 indicated and I quote once again, "To date we have not had a response and I need to know now; or maybe you have changed your mind about your design being used." End of quote.

His then latest letter suggested that I did not respond to his faxed letter dated December 29th 1998, when I did in fact respond via a phone call and suggested that they make me a financial offer for the use of my logo.

It then appeared that Warner's Local Organizing Committee were seeking the use of my logo free of charge. But it was an official FIFA event, and there was absolutely no way I was going to allow myself to be professionally exploited more than I had already been. And certainly not at the FIFA level, when I knew that the world's governing body could have afforded to pay the full value for the use of my logo.

It was not inconceivable to me, that once I gave the LOC permission to use my logo free of charge, they may have then turned around and billed FIFA for it. Whereby, they would have made a false declaration of the logo being a cost attached to the 2001 U-17 World Cup event, when the LOC itself would have paid absolutely nothing for its use. And in the end, one or more individuals may have been financially enriched at my expense. And I would have never known about it.

So, since no financial offer was made, or seemed to be forthcoming for the use of my proposed 2001 FIFA U-17 World Cup Finals tournament logo, I decided not to waste anymore of my time, and elected not to respond to the LOC CEO's letter dated February 1st 1999. There was no further communication between us thereafter.

STEP ONE TO U.S. RESIDENCY

Having both left for the U.S. in December of '98, my girlfriend Alicia returned to Trinidad in mid-'99. However, I spent all of that year in the U.S. to assist my mother with securing her U.S. citizenship. She eventually obtained it at an official swearing-in ceremony on September 17th 1999. It was another one of those days that saw her beaming with unbridled pride and joy.

During that year in the U.S., I spent lots of bonding time with my daughter who was then 10 going on 11 years old. I remember we attended the huge Net Aid music concert, which was held at Giants Stadium in East Rutherford New Jersey on October 9th of '99.

Performers included, Puff Daddy, Busta Rhymes, Mary J Blige, Sting, Bono from U2, Wyclef Jean and Lil' Kim among others. Quincy Jones also took the stage during Bono's performance. We thoroughly enjoyed the event. Seeing all those megastar Artistes perform live in person, certainly had me wanting to get back into music.

Still, the sport of football and the marketing aspect in particular, remained my preferred career path at the time. But with Jack Warner at the helm back in my homeland, and being that I was then on his "Blacklist", I knew that my long-term professional future was then going to be in the United States.

I therefore decided to file for permanent U.S. residency. And although our relationship was extremely strained at the time, I still decided to do my older brother a huge favor, and also filed for him at the same time at my own expense.

Subsequent to my mother obtaining her U.S. citizenship, I then secured all the benefits for her that she was then entitled to as a senior citizen with disabilities, that she would have needed to survive. And so, apart from the need to upgrade her dwelling, she had all that was necessary for her to live fairly comfortably.

With my then latest New York mission completed, late that December of '99, about a week after my mother's 68th birthday on December 22nd and after almost exactly 1 year, I returned to Trinidad. My major concern continued to be the fact that my mother would still be living alone, as apart from being deaf, she was then also dealing with multiple medical issues.

At a point in time during that year that I was in New York sorting things out for our mother, I was forced to call on my older brother for him to assist in resolving a situation that developed back at my Woodbrook residence. He refused to assist, which created an enormous amount of tension between us upon my return to Trinidad.

The key to the city of Quezon, Philippines, which I received for my contribution to the 1992 Global Youth Earthsaving Summit, in my capacity as a United Nations Environment Program Goodwill Ambassador.

Cecile Alvarez (left) pointing out the location of the Philippines at the United Nations Environment Program (UNEP) New York office, after I received my designation of UNEP Goodwill Ambassador; at right in photo is the late Rolph Warner, journalist, who covered the ceremony.

I am back row second from left, at an event in the Philippines together with other foreign delegates.

Wearing the anti-drugs merchandise for the song which saw me bestowed with the UNEP Goodwill Ambassador designation.

Entertainer Jo Ramos, the then Philippines President's daughter with whom I performed.

In conversation with then top Philippines Hip Hop artiste, Francis Magalona and his group.

313

1994: meeting the king of football himself, Edson Arantes do Nascimento "Pele"; A childhood dream come through.

With Cameroon football legend Roger Milla.   With Peruvian legend Teofilo "Nene" Cubillas.

With French legend Michel Platini.

Performing at Soccerfest Los Angeles, at World
Cup USA '94 at the LA Convention Centre.

Smitten by the beautiful Brazilian samba
dancers, before one of my performances.

My vantage point for the USA '94 World Cup
Semi-Final game between Brazil and Sweden.

Chillin' at the bar at my LA hotel with former T&T national
player Anthony Douglas and the man we called "Zabeda".

Getting in touch with the spirit of MJ on a
visit to the Hollywood Walk Of Fame.

A visit to Vegas on my way back to New York
from the USA '94 World Cup Finals.

Me in red at a meeting with several of Trinidad and Tobago's top sports administrators and football coaches to discuss football matters.

With three of my all time favorite Trinidad and Tobago football players (all long retired); In photo at left; with Russell Latapy (center) and Leonson Lewis (right). In photo at right, Dwight Yorke, Manchester United legend being presented with a gift of my Nosila brand merchandise.

A visit to ground zero to pay my respects in the immediate aftermath of the September 11th 2001 New York terrorist attack.

With my then very close friend and well known T&T sports enthusiast TansleyThompson.

Me in white socks, with members of one of several "fete match" football teams I would have helped formed and played with.

Photo at left: the house at Luis Street, Woodbrook where I resided, the front portion which I was converting into a store space called the "dressing room" to fulfill one of my ambitions to sell football gear under my Nosila brand; photo at right shows what the space was shaping up to look like; inset is "The Maga Mass crew" Carlyle Mason (front) Rory Loregnard and yours truly.

317

2003: returning to the place that helped shape my character, the Mahaica Oval Point Fortin, in an effort to give back some of what it had given me; this was in the form of my charity youth football camp, which I named after my local childhood football idol cum Trinidad and Tobago football icon and Point Fortin resident Leroy De Leon, who was also the camp's chief coach.

The camp was also staged in Port of Spain; In the above photos, girls and boys who were involved in that leg of the camp.

In photo above from left to right, the former Trinidad and Tobago Minister of Sports & Youth Affairs, Leroy De Leon and former T&T football team captain Dexter Francis inspecting the Italian made prototype of my Nosila brand football boots; In the background looking on is Tansley Thompson.

Getting a tour of the office of Gordon Taylor, then chief executive of the Professional Footballers Association in Manchester England, during my visit in 2007 to solicit support for the Football Players Association of Trinidad & Tobago; a mission that I successfully accomplished.

Meeting Jermain Defoe (photo left) and Robbie Keane (photo right) after witnessing the Sunderland vs Tottenham game during my UK visit.

Hanging out with T&T legends and then Sunderland players Carlos Edwards and Dwight Yorke (not in photo).

At the 1993 wedding of my younger brother Brian; In photo from left: my older brother Evans, me, my mother, a family friend, Brian and front, my deceased sister Cheryl.

My sister Carol Mason.

With my brother Evans and sister Sandra.

My sister Cheryl Mclawrence.

With my favorite cousins, brothers Michael aka "BoPeep" (photo left) and David (photo right).

Photos above; my daughter Lenecia during her early stages of growth.

Lenecia and I.

My wife Alicia.

321

Posing with my NOSILA 6 panel comet football, which was manufactured in India.

CHAPTER FIVE

2000 AND BEYOND

A BUSINESS VENTURE ON HOLD

With my business relationship with Jack Warner then history, and with my U.S. permanent residency process likely to take up to 4 years, 2000 started off with my intention to finally open up my Dressing Room Sports Store in Trinidad, which would sell my NOSILA brand exclusively as originally planned.

I then had inventory, having produced and shipped quantities of initials items, including a variety of T-Shirts, Caps, Tank-Tops and Sweat Pants while in New York, before I returned to Trinidad. I had plans to add a line of NOSILA football uniforms to my inventory, which I intended to get manufactured in Trinidad, before officially opening up the store.

Meanwhile, with the enormous amount of tension then existing between us since my return to Trinidad in late December of '99, the ongoing conflict between me and my older brother continued to escalate. And things eventually came to a head when I was informed via my new lease in mid-May of 2000, that there was going to be a rent increase from June 1st, when the new lease would kick in.

Our relationship was then at the point where we were not even on speaking terms. So, I wrote my older brother a formal letter informing him of the imminent rent increase, which meant that his portion for sub-letting would also have to be increased. In my letter I specified his increase amount and the payment terms going forward, if he chose to continue his occupancy.

I needed all the cash I could get my hands on for my store business. So, in my letter I also made a formal request for him to finally settle some of his outstanding financial debts that he owed to me at the time, including for his plane ticket to return to Trinidad, which was then 3 years overdue. In response, he chose to vacate the premises, without settling any of his outstanding debts to me.

My older brother elected not to tell family members the true story; as according to our sister Sandra, with whom he is extremely close and who also still lives in Trinidad, he told her that I threw him out of the residence for no reason, apart from which he made other false accusations against me.

His blatant lies would be subsequently relayed by the said sister via a letter to our mother, who unfortunately, believed them, which then served to subject me to periodical episodes of verbal abuse from our mother, on account of my older brother and his lies.

After he left, my older brother was accommodated once again by the same friend who also accommodate him at his Belmont residence many years before. That friend had since relocated to Cocorite in West Port of Spain. My older brother had lived with me continuously at my Luis Street Woodbrook residence since returning from the U.S. in 1997, making it a total of 3 years.

At the time he vacated, the transformation of the entire front portion of the residence into the sports store space had been almost completed. It was then just a matter of installing slot boards, shelves, and racks, and purchasing manikins to display specific product items.

The first phase of my marketing strategy for my NOSILA brand, was to use local Trinidad and Tobago born sports men and women of the past and those who were active, with local, regional and international name and where applicable face recognition, for advertising and promotion, to first establish the brand in the local market, and thereafter the regional and eventually the international market, with the inclusion of regional and international male and female sportsmen and women.

It was a strategy that I based on the historical fact that our elite level sportsmen and women had always been, and had continued to be as good as any and better than many. Therefore, in my professional opinion, they were marketable enough to successfully promote the brand.

Towards the aforementioned initial marketing objective, my company then initially entered into endorsement agreements with several local football superstars, including Russell Latapy, Leonson Lewis, Stern John, Arnold Dwarika and Brent Sancho. At the time, all but one of them plied their trade in European leagues.

Dwight Yorke, who then had the highest profile and name and face recognition amongst our foreign based players on the local, regional and the international scene, as member of the universally famous Manchester United Football Club in England, had also pledged to help promote my NOSILA brand.

In fact, Dwight was actually the very first high-profile Trinbagonian football player that I approached, when he was then a star of the Aston Villa team. That was way back in 1995, when the very first NOSILA product item, a red, white and blue track suit was produced locally.

Minus Dwight, since we did not enter into a formal agreement, there were photo shoots done, involving all of the other players wearing the NOSILA brand, which were to be used in components for the advertising campaign. Sheldon Monderoy, the then world ranked Trinidad and Tobago long distance runner, was also added to the list of endorsers. I also intended to involve Hasely Crawford, Trinidad and Tobago's 1976 Olympic 100 meters gold medal winner, and eventually had discussions with him, to which he was very receptive.

Through one Wally Thompson, I had also tried to secure an audience with the then on fire local sprinter Ato Boldon, to discuss any possibilities that may have existed to also involve him. Wally happens to be the older brother of Tansley, and was then operating his accounting business on the ground floor of the two floor Luis Street Woodbrook residence. Like Tansley before him, Wally and I became very good friends. He was always there to offer words of encouragement, which I sincerely appreciated, because I really needed it at times. "So, Wally, wherever you may be, I say thank you."

But with the then most recent family issue, courtesy of my older brother, I simply could not continue to ignore all the family drama, the extreme amounts of stress, both mental and emotional that accompanied it, especially over more recent years then, and the toll it had been taking on me. It was becoming too much.

I knew that I had been running on fumes for some time, and it was only my innate drive, determination and resilience that was enabling me to keep on going with respects to my own ambitions. Still, at the end of the day, I am only human.

Given the then current situation, in the interest of my own wellbeing, I decided that it was time to take a much needed and well-deserved extended break. My personal wellbeing certainly wasn't worth risking, over achieving my business ambitions.

So, at the point when I was on the verge of fulfilling my Ideapreneurial (from the word "Ideapreneur", which I invented to describe myself as a business professional in the business world) ambitions, I decided to suspend my pursuit of my Dressing Room Sports Store business venture indefinitely.

But as fate would have it, for me that much-needed extended break would only be wishful thinking, because around that same time, just by happenstance, I learnt that my older brother's son, who had immigrated from Trinidad to the U.S. with his mother since about the age of 5 or 6, was incarcerated there, as a result of a run-in with the law.

And since he was only a green card holder, he was going to be deported back to Trinidad in the near future. I believe he would have been in his mid to late 20's at the time. I learnt about his predicament after dialing a U.S. number in my address book that had no name attached to it, thinking it was that of a certain U.S. contact that I was trying to reach at the time.

It turned out to have been my nephew's mother phone number, which I could not readily identify, because I had never called it before. I had not seen or spoken to her for many years. Suffice it to say that in the then given circumstances, she was extremely happy that I called the number, because she was then able to speak to someone who would have known the whereabouts of my older brother, and who would have been able to contact him to let him know what was going on with his son. They lived in Connecticut.

She was extremely distressed about the situation. She was desperate for my brother's support, and wanted him to travel to the U.S. ASAP. But I knew that he couldn't since he did not have a visa, and would have been unable to obtain one at the time to travel to the U.S. I informed his son's mother of that fact, upon which she then made a heartfelt appeal for me to come to the U.S. asap, because she really needed support, which was quite understandable. So, I told her that I would come.

A week later I was on a plane to New York, reuniting with my mother and with my daughter once again. But I knew that I also had another matter to attend to, which I could not reveal to my mother. Given her medical issues, which included HBP, I knew that such news about her first grandchild would have definitely affected her health.

I visited my nephew at a prison that was about a 2½ to 3 hours drive from where they lived, in what appeared to be an upper middle-class neighborhood in New Haven Connecticut. His mother's brother, who also lived elsewhere in New Haven, drove. Accompanied by my nephew's mother, we made the journey to the prison. It was almost night time when we arrived.

I went in alone to visit him. For me it was an extremely sad and disturbing experience, seeing the nephew whom I had taught how to ride a bike back in Trinidad when he was just a kid, in such a situation. Apart from a prison guard who stood several yards off to the side and kept very close watch, we were the only ones in the large room, set up with lots of tables and chairs for such visits to inmates, from friends and family.

I was allowed about 15 minutes with my nephew, during which time he shared some of his prison experiences with me. All I could have done was offer positive words of comfort. He also shared a certain experience he had with his father while his father was still in New York. When the time was up, we engaged each other in a quick embrace and I was off. The image of him sitting across from me at the small table in prison garb, stayed with me.

After spending some more time with my daughter and mother, I returned to Trinidad, which was about three weeks later. The telephone communication between me and my nephew's mother continued, since for some reason, his father really didn't seem to care. She eventually received their son's deportation date and arrival time, and asked me to pick him up from the airport. Once again, I told her that I would of course.

I contacted my older brother and informed him, and expected him to instantly volunteer to accompany me since it was his son. But to my shock, he did not. I picked up my nephew at the airport on the night of his arrival, and took him directly to my Luis Street residence.

My nephew had only visited Trinidad a couple of times since he had been living in the U.S. So, with very limited knowledge of finding his way around Trinidad in general and Port of Spain in particular, he lived with me for several months, during which time there was no form of support or contributions from either his father or mother. I eventually managed to secure a part time job for my nephew.

But I already had plans to take an extended break. And given all that had transpired most recently then, I definitely needed it. As such, my nephew had to eventually move in with his father, who had relocated from Cocorite. He then lived on the top floor of a two-story residence on Buller Street Woodbrook, not very far from my own residence. I visited periodically.

I had arrived at a crossroads. And as difficult a decision it was to make, I decided to shelve my Dressing Room Sports Store business venture permanently, after years of blood, sweat, stress, sacrifice and substantial financial investment to bring it to the point it had gotten. I just really needed to get away from it all. I needed to reset.

With the store space almost ready for stocking, I vacated the 42 Luis Street Woodbrook residence for what would be the final time in December 2000. I then returned to the Big Apple once again, for another reunion with my mother and my daughter. And not for the first time in the 9 years we had been together as a couple up to that point, leaving Alicia by her lonesome.

However, my trip to New York would be different that time around; as apart from spending time with my mother and my daughter, I also used it as a time for self-reflection and introspection.

Looking back at my life during the process, and having fulfilled my dreams, even in the face of lifelong trials and tribulations, I wanted others to know that pursuing and fulfilling their own dreams, whatever they may be, was also possible in spite of having to deal with their own trials and tribulations. I wanted to use myself as an example, and needed to find a way to do it.

The next thought that then entered my mind was, hey, then why don't I also use the time to start writing a book about my life? The thought was so extremely stimulating; psychologically, emotionally and spiritually that it turned into action. I then started putting pen to paper and began to record events and experiences from my very early childhood that I could recall. It then progressed from there.

I was also fortunate that my mother was there to answer lots of the questions I had about those very early years, especially those for which I had little or no recollection. I eventually transferred what I had been writing down on paper to a laptop. From that point onwards, I continued working on and off on what to me would be my most significant lifetime undertaking.

And as much as I really needed an extended break, my natural drive and ambition just would not allow me to take one. My vision and steadfast commitment to the purpose for bringing my NOSILA sports brand to the market, saw me continuing to work on it.

Having permanently vacated the residence where the store space was already set up, my plan then was to get my NOSILA brand into local sporting goods retail outlets. So, while in New York, I designed and had a full color introductory NOSILA catalog produced, displaying initial items under the brand. I also had a website constructed but only as a showroom at that point.

I returned to Trinidad in May of 2001 and took up temporary residence in Tacarigua in east Trinidad. I then had a quantity of samples done locally of the first in the line of my NOSILA football kits, which was the NOSILA football kit signature design, utilizing the 3 action lines devise contained in the NOSILA logo.

Unfortunately, the official Trinidad launch for my brand suffered yet another setback not long thereafter. I then decided to rethink my entire NOSILA business plan and especially the marketing strategy. However, I remained steadfast in my commitment and determination to see the venture come to fruition.

In August 2001 I returned to New York; the place where I always find inspiration. About a month later, Alicia visited for a 3 weeks vacation. She arrived on Sunday September 9th. She stayed in Harlem at the residence of my daughter's mother.

Alicia and I had plans to visit the Statue of Liberty on the Tuesday morning after she had a full day's rest on Monday. We were supposed to be there before 9:00 a.m., since we wanted to get the early tour, that would have taken us all the way up to the crown of the statue.

But I had forgotten my camera back at my mother's apartment in Brooklyn. So, I decided to travel back to Brooklyn on that Monday night of September 10th to pick it up and return to Harlem early the following morning Tuesday, when we would then head down to the Statue of Liberty as planned.

But as fate would have it, I overslept. I was only jolted out of what was a deep sleep, when the telephone that sat on a small table beside my bed rang. It was my sister Cheryl, who, as mentioned earlier, lived only a half block away. "Ali! Ali! Put on de TV quick! Put on de TV quick!" She said in an overly anxious tone of voice.

With very heavy eyes and still holding the phone to my ear, I scrambled down to the foot of the bed and reached for the knob that turned on the television, which had no remote control. "Click." The television came on after a few seconds.

The picture on the screen showed one of the two Twin Towers in downtown Manhattan bellowing smoke. It was surreal. "Yuh seeing wuh going on!" my sister continued nervously. "Yeah," I replied in total astonishment, after which we hung up the phones.

At that precise moment, with my eyes glued to the TV, I saw a plane crash into the second tower. "Buh wuh de hell goin' on dey boy?" I nervously asked myself. I could not believe what I was seeing. It couldn't be real I thought to myself. I kept on staring at the television screen trying to wrap my mind around what I was actually seeing, during which time it was revealed that it was a terrorist attack.

I jumped out of bed and went to the kitchen to call my mother into the bedroom to see what was happening. Then there were subsequent reports with accompanying images of the Pentagon also being under attack. The images were terrifying.

My mother and I spent all day into the very late night in front of the television set, watching the day's events as they unfolded, over and over and over again in total disbelief. But it would all eventually sink in.

A few days later, Alicia and I visited the site that would become known as "Ground Zero". Suffice it to say that her vacation was most definitely affected by that dreadful September 11th event. She returned to Trinidad as scheduled. Assured that both my mother and my daughter were doing fine, I returned to Trinidad and my temporary residence in east Trinidad in late 2001.

In early 2002, after obtaining his number from my cousin BoPeep, I contacted my childhood Point Fortin and Trinidad and Tobago football idol, Leroy DeLeon. He lived in Arizona at the time, and was then attached to a local football club there as a youth team coach.

My cousin BoPeep lived in Florida. Apparently, he spoke to Leroy often and had told him about my NOSILA sports brand, which as mention earlier, was focusing mainly on football apparel and equipment. Leroy had since visited the NOSILA website and had seen the NOSILA signature uniform on the website showroom, and liked what he saw.

Upon contacting him, Leroy requested samples with a view to my company possibly doing business with his Arizona club. The samples were sent off to him within 24 hours. Once he received the package, which included the cost per kit, minus the socks, which was being imported from Italy, he then presented it to his club President and Board Members. He subsequently reported that they were all very impressed with our "Made in Trinidad" product.

I could not have been more excited about the prospects. But my then Trinidad based company was going up against some U.S. companies, who were also vying for the Arizona football club's business. So, I simply had to keep my fingers crossed and wait patiently for their final decision. And so, I did.

THE MULTI-MILLION DOLLAR GOVERNMENT PROJECT: MY EXPERIENCE WITH THE THEN MINISTER OF SPORT

Meanwhile, having already made the decision to immigrate to the U.S., and with the process ongoing, I had the option of simply staying on in the U.S. during any one of my visits there, while I awaited documentation to legally reside there. However, my girlfriend Alicia was still in Trinidad. And I was also still desirous of continuing to serve my homeland. Those two factors were the reasons that I kept going back and forth.

Having long made the decision to serve through the sport of football, and refusing to be deterred from doing so by Jack Warner & Co., I conceived an idea that was based on the premise of reviving the local game at the community level across the twin Islands.

The then "powers that be", who had been the overseers of the local game for decades, had taken it away from the communities and by extension the people, which in my humble opinion, contributed significantly to its continued rapid decline over those years.

My idea was to introduce the Trinidad & Tobago Minor League Football Championship, where in addition to cash awards, teams would have been competing for the "NOSILA CUP", named after my company's sports brand, which would have been sponsoring the specially designed trophy.

The competition would have become known and marketed as "THE NOSILA CUP". I announced my company's intention to introduce the competition in 2003, through a press release in the local daily newspapers in 2002. And after months of hard work and preparation, I was ready to launch the initial phase of the marketing campaign for the competition.

One of the primary objectives of the competition was to involve the nations youths in constructive recreation, as against seeing them involving themselves in destructive activities. As such, it was scheduled to begin in late June / early July, when most local schools would have then been closed for 2 months for the annual July to September vacation.

With a view to achieving the stated objective, each team would have been required to include at least 5 teenage players, who were deemed good enough to participate, with the aim of also discovering young talent.

Being that it was going to be a nationwide competition with a focus on youth involvement, I thought that it would have been a good idea to obtain the official endorsement of the Trinidad & Tobago Ministry of Sport and Youth Affairs for my project. To that end, I secured an audience with the then Minister of Sport and Youth Affairs, who I would have been meeting for the very first time.

As had become the norm for such, I invited and was accompanied by Tansley Thompson to the meeting. That meeting with the then Minister of Sport and Youth Affairs, was held on February 5th 2002 and began at 3:45 p.m. Also in attendance was one Anil Roberts. Like the then Minister, I was meeting Anil Roberts for the very first time.

Roberts' engagement in the proceedings was minimal. After I introduced myself and Tansley, I shared my professional background with the then Minister. I then revealed what was then considered confidential details of my "NOSILA CUP" project.

But what would have seen the project assume even more significance, was its potential to have a positive social impact, especially in communities where unemployment was a major social issue, thereby making said communities more susceptible to illicit drug trafficking and other crimes. As such, I was incorporating an integrated Anti-Drugs / Anti-Crime Advertising Campaign into my project, details of which were also revealed to the then Minister.

The then Minister could not suppress his excitement over what was being presented to him. So much so, that he interrupted me a few times during my presentation, to express his enthusiasm over what he was hearing at that juncture.

Before I had a chance to finish my entire presentation, the then Minister interrupted me for what was the final time, indicating that he had heard enough, upon which he expressed that he was very impressed with my idea and presentation.

He then promptly asked if I would agree to adapt my original project idea to other sports, more specifically, small-goal football, basketball, wind-ball cricket and net-ball, to be implemented as a project of the Ministry of Sport and Youth Affairs. In other words, will I agree to have my original idea adapted to the sports he specified, then have the project implemented as his Ministry's idea, which would then be called "The Community Sports Festival". He also offered a slogan for the project, which was "No Time For Crime".

I viewed working together with the Sport Ministry on such a meaningful initiative, as an opportunity to make my ultimate contribution, which was to utilize the power of sports to positively impact local youths and communities, and by extension, the entire Trinidad and Tobago society in general.

I therefore verbally agreed to grant the Minister his request, but under certain terms and conditions; the most significant of which was that I would be contracted to oversee the nationwide implementation of what would then be "the government's project", to ensure a professional level of execution, for which I would be paid for the use of my idea, as well as for my professional services relative to overseeing its implementation.

Upon reaching our verbal agreement, I was immediately commissioned by the then Minister to develop a detailed proposal for "The Community Sports Festival" project, inclusive of the budget. He informed me that the proposal would then be presented to the top executives from the energy sector companies at a breakfast meeting, for the purpose of securing funding for the project.

His plan for funding the project immediately raised a red flag. I could not understand why the funding wasn't coming directly from the Government coffers, especially given the fact that from all reports, addressing the then very serious and rapidly escalating crime situation in the country, was to have been "a government priority".

I thought, if so, then isn't the project critical enough to warrant total funding from the government itself? From that initial thought, and being the very deep thinker that I am, other questions then entered my mind. For example; did the then Minister himself really believe in the initiative and its "No Time For Crime" message? Was it all simply just another political gimmick for the purpose of scoring political points, and for which I was going to be used?

My perceptive instincts subsequently kicked in to provide the answers to those questions. Still, I was trying to convince myself that my instincts were wrong on that occasion, because if they were, then my involvement would certainly have been well worth the time and effort.

Following our meeting, which lasted for just over an hour, the then Minister arranged for us to meet immediately with Hasely Crawford for a second meeting. The Trinidad and Tobago 1976 Montreal Olympics 100 meters gold medalist, held a position at the Ministry at the time. Tansley and I were both already acquainted with Hasely.

I was instructed by the then Minister to brief Hasely about what was discussed, and the decision that was taken in the meeting with him. I complied. The meeting with Crawford lasted for about 15 minutes. After the Crawford meeting, the then Minister then instructed us to meet with Anil Roberts, who, it then became clearer, was also attached to the Minister's office in some capacity at the time, for a third and final session. He and Tansley appeared to have already known each other.

In that meeting, the discussions were focused on my preparation of the budget and funding for the project. But it was what Anil Roberts himself instructed at the end of our session with respects to the budget, that left me speechless.

He, Tansley and I had exited his office and were approaching the building's elevator, when he looked me in the eyes and directly instructed, and I quote, "an' put something in dey fuh meh eh," he paused then he continued, "an' fuh he too," meaning Tansley. Anil Roberts was instructing me to add an undisclosed amount of money to the budget, which would go to him.

With my initial budget estimate for the project, which was discussed in our meeting, amounting to millions, I could have only concluded that by "something" he meant a substantial amount. I did not respond. I could not respond.

Here it was where Anil Roberts and I were meeting each other for the very first time; and we were doing so for the sole purpose of his then employer, the Government of Trinidad and Tobago, through its Ministry of Sport and Youth Affairs, which he was representing, addressing the extremely serious social issue of the escalating crime situation in the country, through an extremely critical initiative. But clearly, Roberts was also viewing the project as an opportunity to enrich himself; and wanted to use "poor me" to do so.

It was obvious that he was assuming that everyone he came into contact with under such circumstances, was into such illegal and unethical business practices, which was to him quite normal, it seemed. I most certainly wasn't. Therefore, I had absolutely zero interest in being initiated into his world.

Upon Roberts giving his quite damning instruction, a second red flag was raised. It most certainly gave me a bit of insight into how corruption worked at the political level in my homeland. I was more than grateful for that bit of political education.

With two red flags raised, I was then having second thoughts about my involvement with the project. But I had already exposed my documented idea in detail to the then Minister, and had left a copy of the document with him. As such, I felt that I should complete the assignment, because I was 100% certain that if I aborted it, my idea would have been plagiarized and implemented anyway, and I would not have been paid for its use. As such, I completed and delivered the proposal document to the then Minister.

It was a very comprehensive project document, with the cost of implementation at an estimated TT$24 million. I was then pumped and ready for the presentation to the representatives from the local energy sector. But there would be disappointment.

After working day and night to complete the document by the initially set deadline, I was subsequently and might I add, very casually informed by the then Minister, that the breakfast meeting was postponed to a later date. The reason he gave was that it was difficult to get all the invitees to attend on the initially scheduled date.

I thought, okay, fair enough. But then there was more. The then Minister felt that $24 million was asking much too much from the multi-million and possibly multi-billion-dollar energy corporations. Given the significance of the initiative, I most definitely did not share the then Minister's opinion, but kept mine to myself. So back to the drawing board I went.

Five and a half weeks, four proposal re-dos, with each coming in at TT$19 million, $12 million, $9 million, and $6 million respectively for implementation, and a mountain of frustration and stress later, the then Minister then decided that the TT$12 million version of the project was acceptable.

Even more frustrating and distressing, was the fact that I had absolutely nothing to show for all of my time and hard work up to that point. I then felt that I should not waste any more of my time and energy, cut my losses and simply head back to the U.S.

So, I contacted the then Minister to inform him that I could not just simply wait around any longer for the meeting to happen, so I was returning to the U.S. It was only then that he informed me, that he had finally gotten confirmation from all of the invitees, and the breakfast meeting was definitely on. I noted that he did not even see it fit to contact me to relay that information.

It was being held at Hotel Normandie in St Anns. Being that it was a breakfast meeting, I had planned to set up for my presentation the night before. So, I made a request for 3 fairly large presentation boards that belonged to the Ministry, to be transported to the venue late in the evening the day before the event, which was scheduled for the morning of March 20th 2002.

I waited all evening and all night into the wee hours of the morning of the event, for them to arrive on site. They never did. An hour before the event was to have started, they still did not arrive. I then decided that I'd had enough, and was no longer going to be involved. I therefore did not change into my professional garb.

I then retreated to my room at the same hotel. Half an hour before the meeting was to have started, I went back down to inform the Minister of my decision. That's when I discovered that the presentation boards had finally been delivered. I personally felt it was an effort to sabotage the meeting, given what had transpired during my efforts to secure them in the first place.

With the help of a friend, I proceeded to mount the presentation. While we were completing the task, attendees were arriving for the meeting, which was not a good look at all. But I simply did not care at that point; because by that time I was literally "out of it", physically, mentally and emotionally. I did not want to be there. And I definitely did not want to be involved with the project any more.

My head and more importantly, my heart, was no longer in it. And I was fully aware that given my then state of mind, there was a real possibility that my presentation could turn out to be poor. However, I decided that I would simply go through the motions of my presentation, to ensure that I would receive what would represent my initial payment for the project, which would be for preparing the proposal document.

After the presentation materials were mounted, I went back to my room, took a shower and did the image transformation thing. And as I expected, by the time I returned to the venue the meeting was already in progress. It was well attended. I took my seat at the head table. One Ashwin Creed was addressing the meeting at the time. The then Minister followed. At the end of his address, which included excerpts from my Community Sports Festival proposal document, he introduced and invited me to the podium to make my presentation.

Because I then had zero enthusiasm to do so, my presentation was weak. No one had to tell me. I knew it myself. It certainly did not enhance any chance I may have had of being a political spokesperson, if I was ever entertaining the thought. Fortunately, I would never be interested in such a job.

More seriously though, making presentations had always been one of my strong points. During the almost 15 years I had spent in the

Advertising / Graphic Design industry and thereafter, I had made countless successful presentations.

And as one who always take a great amount of pride in any and
everything I do; I knew that I had not done myself justice. And I imagine
that I did not do the "Honorable Minister" any favors that morning of
Wednesday March 20th 2002. But all things considered, neither bothered
me one bit.

At the end of the meeting, each corporate representative in attendance, received a copy of the "Community Sports Festival / No Time For
Crime" project proposal document in which full details were outlined, to
take with them for their consideration for funding for the project.

I subsequently wrote a letter to Anil Roberts, directly addressing the
matter relating to his "an' put something in dey fuh meh eh," instruction.
I delayed its delivery, because I wanted to ensure that I was first paid for
my work before I delivered it to him.

Once I was paid, which took a few extremely frustrating weeks, upon
returning to New York once again shortly thereafter, the letter was then
faxed to Roberts at the office of the Ministry of Sport and Youth Affairs.
I kept the original letter, which I still have in my possession.

Whilst surfing the internet while in New York several months later,
lo and behold, I came upon a press release from the Ministry of Sport and
Youth Affairs in one of Trinidad's daily newspapers. I read in fair detail
about the said Sports Ministry's and more specifically the then Sports
Minister's plans to work together with the Trinidad and Tobago Football
Association, to introduce a "community football league".

The plan read exactly like the one I revealed in confidence to the
then Minister at our very first meeting several months before. As a matter
of fact, in the newspaper article they even used the word "Conference",
which was the exact terminology I used to describe the specific zones in
my original "NOSILA CUP" idea. I could not believe it! "Hell no!" I said
to myself, sitting behind the computer.

Not very long thereafter, I was back in Trinidad. Once there, I delivered a letter to the then "Honorable Minister", drawing his attention to the specific article and its contents, and requested an audience with him, to allow him the opportunity to explain the unquestionable similarity to my original idea, which was revealed to him in confidence, several months before. For the obvious reason, he ignored my request.

However, a former colleague from my time in the Trinidad Advertising / Graphic Design industry, who was then employed at the Ministry, subsequently confirmed that the then Minister had in fact extracted original ideas from both my "NOSILA CUP" and "Community Sports Festival" documents, and included them as his and his Ministry's, in the official national sports policy document of the Ministry of Sport and Youth Affairs.

That fact would be reconfirmed by the then Minister himself years later in June of 2005, on the television sports program called Spalk. I heard it with my very own ears, when he revealed on the program that ideas from the 2002 Community Sports Festival project were included, and would in fact be implemented, as part of the Trinidad and Tobago Government's National Sports Policy. The Spalk program where he made the revelation was hosted by none other than Anil Roberts, his former Ministry associate, on the Gayelle television channel.

Roberts himself made specific reference to me, when addressing the 2002 Community Sports Festival matter, in an article he wrote that was published in the Trinidad Guardian Sports Arena dated Wednesday June 8th 2003, where he was extremely critical of the then Minister's handling of the project.

Having used my idea(s) for the 2002 Community Sports Festival initiative without financially compensating me, the then Minister did in fact breach our verbal agreement, whereby we agreed that I would have been paid for the said use.

By his very own admission, the then Minister effectively plagiarized my ideas. Additionally, the then Minister also included written excerpts from my documented ideas for which he possessed a copy, as part of the government's National Sports Policy without my consent, thereby committing an act of copyright infringement against me.

Like so many other highly creative Trinbagonians, who earn a living through conceiving, developing and selling ideas, whether they be visual or otherwise; tangible or intangible, I have been a victim of plagiarism in my homeland. In some instances, by people in high places as revealed in this passage, with no recourse except for if one decided to physically confront the individual engaging in the act, and or expose them publicly, as I am doing here and now.

In a land of an estimated 1.3 million people, where creative minds abound among the common folks such as myself, sadly, the harsh reality is, it also happens to be a land where creativity and the creative arts are grossly underappreciated and undervalued, by those whose agenda is simply to exploit it.

WIL' AND J-WILLI': AWAKENING "THE BEAST"

After my unpleasant experiences with Jack Warner & Co. years before, I will admit that I very foolishly chose to ignore the lessons that I was supposed to have learnt from them. And so, being a patriot who was also a committed self-confessed servant of the local game, I was suckered in again. That time around, by two seemingly respectable millionaire owners of two different professional football clubs. They however, turned out to be nothing more than two unscrupulous millionaire businessmen.

I refer to them throughout this passage as "Wil' and J-Willi'"; shortened versions of their first and last names respectively, because to me personally, those versions totally fit the two dishonest, shameless characters I would come to know. They would actually inspire me to write a song about them.

J-Willi' was the one who approached me. And I may have been suck-ered in again because of the fact that I had known him from back in the 70s. I actually knew his entire family. One of his older brothers also attended Vessigny Secondary School during the time I was there. I was one class ahead of him. I guess I assumed that J-Willi' had retained the core values, that I am certain was inculcated by his parents while he was growing up.

His approach then led to a telephone conversation on Tuesday March 26th 2002 to be exact, and two subsequent meetings at a Chinese Restaurant at the Valpark shopping Plaza Valsayn, in east Trinidad. My first meeting with him was unproductive. He used that session to mostly vent about Jack Warner, whom he claimed then owed him TT$560,000.00, after his club had won some local competition during the 2001 football season, and was not paid the prize money.

For our second sit down however, to my surprise, two other individ-uals were also in attendance on the night. One was the very well-known and highly respected high-profile local coach Jamaal Shabazz, with whom I was already very much acquainted.

The other individual was a local Caucasian looking gentleman whom I never saw before. J-Willi' introduced me to him, upon which he informed me that he had a stake in one of the teams. I will refer to him as Wil' as stated earlier. Like both Wil' and J-Willi', Jamaal Shabazz was also directly and closely attached to a club in the then local professional football League.

Disappointingly, Jack Warner was on the agenda once again. And as it turned out, as many others also were I'm sure, those three gentlemen were of the impression that I was fired by Warner, from my previous mar-keting positions with his various football entities.

J-Willi' began to delve into that particular matter once again. But to avoid turning it into another meeting about Jack Warner, I quickly sug-gested that we focus on the item that was supposed to be on the agenda, which was their desire to employ my professional marketing services, for what was in essence going to be a new professional football league.

Apparently, Jack Warner, who everyone knew financed the local game for his own intents and purposes, had decided to pull his finances after the 2001 season. The league was then in crisis. So, the clubs themselves were then going to be taking over the operations.

They were in desperate need of my professional services, but J-Willi claimed that "de league eh hah no money tuh pay mih." So, there they were; J-Willi', an extremely successful millionaire businessman and professional football club owner; and Wil', a total stranger to me, whom I would later learn was also a very successful millionaire businessman himself, sitting around a dinner table in a Chinese Restaurant at Valpark Shopping Plaza, with one objective in mind, which was to unashamedly try to persuade me to provide my professional services to their "Professional Football League" for free.

I quickly figured out their strategy, since Jamaal had mentioned very early in the session, that they felt that I would have wanted to prove something to Jack Warner, after the bad treatment I got from him, and I was then being presented with the perfect opportunity to do so.

Jamaal and I had established a good professional relationship and solid acquaintanceship over the years. I had never had any problems with Jamaal. I gathered that he was at the meeting voluntarily or otherwise, primarily because it must have been felt that his presence could have somehow help persuade me to "work fuh free", based on the aforementioned theory.

In J-Willi's case, he may have felt that he could have taken advantage of our long-standing acquaintanceship and hometown connection. And perhaps more telling, an ill-conceived notion that I may have wanted to be associated with him because of his "Mr. Millionaire" persona, and his popularity as a result of his new-found status within the local football fraternity. He was very wrong. As for the Wil' character; his presence was to me nothing other than repulsive.

In the given circumstances, I managed to remain quite polite in making it quite clear, that while I was willing to continue to contribute in the interest of the local game, I was not going to work for free. Our meeting was taking place with the start of the new football season then only 2 weeks away. And so, in the said interest of the local game, I decided to take on the assignment to sell it once again. It was a decision I would live to regret.

With time then of the essence with the start of the new season a mere 2 weeks away, I immediately proposed a launch event, with the objective being to fulfill the urgent need of creating high profile public awareness of the fact, that the new season was going to start in 15 days.

That objective was going to be achieved from the subsequent media coverage, exposure, and publicity. The three gentlemen all approved of the idea there and then. There was then a mutual verbal agreement, that I would receive payment no more than 48 hours after the event. I left the amount up to them.

J-Willi' was so happy with my decision to continue to serve the local game, he then also commissioned me to develop a marketing action plan for the league itself, which he assured me that he would personally pay for. The meeting ended on that note.

Every day following that final meeting of Thursday March 28th 2002 up to the day of the event, I was in constant communication via phone calls to and from both Wil' and J-Willi', but more so with Wil', who appeared to have been charged with the responsibility of following up with me.

The launch event was scheduled to take place on Thursday April 11th, indoors at the Jean Pierre Sports Complex starting at 8:00 p.m. That left me with 10 working days for organization. But I got the job done as always.

The Fire Services Band played the national anthem to kick off the proceedings on the night. The event program for which I was totally responsible, also included addresses by several high-profile individuals;

the unveiling of the league's new logo, which I offered up as part of my contribution package; a presentation of the teams; and an entertainment segment featuring top Soca artistes Bunji Garlin and Onika Bostic, to end the night's proceedings.

The MC was Phil Simmons. Other presenters on the night included Allyson Hennessy and DJ Jus Jase. As mentioned earlier, Phil's and Jus Jase's professional services, I usually employed. I also usually hired Rent-a-Amp Sound System for all my events. The company's owner Davy, was another really cool individual that I had met during the time I operated my business.

The launch was an overwhelming success in terms of its production and achieving its objective. The following is an excerpt from a newspaper report by one of Trinidad and Tobago's top sports journalist Lasana Liburd, that was published after the event.

I quote Liburd, "The launch itself was impressive for its speed and quality, from the Fire Services Band who started the proceedings with the national anthem, to the speakers, who included interim Pro-League chairman David John Williams and Trinidad and Tobago Football Federation President Oliver Camps. Those speed and quality are two characteristics that the eight competing teams would hope to copy if they are to present a product of sufficient quality to snare a major financial partner". End of quote.

Alarmingly, the then Trinidad and Tobago Minister of Sport, who was invited, chose not to attend the event. I subsequently learnt that it was because there was some type of political fall-out between himself and Wil', who because of his social class and business and financial status, would have been politically aligned, since it is alleged that those of his ilk are the ones who actually runs the country.

I expected phone calls the very next day from both Wil' and J-Willi'. But those calls never came, if only to say thank you or to commend me for a job well done, let alone to say "come pick up your cheque", which I was then assuming they would have been more than happy to do, given the success of the event.

In fact, the phone calls that I was receiving daily from both men prior to the event ceased completely once the event was over. And the reason was quite clear. It was then time for me to be paid, and they had absolutely no intension of doing so. The event was then over, but my headache was just about to begin.

To add insult to injury, neither Wil' nor J-Willi' were even accepting or returning my phone calls to their cell phones, or responding to my faxes to their respective offices. Those two well-known local millionaire businessmen, were both then avoiding me. I had worked extremely hard and had earned every cent of that pay cheque, whatever the amount might be. So, I was very persistent and eventually I was finally able to catch up to both men.

In the case of J-Willi', it was only because he needed the marketing action plan, he had commissioned me to prepare. And still he gave me a real run-a-around before I eventually got paid. The agreement with respects to the marketing plan was that once approved by the Board, I would have been given the contract to implement it. Wil' and I were supposed to have worked out the final agreement.

I was also informed by J-Willi', that Wil' was going to be the one paying me for the launch event. So, after also finally catching up to him, he began inviting me to meet at his business establishment located behind the Port of Spain Central Market, as well as at the mansion where he lived next to Queens Royal College (QRC).

Wil' was supposedly doing so firstly, to propose and finalize the amount and hand over my payment cheque for the launch event, and secondly, to discuss the terms and conditions and compensation package, with respects to the assignment to implement the marketing plan, that I was to undertake for their new professional football league.

But on those occasions when we met for the sole purpose of addressing those two specific matters, Wil' would instead engage in empty rhetoric. It suggested to me that he was using his "come let's meet at my sprawl-ing business establishment and St. Clair mansion" strategy, thinking that I would have been in awe and overwhelmed by it all. He appeared to have been thinking that I would have become so stupefied, that I would have then decided to forego payment for my work on the launch event, which seemed to have been his objective.

Given my past experiences with those of his ilk, I was highly offended by what I deemed to be Wil's massa day mentality towards me. In fact, it infuriated me. I was really itching to say something about it. But as I usually did in such situations, I held my tongue and kept calm, cool and collected, while maintaining my professional decorum.

It was then late May, almost two months since the launch event, and I was yet to be paid for organizing and producing it. Utterly fed up with the run-around and Wil's empty rhetoric, which I knew was his strategy to avoid paying me, I proposed a paltry sum of TT$10,000.00 as my compen-sation, simply to get it over with. For the obvious reason, Wil' was more than happy to accept my proposal. Actually receiving the cheque was a whole other story.

It was absolutely unbelievable, the extent to which that millionaire crook was prepared to go to avoid paying me the measly $TT10,000.00, as he went MIA once again. After almost 2 months of running me around, and after finally catching up to him once again after his latest MIA stunt, he advised me to pick up my check at his office the first thing on the morning of Friday May 31st. I arrived at his office that morning as he advised. I waited, and I waited, and I waited. Wil' never showed up.

But unknown to me at the time, he was communicating with his personal secretary during the time I had been waiting, to find out whether I was still there. That shameless, classless, "wanna be football jefe", was hoping that I would have eventually left, whereby he would have then gotten away with not having to pay me, since I had informed him that I was going to be returning to the U.S. that same day. But little did he know that in anticipation of his expected unscrupulous act, I had already rescheduled my departure, given his elusive tactics after the event.

While waiting, I was informed of that despicable man's despicable tactic by one of his very own employees, who unlike him, had a conscience. I then staged my very own counter tactic. I pretended as if I was finally leaving. I informed his secretary, with whom he was in constant contact, that I was in fact leaving as I had to catch my flight back to the U.S. I assumed that would have been immediately communicated to him.

I then got into the vehicle I was driving and left the compound. After driving at a slow speed for about a minute or two, I turned around and headed back to Wil's business establishment. It was then about 2½ to 3 hours later. I had arrived at his office around 8:30 a.m.

Upon arrival, I re-entered the expansive building and walked down the long corridor leading to his office. As I was approaching the doorway, which was wide open, Wil' was just exiting. Apparently, he had been hiding out somewhere in the building all this time. I cannot begin to describe the look on that crook's face when he saw me.

Standing face to face a mere 2 to 3 feet apart just outside his office, Wil' instantly went into a verbally abusive guilt-ridden tirade in the presence of his employees. Maybe he felt that I would have been intimidated by his shocking outburst. Or like many others before him, maybe he too was also fooled by my small stature and cool, calm and collected demeanor.

The man even tried to involve his innocent secretary, by openly and falsely accusing me of calling her on the telephone and harassing her about the matter. His secretary, whose name was Rhonda, surprisingly and bravely I might add, quickly dispelled the man's blatant lie.

Wil's was a perfect example of a Jekyll and Hyde transformation. And though wanting to absolutely explode on the man, I managed to maintain my composure as usual, and calmly and politely told him that I was there to collect my cheque as he advised me to, and I was not leaving without it.

He went on and on, making up excuse after excuse as to why I could not receive my cheque that day, knowing fully well that I was supposed to return to the U.S. that very evening. I very calmly repeated to the man that I was there to collect my cheque, and I was not leaving without it. I then side stepped him and walked into his office and sat down in one of two chairs that were at the front of his desk. My display of defiance seemed to anger him even more than he had already demonstrated.

I vividly remember one particular statement that he made to me that day, and I quote, "ah now see how yuh become so successful." End of quote. Now, this was an individual who didn't know me from Adam. So, like many others, what he may have known about me, would have been what he may have been told by someone, or what he may have read in the newspapers, which reported some of my achievements through various articles over the years.

Dear Wil', I can unequivocally boast that whatever successes I achieved in my life, came directly through the utilization of the gifts and talents that was bestowed upon me by "The Higher Power", and extremely hard work. I can also unequivocally boast that said successes were achieved without deception, dishonesty or engaging in corrupt activities, and equally important, without causing hurt, distress or misery to, and without exploiting anyone. It is all laid out in detail in this book. So then, Millionaire Wil', can you make similar unequivocal boasts about your successes?

On top of all the verbal abuse I was receiving, Wil' apparently felt that it was not enough. So, he then decided that he would attempt to humiliate me in front of his employees. "I would like you to leave," he insisted. With those words, "Millionaire Wil'" had finally hit the nerve that triggered a temper that I had won the lifelong battles to control and suppress in such circumstances. Yet somehow, I still managed to stay cool, calm and collected.

Sitting quietly, but absolutely overflowing with rage, I began thinking to myself that after a lifetime of working hard on and succeeding in controlling my extremely explosive temper, choosing instead to be a decent, hardworking, upstanding, productive, law-abiding citizen, this man was about to change it all.

In that moment, the more I thought then about how hard I had worked to put on a successful event for those two millionaire crooks, the more rage was building inside me. It eventually got to the point where I was ready to do something to the man that he would have remembered me for; every minute, of every day, for the rest of his life.

He continued spewing insults at me, while I sat in his office awaiting the cheque that I had earned. He eventually left his office and left me sitting there. With his many insults and disrespectful statements resonating in my head, I remember beginning to feel overwhelmed by the rage that was building inside me at the time.

It was getting to the point where I felt like I was being pushed by some unknown force to act on the rage that I was feeling. It seemed uncontrollable at that point. I already had my eyes on the weapons that I was going to use, both of which were in a tray that was on his desk. Being that he was a "big-time business man of a certain ilk", I presumed that he might have been carrying a firearm, which would have given him a sense of absolute security.

I therefore factored in my presumption into my plan for my physical assault on the man. I knew that I could not have given him any opportunity to retaliate. And I wasn't going to. I also knew that I had the element of surprise as an advantage. I was all set to launch my attack when I heard his voice, as he was coming down the corridor that led to his office.

At that precise moment "The Higher Power" must have surely made a personal appearance; because just then, I heard Millionaire Wil' blurt out to his secretary, "Rhonda! Call and see if "this boy" cheque could be organized sometime this evening fuh mih," as he walked into her office, which was facing his on the other side of the corridor.

Since we had been first introduced by J-Willi', we had been respectfully addressing each other with Mr. in front of our respective last names. But I noted on that occasion, he referred to me as "this boy". He had therefore, finally revealed his true self, which was not a surprise to me at all. And thus, my reason for describing my personal feeling about his presence at the March 28th meeting as repulsive.

After a short verbal exchange with his secretary, which I couldn't quite decipher, he then returned to his office where I was still sitting calmly. "Come an' pick up the cheque two o'clock dis afternoon," he said in his still angry tone, not even inquiring about the time of my flight to determine if two o'clock might be cutting it too close, because he simply did not care. And I fully understood that.

My parting words were simply, "Mr. E (last name called), please doh leh mih come back here two o'clock an' eh geh mih cheque eh," after which I left his office and exited the building. I returned to his office at 2:00 p.m. sharp. He was not present when I arrived. But more importantly, my cheque was ready, which I collected from his secretary.

I had then been twice bitten by the Trinidad football wolves in sheep clothing. But having long decided to serve my beloved country through that sport in particular, and as a product of the sport myself, I decided thereafter that I would not allow them to deter me either, from continuing to make my contribution in the future. However, I would do so under my very own terms and conditions.

But I did learn something meaningful from that particular experience. What I learnt was that serious physical violence against another person or persons is an act that could simply be triggered. And as such, one does not necessarily have to have a violent background to commit such an act.

I certainly did not have a history of violence, nor did I ever commit any violent acts, serious or otherwise against anyone. Yet, I came extremely close to doing so. Therefore, based on my personal experience, I have concluded that to commit such an act, there is one prerequisite and one prerequisite only. And that is; one needs only to be a human being that is triggered by a certain word, or certain words, or a particular action, situation or circumstance. Following are the lyrics to the song I wrote, which was inspired by my experience with Wil' and J-Willi'.

SONG TITLE: WIL' AN' J-WILLI'

Verse 1
Wil' an' J-Willi'
Pro ball business looking bleaky
Wil' and J-Willi'
Need my services desperately
Agree to work for these Big Shots—Jamaal was there
Deep down I knew that I would regret
Already been where the wolves at—Sheep clothes they wear
Did their work time to write meh cheque

Chorus
Wil' and J-Willi'
Say dey start tuh hide… Dey start tuh hide from me
Wil' and J-Willi'
Say dey start tuh hide… Time to pay currency
Wil' and J-Willi'
Ah say dey start tuh hide… Trying tuh avoid me
Wil' and J-Willi'
Say dey start tuh hide… No shame no decency

Verse 2
Wil' so funny
Come with Massa mentality
Doh wanna pay no money
Think him working psychology
Inviting me to his big flat—In St. Clair
Adding insult tuh injury
Doh give a damn about all dat—Wil' kiss my rear
Look put that clown in ah Jim Carey movie—CHORUS

Verse 3
You J-Willi'
Because I knew your whole family
True J-Willi'—Your brother Termite
Even went the same school with me
Just didn't know you were a ball quack
No professional integrity
How were you any different from Jack
Seems that you were just about football money—**CHORUS—END**

A BREAKTHROUGH FOR MY NOSILA SPORTS BRAND

After spending about 5 months considering proposals from the other companies that were based in the U.S. and vying for their business, the Arizona football club chose my then Trinidad based company as their official uniform supplier.

Given that it was going up against U.S. companies, their choosing my NOSILA brand represented a major breakthrough. I felt extremely proud as well as excited in that moment. By that time, and with the future in mind, I had taken the initiative and NOSILA Sportswear was then a registered business entity based in Orlando Florida, with my cousin BoPeep as a partner.

The Arizona club was huge. It was made up of many youth football teams comprising of both girls and boys in different age groups. Their very first order for kits was also huge, and was divided into two parts in various sizes, in two color combinations of red and white and black and white. Each jersey and shorts also had to be numbered.

Since the kits were then being produced in Trinidad, over the next couple of months I would be a very frequent flier between Trinidad and the U.S., delivering parts of the order as required, which I was transporting to Florida, then shipping via FedEx to Arizona.

We delivered on the first part of the order. The club was extremely satisfied with both the product and service. We were to deliver the second part of the order not very long thereafter. However, the Trinidad supplier who was an entrepreneur like myself, and whom I was actually giving the huge business opportunity to produce the entire order, messed up the second part big time.

With that big mess up came an even bigger challenge, as valuable time was lost. It then left me in a situation where I was under a tremendous amount of pressure to deliver the second part of the order by the expected delivery date. I certainly did not want to blow such a huge business opportunity that could turn out to be long term; especially not after all the years of extremely hard work and sacrifice to get to that then current point.

So, with very limited time to deliver the second part of the order, I then had no other choice but to hop on a flight out of Trinidad to Florida, in a desperate search of a new manufacturer who could deliver it on time. But I was unsuccessful in my Florida search, which was over a few days.

With no time to waste, I then flew to New York where I managed to source a manufacturer out of Mexico. I managed to deliver the second part of the order with absolutely no time to spare. But issue was taken with the new fabric used, which, although of good quality, was different from that which was used to produce the first part of the order.

While they accepted it, and the respective teams did in fact use the uniforms, we were conducting business with a U.S. client. So, I totally understood it when they were refusing to pay the full amount on the outstanding balance on the order, because of the use of the different fabric.

Our pursuit of the full payment balance led to an initial legal course of action. But given what it may have cost in legal fees to go to court, I eventually decided it would not have been worth it. Through no fault of mines, except that I decided to give a local entrepreneur like myself an opportunity, the Arizona business relationship that looked oh so very promising, ended on that note.

Since its conception back in 1994, and with an unwavering commitment to my vision, I had made, and was then still, stubbornly I might add, continuing to make every possible effort to put an undeniably distinct Trinidad and Tobago stamp on my NOSILA sports brand. But in the end, with the loss of the huge Arizona business opportunity, it proved to be my undoing. I had then been pursuing my NOSILA business venture for 7 years at that point.

That then most recent development dictated that I finally accept that I had then totally exhausted those efforts, for which I paid the ultimate price for my insistence. But for me, giving up was not an option. Giving up was definitely not a part of my DNA. To me it simply meant that it was time to rethink my original vision.

It was then time to begin to explore the possibility of launching my NOSILA brand in the U.S., which presented a whole different proposition of course. As such, I knew that I would have had to quickly pick myself up, dust myself off, and start all over again. It would not have been the first time. With the desire and a renewed sense of purpose, I was certainly up for the challenge.

MY 4 MONTHS STINT AS THE GENERAL SECRETARY OF THE FOOTBALL PLAYERS ASSOCIATION OF TRINIDAD & TOBAGO

Following our historic feat of qualifying for our first ever FIFA World Cup Finals, which saw my beloved twin island nation's participation at the 2006 event in Germany, where we gave a very credible showing, most of the local stakeholders would have been then hopeful for a "Diamond Era" for the local game.

With Jack Warner at the helm and then at the peak of his powers, he would have been the one to orchestrate and usher in such an era. And given his then undeniable status and power within the world's governing body of the world's most popular sport at the time, the local stakeholders optimism would not have seemed misplaced.

But remaining true to himself I guess, Warner continued to allow his ego, which was being fed by said status and power, to influence his decision making. As a result, he elected to flex his well-established administrative muscle to quickly render all the local stakeholders optimism, one more of wishful thinking than a realistic goal.

And that was primarily because Warner instead decided to turn the opportunity into yet another dark period in our country's football history, as he conspired to turn what was a fairly straightforward financial compensation matter with the players who were involved in our afore-mentioned historic FIFA World Cup Finals appearance, into one of such contention that it made world headlines.

So, what in my personal opinion should have represented a plat-form for development and the springboard for sustainable success for the local game and by extension, success on the international scene, turned into an administration of one, being the catalyst once again for leading the local game into yet another one of several dark, low periods, that it experienced over the years under his watch. He obviously did not feel the need for redemption.

It was during one of those periods that a courageous group of Trinidad and Tobago's then overseas based professionals, who were then also members of our Senior Men's National Team, decided to take a bold initiative. They had decided to establish a local football union, that would represent the interest of all the locally based professional players, and play-ers who were members of the Senior Men's National Football Team. And so, the Football Players Association of Trinidad and Tobago (FPATT) was born.

I was not aware that such an organization even existed in my home-land, until I got a phone call in late April of 2007 from one Brent Sancho, who was one of FPATT's founding members. At the time, I was just about to head back out to New York after being in Trinidad to make initial preparations, to stage my revolutionary Goal Points Football League com-petition the following year, as a way of continuing to make my personal contribution to the development of the local game.

I had met Brent for the very first time in the very late 90's, while I was at a Senior Men's National Team training session at the Hasely Crawford Stadium. He was dressed in full training gear and sitting alone dejectedly, on the short yellow railing that encircled the athletic track that was constructed around the football field.

He had returned to Trinidad from Finland, where he had been ply-ing his professional football trade, with the hope of obtaining a try-out with the Senior Men's National Team. But the then national team coach Bertille St Clair was an extremely strict disciplinarian, and had adopted a policy that did not allow Brent to participate.

That policy was that he would have had to cut off the dreadlocks hair style he had, before he could do so. Since I was meeting Brent for the very first time then, I could only simply have offered words of encourage-ment to him and did so.

Subsequent to that initial encounter, I would come to learn that Brent was actually the cousin of my girlfriend cum lifetime partner, Alicia. It was on the basis of being my girlfriend's cousin, and also continuing to make my contribution to the local game, that I began to facilitate him with favors of pro-bono professional services, whenever he requested same from me.

One such occasion was when I was asked by Brent to be a member of the Organizing Committee, to promote, produce and manage the 1st Annual Mickey Trotman Memorial Football Match event in December 2001. I was extremely honored to do so, in memory of the former Senior Men's National Team member, who died in a vehicular accident on October 1st 2001, at the age of 26.

Brent's late April 2007 phone call was from England, where he was playing and residing at the time. It was for the purpose of employing my professional services, as the founders wanted to relaunch FPATT in a big way. So, Brent had called to commission me to do the relaunch assignment.

The primary objectives were to create high profile awareness among all the Trinidad and Tobago based professional football players, whose interest the organization was intending to serve, as well as among other stakeholders including local supporters and the public at large.

It was also around that time that Brent introduced me via e-mail to a Kevin Harrison, who was a Caucasian Englishman living in England.

Brent informed me that Harrison would be directly involved with FPATT in some then yet to be decided capacity.

The first important duty I would perform relative to the commissioned assignment, would be to design the official logo for the FPATT organization. Another major part of my assignment was for me to conceive an official launch event, which I would then have the responsibility of organizing, producing and managing. I came up with a "FOOTBALL-FUNDAY" event, with a play on the words "FUN and FUND", which, while serving to relaunch the organization, would also serve as a day of "FOOTBALL FUN", while raising "FUNDS" for the organization.

The event would involve a football game between the Trinidad and Tobago team that participated at the 2006 FIFA World Cup Finals in Germany, and a local celebrity team made up of popular radio DJ's, sports, entertainment and other high-profile personalities.

But as was usually the case whenever I was called upon to render professional services to football entities in my homeland, there was one major problem, as Brent informed me that there were no funds available for staging what was going to be a major undertaking. However, I decided to still facilitate Brent and the other FPATT founders anyway.

I did so for one reason and one reason only. That reason being that it was a cause that I believed in and was very eager to work for. To me, FPATT represented and signaled the coming of the long overdue revolution, that the local game so desperately needed.

Moreover, I had knowledge of the history of the bad treatment that was meted out to players by the local administration dating back to the 60's, and had always wanted to contribute in any way that I could to any such local football revolution, for which the players interest was at its very core and would be served.

I always wanted to be a part of any such movement that sought to seriously challenge the Modus Operandi of the then local administration as it related to the players under its charge, since it had a well-established reputation of exploiting and being extremely disrespectful to said players.

FPATT therefore represented the cause that I was extremely passionate about. As such, and not for the first time, I was prepared to take a hit with respects to compensation for my professional services.

With no funds available, I had to try to secure sponsorship for the launch event. But securing sponsorship for football related events always posed a major challenge, since corporate citizens did not really want to be involved with the sport, as a result of the "Jack Warner Effect". Being commissioned to undertake the assignment a mere 2 1/2 weeks before the relaunch date, I had only managed to secure TT$7,500.00 in sponsorship. It came from Toyota through one Andre Baptiste, who is also a top Trinidad and Tobago sports commentator, journalist and sports fanatic.

So, also not for the first time, I was being asked to undertake a major football related assignment, but with only very limited funds to get the job done. With no other choice however, contributions eventually had to come from several of the World Cup players themselves, for the event to be staged.

I subsequently organized an official media conference to announce it, at which several overseas based players were present. The media conference was held at the Hasely Crawford Stadium VIP Room. The "FOOTBALL-FUNDAY" event to relaunch the FPATT organization, took place on May 20th 2007 at the Hasely Crawford Stadium, and was a resounding success based on its primary objectives being achieved.

Kelvin Jack, one of FPATT's founding members and the then national team Goalkeeper, in expressing his amazement at how one individual could have delivered such an assignment remarked, "Alison, yuh do ah job that would usually take ah whole team ah people to do? I am very impressed." Kelvin Jack's personal recognition of my hard work under extremely challenging circumstances was well received and appreciated, especially since he was the only individual to do so.

A second leg of the FPATT relaunch event was also held on the Sister Island of Tobago. But it turned into a bit of a fiasco, as one Peter Granville, who wanted us to bring the event to the Sister Isle, did not honor his word with respects to making all the necessary arrangements for travel and suitable accommodation, for the entire party that would have been travelling from Trinidad.

The Englishman Kevin Harrison had traveled from England for the Tobago event. He, Tansley Thompson, my girlfriend Alicia and I were staying at the same accommodation. With Tansley being the designated chauffeur, and with Harrison, Alicia and I being passengers, we were just having casual conversations among ourselves during a journey, when out of the blue Harrison posed a question.

Referring specifically to Tansley and myself he asked quite bluntly, "So guys, what are your respective personal agendas with regards to FPATT?" Huh! We had literally only just met, so the man didn't even know us, yet he seemed to have been suggesting that we had personal hidden agendas with regards to our involvement with FPATT? I personally took offence and immediately responded, "what's yours?"

In his also blunt response, Harrison, who told us that he was attached to a football club in England, revealed that since he had met Brent and some of the other local boys back in England, he saw that there was the opportunity to use them to elevate himself, relative to his involvement in the football world. Again. Huh! I was appalled at Harrison's revelation. But since it was clearly obvious that Brent and company totally trusted the man, I simply kept his revelation to myself; that is, until now.

Once we returned to Trinidad, Brent asked me to, and I subsequently picked up Harrison from the airport upon his arrival in Trinidad from Tobago in a taxi I hired. I usually hired my good friend Abdul Muhammad (formally Milton Archibald) who owned a Taxi, to take me around whenever I was in Trinidad, so I also hired him on that occasion. We then took Harrison to the Kapok Hotel where he checked in.

Brent then also charged me with the responsibility of introducing the Englishman to the Trinidad and Tobago public and football stakeholders. To that end, I arranged an extended television interview for him at Trinidad and Tobago Television (TTT). That interview was conducted by

Rolph Warner Jr, my very good buddy Rolph Warner's son, who worked there at the time.

I also arranged for him to meet with the then Trinidad & Tobago Pro League boss Dexter Skeen. Harrison, with me acting as his chaperone, was being chauffeured around over several days from his pick-up point at the Kapok hotel in Abdul's hired taxi at my personal expense, including taking him to the airport for his return trip to England. He had then gotten the start he needed, towards ultimately fulfilling his personal agenda.

I was extremely motivated to work for the FPATT cause for the reasons stated earlier, and wanted to do all within my power to ensure the organization's success. So much so that on June 4th of that year 2007, just one week after the Tobago relaunch event, and upon my very own initiative, I arranged to and met with the then Minister of Sport, to solicit financial assistance from the government for the organization.

I had informed Brent Sancho, who agreed to give me a ride to the Minister's office on the day, but did not wish to attend or participate in the scheduled session with the Minister, citing that he was not properly attired. He was wearing a T-shirt, shorts, and sneakers. But I persuaded Brent to attend.

The meeting was a very productive one, at the end of which I was asked to submit a budget for projected FPATT expenses over its first year of operations. Two days later, on June 6th 2007, the then Minister had the document in his hands, upon which he informed me that the next step would be for him to take it with a note to Cabinet, for consideration and approval.

That night of June 6th, FPATT held an Annual General Meeting at the offices of the West Indian (Cricketers) Players Association (WIPA) located on Edward Street Port of Spain. FPATT members present at that meeting were Brent Sancho, Cyd Gray, Clayton Morris, Leslie Fitzpatrick and Leonson Lewis, all then current or former members of the Senior Men's National Football Team. I was well acquainted with all of them, but I will single out Leonson more as a very good friend.

Invited persons present at the meeting were Philip Nunez, Carla Herbert, Tansley Thompson, Darren Millien and me. Out of those four, Tansley was the only individual I knew at the time. The then outgoing president Brent Sancho chaired the meeting.

At that meeting I was offered, accepted, and was appointed to the position of General Secretary. I personally considered it the most significant job I would have, relative to my then ongoing service to the local game. And that was simply because it was one that was going to be all about representing the interest of the local players.

Because I then resided in the U.S., I would have been required to relocate to Trinidad to take up the position. And since FPATT could not afford to pay me a full salary at the time, I simply asked for my Trinidad living expenses to be met. The meeting agreed that I would have my Trinidad living expenses met by FPATT, until such time that the organization could afford to pay me a full salary.

However, Brent and Co. would have problems coming up with the funds to cover my Trinidad living expenses as agreed. That cost was set at TT$10,000.00 per month. As such, Brent then informed me that he would request contributions from some of the World Cup players, through one of two bank accounts they had at the time, to make up the first payment.

I was extremely uncomfortable with that arrangement, because to me it felt like they were going to be hassled for cash on my account. I communicated those feelings to Brent. He then assured me that he would discuss it with them beforehand, so that they would know the reason behind it, and I would then simply follow up. He subsequently gave me the phone numbers for specific players that I was to make follow up calls to.

But it appeared that he set me up in some cases, because those players were not aware when I called. One player said he wasn't contributing because he did not trust Sancho. Given the utter embarrassment I felt during the process, I transferred the full responsibility back to Brent.

I was eventually able to access my then overdue June payment through one of the bank accounts in mid to late July. I then informed Brent that I was returning to New York until my living expenses issue could have been sorted out. I left for the U.S. thereafter.

As his local marketing representative at the time, I had been invited to England by Carlos Edwards, then a member of the Trinidad and Tobago Senior Men's National Football Team and English Club Sunderland AFC, to witness a game involving Sunderland at any time during that 2007 season.

Sunderland would have been participating in the English Premier League after gaining promotion that year. Stern John, another member of the Trinidad and Tobago Senior Men's National Football Team, was then also a member of Sunderland at the time.

I continued the work of FPATT while back in the U.S. Subsequent to my return, I contacted the then Minister of Sport from my New York base, to follow up on the status of the grant I had requested from the government, on behalf of FPATT.

Unknown to me, the Minister was at a Florida medical institution for a medical procedure at the time. He informed me that the grant request would have already been submitted to Cabinet by his Permanent Secretary for consideration and approval, which was great news, as progress was being made.

I was very mindful that FPATT would inevitably be locking horns with Jack Warner, and that we would have needed serious backing when it occurred. So, I got down to doing some research while at my New York base. I then came up with an idea. I contacted and shared my idea with the then recently appointed FPATT President.

The idea was for me to travel to the UK to meet with one Gordon Taylor, the then Chief Executive of the (English) Professional Footballers Association (PFA) and Honorary President of FIFPro, with a view to securing support for FPATT from both those organizations. FIFPro is the worldwide representative organization for professional players and player's organizations such as FPATT. I had first heard about FIFPro from Kevin Harrison, the Englishman.

The then FPATT President immediately acknowledged my idea as being a brilliant one. He indicated that he would begin the process of securing an audience for me with Gordon Taylor, whom he knew personally.

I was an avid fan of the English Football League since the very early 70's, when I started watching it on television in Trinidad as a youngster. Witnessing an English Premier League game in person was an experience that was on my bucket list.

But while I was still undecided about when exactly I might have taken up Carlos' invite to witness a Sunderland game, the possibility of embarking on that important FPATT mission, most definitely provided more impetus for me to want to make the trip across the pond. As apart from witnessing a Premier League game in person, featuring my Trinbago home boys Carlos, Dwight Yorke and possibly Stern John, the FPATT mission would have made the trip even more worthwhile.

The then FPATT President secured the meeting for me with Gordon Taylor as promised. I then contacted Carlos to let him know that I was going to be making the trip to England from the U.S., to meet with Gordon Taylor, and would be taking him up on his invite to see him play in the Premiership.

On Tuesday August 7th 2007, I was on a flight bound for the homeland of my grandfather for the very first time. My excitement could not have been more elevated. I stayed with Cheryl Mclawrence, my sister by father, who still lived in London at the time.

After immediately contacting his office upon my arrival, the meeting with Gordon Taylor was confirmed for 1:00 p.m. the following day Wednesday August 8th. Within 24 hours of my arrival in the UK, I was on a train to Manchester where his office was located, to meet with the then Chief Executive of the PFA and Honorary President of FIFPro, in my official capacity as FPATT's General Secretary.

My well-tailored Italian navy-blue pinstriped designer suit, ensured that I looked the part. Upon my arrival, I was escorted to a boardroom where I was joined by one Mick McGuire, the then Deputy Chief Executive of the PFA. Mick informed me that unfortunately Gordon was unavailable to meet with me at the time, so he would be filling in for him.

After the usual introductions and pleasantries, I told Mick the reason for my visit. I then presented my credentials to him, which were displayed in an impressive professional grade presentation folder. After flipping through the first few pages, Mick asked me to hold on for a moment.

He then got on the phone that sat on the boardroom table and made a call. "Hello Gordon? I really think that you need to meet with this guy," he stated. To me, that phone call was validation of my credentials. After advising me to leave my belongings on the boardroom table, Mick then escorted me up to Gordon Taylor's office on the floor above.

Upon arrival, Mick formally introduced me to the man who was playing a pivotal role in the English game. Gordon then proceeded to give me a tour around his office, where he had lots of football collectables and memorabilia on display in several glass cases.

Gordon, Mick, and I then got down to discussing the serious business for which I was there. During our discussion, Gordon called in a photographer who took several photos of us together. At the end of the session, he presented me with several gifts, including two PFA neck ties and a few books about the history of the English game. He then had a few words with Mick, after which he advised me that Mick will finish up with me downstairs. He then bade me farewell.

Mick and I then left his office and headed back down to the boardroom. On the way there, we ran into former player Mike Berry, to whom I was introduced. Apart from his role at the PFA, I believe that Mike was also the agent of several Trinidad and Tobago players who were then plying their trade in the UK.

Once back in the boardroom, Mick and I immediately began working on the draft of a letter that was going to be sent to one Theo Van

Seggelen, the then General Secretary of FIFPro (International Federation of Professional Footballers) World Players' Union, expressing FPATT's interest in becoming a member. FIFPro headquarters is in Holland.

With the final draft in my possession, the process of FPATT becoming an official member of FIFPro had begun. I left Manchester absolutely bursting with pride, knowing that I represented not only FPATT, but by extension Trinidad and Tobago exceedingly well. The then FPATT President never mentioned anything to me, but I assumed Gordon Taylor would have subsequently conveyed that to him.

Meanwhile, after initially speaking with him on the phone, I met Kevin Harrison in down town London the morning of Thursday August 9th. During our telephone conversation, he had indicated that he had a few meetings lined up with "some" London based businesses, who had interests in partnering with FPATT that he wanted me to attend.

As it turned out, we actually went to only two locations. The first we went to was a company called Travelex, which was involved in the business of international currency exchange and transfers. But there was no meeting. And it was also obvious that no one was expecting us.

We simply dropped in, I was introduced to one of the employees who Harrison seemed to have known, and with whom he then exchanged a few words. We then took a few quick photographs and that was it. It was unproductive, and quite frankly, a waste of my time.

The second location we visited was smack-bang in the heart of downtown London. It appeared to be a football related entity. Again, it was obvious that no one was expecting us. In fact, no one even came out to greet us upon our arrival.

It was only after Harrison blurted out hello a few times to get someone's attention, did an individual eventually come out to us. The individual did not seem to know Harrison. And again, there was no meeting. The gentleman simply invited us to have a look around and disappeared back into his office.

I left that location with a poster of my childhood football idol Pele, which made that trip worth it somewhat. All in all, it was a very unproductive few hours spent with Harrison. I was unimpressed, and in fact felt embarrassed for him. Fortunately for me, what would turn out to be a quite enjoyable part of that day's activities, was actually still to come.

And that was when we then headed to The Brit Insurance / Kennington Oval cricket ground to meet one Mike Townley. Townley was the London based Attorney who was representing Trinidad and Tobago's 2006 World Cup players, in their financial compensation dispute with Jack Warner. Upon our arrival, England was engaged in a cricket Test Match with India.

While I attended several tests matches back in Trinidad at the famous Queen's Park Oval as a supporter of the West Indies cricket team during the Clive Lloyd, Vivian Richards and Brian Lara eras, never did I ever imagine that I would have witnessed any part of a cricket test match in England in my lifetime. That was a big bonus of my trip.

Mike Townley most definitely appeared to have been someone of fairly high status, because upon meeting him, he escorted me to what appeared to be a VIP lounge. There, he and I chatted and got to know each other a bit.

Unknown to me until I was informed while at the cricket ground, there was a dinner meeting planned for later that evening involving FPATT founders Brent Sancho and Kelvin Jack, Mike Townley, Harrison and me. In between time, I simply enjoyed the cricket, holding up my 4 runs placard when a 4 runs boundary was hit, by whoever was at the wicket at the time.

Mike Townley, Harrison, and I left before the close of play, and met up with Brent and Kelvin outside the Oval. We then headed to a nearby restaurant where the meeting was held over dinner. There were several items on the agenda, including an impending trip to Trinidad by Mike Townley.

As the representative of the 2006 World Cup players in their compensation matter with Jack Warner, he had a court appearance in Trinidad, which was scheduled for Friday September 21st. At the meeting I agreed to be his host while he was in Trinidad. We enjoyed our respective meals and departed for our respective places of abode thereafter.

MY UNFORGETTABLE DAY AT
SUNDERLAND AFC's STADIUM OF LIGHT:
CONTINUING THE WORK OF FPATT

Once back at my sister's apartment, I was quickly off again the following morning Friday August 10th; that time on a train to Sunderland. The real excitement was then only hours away. As pre-arranged, I was picked up at the train station in Newcastle by Carlos that evening in his black Mercedes SUV. I was so happy for and extremely proud of my home-boy, especially since I knew and could appreciate how hard he would have had to work for his success. I communicated such to him.

In less than 45 minutes we were at his residence in Sunderland, which was very close to a beach. His wife, with whom I was already very much acquainted was at home with their new born when we arrived. Silvio Spann, another Trinidad and Tobago Men's Senior National Team player at the time, was also at Carlos' residence when we arrived. He was departing that same evening, after staying at Carlos' during a trial at Sunderland.

Carlos and his wife wanted me to have a taste of the famous English Fish and Chips, so I accompanied her to go pick up some for all four of us to have for dinner. Upon our return to the residence, we all sat watching the tele and chatted together while enjoying the English staple, which, as a very finnicky eater, I must admit was really good.

Silvio eventually left, after which Carlos and his wife retreated to their private quarters. Carlos indicated that he would have been leaving sometime during the night, to link up with his teammates at a hotel to prepare for their season opener the following day Saturday, which was going to be against Tottenham. After watching some more television, I then had a shower and retired to bed.

I was up early in anticipation of the day's events. Kick-off was scheduled for 12:30 p.m. I had breakfast, after which I had a shower. I then got decked out in my Sunderland replica jersey, which was provided by Carlos and his wife. It was then off to the game together with Carlos' wife and their then newly born daughter, safely tucked into her car seat in the back.

As we got closer and closer to the match venue, there were droves and droves of Sunderland supporters all dressed in their red and white striped replica jerseys, descending upon the stadium. It was a sight to behold and had my excitement mounting.

With Carlos' wife having special VIP privileges for obvious reasons, we sat only a few rows behind the substitute's benches. One of Carlos' close English friends, a gentleman who perhaps like me then, could have been in his 40s, sat with us.

The field was in absolutely immaculate condition. With my camera at the ready, I began surveying the spectacular "Stadium of Light". I immediately spotted a Trinidad and Tobago flag hanging from the lower level of the stands close to the corner flag off to our right. "Click click. Click click," went the shutter. The first couple of shots were in the bank.

It did not take very long for the stadium to be filled to capacity, upon which the customary loud chanting of various songs adapted for the occasion began. The opponents, Tottenham Hotspur FC was one of the biggest English clubs with a rich football history. In fact, one of Tottenham's legends Glen Hoddle, is one of my all-time favorite English players. But that day I was a Sunderland supporter without question.

Almost deafening applause and cheers broke out when the players emerged from the tunnel and walked out onto the field. "Click click. Click click. Click click." The sound of the shutter of my camera continued, as it did throughout the course of the entire game; as did the increasingly loud chanting from the supporters.

My camera's view finder was trained on both Carlos and Dwight Yorke, who both started the game. Dwight was substituted about fifteen minutes into the second half. Unfortunately, Stern John did not play any part in the proceedings.

The game was a very exciting affair, and got into time added on seemingly headed for a 0-0 draw. Then it happened. A cross from the right side fell to substitute Michael Chopra; with a deft first touch he killed the ball just to left of the penalty spot with his right foot, and with his second touch with the same right foot, dispatched a low drive to the Tottenham keeper's left into the back of the net. It was almost the last kick of the game.

The Sunderland supporters; 40,000 plus, including me of course, leapt to our feet in unison with the loudest naturally orchestrated eruption of voices that I had ever heard. Delirium took over the entire stadium, as supporters went into a state of total rapture, as Chopra sprinted off in celebration with his team mates in hot pursuit. Carlos' friend held me in a brief bear hug in his initial moment of delirium. What a moment. What an experience.

Then again in unison, the 40,000 plus Sunderland supporters, made up of grandparents all the way down to their grand-children, and perhaps even their great grandchildren, broke out in song at the very top of their respective lungs, singing the hook line from the Beatles' monster hit Hey Jude repeatedly, replacing Hey Jude at the end of it with another name. "Naaaah! Naah! Naah! Nah! Nah! Nah! Naaaaaah! Nah! Nah! Nah! Naaaaaah! Keeenoooo!!!!

They were celebrating their Sunderland coach, Manchester United legend Roy Keane in song. The whole atmosphere literally gave me goose bumps; it was so filled with emotion. It was an unforgettable experience indeed.

After the game I had brief interactions with some of the players from both teams in the players' lounge. There was a feeling of extreme pride seeing the homeboys Carlos, Dwight and Stern in their true professional element.

On the way out to their vehicles, which were parked in the players private car park, there were throngs of fans lining both sides of a barricaded pathway seeking autographs from the players. Carlos signed several whilst on the move at a fairly brisk pace as he headed towards the car park, fearing that if he actually stopped to do so, he would have been there for quite a while. That was fun and also telling to witness, as it gave me a real sense of how the players were genuinely celebrated, and treated as the true superstars they were by the fans.

The day ended with a "lime" (to hang out) at a former Sunderland player's house, where I hung out with Carlos and Dwight among a few other folks. After hanging out for about an hour, all the guests departed.

But my UK mission was not quite done yet. You see, immediately after the game, I had set up a meeting with Dwight for the following morning Sunday at the Sunderland training ground to solicit his support for FPATT. Brent, whom I had told about my intention to do so, had stated that there was no way I could pull that off, giving the impression that he knew Dwight well enough to know that he would have spurned my approach. Brent even decided to put a £100 bet on it.

What Brent did not know was that I had established really good relationships with most of the players from the 1989 Road To Italy cum Strike Squad era, during and post the Road To Italy World Cup Qualifying Campaign over the years, including Dwight.

And while I certainly was not taking him for granted, I was sure that Dwight would not have spurned my approach, since he knew that I was "a true member"; meaning that he knew that I was one of those within the local football fraternity, who was a genuine servant and who could have been trusted.

In fact, I became somewhat acquainted with Dwight since he was a member of the Trinidad and Tobago U-16 team. He sometimes stayed at my then girlfriend's aunt, Dorma Bennetts' residence, whenever he came over to Trinidad from Tobago where he resided, to train or for games. My then girlfriend's aunt had a son, Sheldon, who was also a member of the national U-16 team at the time. He and Dwight were very good friends during those days.

Carlos would drive me back to the Newcastle train station that Sunday morning. He first took me to the Sunderland training ground, where the first team players had a meeting. The second team was training when we arrived. So, while he attended the meeting, I went over to observe the training session, which was an 11 vs 11 full blown game.

Stern John was involved in the game. There was absolutely no holding back by the players. The running was hard and the tackles were fierce, simulating a real game situation. It was extremely intense. And I mean extremely intense. One would have sworn that 3 Premier League points were at stake. It most definitely served as an eye opener for me personally.

Dwight and Carlos eventually emerged from the building where the first team meeting had taken place. I then met with Dwight about him getting involved with FPATT, by way of him being the first to sign on as a member. Being as he put, "that he knew what I was all about", he immediately signed on, thereby becoming the FPATT organization's first official member and the highest profile one at that. Less important was the fact that Brent had lost his bet. He never paid up anyway.

After taking care of that final piece of my FPATT business in the UK, which was on my very own initiative, Carlos then took me to the train station. On the way there he took me to the Sunderland merchandise store at the stadium and gifted me several replica jerseys. I specifically requested one with his name and number, which I still have in my possession today.

No sooner, was I on a train heading back to London. Carlos and his wife were excellent hosts. They made me feel most welcome and extremely comfortable during my relatively short stay.

Once back in London, I used the next day Monday to draft my report, relative to my FPATT UK mission and what had been accomplished. The following day, Tuesday August 14th 2007, which was my 48th birthday, I was on a British Airways flight heading back to New York.

The following day Wednesday, I contacted the then FPATT President. He informed me that things were not looking to promising with respects to my returning to Trinidad to continue my duties as FPATT's General Secretary, because there were no funds available to cover my Trinidad living expenses as agreed.

I then assumed that as short-lived and as productive as my FPATT tenure was up to that point, it was then over. Still, given its importance I continued working, completing and sending off the final letter via overnight courier to Theo Van Seggelen at the FIFPro Holland headquarters at my own expense, so as to not stop the process of FPATT becoming a member of FIFPro.

Then in very late August, even as I wasn't being paid during the period since I had returned to New York, I received a phone call from the then FPATT President, upon which he charged me with the responsibility of an extremely urgent and important assignment.

It was an assignment that would determine the club future of one of Trinidad and Tobago's then Senior Men's National Team members, then plying his professional trade in England. The call came in just after 5:00 p.m., U.S. Eastern Standard Time, which was just after 10:00 p.m. UK time.

The then Trinidad and Tobago Football Association, had flatly refused to submit a letter to the English Football Association, that would have served to complete that player's transfer to another club. Without the said letter, the transfer would not have been possible, thereby, resulting in the player then staying at the club where he was at the time in the

English championship division. But thankfully, FPATT was there to save the day.

Because the English FA then recognized FPATT as a legitimate organization representing the interest of both Trinidad and Tobago's local and overseas based professional players, largely due to my trip to Manchester, they were prepared to accept the letter from FPATT.

And so, in my capacity as FPATT's General Secretary, I was then charged with the responsibility of preparing the said letter on behalf of the player, and getting it into the hands of representatives in England before the midnight transfer deadline UK time. As usual, I got the job done. The player's transfer then went through before the midnight deadline.

He then made his dream move from Southampton Football Club, who were then in the English second division, to Sunderland AFC in the Premier League. The player was Kenwyne Jones. Such assignment, was the very reason that I was so extremely motivated to work for the FPATT cause. I was extremely happy to have played such an important role in the career of one of the sons of the soil. More so, since I wasn't even certain that I would have been continuing to be involved with the organization.

But I guess that my performance up to that point spoke for itself, because the then FPATT President then promised that he would work something out regarding payment of my Trinidad living expenses as initially agreed, since he wanted me to continue the work of the organization.

At the time I was then owed my July and August payments, amounting to TT$20,000.00, since I had continued working over those months. And having finally learnt my lesson, I certainly was not going to be working for free, especially since I was delivering big time on many fronts. And I had in fact paid out of my very own pocket for the UK trip, during which FPATT business was given priority.

I then received another call a few days later from the then FPATT President. On that occasion he called to urge me to return to Trinidad, as he was arranging to get some funds to me upon my arrival; and thereafter, he would make the necessary arrangements to ensure that I continue to receive the funds for my monthly Trinidad expenses as initially agreed, while I continued the work of FPATT. I took him at his word and therefore agreed to return to Trinidad.

After ensuring that my mother would be okay, I returned to Trinidad on the night of Sunday September 9th, almost 2 months after I had left, ready to continue the FPATT grind on home soil, where it had all started. The then FPATT President kept his word. That very night, upon my arrival at the Trinidad apartment, his father dropped off US$2,000.00 in cash, which at the time was equivalent to TT$12,000.00.

However, having been paid the very first payment of TT$10,000.00 for June from the players bank account, I was still owed TT$20,000.00 at the time for July and August. But in recognition of the effort of the then FPATT President, I elected not to bring up that issue at the time. I had to use the TT$12,000.00 cash that was provided by the then FPATT President to cover my September Trinidad living expenses.

So, I was then owed TT$18,000.00 for July and August, with TT$2,000.00 from the $12,000.00 going toward that outstanding payment, since that was the excess being that TT$10,000.00 was the agreed amount to cover my living expenses.

My Trinidad accommodation was arranged by one Darren Millien, who had since been appointed FPATT's Marketing Director. The rent was TT$4,500.00 per month. According to his e-mail, which I received while in New York, it was supposed to have been a fully furnished 1-bedroom apartment located in St. James, containing all the necessary appliances, including a stove most importantly, since I had planned to prepare my own meals.

However, upon my arrival at the "1-bedroom apartment" on the night of September 9th, I was left most disappointed. It turned out to be a claustrophobic two level "self-contained" annex. The "so called" bedroom, which was on the upper level, was itself a health hazard.

There, one could not walk freely, as they had to always watch their head in a certain area that was very low with a concrete beam running across a particular area. The accommodation most definitely was not worth the whopping $4,500.00 rent.

Most notably, there was no stove as expected. That meant that I had no other choice but to purchase lunch meals on the outside on a daily basis, which proved to be a quite expensive proposition. And the refrigerator was one of those mini-type versions that could only hold a very limited amount of food items.

The then FPATT Vice President, Clayton "JB" Morris, who had cause to pay me a visit on one occasion, could not believe the claustrophobic conditions under which I was being asked to function, and could certainly attest to the aforementioned facts.

I did not complain to the then FPATT President or anyone else about the living conditions, which left much to be desired, or about the fact that I was in desperate need of a computer. I simply got down to work, by footing it back and forth in the blazing sun several times a day to an internet café in the area to execute my duties.

One of the first actions I took was to reapply for FPATT's original certificate of registration document, which was then non-existent. That took several visits to the relevant office located in the Riverside Plaza. I also requested and obtained other critical information to ensure that the organization would have been legitimately set up for its operations, which would have been required to conduct any official business.

While involved with that process, I simultaneously began FPATT's membership drive, while also following up on my initiative of seeking financial assistance from the government. The membership drive took me to the different parts of the country, where the clubs then participating in the local professional football league were based.

As earlier mentioned, whenever I visited Trinidad, I usually hired my very good friend Abdul Muhammad (formerly Milton Archibald) to take me around, since I did not have my own means of transportation and he owned a taxi. So, I also hired him to take me around when conducting

FPATT business, which included taking me around to the clubs. I was paying him out of my own pocket.

During that initial period of the FPATT membership drive, Mike Townley, the English Attorney representing the Trinidad and Tobago 2006 World Cup players in their financial compensation matter against Jack Warner, had travelled to Trinidad as expected for his court appearance.

He arrived on Wednesday September 19th. And as was previously arranged, with Abdul as my hired chauffeur as usual, I picked him up at the airport and ensured that he checked-in to his Port of Spain hotel without incident.

But while I was simply supposed to be his host cum chaperone, I would play a much more critical role, relative to the purpose of his visit. Before he met with the local Attorneys representing the players to dis- cuss their strategy for the hearing that was scheduled for 11:45 a.m. on Friday September 21st, he asked, and I advised him about what he should expect both in specific and general terms, for which he expressed much appreciation.

But I would be exploited yet again. However, given the circumstances, I would never have expected to be on that occasion. In that instance, a press conference was to be held after the court hearing. It was scheduled for 3:00 p.m. that same afternoon. The venue was the Crown Plaza Hotel on Wrightson Road Port of Spain.

Although I was more than capable of doing the job, Brent Sancho had decided to solicit the services of an outside source to organize the press conference. The reason he gave was that he did not want to give the impression that FPATT had anything to do with it and by extension, that FPATT had anything to do with the then ongoing players dispute with Jack Warner. And in truth and in fact FPATT did not on both counts.

However, the fee that was being charged for the assignment by the individual whom he had contacted was TT$40,000.00. So, he then made another one of "those calls" to me, because he felt the individual's fee was as he put it, "too exorbitant". I had only about an hour and a half to do so. I delivered, with some assistance from his father Keith Sancho.

Because of the short notice and me having to get to work right away in order to pull it off, we neglected to discuss the fee that would be attached to my services for organizing the event. I took it for granted that since he knew that the assignment had absolutely nothing to do with FPATT, Brent would have known that I had to be paid for my services; especially since he had the TT$40,000.00 figure as a benchmark, which was the fee that he would have had to pay the other individual. However, I was never paid one cent.

Staying true to form, I decided to maintain a passive position on the matter, to avoid any possibility of an unpleasant confrontation that may have resulted if I didn't. But as attested to in some of the prior passages, Brent would not have been the first of those who would try to play me for a fool, nor would he be the last to do so.

And I was undoubtedly extremely good value for no money, because as it also turned out, the advice that I had given to the players English Attorney Mike Townley, did actually serve him in very good stead.

So much so that then back in London and in recognition of same, in a formal memo to the Germany 2006 World Cup players themselves, dated September 24th 2007, he wrote and I quote, "Can I say that Alison did a great job with everything, and without him and Abdul I would have been truly lost, and the outcome would not have been as positive as it had been. To be clear, I do consider what we now have as a real achievement." End of quote.

Because I was 100% committed to the FPATT cause, I was not at all deterred by Brent's mistreatment. There was a more important mission to focus on and to be accomplished. And so, I continued full throttle with the FPATT agenda into the month of October, although not having received any funds whatsoever for that month's living expenses, and still being owed the TT$18,000.00 balance for July and August.

But I was very much encouraged because progress was most definitely being made. You see, as a result of my Manchester initiative, FPATT had gained Candidate Membership from FIFPro. As such, FIFPro was expected to provide a grant of US$10,000.00 to FPATT, for which the then equivalent was approximately TT$60,000.00, to give the organization a start. I was advised that I would receive all outstanding living expenses payments owed to me from the FIFpro funds when it arrived. The total figure then stood at TT$28,000.00.

On Thursday October 4th 2007, the FIFPro grant arrived into the FPATT account at Scotia Bank St James. So then, in addition to the TT$7,500.00 sponsorship I had managed to secure from Toyota, the beginning balance in the FPATT account was TT$68,998.42.

Upon the news that the grant had arrived into the FPATT bank account, three of the five members of the FPATT hierarchy (they know who they are), who had made personal financial contributions towards the relaunch event of the organization, immediately requested partial reimbursements. Kevin Harrison also made a request for reimbursements for travel expenses etc., from London.

I was most definitely taken aback by their respective requests, since I thought that they had all made those contributions because they all had vested interests in seeing FPATT survive in the first instance, and thereafter thrive as an organization, especially given its purpose. Their requests most certainly gave me food for thought.

Then, while I was still owed living expenses payments for July, August and October, during which time I had been working my ass off, Kevin Harrison the Caucasian Englishman, received reimbursement forthwith from the then FPATT President's own resources, upon which he then gave me instructions to reimburse him out of the FIFpro funds, since he had reimbursed Harrison out of his very own pocket.

I had made no request for reimbursement for my own out of pocket expenses up to that point. I instead reminded the FPATT principals via e-mail of the purpose of the FIFPro funds, which as I understood it, was to get FPATT up and running. And I reiterated that by posing that rhetorical question directly to the FPATT Board. For example, I badly needed a computer, but apparently that was not a priority, as no consideration was being given to purchasing same.

I then suggested via e-mail that we all hold off on receiving any out-of-pocket reimbursements due, until the organization was in a position to afford reimbursements. But it appeared that Harrison was allowed to dictate proceedings and as such, my suggestion fell on deaf ears. I could not and did not hide my displeasure. It was at that point that I decided that it was finally time to stop people trying to play me for a fool.

So, since I was actually the poor one out of the lot, I then decided to formally request all the funds that was owed to me, including reimbursement for my own out of pocket expenses, to which like Harrison and the others, I was also entitled. I furnished the then FPATT Vice President with all the necessary receipts to substantiate my reimbursement claims, which he in turn forwarded to the then FPATT President for approval.

Via e-mail, the then FPATT President fully scrutinized all of the items for which I was claiming reimbursements. Some of my claims were being questioned by him. I had absolutely no problem with that as I am, always was, and always will be an advocate for total transparency, a fact to which one of my prior e-mails to the FPATT Board attested.

And while admitting that he was not privy to all of my FPATT activities, the then FPATT President still made the decision that I was not going to be reimbursed for the items that he admitted that he knew absolutely nothing about, since they were performed before he was appointed President. I noted that none of the individuals who were well aware of the said activities, did not stick up for me.

One of my claims was for 50% of my New York to London return airfare, which was on the basis that at the given time, the FPATT agenda provided the real impetus for me making the trip at the particular time, and was given high priority during the said trip. That claim was flatly turned down by the then FPATT President.

He claimed that I was going to be in the UK on "personal business" (re the invite from Carlos Edwards) anyway and as such, I should not have to be reimbursed the 50% of the air fare. So, once again, to avoid confrontation, I accepted the decision.

Meanwhile, Harrison was reimbursed his full return air fare from England by the then FPATT President, for what was a vacation to Tobago and Trinidad as far as I was concerned. I simply couldn't stop thinking about the fact that while my claims were being subjected to extreme scrutiny before I could be reimbursed, on the other hand however, those from Harrison were never subjected to any such process; he having received his reimbursement promptly, directly from the then FPATT President himself.

In requesting his reimbursement, Harrison claimed that he had an urgent need to pay his mortgage back in England. Adding insult to injury was while I was being denied legitimate claims, Harrison even received reimbursement for what the then FPATT President listed as "miscellaneous expenditure".

The then FPATT President's noble, well intended gesture towards Harrison, had me questioning myself as to why the same courtesy was not extended to me, "the local fella", who, like the Harrison fellow from England, also had bills to pay. While I didn't have any mortgage to pay back in the U.S., I still had to eat and was then owing the $4,500.00 October's rent in Trinidad.

Harrison himself even had the audacity to question my request for reimbursement for as he put it, "taking taxis". The reimbursement I was requesting was for the taxi, Abdul's, that I usually had to hire for hours on those respective days, or for an entire day to conduct FPATT's business. Such was the case when I had to visit the Pro League teams during the membership drive.

Such was also the case, when Harrison himself was being chauffeured around Port of Spain to do media interviews and attend meetings, including the one with the then TT Pro League CEO Dexter Skeen, all of which I arranged for him. It cost me a few thousand dollars out of pocket in total over those periods I had to hire the said taxi, to conduct FPATT's business in my capacity as its General Secretary, while in Trinidad.

It was then crystal clear to me that Harrison was being given more respect, being perceived as more trustworthy and ultimately, also being perceived as a more valuable asset to the FPATT organization than I was; and thus, was being given special treatment.

And that was in spite of the fact that I was doing the majority of the work and producing results, and was the then driving force behind the organization literally speaking; points that were made by Harrison himself in some of his e-mails to me, although I certainly did not want or need any commendations or validation from him. In one such e-mail, Harrison even suggested that the then FPATT Board should be replaced, since they were not doing much.

Because I knew with 100% certainty that I had absolutely nothing to hide, I was more than willing to be open to, accept and be subjected to the extreme scrutiny of my reimbursement claims that was being conducted by the then FPATT President.

What I wasn't prepared to accept or subject myself to, was the discrimination and what I felt was not only professional, but personal disrespect. Not for the first time in my homeland, did I not only hear the message that was being sent; I also saw quite clearly, the message that was being sent as well. With my steadfast intolerance for such, I knew then that my exit from the organization was imminent.

And so, on Friday October 19th 2007, after just over 4 months as its first General Secretary, I tendered my resignation to the FPATT Board. Subsequent phone calls from both Brent Sancho and the then FPATT President went unanswered.

I did however, take a call from the then FPATT VP, whom I had always known to be a very upstanding and serious minded individual. He tried to persuade me to stay on. But given all that had transpired over the course of my short tenure, culminating in the reimbursement issue, I let him know that my decision to resign was final.

A few days before I had resigned, I had contacted Mick McGuire in the UK to get a first-hand update on FPATT's FIFPro membership application, since that initial news came from another source within FPATT. The following was Mick's e-mail reply sent Thursday October 25th 2007, which I cut and pasted for the purpose of authenticity.

Alison

Thank you for your email.

I can confirm that FIFPro are looking to offer you candidate membership which I believe is on a two-year basis following which you would become a full member.

As a full member you would be entitled not to a grant but to benefit from a solidarity payment and a payment for FIFPro's use of your logo. In addition you would also receive payments for supporting the interactive computer games endorsement but the amount you receive is dependent upon your status and the amount your players are used in the computer game.

I believe you have been invited to FIFPro Congress in Barcelona at which information will be given to you in relation to all aspects of being a member of FIFPro.

I look forward to seeing you in Barcelona.

Regards
Mick

Prior to my resigning, and with respects to the closing line in Mick's e-mail, the then FPATT President, FPATT Vice President and I were going to be traveling to Barcelona Spain that November to attend the FIFPro Congress. In an e-mail message to me on the subject, the then FPATT President stated and I quote, "I think you'd be a fantastic asset to have there." End of quote.

The then FPATT President further stated that he would be personally covering all my expenses for the trip. That then gave me reason to believe that he may have gotten feedback from Gordon Taylor about my meeting with him in Manchester after all, which may have possibly included me getting a personal vote of confidence from Gordon himself.

However, and I hasten to add not surprising to me, having revealed his agenda to Tansley Thompson and myself, Kevin Harrison, though not selected to go on the trip, inserted himself into the Barcelona picture. Being that I was someone who was never pushy, or to ever even entertain, much less engage in any such debate, I then simply withdrew myself from the Barcelona picture also by way of my resignation, to allow the Harrison fella to have his "Reign in Spain".

When all was said and done, with no other choice but to accept my resignation, which official acceptance came via e-mail from the then FPATT President, I was subsequently paid a portion of the total of the living expenses payment that was owed to me. And I was only paid reimbursements on the items that the then FPATT President deemed to be legitimate claims. The FPATT chapter was then closed. I returned to the U.S. shortly thereafter.

And remember that government grant that I had solicited on my very own initiative from the Ministry of Sport on behalf of FPATT in June of 2007? Well, TT$3.25 million got Cabinet approval in late 2008. But by that time however, the organization had apparently been in limbo. Yet another yeoman's effort had completely gone to waste.

I personally viewed the existence of an organization such as FPATT as necessary in my homeland. To me its non-existence meant that a monumental opportunity had been lost to finally empower the local football players, who, over generations continued to be powerless.

I had returned to Trinidad earlier in 2008, to continue my personal mission of making a positive social contribution in my homeland through the sport of football, but under my own terms and conditions. My then latest project was in the form of a community football league, based on a revolutionary points award system I invented.

And so, in June 2008, I introduced the "GOAL POINTS FOOTBALL LEAGUE" (GPFL), to give back as I did to Point Fortin, to another place that I lived for many years; that place was the vibrant community of St. James, Port of Spain.

Before the league kicked off, I first ensured that the playing field, which needed a fair amount of work, was upgraded. I also employed the services of qualified match officials for every game. They each received financial compensation for their services.

The league, which had 12 participating teams, was conducted at the well-known St James Infirmary facility over a period of 3 months, and was run in a highly professional manner, with rules and regulations, which had to be strictly adhered to. The league was a resounding success, and got national media coverage, with big crowds attending games, to which admission was free of charge. I made efforts towards launching a similar initiative in Curepe, because I also wanted to give back to the Curepe community. However, and very regretfully I might add, it never materialized.

Thus, the 2008 GOAL POINTS FOOTBALL LEAGUE, could well turn out to have been my final act with respects to serving my beloved homeland, utilizing the vehicle of sport, and football in particular.

If so; and in spite of the many challenges faced with respects to my many undertakings, I would hope to have left a legacy defined by unquestionable integrity, professionalism, creativity and innovation; and by not only always getting the job done, but getting the job done to the very highest professional standards, in my pursuit of professional excellence, epitomized by my personal 4 P's motto; PRIDE. PURPOSE. PASSION. PATRIOTISM.

THE AYRES
GOAL-POINTS SYSTEM

© 2006 Alison C. Ayres

"Score Goals! Score Points. More Goals! More Points™"

Under the Ayres Goal-Points System™, points will be awarded as follows:

WINS

For a win where a team scores 1 goal, that team will be awarded 3 points.
For a win where a team scores 2 goals, that team will be awarded 3 ¼ points.
For a win where a team scores 3 goals, that team will be awarded 3 ½ points.
For a win where a team scores 4 goals, that team will be awarded 3 ¾ points.
For a win where a team scores 5 goals or more, that team will be awarded 4 points.

DRAWS

For a scoreless draw, the teams will be awarded 1 point.
For a draw where the teams score 1 or 2 goals, the teams will be awarded 1 ¼ point.
For a draw where the teams score 3 goals, the teams will be awarded 1 ½ point.
For a draw where the teams score 4 goals, the teams will be awarded 1 ¾ point.
For a draw where the teams score 5 goals or more, the teams will be awarded 2 points.

LOSSES

For a loss where the team does not score, that team will be awarded 0 points.
For a loss where the team scores 1 to 4 goals, that team will be awarded 1/4 point.
For a loss where the team scores 5 goals or more, that team will be awarded 1/2 point.

I submitted a proposal for my AYRES GOAL-POINTS SYSTEM™ for consideration by the International Football Association Board (IFAB), the organization that makes decisions on rules changes etc. for the sport. On the following page is the IFAB's formal response. I actually traveled to Trinidad and met with the then Trinidad and Tobago Football Association President William Wallace and requested support for my proposal as was required. His verbal response was in the affirmative, but it was never followed up with action, which was not at all surprising to me.

To
Mr. Alison C. Ayres
By e-mail: nosila2000@hotmail.com

Zürich, 18 February 2019
SEC/2018-L268/bru

Your proposal

Dear Mr Ayres,

On behalf of The International Football Association Board (The IFAB), I would like to thank you for your correspondence dated 7 January 2019 and your proposal on how the Laws of the Game could be improved.

We are always pleased to see that people the world over truly care about football and share a passion to develop and enhance the game with new approaches.

While we have read your correspondence with interest, we would like to inform you that The IFAB can only consider proposals that are supported and then submitted by the respective national association on your behalf. Therefore, we suggest you get in touch with your national association in order to potentially take your proposal further.

We wish you all the best in your future endeavours and thank you once more for the interest shown.

Yours sincerely,

The International Football Association Board

Lukas Brud
Secretary

The International Football Association Board
Münstergasse 9   8001 Zurich   Switzerland
T: +41 (0)44 245 1886   theifab.com

FAMILY MATTERS

JEALOUSY AND DYSFUNCTION

Publicly revealing or sharing one's unpleasant personal experiences with one's family, and more specifically, those involving one's parents and or siblings, has forever been considered Taboo in my homeland.

Airing any such so called "dirty laundry" for public consumption, as truthful as the experiences may be, would usually see the individual airing said dirty laundry, being heavily criticized by said family members as well as relatives, friends, acquaintances and even members of the public at large.

The individual could ultimately become an object of scorn and be treated as a family outcast, because the general rule is that such dirty laundry should be kept within the confines of the household and family circle. As such, most are not prepared to risk being the said object of scorn and a family outcast, and so choose to remain silent on the issue while suffering in said silence.

And that is quite understandable; because like in many other cultures, we are brought up from the time we leave the womb, to believe that family is the most sacred of all social institutions, and should be defended and protected at all cost, to eternity.

Like in many other cultures, we are brought up to believe that family would provide the most joyful of joyful life experiences, and the most cherishable of cherishable lifetime memories during the course of our respective lives. And the truth is; family does that.

And above all else, like in many other cultures, we are brought up to believe that family will be there for us, especially in times when we are in most need. And here again the truth is; most times they are. We hold those truths to be self-evident, and so, live by those creeds.

But on the other hand, and being very mindful that all of our respective families and family experiences and dynamics are not the same; how many of us are ever told about the other side of the family coin?

I refer to the other side of the coin where the harsh reality is, that as joyful and as cherishable as the family experience can be; it can also be equally as painful as a result of the unpleasant experiences. Experiences that can inflict the deepest emotional and psychological wounds that one would ever have inflicted upon them, during their respective lifetimes; wounds that can leave one scarred for life, or for the rest of their life as the case may be.

From childhood to adolescence, into and during young adulthood and beyond, I had been continuously learning firsthand, that life was filled with seemingly never-ending trials and tribulations. But never ever did I, would I, or could I have ever imagined that at some point, it would actually be members of my very own immediate family; my very own blood; who would be the absolute root cause of my life's most extreme trials and tribulations. As such, as stated in the opening line of my book, and more specifically in the prologue, and I quote, "My life always revolved around family, especially my single parent mother and older brother."

In the prologue I also state that because of all the sacrifices that our mother had made to provide for her children while we were growing up, I personally wanted more than anything, to repay her by making her both proud and happy one day. And so, I embarked upon a life journey of pursuing my childhood dreams, but with the higher purpose of personally repaying my mother for the debt that I felt I owed her.

Once I had successfully completed my studies at Pratt in 1985, whereby I then had a higher earning potential, that life ambition came into focus. I literally began living my life for my mother; doing any and everything to please her and to make her happy and proud. As such, I was always very mindful of not doing anything that would cause her worry, embarrassment, hurt or harm.

But as my book would attest, I also extended myself above and beyond for my older brother in particular and to a very significant degree, my other two older siblings in general. I did so despite the fact that none of my older siblings ever offered me any type of support, moral or otherwise, while I attended Pratt, when I desperately needed it. Yet they would all come to benefit from my Pratt exploits.

I do fully understand the cultural Taboo in my homeland of not airing one's so-called family dirty laundry in public. I also do fully understand the possible consequences of doing so.

But my book is about my life, which mostly revolved around my family, where during the first 25 to 30 years there were indeed many joyful experiences and memories to cherish, most of which occurred when we were all growing up together in Point Fortin. They were sporadic thereafter, and were made up mostly of time spent indoors, when I would visit either of my family members at their respective places of abode over those years.

But the fact is that I have also had some extremely unpleasant family experiences, from early middle age, between 40 and 50, but more so during my late middle-age years, between 50 and 60; experiences that were at times overwhelmingly painful; experiences that left deep scars.

I will not exclude them from my book only for reason of conforming to some cultural Taboo, or for reason of preserving the perception among relatives in particular, and so-called friends, acquaintances, and the public in general, of a seemingly close-knit family. Although it once was, the reality is that it became increasingly dysfunctional the older we grew, when we began resenting each other for our own respective reason or reasons.

Until this book, and conforming to the Taboo I guess, I was very much guarded about my personal and family life. By now making both public, my culture assumes that I will be bringing some degree of embarrassment upon myself and family members, especially in the eyes of those in my homeland, and among those from my homeland residing elsewhere, who choose to read my story.

I reiterate. This is in fact my life story, wherein there were some extremely unpleasant family experiences. Given the effects of those experiences, it would be very remiss of me not to share them. Furthermore, my life has never been about deception, pretending, or about trying to impress, or creating false impressions. Therefore, the perceived consequences of revealing its harsh realities does not matter to me. The only thing that does...is being truthful.

"THE SIBLING LETTERS"

Because of my upbringing, the "Family First" philosophy, which was inculcated from very early on, was always upper most in my mind. Therefore, my family was always my number one priority in my life.

As such, after graduating from Pratt Institute in 1985, and subsequently embarking on my Advertising / Graphic Design career in earnest, major professional and personal life decisions were determined by how they would have affected my ability to achieve my life ambition with respects to my mother in particular; and to assist my siblings in general.

And so, over the next 3 decades, even when I could not afford to say yes to various requests from family members, which were usually of a financial nature, and often had far reaching consequences for me personally, I never said no.

During the 9 post Pratt years that I worked the 8 to 4 jobs in Trinidad before I became self-employed in 1995, that meant having to request advances on my monthly salary on numerous occasions from my respective employers; or I would simply do without something that I wanted or needed for myself to facilitate them.

Given the extremely rough life we all had whilst growing up, I was just happy to have been then in a position, where I could help the members of my family when called upon. I did so genuinely. I was totally committed to my family without reservation.

Then one fateful day in late 2002, during what was supposed to have been a brief visit to New York from Florida, I discovered some letters from one of my two older siblings living in Trinidad to our mother in New York. The discovery of those letters was a major defining moment, as it would dramatically change my whole concept of what family meant to me personally. Following are the circumstances surrounding the discovery.

Having started my NOSILA Sportswear business in Orlando Florida that year with my cousin BoPeep as a partner, I was based there at the time. That September, I had to make a trip to New York to source a supplier as a matter of urgency, as I explained in an earlier passage. I had my own keys to my mother's apartment and mail box. Upon arrival, before heading up to the second-floor apartment, I first checked the mail box on the ground floor.

That procedure became almost natural, because by some strange coincidence, I always came upon some piece of correspondence related to some important matter, that I would have needed to address on my mother's behalf, which she could not handle herself. That September 2002 trip was no different.

But on that particular occasion, I retrieved a piece of mail that was most disturbing. It contained court documents, indicating that my mother was going to be evicted in a couple of weeks for the non-payment of rent dating back many months. That also meant that I would have then needed alternative accommodation, for which I had no options.

My mother would have needed to appear in court to defend herself against her then Landlord's claim, which I had to avoid because I found out that she was in fact owing rent. The amount left me totally shocked.

So, I was then faced with yet another extremely distressing situation related to our mother in New York, which I had to resolve on my own, because I knew that assistance from my two older siblings living in Trinidad would not be forthcoming. They had never offered any when such situations arose in the past, and I did not think that I should have had to ask them for assistance for our mother anyway.

Consequently, the stress started almost from the moment I arrived in New York that day in late September 2002. Then not to long thereafter, my sister Cheryl, the eldest of my mother's 5 children who lived a half block away, fell seriously ill and had to be hospitalized.

With Cheryl then hospitalized, and with my mother needing to vacate the apartment before being evicted, I made an urgent request to the elder of my sister's two daughters who lived at the apartment with their mother at the time, for their grandmother to stay at their apartment, until I could sort out the situation.

I was left absolutely dumbfounded, when I was told that my mother (her grandmother), could not stay at their apartment. I could not believe my ears, especially since it was in fact a real crisis, and her mother's bedroom was then available, with her then being in the hospital.

Whatever her reason or reasons for not wanting to accommodate her grandmother, I still felt that she should have been accommodated if only because of me personally, given the fact that I had been there for them and their both parents in times of need. I was therefore left a bit stunned by the decision. But the situation was such that there was no time for me to dwell on it.

So, I immediately started making arrangements with my other niece, my older brother's daughter, who lived in Washington, for our mother to stay with her and her family, until I was able to sort things out. Interestingly enough, my niece who turned down my request for her grandmother to stay at their apartment, which was a half block away, was more than happy to drive her to Washington and did so.

That now brings me to how I discovered the "Sibling Letters", which would dramatically change my whole concept of what family meant to me personally. While going through stuff to dispose of to clear out my mother's apartment to vacate, I came upon a fairly large pile of mail, which was being stored in a plastic shopping bag. Not sure about how much of it would have been worth keeping, I decided to sort through the pile.

During the process, I came upon some letters from one of my two older sibling living in Trinidad, to our mother. Out of curiosity I decided to scan through the letters. While doing so, I discovered that I was being referred to in most of them, and upon closer examination, I realized that I was the primary subject in a particular one. Upon reading that particular letter, almost impulsively, I immediately recalled a conversation that I had with an associate in Trinidad (initials HP) not too long before, during which we were discussing life in general, when the topic of family came up.

While the relationship between my two older siblings and I had already been deteriorating, during our conversation I was still pledging my love, loyalty, allegiance, and commitment to my family. "FAMILY!?" HP exclaimed, in a tone that clearly suggested that he perhaps wanted nothing to do with his.

For some strange reason I had never forgotten his response that day, which was obviously one he could have justified if he needed to, I'm sure. But his one-word verbal response and the tone used to express it said it all. I could not fully understand his response at the time, that is, until I read my older sibling's letters.

She had written them during a sequence of correspondence between herself and our mother dating back to 1998. I had also brought Alicia to New York in December that year to meet my mother. In her letters, my older sibling was telling our mother things about me, which for her own intents and purposes, was clearly intended to turn our mother against me.

In her letter, wherein I was the main subject, my older sibling expressed views and opinions with unbridled resentment about a "Big Shot" lifestyle, that she and other family members and some relatives perceived I was living in Trinidad with Alicia. Based on her letter, the views and opinions she expressed, appeared to have been supported by my older brother in particular.

She went so far as to let our mother know that my older brother and I were not on good terms, and that she herself had planned to never speak to me again for whatever reason. She would eventually reveal her reason in another letter years later. I was also not supposed to have seen that letter, but I did.

She said a lot of very unpleasant stuff about me to our mother in her letters. It was very clear that she was harboring deep resentment towards me. Yet she continued communicating and visiting me with a big smile on her face whenever I was in Trinidad, since she was not aware that I had discovered her letters.

It was also only upon reading her letters, that I realized that my sister had been continuously requesting money from our mother, as well as making numerous other requests for our mother to "sen' a barrel" with stuff for her, all of which our mother fulfilled.

That was a major part of the reason that our mother was then in the eviction predicament I met her in, upon my arrival from Florida. Instead of paying her rent, our mother had been sending money and barrels of stuff to my sister.

For many years I had been willingly sharing, and they were all enjoying the benefits of my blessings. So, after reading the contents of her letters, the question then arose in my mind as to whether jealousy was at the root of the issues, that my two older siblings were having with me.

In my older brother's case, that question would be answered years later with "the slip of the tongue" of his own daughter. And as it turned out, one of my sister's letters revealed that my older brother was the instigator, relative to the issue that had her resenting me.

The issue revolves around me filing for permanent U.S. residency for myself and my older brother, whom, although we were not on good terms, I decided to do that huge favor at my own expense. Because I did not do the same for my sister, she has been holding it against me ever since.

It is an issue that my mother would also come to hold against me and also resent me for, after my sister complained to her about it in one of her letters, and for which I would eventually receive years and years of verbal, emotional and mental abuse from my mother, which in turn would also eventually see the relationship between me and my mother being adversely affected.

What really irked me about that situation was the fact that my two older siblings were the architects of their own immigration problems, after they both chose to overstay in the U.S. illegally. Furthermore, like myself, they were both adults in their 40's at the time I filed. It was their very own responsibility to act in their own interest towards their eventual immigration to the U.S. I was under no obligation to act on their behalf, but still decided to do my older brother that huge favor.

It so happened that the same year that the letters started from my sister, which I wasn't aware of at the time, was the same year I took Alicia to New York to meet my mother, which was back in December of '98. Alicia and I had already been a couple for almost 8 years at the time.

After Alicia had left New York, our mother, in a letter in response to one from my sister, expressed that she didn't want Alicia in the family. In the said letter, our mother vowed that she was going to break up the relationship between Alicia and I through "spiritual means". In Trinidad terms that means by "wuking Obeah". In the U.S. it is more widely known as Witchcraft or Black Magic.

I simply could not believe or even begin to wrap my mind around what I was actually reading in the letters. And that was because what I was reading was that my very own sister, who was influencing our mother, and whose views and opinions it appeared, was being supported by my older brother, were conspiring to create major strife in my life, for reasons I could not understand at the time.

Some of my very closest adult relatives were also fully aware of all that was going on, which was also unknown to me until I discovered the letters. Still, while it became clear that they were all ill speaking me behind my back, they all had broad smiles on their faces whenever they saw me.

Having then read, absorbed, and processed all the malicious and defamatory contents and intents in the letters against me, it became extremely difficult for me to be around my very own family and those relatives who were involved, because they had then totally lost my trust. And so, I avoided them as much as possible.

Professionally, because of all that was then going on, and at the time when I was also in the midst of having to deliver football kits to the Arizona client, I had to quickly come to the realization that my NOSILA business venture, was then at risk of being totally derailed once again because of family issues. My stress was mounting.

We then found out that my sister Cheryl was in fact terminally ill and could die within a few months. With my mother in Washington, I then had just a couple of days to vacate the apartment. I would then have had no place of abode except to incur the expense of a hotel, which was totally out of the question.

Compounded by the things I had then only recently read in the correspondences between my older sibling and my mother; my distress level was way up there. Each day I faced became a severe test of my mental, emotional and spiritual fortitude.

And like in similar situations over the years, I never once complained to, or laid my burdens down on anyone. I simply endured my personal and professional trials and tribulations in silence and kept it moving, usually with a smile on my face.

My then immediate priority was to secure a place to stay while I was in New York. Given the circumstances under which my mother had to vacate, staying at the then current apartment did not seem to be an option at the time. But with no other choice, I simply swallowed my pride and contacted and requested an audience with the landlord, with a view to addressing and resolving my mother's rent issue.

When we met, I informed him that my mother had in fact already vacated and was then in Washington, but because of my sister's prognosis, both she and I needed to be physically present. I offered to pay off all of the rent that my mother owed, which would have allowed that to happen, since we had no other place to go. I was literally begging the landlord to accept my proposal.

Sensing my personal desperation, he eventually agreed to rent the apartment to me personally, but for one month only, without me having to pay off my mother's back rent, and on the condition that she would not be reoccupying the apartment while I was there. I agreed and the deal was done. I had secured accommodation, but only for one month.

To my shock, about a week after my mother had left for Washington she was back in Brooklyn. Given that we had to vacate and not knowing whether I was still there or not, she decided to go straight to a friend's apartment upon her return.

I then had no other choice but to allow my mother to return to the apartment, which was a breach of my agreement with the landlord. My mother had gotten the news that her daughter was still hospitalized, so there was no way she would have ever stayed in Washington knowing that anyway.

But as challenging as it was for me to do so with all that was going on at the time, I still had to try to focus on keeping my business going, then having that huge order from the football club in Arizona to finish fulfill. I still managed to meet that challenge, details of which were revealed in a previous passage.

With my then mounting stress, to try to get my mind off all that was going on at the time, I just continued working on designs for my range of NOSILA products, including the final design for what was to be the first in the line of my NOSILA brand of football boots, which was being called the Nosila MVP.

Not wanting the landlord to discover that my mother was back in the apartment, which would have been grounds for my immediate eviction, a game of cat and mouse ensued. I was then desperate to find us another. With my paperwork for permanent U.S. residency already being processed, I intended to then also be on the lease for any apartment that I was able to secure.

Then in late October there was a ray of hope. Another of my mother's friends who knew that we were in desperate need of living accommodation, brought us a housing application, but it was for Senior Housing.

That meant that if we were able to secure an apartment in such a facility, I could not be on the lease until I was 62 years old. I was only 43 at the time. But while I could not have been on the lease, if we in fact secured a Senior Housing apartment, as my mother's caregiver, I would have been able to live at the apartment legally, which was all that really mattered, given our then desperate situation.

So, I filled out and submitted the application together with some other paperwork, which was only the first step in the process. The building in which we were applying for the apartment was in the final phase of completion, and was only months away from being ready for occupancy.

But there was bad news. My mother, who would be the leaseholder, was found ineligible to rent an apartment because her monthly SSI income was much less than what was required for eligibility. I decided not to give her the bad news. But since it represented our best chance of securing an apartment, and one that would be very affordable, I refused to give up.

I contacted the offices of the organization that owned the building via telephone and spoke to a female representative. I was honest about our situation. She informed me of what was needed to make my mother eligible to rent an apartment in the building, and advised me to re-submit a new application once I was able to meet the specific requirements, which had to be supported by legitimate documentation. I complied. Thereafter it was a wait and see scenario.

But the ultimate bad news came eventually, with the passing of my sister Cheryl on January 15th 2003. At that point in time, with all that was going on otherwise, I swear that I was on my absolute last, mentally, and physically.

Meanwhile, the initial month-long rental agreement I had entered into with the landlord had since turned into four. He gave the extensions only because my sister had continued to be hospitalized with her terminally ill prognosis. During that time, she was visited daily by family and friends, as the vigil continued from early October when she was admitted, into the peak of the winter season. Her funeral took place on January 20th 2003, on what was a very cold winter's day.

The game of cat and mouse continued between me, the landlord and my mother over the 4 months we occupied the apartment, to ensure that she wasn't discovered. My stress level stayed at maximum through-out. Once my sister's funeral took place, he advised that there would be no further extension on our rental arrangement. He let it be known that January would be the absolute final month before I myself would have to vacate.

We had since been formally notified via a letter, that my mother was then eligible to rent an apartment from the organization, after all the necessary paperwork that was submitted was found to be in good order, upon which the new application had been approved.

I was then anxiously anticipating the next step, which was the inter-view that could possibly see us secure what would be a brand-new apart-ment. The appointment was set for January 24th, just four days after my sister's funeral.

At the interview, apart from the fact that she is deaf, as my mother's caregiver I answered all the questions and provided any other informa-tion that was needed. If the interview was successful, the final part of the process would be paying the first month's rent together with the security deposit, and having my mother sign a one year or two years lease and other relevant documents.

And there was great news on that front, when we were subsequently notified via a phone call from the female representative who had been engaged with the entire process, that we had in fact secured an apartment. Securing the apartment took that extremely heavy weight off my shoul-ders, and gave me the peace of mind that I needed on that front for two main reasons.

The first was knowing that my mother would then be living in a very comfortable environment and situation from then onwards, and would never have to worry about ever being displaced again domestically at any time in the future. The second reason was knowing that I myself would not have to worry about where I was going to live when I eventually immigrated.

The apartment lease was signed on January 30th 2003; 4 months after the extremely stressful process of securing the new apartment started. With the deadline to vacate the other apartment then upon us, I moved over all the necessary stuff that very day. The next day I took my mother to see the apartment, which was just two and a half blocks from the residence she had lived at on the very same street for almost 5 years, and the very same area she had lived in for more than a decade at the time.

When we got there, I put the key in the key hole and left it to her to simply turn it to open the door. She did. She then stepped inside the apartment and began surveying it in its entirety. Her expression said it all. She was the absolutely happiest mother in the world. As such, I was then the happiest son in the world. The day was Friday January 31st 2003. We were the very first to occupy an apartment in the building.

And so, through a combination of initiative, an innate never ever give up attitude, and what I once again believed was "Spiritual Orchestration", I had managed to secure a brand-new apartment in which our mother could live very comfortably for the rest of her life. In doing so, I was then also delivering on another promise that I made to myself many years before.

I had since completed the final design for the NOSILA MVP football boots, and had sent it off to a company in Italy to have the first prototypes made, at a cost of US$2,000.00. I was really excited and could not wait for them to be delivered.

Meanwhile, apart from having to be there to prepare for an Inaugural Charity Youth Football Camp Event that I was putting on in August that year, I had since received notification from the United States

Citizenship and Immigration Services (USCIS), and would have needed to be in Trinidad to receive future correspondences. So, I had to return to Trinidad.

Once I was satisfied that my mother was settled into the new apartment, I left for Trinidad on February 21st 2003. And after a relatively short second stint at my then temporary Tacarigua east Trinidad abode, I once again relocated to Fort George Road in St James, where Alicia joined me as she continued to be my live-in spouse.

My older brother had himself since moved back there and occupied one bedroom of the three-bedroom residence. I occupied another with the third being unoccupied. The rest of our top floor residence remained common areas as was always the case.

Being in the presence of my older brother on a daily basis, with the thought of the malicious contents of my other older sibling letters to our mother swirling around in my head was killing me inside, knowing then that he was a part of it. Since discovering the letters, I had been silently dealing with my "Sibling Demons", struggling to understand why they had so much ill-will towards me, after I had been so good to them.

Because I knew that I had done absolutely nothing to any of them, the only answer that made sense was my jealousy theory on both of my older siblings' part; that natural human trait that often surfaces in others in the face of someone else's success, if they too are not as, or more successful themselves. Still, the thing is, it was not like I was getting rich from my success; far from it.

Was it because of not only the successes that I was having in my life, but more so the magnitude? I asked myself many questions over time, while trying to come to terms with their obvious feelings of ill-will towards me, which would have been very easy for me to understand and accept if I had been selfish with my successes. But I most definitely was not. Instead, I was the exact opposite.

The first NOSILA MVP football boots prototypes for both dry and wet conditions arrived in Trinidad from Italy via FedEx in mid-May 2003.

I was forced to take a TT$1,000.00 loan from my older brother, as the local FedEx charge for the delivery of the package was TT$3,000.00. I only had TT$2,000.00 on my person the day it arrived. I paid my brother back within a few days.

The prototypes were produced in the latest materials on the market. The pair for wet conditions was white in color and the pair for dry conditions was produced in black. But being that it would be the first in the NOSILA line, I first wanted to offer a signature product in the mold of the Puma King and Adidas Copa Mundial. I mostly wore the Puma King myself, because it was also the boots my childhood idol Pele wore during his playing days.

So, I then reordered additional prototypes using the original NOSILA MVP design to match that mold in terms of material, construction and craftmanship. They arrived one month later. Thankfully, I didn't need to ask my older brother for another loan when they arrived. With a bit of tweaking, we were ready to go to the second stage of the prototypes production.

I actually gifted one of the first two prototypes that were delivered, to a participant of my Inaugural August 2003 Charity Youth Football Camp, who did not have any football boots, but badly wanted to participate. He did not know it, but the price tag on the pair of boots he wore during the camp and thereafter owned, was US$1,000.00, which was equivalent to almost $7,000.00 TT dollars. I also gifted the other pair to Alicia's cousin, with whom I used to play on a regular basis with other youths from the area where they lived.

Meanwhile, my final U.S. permanent residency paperwork was eventually received in late 2003. After spending one year in Trinidad, I departed Trinidad for New York in February 2004.

Although I had lost a great degree of respect for my two older siblings and some relatives, I still was not disrespectful to them. I would eventually reveal my discovery of the letters to my older brother, and impressed upon him the fact that I knew how he and his sister felt towards me, so they need not pretend otherwise. I knew that my revelation was in no way going to help our situation going forward; and it was not meant to. I just needed him to know that I knew.

With my mother since being made aware of the dysfunction between my two older siblings and I via the letters from my sister, but not wanting to hold her two older children accountable, my mother then decided to use my girlfriend Alicia as a scapegoat.

She raised the issue quite frequently, upon which she would state angrily that it was Alicia who was causing the problem, and that Alicia was "mashin' up de family". She usually followed up that statement by verbally abusing me in defense of my two older siblings, and demanding that I end my relationship with Alicia.

My mother simply did not want to accept the fact that her two older children, over many years, had themselves conspired to, as she put it, "mash up de family". And sadly, it may have all come about because of what seemed to be another case of sibling jealousy, which often times results in once close-knit families being the casualties, as it was in this case.

But one thing was for certain. I was not going to end my longstanding relationship, which was going very strong and was without any major issues, simply because my mother wanted me to. It was the one time she was not going to get her own way with me. I was definitely not going to choose my two conniving older siblings over Alicia.

With that defiance in addition to what continued being fed to her by my sister through more letters, the relationship between my mother and I would also gradually begin to deteriorate over time. Still, it did not deter me from continuing to take care of her.

The thing is, while I had been always there for that particular older sister in her times of need, be it financial or otherwise, she has never done anything of significance for me throughout her entire life.

I have never even received a phone call or a birthday card, much less a gift from her on my birthday over the course of our lives. It was the same with my older brother; except for the fact that we had been doing each other financial and other favors over most of our adult lives.

OUR MISSING OLDER BROTHER

Enter June 2012. Late that month, I was at home in New York when a call came from Trinidad. It was my sister, which was very unusual. She stated that no one had either seen or heard from our older brother for what was then going on one month. She said that he was not answering his phone; not even calls from relatives residing in different parts of North America with whom he was close, who had since also become aware of the situation.

Several relatives based in Trinidad also paid several visits to his Cocorite residence, with absolutely no response from him when banging on the door and windows of his ground floor apartment. They said that even his neighbors said they had not seen or heard from him during that time. I said nothing to our mother, since I knew that sharing such news could have had serious consequences, given her medical conditions.

Long before he went missing, I was engaged in a legal matter which was then before a U.S. Civil Court, from which I was likely to walk away with a decent sum, that was earmarked for my NOSILA business venture. After then 17 years of fits and starts, there was no giving up on bringing it to reality.

I had initially hired an Attorney. But because of financial constraints, I was eventually forced to represent myself in my court matter. That meant that I then had to learn the ins and outs of the law and the court process relative to my case. So, I buckled down and studied online, and through educational material at the Brooklyn Central Library, where I spent many hours, over the 2 1/2-year period it took for the case to be brought to trial.

I thoroughly enjoyed the learning process and representing myself. It was an extremely valuable and empowering experience. During that time, there were notices, answers, replies, affidavits, motions, et al., filed by me the Plaintiff on my own behalf, and the Defendant's Attorneys on the Defendant's behalf.

As part of the proceedings, I also underwent a deposition that was conducted by the Defendant's Lead Attorney. It lasted exactly 3 hours and 4 minutes, during which time I was asked a total of 764 questions. The deposition left me with a feeling of absolute pride, because it brought to bare my professional integrity, and confirmed that it was unquestionable.

With the news about my older brother, I had begun preparing for my mother and I to travel to Trinidad as a matter of urgency, if no one heard from him by 9:00 a.m. on July 2nd 2012, which was also the day of the trial. I did not reveal anything about the possible trip to our mother for obvious reasons.

I set the 9:00 a.m. deadline since the trial was supposed to begin at 9:30 a.m. on the day, and it would have then given me the opportunity to make an informed decision with respects to whether the trial could proceed, or if I would have needed to request an adjournment to a later date.

The 9:00 a.m. deadline arrived, but no call came from Trinidad. I therefore had to assume that no one still hadn't heard from or seen my older brother. My thought then was that my mother and I would have had to leave the U.S. within a couple of days.

I was well prepared for the trial, and quickly gained the upper hand upon giving my testimony and providing my mound of evidence relative to the matter. I was winning hands down in Court on the day. The Judge eventually gave us the option to try to reach a settlement.

Because getting to Trinidad as soon as possible was then the priority, I agreed to do so, and accepted an offer that was significantly less than the figure I was likely to have been awarded by the Court, if I had let the trial run its course.

The plan was to purchase the plane tickets once I got back to the apartment, for me and my mother to leave New York for Trinidad within 48 hours. On my way out of the building, the call that I had been waiting for from Trinidad before I appeared before the Judge, came. My older brother was finally located. But I had already agreed to a settlement in the matter.

It was very much a bitter sweet moment for me personally; because while it was in fact good news, unbelievably, it turned out that my older brother had simply been locked away in his apartment all the while, in what turned out to be self-imposed isolation.

He had been ignoring everyone's phone calls etc. on purpose; all of whom were obviously extremely concerned about his wellbeing. I quickly figured out that during his self-imposed isolation, he would have been engaged in one of his extended meditation rituals, related to a certain religion he had been involved with for many, many years.

With that knowledge, any anxiety that I harbored over his perceived plight, quickly turned into anger. His then latest of June / July of 2012, basically had all and sundry thinking that he could possibly have been dead somewhere.

Once that entire episode was over in very early July, my older brother informed me that he was owing months of back rent and requested some funds to pay it off, since he was not working at the time. I forwarded the funds to him immediately. Between that time and late August, he made two more requests for funds, which I facilitated.

That October, I made an impromptu trip to Trinidad. There were two specific reasons that I made the trip. One was to tie the knot with Alicia. The other reason was to take over handling a matter relative to our deceased father's estate, after my older brother had asked me to, because our father's widow was being dismissive of both him and his sister, and was dragging her feet with regards to delivering our legal entitlements, since the deceased did not leave a Will.

I traveled to Trinidad on Friday October 12th 2012. And while I did not intend to, upon his invite, I decided to stay at my older brother's place. It was obvious that his invitation was as a result of the financial favors that I had done for him recently. So that was my pay back, I guess.

During my visit, which turned out to be 3 months long, because of the legal matter that I was also there to handle, I learnt that not for the first time, my older brother had been unemployed by choice. I also learnt that he had been making arrangements behind my back, to have our mother placed in a home for the elderly, as against sharing caregiving responsibilities with me, which we had planned out years before.

But most importantly, if I had any doubts, I learnt from the horse's mouth, exactly what he thought about me, during a really heated verbal altercation that we had over a few matters. Personally, I happen to believe that in anger truth is spoken.

As for the matter involving our legal entitlements? The matter was concluded in late December 2012, upon which my older brother, sister, younger brother, and myself each received an equal amount of cash from a substantial entitlement total. I had offered to get my younger brother's funds converted and delivered to him in U.S.

However, his wicked sister somehow convinced him to leave it in Trinidad in her care; and so, he did. What he did not know, was that she did so with an extremely sinister plan in mind. She ended up stealing TT$45,000.00 of his money.

I returned to New York on January 22nd 2013. I intended to purchase my own place in Florida and relocate there from New York. The plan was to then restart my NOSILA Sportswear business in partnership with my cousin BoPeep once again, which we had already discussed.

But apart from the possibility of physical and other forms of abuse, I knew for a fact that my mother would never have been comfortable or happy living in a home for the elderly, as was my older brother's preferred solution, as against sharing the responsibility of helping me take care of her. I knew then that I had to make another huge life decision in the interest of our mother's welfare and wellbeing. And so, I did.

I thus cancelled my plans to relocate to Florida and remained in New York to continue to take care of her, where winter challenges aside, she absolutely loves living, because of its many conveniences. But more importantly, it is where she has her friends and relatives. And I must admit that I too love New York more than I do Florida.

Meanwhile, with our relationship all but officially dead, I would however, do my older brother one more good deed, that was extremely critical for him to obtain his permanent U.S. residency. His U.S. immigration process had been in limbo for years because he needed a Joint-Sponsor, which he was unable to secure himself, although having his daughter and some very close friends residing there for many years; all Trinidad born who had become American citizens, and doing well for themselves.

Our mother did not meet the USCIS's requirements for her to be his sole sponsor, in order for the process to have continued. So, little brother stepped up once again. I made a request to Carol, our sister by father, with whom I had gotten extremely close over the years, to do it for him as a special favor to me. Without any hesitation whatsoever, Carol agreed to be his Joint-Sponsor. And so, my older brother's ambition of obtaining his permanent U.S. residency was then on course in earnest.

I next visited Trinidad in March 2014. I arrived on March 18th. I was there for the sole purpose of taking our mother back to the U.S. It was one of only two occasions over the years, that our mother visited Trinidad and stayed with my older brother over an extended period.

My older brother and I had come to an agreement back in 2008, whereby she would have done so on an annual basis once our mother was able to travel, which she obviously would have been able to do over those years, so that I would have then gotten some much needed relief, to totally focus on my NOSILA business pursuits during those periods. He did not honor our agreement.

During what was a 3 weeks trip to Trinidad, I would have what was a chance encounter with the then Trinidad and Tobago Minister of Sport and Youth Affairs. The encounter happened at an event which was held at the Ballroom of the Cascadia Hotel in St Anns on April 7th. The event, which targeted the country's youths, was put on by one Valentino Singh, a former sports editor of the Trinidad Guardian newspaper.

My encounter with the then Minister of Sport and Youth Affairs that day, would lead to me making what turned out to be another highly regrettable professional decision. That decision was to agree to undertake an assignment for and on behalf of his Ministry.

The assignment was for me to conceive, develop and deliver an implementation plan for another National Community Anti-Crime Sports Initiative, based on the similar assignment I undertook for one of his predecessors, with whom he worked at the time back in 2002. I had two weeks to deliver the new assignment.

I took my mother back to the U.S. on April 11th as scheduled. Over the next two weeks while back in New York, I worked almost round the clock in order to conceptualize, develop and complete the assignment document. I achieved that objective and returned to Trinidad on Monday April 28th to deliver it to the then Minister. I stayed at my older brother's place, anticipating that I would have been in Trinidad for about a week or two at the most.

But the originally scheduled presentation meeting for the following day Tuesday April 29th had to be rescheduled to May 5th, because of the passing of former Prime Minister and President, A.N.R Robinson. And so, on May 5th, I presented and delivered the assignment to the then Minister at his Abercromby Street Port of Spain office, in the presence of some of his colleagues.

He approved the idea and implementation plan, which he described as excellent. He then instructed me to meet immediately with Ashwin Creed, who was then Permanent Secretary at the Ministry, to brief him of what transpired at our meeting, and to submit my already prepared invoice to him. I complied, upon which Creed asked me to hold on to the invoice for a few days. One Colin Borde was with Creed when I arrived in his office, and was privy to my conversation with Creed.

I expected to be paid within a week or two, and return to the U.S. immediately thereafter. But that did not happen. I encountered major problems regarding the said payment for my work, even as the then Minister knew that my stay in Trinidad was supposed to be brief, being that I was the caregiver for my mother, which I shared with him.

Consequently, what was initially expected to be a very short visit to Trinidad, turned into an almost 6 months stay, in my tireless efforts to get paid from the Ministry of Sport for my work; at the end of which I still did not get paid.

But I had had more than enough of that type of disrespect, by those who had solicited and employed my professional services, whenever I visited my homeland over the years. And that then most recent occasion involving the then Minister of Sport, would be the very last straw. The events that followed, would be revealed in the penultimate passage of my book.

Our mother had been anxiously calling me a few times a week to find out when I was coming back to New York, when she realized that I had not returned as originally scheduled. Since she could not hear my response herself, I would usually call her neighbor thereafter to relay it to her. That neighbor, over the years, had learnt how to communicate with my mother. At times she would call with that said neighbor present, through whom I would then deliver my response to her.

She usually called when she knew my older brother would be home so she could talk to him also. Sensing her anxiety because of her constant phone calls over the initial period of about a month, and with me then not actually sure when I would have been returning to the U.S., my older brother had decided that he would arrange for our mother to travel to Trinidad while I was still there.

The plan was that I would simply take her back to New York with me whenever I was returning. I relayed that news to our mother, who was naturally excited about it and looking forward to the trip. But it all ended in a huge disappointment for her, as the promised trip never happened.

Meanwhile, as the time past, it grew increasingly uncomfortable staying with my older brother. His attitude towards me was clearly signaling that I was overstaying my welcome, especially given the already existing tension between us.

I eventually returned to the U.S. on October 7th 2014 accompanied by my lifetime partner Alicia, with no plans of returning to Trinidad anytime soon. And I really would not have had a reason to, because having since filed for her, Alicia had received her final documents for permanent U.S. residency.

Unfortunately, however, and disturbingly so I might add, after she had spent what she herself admitted was an enjoyable 6 months with me and Alicia in Trinidad back in 2009, which was the last time they saw each other, my mother had continued to be unaccepting of her without reason or justification, except the ones she conjured up in her own mind. She was always going on about my lifetime partner depriving her and my two older siblings of things that they would have otherwise been receiving and enjoying courtesy of me, if Alicia was not in my life.

So, being that Alicia had accompanied me on my return to the U.S., and would have been residing permanently with me at the apartment, I decided that we should head to Florida instead, after we had already actually landed in New York. It was an impromptu decision that was made so as to avoid my lifetime partner being subjected to any sort of embarrassment from my mother, because I wasn't sure how my mother would have received her.

I was then seriously reconsidering my original plan to settle in Florida, after shelving it a couple of years before to continue to look after my mother in New York. I intended to purchase a unit in the same condominium complex where my cousin BoPeep lived.

AN UNFORGIVABLE TRANSGRESSION: SEVERING TIES WITH MY TWO OLDER SIBLINGS

Having promised our mother a trip to Trinidad while I was still there and disappointing her, my older brother decided that she would travel to Trinidad on that promised trip that November of 2014, so that they could spend some time with each other. He knew that she was then living alone in New York, being that I was in Florida together with Alicia at my cousin BoPeep's residence at the time, with no intentions then of returning to New York.

With our communication lines still open, my older brother confirmed via a text message that our mother would be traveling to Trinidad on Friday November 28th. She would have been there for 6 months or more if necessary, during which time we anticipated that my older brother would have received his final U.S. immigration paperwork. He and our mother would have then traveled to New York together, where he would have then been residing permanently with her at the apartment, whereupon he would have taken over caregiving duties from me.

Towards that end, and with the expressed intention of returning to Florida, I left Alicia there and traveled to New York in early November. I did so specifically to perform the usual necessary duties that my older brother knew I would have had to perform on behalf of my mother, whenever she had to travel to Trinidad, especially for a prolonged period.

Critical to those duties was taking our mother to get a thorough medical checkup and travel clearance from her Cardiologist, and obtaining at least a 6 months' supply of each of the 5 different prescription medications she takes, which is a process in itself, since it needed to get approval from her insurance, as her usual maximum supply is in 3 months increments.

My mother was naturally ecstatic when I told her that her eldest son had finally confirmed that she would be traveling to Trinidad on

November 28th. He even sent some funds for her subsequent to my arrival in New York, so that she could have done a bit of shopping for her trip.

My older brother indicated that he was expecting his daughter to travel to Trinidad with her family for a week for Christmas, which my mother was also excited about, being that she would have been seeing them. All plans for our mother's trip were moving along very smoothly.

The week for our mother to travel to Trinidad had arrived. One of her grand-daughters was accompanying her, because her doctor advised that she not travel by herself. She had shopped and was all packed and ready, and was both anxious and excited at the same time.

The only thing left was for her ticket to be paid for. My older brother was supposed to have purchased our mother's ticket. But that week he suddenly stopped communicating with me. He was not responding to my text messages or answering or returning my phone calls.

I gave him the benefit of the doubt, and went ahead and purchased our mother's plane ticket, upon which I then texted him our mother's flight information, assuming that he would simply reimburse me. But to my absolute shock, after a period of very civil, cordial, and respectful communications between us relative to our mother's trip to Trinidad, it all then suddenly went "totally left", as the saying goes.

His text response to the news that I had purchased our mother's plane ticket not having heard from him at such a critical time, quickly went from being civil, cordial and respectful to an instantly angry tone. "Why yuh do dat!?" he asked, which to me was quite perplexing to say the least.

I simply could not wrap my head around his question and suddenly hostile tone, being that he had promised to fly our mother to Trinidad since I was there, and had only recently finally confirmed her travel date for November 28th via text while I was in Florida. So, our mother had in fact been anticipating the trip for a while. His follow up text messages then began reflecting our then extremely volatile relationship.

With her ticket then having been paid for, accompanied by her grand-daughter, whose ticket I also paid for, my mother traveled to Trinidad on Friday November 28th 2014, as previously arranged by my older brother. I texted her arrival time to him, upon which he replied, "I would not be responsible for her when she reach Trinidad," which, in any event, given his sudden hostile attitude, he wouldn't have had to be, since I had already made alternative arrangements for her.

Following through on his statement to prove a point I suppose; my older brother was not at the airport to receive or welcome our mother. He claimed that he was in Tobago at the time. Mind you, it's just a 20 minutes flight to get from Tobago to Trinidad. And he would have flown in to the very airport where our mother came in.

But I had already anticipated that out of spite that he would not have shown up anyway. Thus, arrangements were already made for her grand-daughter to take our mother with her to Point Fortin, where our mother would stay with a relative there.

Having already spoken to that relative, Aunty Muriel as we called her, it was decided that my mother would only have stayed in Trinidad until Christmas, which was just over 3 weeks away, after which she would have returned to New York. Incidentally, Aunty Muriel was the person who arranged for us to stay with her then neighbor "Sando", the church organist, when we were thrown out of the house by our grandmother back in the 70s.

She told me that she was happy to hear my voice, since she hadn't spoken to or seen me for many years, and that she was looking forward to receiving and spending some time with our mother, whom she also hadn't spoken to or seen in many years as well. And especially since she herself was experiencing some serious medical issues also.

Aunty Muriel is the same Mother Muriel Austin "SuperBlue" Lyons referred to in his song "Get Something an' Wave", which won him the Road March title by a landslide that year. Austin has a son with my cousin Annmurie, the older of Aunty Muriel's two daughters.

I assured Aunty Muriel that I was arranging to send funds to Trinidad for them in a couple of days, to ensure that both our mother and her would have enjoyed a very happy holiday season, which would have included a little surprise 83rd birthday celebration for our mother on December 22nd.

But my older brother, who did not buy our mother's plane ticket; did not meet her at the airport; wasn't providing accommodation for her; and clearly stated via his text message that he would not have been responsible for our mother while she was in Trinidad, on his very own account, and to satisfy his ego I suppose, decided that he was going to spoil those plans.

The already extremely fragile relationship between my older brother and I, was about to finally reach its absolute breaking point. It got there as a result of his and his sister's, absolutely despicable, intolerable, inexcusable, and inhumane treatment of our mother.

And it was all instigated by my older brother. I had since come to learn that he had also been the instigator of many of his sister's unpleasant discourse that was directed towards me in her letters to our mother over the years.

So, it had long been my older brother's Modus Operandi, to simply feed the beast and then let loose his wicked sister to do all the dirty work, while he simply stayed in the background, pretending to be Saintly and innocent.

And so, staying true to form, less than 24 hours after our mother arrived in Trinidad and at Aunty Muriel's residence; and to our mother's and Aunty Muriel's utter disbelief, my older brother sent his sister to inform our mother that "he" was sending her back to New York on the next available flight. But his sister did much, much more. She cursed out and verbally abused our mother to the point that left both our mother and Aunty Muriel extremely distraught, traumatized and in tears.

Listening to our mother on the phone after I called to check up on her that morning after she arrived the night before, it was clear that she was. Crying uncontrollably, she said, "Son, yuh sister jus' come here an' cuss mih up bad yes. Is yuh brother who sen' she. He eh even come tuh look for mih. He sen' she tuh post mih back to New York like ah barrel yes."

Aunty Muriel then confirmed all that my mother had said. She had spoken to my older brother over the phone before I had called. And he was quick to follow through, having his sister purchase the plane ticket almost immediately, with our mother's return flight to New York then scheduled for Thursday December 4th, 5 days after she had arrived.

But being that he had made his spiteful declaration that he would not bear any responsibility for our mother while she was in Trinidad, I then intervened. With his December 4th return travel schedule, our mother would have been traveling all by herself, since he flatly refused to pay for her grand-daughter's ticket to accompany her back to New York.

And to make matters worse, the flight they booked would have been seeing our mother arrive at JFK in New York at 10:00 pm, all by her-self. But he did not care. He just wanted to get her back to New York. I instructed my niece to totally ignore any travel arrangements my brother had made. I then made alternative arrangements for both her and our mother to return to New York.

Her son, my older brother, did not even see it fit to pay our mother as much as one visit during her very short stay. And given the declarations he made to both Aunty Muriel and my niece, when I spoke to them on the phone, I knew that his rejection of our mother was for real.

I quote Aunty Muriel who has since passed away. "Yuh brother tell mih he doh wuh no part ah he mudder." End of quote. He repeated a similar sentiment to my niece Keithann, who had escorted our mother to Trinidad and was also escorting her back to the U.S. I quote my niece. "He say he doh wuh nobody around him tuh make he life miserable." End of quote. The "nobody" my older brother was referring to in that instance was our mother.

And yes, our mother did make each of her children's lives miserable at different periods of our respective lives. But certainly, mine more so than any of the others, since I had been spending the vast majority of the time with her.

And as miserable as she was making mine, which was purely in her defense of my same older brother and sister, I never ever abandoned her. And as a result of what transpired during her Trinidad trip, the worst was yet to come for me, as I would come to experience my mother's full "Spiritual Wrath".

Given his statement, one would be inclined to believe that my older brother has never made other people's life miserable during the course of his. He definitely made mine extremely miserable, as attested to throughout some of the passages of this book, and was still continuing to do so at the time.

I had already totally severed ties with his sister since early 2013; and after their then latest episode with the ill-treatment of our mother, I then also totally severed ties with my older brother.

Once I had confirmed the flight arrangements, I informed my mother's neighbor and good friend, whose name is Miss Martin, who lives 2 doors away from my mother's apartment, that my mother was returning to New York in a few days because of developments in Trinidad. She couldn't believe it, since my mother had excitedly informed her and others, that she was going to Trinidad to spend 6 months with her oldest son.

Miss Martin knew I was supposed to have been returning to Florida, once our mother left for what should have been an extended stay in Trinidad. She also knew that our mother couldn't really fend for herself, especially during the winter months that was then already upon us.

So, out of concern for my mother, Miss Martin strongly advised me to bring Alicia to join me in New York, as against returning to Florida, so that I would have been still there to continue to look after my mother, especially given her then traumatized state at the time. Miss Martin assured me that she would let my mother know that she was the one who told me to bring Alicia to New York.

As precarious as I knew the situation would be, I took Miss Martin's advice because it made sense, since I certainly did not want my mother to be living alone; even more so after her horrible Trinidad experience. But I also wasn't just going to leave Alicia in Florida either. So, she traveled to New York to join me the same night that my mother was returning.

Given all that had transpired over the years, during which my older brother in particular, for his own intents and purposes, deceived, manipulated, used, had taken advantage of me, and betrayed my trust over and over again, all matters between us had then become personal. And I mean extremely personal.

I communicated my feelings directly to him via e-mail, knowing full well that he would have shared its contents with his sister, for whom I already had absolutely no respect. I am certain that they both already knew that such a day would have eventually come.

They both know what they did in cahoots over the years to have brought it to that point. I know there will never be any reconciliation. There will be absolutely no Kumbaya moment between my older brother and sister and me, at any time during the rest of our respective lives. I trust that they know that too; especially after their then most recent unforgivable transgressions against our mother.

Our mother, accompanied by my niece, returned to New York at around 9:00 p.m. on Saturday December 6th 2014. She arrived at the apartment at around 10:30 p.m. She was the most distraught that I had ever seen her in her entire life, as a result of the treatment meted out to her in Trinidad by her two older children.

Alicia was at Miss Martin's apartment when our mother arrived. With my mother being so very distraught, I immediately took her over there to see Miss Martin, hoping that Miss Martin could offer some form of additional comfort to her.

I was extremely shocked, but at the same time also extremely relieved, when upon seeing Alicia, my mother greeted her with a big hug. My very first thought was, maybe she was just happy for anyone to console her at the time; even someone that she did not want to accept as her daughter-in law.

So that night, which is a night I will never forget, Miss Martin, my lifetime partner and I, did our best to do just that. And after we left hers, Miss Martin eventually came over to our apartment to continue to do so. But my mother was inconsolable; and understandably so.

Unable to sleep, my mother cried all through the night into the early morning hours, which naturally also kept Alicia and I up as well. The inhumane treatment meted out to her by her daughter, in addition to being totally rejected by her oldest son who she absolutely worships, was clearly unbearable.

Our mother remained distraught for weeks, during which she had episodes when she would talk to herself about her Trinidad experience over the course of a couple of hours, and eventually broke down and cried. There were occasions when the situation required visits to the ER or her private doctor.

I knew then that I most definitely could not have returned to Florida. Her emotional episodes continued for months whenever she recalled her traumatic Trinidad experience, upon which she had to be consoled, some-times with the help of our neighbor, Miss Martin.

During that time, everything was just fine between her and my lifetime partner. She accompanied my mother to the Supermarket and almost everywhere else. They certainly seemed to have been bonding. It most definitely gave me the peace of mind that I needed, relative to that particular issue. It made me extremely happy, as it appeared that my mother had finally accepted her. Life was good.

Then it all suddenly changed after about 6 months. I attributed it to the extreme pain that my mother had been feeling since her Trinidad visit, which was then turned mercilessly on me and my lifetime partner.

I guess she had to take it out on someone. So, my lifetime partner and I became the undeserving victims.

Miss Martin had already told my mother that it was she who told me to let Alicia come to New York, and the reason she did so, which was in my mother's best interest. But that did not seem to matter to my mother then.

So, while I had already been personally experiencing it for years, from the 6 months period onwards, Alicia also became a target, whereby we were both being verbally abused by my mother on a regular basis. My mother was then saying that she did not want Alicia in the apartment, because believe it or not, she wanted my older brother to live there with her whenever he got his permanent U.S residency. Yes; that same older brother who posted her back from Trinidad to New York like ah barrel months before.

But the apartment was also my permanent place of abode; with the operative word being "permanent". And there was no way that I was ever going to just up and leave at any point, especially at my very own expense, to accommodate my older brother. Period.

Not after all the blood, sweat, tears (yes tears), stress and cash it took on my part to secure it in the first place, and thereafter to maintain it, sharing the rent, and paying all of the other bills since my mother and I had been residing there together. So, all things considered, there was absolutely no way that I was ever going to submit to my mother. My older brother would have to find his own accommodation wherever, whenever the time came.

And although she didn't need it; my older brother also felt that he should then give our mother another fictitious reason to continue to verbally abuse me and my lifetime partner, by telling a blatant lie surrounding the circumstances of her visit to Trinidad.

Unfortunately for me, my mother and other family members and some relatives believed his lie, which caused her to then turn around and blame me for him totally rejecting her during her short-lived Trinidad visit. During her abusive tirades she would often say and I quote, "Is because of you yuh brother sen' mih back an' never come an' look fuh mih when ah went Trinidad." End of quote.

Then she found out that Alicia and I were actually married. Well, boy! That news just made matters between our mother, me, and my life-time partner much, much worse. Her finding out was orchestrated by none other than "the instigator himself", my older brother.

He was one of 3 witnesses at the ceremony, and the only family member who was supposed to know about it, until I myself decided to reveal it to the selected few that I wished to share it with.

Telling him and actually inviting him as a witness to what was a very simple and brief ceremony performed by an official at a building located at South Quay Port of Spain, turned out to be a really big mistake on my part.

For obvious reasons, my mother wasn't supposed to know about it, until I myself decided to tell her. I specifically told my older brother that. But he just could not resist. Staying true to his backstabbing Modus Operandi, he simply fed the beast once again, and his sister did the rest her usual way, "via air mail".

And so, my lifetime partner and I were then also having to deal directly with my mother's "spiritual wrath", in the form of various types of spiritual rituals, that she began perpetrating against us subsequent to her first meeting Alicia back in 1998, in her nonstop efforts to break up our ongoing relationship, which she had vowed to do way back then. She was then more determined than ever to do so, once she found out that we were married.

As such, my mother then took her efforts to break up the relation-ship to a whole other level; expending substantial amounts of cash, which she really could not afford to expend, to engage the services of other "spir-itual workers" (one Latino) to achieve her objective.

It was not unusual to discover weird looking mini effigies and other spiritual articles contained in various types of vessels, with both Alicia's and my name inscribed, or written on parchment paper and attached to them, all around the apartment for that expressed purpose. Absolutely none of it scared me personally. Such is my belief and extent of my faith in "The Higher Power".

But it got to the point where my lifetime partner usually left the apartment during the morning period, and returned late in the evening into night time, to get away from it all. She spent that time constructively at the library engaging in and completing various courses. I joined her eventually. But my mother was always ready and waiting to continue to unleash her verbal wrath upon us, whenever we returned to the apartment.

I usually just ignored my mother during her verbally abusive tirades. But when it became too much, since I knew how to communicate with her, I would engage her verbally, in defense of myself and my lifetime partner, who never ever responded to my mother. She always handled herself very well, as regular as such situations occurred. She just simply remained silent.

It all came to a climax for me during one such episode in 2016. With total disregard of the possibility of the extremely serious consequences to me, my dearest mother left the apartment in a rage, and went to one of her neighbor's and had that neighbor call the cops on me on her behalf. My mother had told the neighbor that I had physically assaulted her.

I became aware of the situation when two cops from the unit that deals with such incidents, came to the apartment in a rush from straight off the streets, only a few minutes after my mother had left. In the U.S. as we all know; the law takes such situations very seriously. I was not at all fazed by the presence of the cops, because I knew that I did no such thing.

I had absolutely nothing to hide, and told the cops everything that they wanted to know. That information included a brief history of the ongoing family feud, leading up to the then most recent verbally abusive tirade from my mother, that occurred only a short while before they showed up.

But they had their jobs to do. So, the Cops did an inspection of my person to see if there were any marks, such as scratches on certain parts of my body. They then did an inspection of the entire apartment. As expected, they found absolutely no basis upon which to make the arrest that they had probably anticipated they would have been executing, when they rushed to the apartment off the streets.

Still, while my mother's allegation was unequivocally untrue, the mere thought of how things could have possibly turned out for me that day, made me detest my two older siblings even more than I already had.

I felt that way because I knew that our mother was acting out primarily as a result of the pain that my two older siblings, and older brother in particular had inflicted upon her, when totally rejecting her upon her visit to Trinidad, after which he lied, causing her to blame it all on me.

And I also felt that way because I knew he had done it for the sole purpose of being spiteful, with his objective being to make me look bad in the eyes of family and relatives, in continuing his unjustified, ongoing, personal vendetta against me. And he simply didn't care that he was doing so at the expense of our mother's wellbeing.

Given how it all unfolded over the years, I was absolutely convinced that the ill-will that my older brother developed toward me, was in fact born out of nothing more than pure jealousy. I also do sincerely believe with every fiber of my being, that my two older siblings and especially my older brother, did not wish to see me succeed more than I already had.

Throughout the course of my life, I was always loyal to and trusting of my immediate family members and a few close relatives in general. But I was undeniably loyal to and trusting to a fault of my older brother in particular. And so, I paid a heavy price.

I had never even once entertained the thought of questioning his motives or agenda, until I came to realize that he did in fact have ulterior motives and hidden agendas. He, his sister, and a lot of my relatives betrayed my loyalty and trust, and it hurt terribly. It can never be regained.

425

While being made into the scapegoat over the years, my lifetime partner has been "ride or die" as they say in the Hip Hop culture. And through it all, have not even once been disrespectful to my mother or any other member of my family or relatives, in any way, shape or form. Evidently, it has not been an easy journey for us over the years, in the face of my two sibling haters and my mother's continuous verbal, emotional and mental abuse.

My lifetime partner has been with me, and has always been there for me since 1991. She has without question, been my most genuine and significant means of support since that time, relative to every aspect of my now 64 going on 65 years old life.

She has experienced all of those aspects, the good, the bad and the ugly; the ups, the downs; the ebbs, the flows; walking steadfastly beside me for half of it at this juncture. My love and appreciation for her is of the utmost sincerity, unconditional and immeasurable.

My "so called family"; my very own blood; as well as a lot of my relatives, have most certainly served up my ultimate lifetime reality check. My mother had always been, and still remains very much unaware, of the extent of the personal and professional sacrifices I have made to assist all of my siblings in general; and my older brother in particular, financially and otherwise over the years, and even up to the time I decided to completely sever ties with him back in November 2014.

Through his sister's letters dating back to 1998, and up to that time, they had both conspired to turn our mother against me. And considering how I had been treated by her for the majority of those years and beyond, their efforts proved successful in accomplishing that mission. So, I guess they should be both proud of themselves.

But neither he nor his sister was ever honest or even grateful enough to mention to our mother, or to any other family members, or even relatives for that matter, about the countless times, I, as their younger sibling, was there for them in their times of dire need and otherwise, during the course of our respective lives.

I now hereby speak for myself and myself only. Given my very own personal life experiences, I no longer view my family, which was supposed to be the most sacred of all social institutions, as such anymore. And never will I ever again.

In my personal opinion, to do so, would be to foolishly ignore the very critical life lessons, I was supposed to have learnt and be guided by, by my extremely unpleasant family experiences. I have forgiven each one of them for their respective contributions to those experiences. But never will I forget.

As for my mother, apart from the episode she suffered back in 1995, which left her with a limp and limited mobility in her left leg and arm, her other medical conditions include severe coronary heart disease, aortic insufficiency, hypertension, chronic kidney disease, acute arthritis, chronic constipation, anemia and cataracts in both eyes, which is affecting her eye sight. Her Ophthalmologist has decided against surgery thus far.

In addition, she has also been suffering from shortness of breath and extreme nasal congestion for many years, which her doctors have not found a permanent solution for. It leaves her feeling miserable daily, especially during the winter months. Even Flu shots no longer give her any significant relief.

Over the many years that I have been her caregiver, I did whatever I needed to do, to ensure that she live as healthy and as comfortably a life as her medical conditions would allow. I cannot even begin to tell you how many hours I have spent in at least 4 New York medical institutions over those years. One of them is New York Methodist Hospital (now New York Presbyterian / Brooklyn Methodist Hospital), which is the one I have been taking her to since around 2007.

In addition, I also spent countless hours with her at her Personal Care Physician's Office over those years; a brilliant Cardiologist whose name is Dr. Atul Chokshi, who retired in 2018. Her current Cardiologist, Dr. Vinod Patel, who once worked together with Dr. Chokshi, is also top notch. I continue to take her to him for medical visits as needed.

Thankfully, she is still able to walk on her own with the use of a cane indoors, and a rollator walker outdoors, although now only for very short distances at a time at snail's pace, and not without very heavy breathing and pain from her hips, both knees and both ankles, which limits her to those very shorts distances upon which she must rest. She also cannot stand for very long. The feet that once carried me and her other children over miles of Trinidad asphalt during those very early years, can now only carry her very limited distances, but she always completes those journeys.

Back in the prime of her life, those same feet would have seen her dashing through the Toronto and New York snow on extremely cold winter days to get to a job, which meager pay would feed and clothe us all back in Trinidad. Her arms, that held us all safely and securely as infants and toddlers, and especially the left, can still perform, but now, only limited chores. Overall, her endurance is very limited as is to be expected.

Now, simply sitting and getting up off her recliner or bed, dressing herself and putting on her socks, shoes or sneakers and tying the laces, are tasks that are almost impossible for her to perform, and or complete on her own. But she continues to be the absolute fighter that she always was, and that I have always known her to be. The fighter that never ever gives up.

And until death do either of us part, I will always be there, fighting together with her all of the way, as I continue to perform my labor of love, taking care of our mother 24/7. And finally, with some assistance from another family member, my younger brother Brian, who moved back to Brooklyn in July 2017, after living in California for just over 10 years. Brian and I always had a good relationship.

He would bear witness to the verbal, emotional and mental abuse me and my lifetime partner were suffering from our mother. He would also witness her verbal abuse escalate to the point where she would physically assault me on a few occasions. And although not to the same degree, my younger brother also became a victim of verbal, emotional and mental abuse from our mother.

He would eventually receive a phone call from our older brother, which I was privy to, which revealed that our older brother did in fact plan to live in the apartment once he immigrated to the U.S. But he knew full well that could only have happened if I was not there anymore. Our mother knew that as well.

It turned out that the escalation of her verbal abuse and spiritual shenanigans against my wife and I, was also her way of trying to force us out to accommodate my older brother. I had then gotten wind of the plan; and so, refused to capitulate.

At the ripe old age of 91 going on 92 years at the time of the publication of my book, and even as she is dealing with all her various medical issues, my mother continues her ongoing mission of trying to break up my now 32 years ongoing relationship with Alicia, through "Spiritual Means". Such is her determination.

She had also been joined in her efforts to do so by some of our relatives, who I did not even know were also involved in the practice. But my mother knew that they were, and had reached out to them. One relative even confessed to me.

None of those relatives have told my mother that what she is doing is totally wrong, and that she should stop. They instead chose to join her. Maybe it's because the cash they receive from her to be active participants, is simply too hard to refuse.

We; meaning our mother, me, my wife and my younger brother, are all paying the consequences on the account of her two older children's misdeeds. In the end, after all that was said and done, and with all that is still being said and done, in the interest of my personal peace of mind, wellbeing, joy and happiness, I simply stopped trying to understand and make sense of it all.

I finally came to the point where I just decided to accept that it must have been already written as a part of my journey, which was a reality that "The Higher Power" deemed necessary for me to experience, and learn from. And boy; did I ever. The following are the lyrics to a song that was inspired by the most painful and unpleasant of my painful and unpleasant life experiences.

SONG TITLE: "CYAR TELL"

Written by Alison Ayres © 2015 Alison Ayres All rights Reserved

Verse 1
I could not have conceived—no
Because ah get ah li'l blessings in meh life
They'd conspire to aggrieve
Manipulate our mother to create strife
I could not have perceived—no
Not after sharing all of my blessings with them
They'd only flatter to deceive
Make it their life mission to cause me problems

CHORUS
Cyar always tell who is haters
Sometimes is your own family not just friends who praying for yuh downfall
Cyar always tell who is haters
They'll be the ones creating your problems but pretending dey love you all

Verse 2
Couldn't believe meh own blood
Who always appeared dey so happy for me
Behind meh back was slingin' mud
Ah rude awakening that definitely
Taught me ah lesson an' ah learn
That I gotta look out for my own interest
Never again will I geh burn
So doh tell mih about no Kumbaya business—**CHORUS**

Verse 3
Ah use tuh put family first
Before I knew they could be so devious
Since then meh family bubble burst
Keeping away from dem has been meh modus
Dey could keep wishing me the worse
Because is in the Higher Power I trust
And who the man bless no one curse
If yuh could relate then sing de chorus—**CHORUS—End**

TAKING ON THE POLITICAL ESTABLISHMENT IN MY HOMELAND: MY MONUMENTAL BATTLE FOR JUSTICE

I will now get into the details with respects to my encounter with the then Minister of Sport & Youth Affairs that I mentioned in an earlier passage, during one of my trips to Trinidad from the U.S., upon which I was approached and subsequently commissioned by the said Minister, to undertake an assignment for and on behalf of the Trinidad & Tobago Ministry of Sport & Youth Affairs and by extension, the then government of Trinidad and Tobago. That was in mid-April of 2014.

The assignment was for me to conceive, develop and deliver an implementation plan for another National Community Anti-Crime Sports Initiative, based on a similar assignment that I undertook for one of his predecessors, with whom he worked at the time back in 2002.

I had delivered the completed assignment document to the then Minister on May 5th 2014. However, his Sport Ministry was refusing to pay me for my work, after I submitted my initial invoice to the then Permanent Secretary Aswin Creed on that said May 5th date, and after a second invoice was submitted on July 1st.

After pursuing and exhausting every possible avenue for an amicable settlement over an extended period of 3 years towards that objective, the Sport Ministry was still refusing to pay. The irony is, that the payment was earmarked for my U.S. NOSILA sport brand business venture, from which Trinidad and Tobago sports would have benefitted, if it did in fact turn out to be as successful as I was anticipating.

I decided then that enough is enough. I was done being a victim. The ultimate rebel in me finally emerged. I was going to take the Trinidad and Tobago government, and more specifically, the Attorney General's Office to court, for the payment that was then owed to me. And I was going to fight to the bitter end to get my just due.

To back up my claim for the payment that was owed to me, I then began to gather my evidence, to turn over to whoever was the Attorney that I was going to select to represent me. During that process, I went to a local phone company to obtain cell phone records of the communications between the then Minister and myself.

I was told by the phone company that I needed a Police Report to obtain the records. I had no idea why I would have needed a Police Report, but I simply followed instructions and went to a Police Station for that purpose. A Police Officer began taking the information. When I mentioned the name of the government official involved, he appeared to freeze a bit and became hesitant and nervous.

There was another Police Officer near us. So, strangely, the one taking the information, then asked me to move further down to the end of the counter away from the other officer. He then informed me that once he entered the report, which his superiors would then check, given that there was a government minister involved, there were a couple of scenarios that could possibly play out as a result.

One was that I could get a knock on my door from Law Enforcement Officers who were the protectors of the particular Minister. And he could possibly face consequences for having entered the report, being that a government minister was being mentioned.

Recognizing the officer's extreme anxiety over the situation, I decided to withdraw my report, more so to save him from the possibility of facing consequences. It was another eye-opener indeed. I still managed to obtain the cell phone records.

I said another eye-opener, because that experience immediately brought back to mind my very first eye-opener in a similar situation back in 2006, when during another one of my visits to Trinidad, I was approached once again and commissioned to do two government assignments, which were to be aired on television.

On that occasion, I was commissioned by my former colleague from my time in the Advertising industry, who was then attached to that particular government agency.

I had worked with one of the country's top video editors, at his home editing studio on the second of the two assignments. I was meeting and working with him for the very first time. He revealed to me that the individual who commissioned the assignment, who had been using his professional services for a while, was grossly underpaying him, which was proven to be true.

So, as one who is totally against any such injustice, having been a victim myself, I suggested that he not hand over the completed assignment, until the individual agreed to pay him what he deserved for his professional services for his part on the assignment. That particular assignment, was to be presented the following day, to the then Prime Minister and his Cabinet Members, who were on a weekend retreat at the time.

The individual who commissioned it, called me and related to me over the phone that the editor was refusing to hand over the completed assignment, which was on a DVD, because he wanted to be paid more. I told the individual that I fully supported the editor's position, given the work that was involved.

To my great shock, the individual then told me that they were then going to arrange for some Law Enforcement friends of theirs, to pay the editor a visit at his residence to execute a most devious and malicious act, which the individual specified, to force the editor to hand over the DVD. I ended our conversation on that absolutely numbing note.

I then immediately contacted and told the editor what the individual had just told me over the phone that they were about to do, and strongly advised that he hand over the DVD to the individual, because it wasn't worth it. He complied. As it turned out, I too was also grossly underpaid for my work on the assignment, upon which I told the individual that I wasn't interested in doing any further work for them.

Now to get back to my 2014 matter. In my efforts to get the payment due to me, over the aforementioned extended period of about 3 years from 2014 to 2017, I had made a request for an audience with the Prime Minister who was then in office, seeking that Prime Minister's intervention in the matter. However, I was only granted an audience with the then Prime Minister's Special Advisor, one Shem Baldeosingh.

Mr. Baldeosingh and I met on Friday July 11th 2014, at the then Prime Minister's St Claire Port of Spain offices. At that meeting, I was very bluntly informed by the then Prime Minister's Special Advisor, that the then administration was not touching any matters having to do with the particular Sports Minister, because of a then ongoing investigation relative to some other matter. The other matter would eventually force the said Sport Minister to resign.

I left a package with Mr. Baldeosingh, to deliver to the then Prime Minister. It included all the work I had completed, and a formal letter dated the said Friday July 11th 2014, requesting the then Prime Minister's intervention. I received no response to my request.

With seemingly no response forthcoming from the Prime Minister, I then met with one Amroodeen Ali on August 8th. He then held the Sport Ministry's highest office, which is that of Permanent Secretary. He instructed me to make a similar intervention request to the then Minister of Sport, one Rupert Griffith, who succeeded the one who solicited and employed my professional services in the first place, and had since been forced to resign. Interestingly, Mr. Ali also instructed me as to what that letter should contain. I complied.

A meeting was subsequently convened on Friday August 15th 2014, where I met with the said Minister Rupert Griffith, Amroodeen Ali himself, and the then Deputy Permanent Secretary, one Ian Ramdahin, to try to resolve the matter.

After reviewing documented communications confirming the commissioning of the assignment by the then Minister, and acknowledging all the work that I had completed, they took the view that there was "no binding contract". They then suggested that I present my case to the Sports Company of Trinidad and Tobago (SporTT).

I subsequently met and or corresponded with at least 2 other Sport Ministry officials, namely, Ashwin Creed and Joan Mendez, who each held that Ministry's highest office at different periods during that time. They all had the authority to settle the matter, and bring my years of ongoing misery to an end. But they all chose not to do so. My concerted efforts towards that conclusion proved futile.

Having then totally exhausted my personal efforts, that September I employed the services of a very high-profile Attorney attached to a highly reputable local law firm to handle my matter, which was before I had finally returned to the U.S. that October accompanied by Alicia, after my 6 months Trinidad stay, in my all-out effort to receive the payment then owed to me. However, I was not satisfied with his initial efforts, and eventually ended that Client / Attorney relationship.

After I had returned to the U.S., I had then contacted another Prime Minister who succeeded the first, by way of a formal letter as well, seeking that Prime Minister's intervention in the matter. But I was simply referred back to the Ministry of Sport and Youth Affairs.

Thereafter, upon a referral from a former Trinidad & Tobago Attorney General, whom I had consulted for possible representation in his then capacity as a practicing Attorney, I subsequently engaged the services of another Attorney via e-mail. I did so on a strict contingency agreement that time around.

I engaged the services of Attorney number 2 in February 2017. He told me that he intended to set up a meeting with the relevant parties from the Ministry of Sport, to discuss an amicable resolution of the matter. He advised that I traveled to Trinidad when the time approached, because he wanted me to attend. I complied and traveled to Trinidad in late July, when the meeting was supposed to have taken place.

However, Attorney number 2 did not set up the proposed meeting as he had said he would, which was an immediate red flag for me. Not wanting my trip to have been a waste of time and money, and in my own interest, I then took the bull by the horns and arranged two meetings myself, with two relevant parties from the Ministry of Sport.

One was with the Ministry's Attorney Tyrone Marcus, and the other was with the then Permanent Secretary Ian Ramdahin, who had been since promoted from Deputy Permanent Secretary. Although informed beforehand for the purpose of him attending, Attorney number 2 failed to show up for both meetings, whereby a second red flag was then raised.

He and I subsequently had our very first face-to-face in early August. I invited my then very close friend Tansley Thompson to attend; and he did. A few additional red flags were raised on items discussed during that session. One being when he strongly advised me to make a Will as soon as I got back to the U.S., and e-mail it to him.

His reasoning was that if I should die during the legal proceedings, then my beneficiaries would be able to receive any financial award that resulted from the matter. I decided to give Attorney number 2 the benefit of the doubt, even after multiple red flags were raised. Given the time that had already elapsed, which was then over 3 years at the time, I wanted him to file my claim with the court forthwith.

But he insisted upon employing his very own strategy. It was one that was similar to what had been already unsuccessfully employed by Attorney number 1, wherein he simply set timelines once again for specific actions to be taken, before he would file the claim.

Apart from the notes that I was actually writing on my note pad, I also took a mental note of the fact that he was ignoring his client's wish to file the claim forthwith. I returned to the U.S. the day after our face-to-face. Once I got back to the U.S., I followed Attorney number 2's instruction and made a Will and e-mailed it to him.

Because of their well-established lack of integrity, history of deceit, their alleged insatiable desire for financial and materialistic self-enrichment through corrupt practices, and penchant for oppressing a particular segment of society, I was never a fan or supporter of politicians, generally speaking. But being as patriotic as I was with respects to my homeland, I always answered their respective calls, in my continued efforts to serve the beloved land of my birth.

It stands to reason therefore, why I feel a profound sense of bitterness towards them, given the grave injustice that was then being perpetrated against me by a clique of the locally bred species, coupled with the complete lack of effort starting with the one responsible, right up to those at the very top of the pyramid, to put that wrong right.

That bitterness is compounded by the fact that such injustice would never be perpetrated against two specific races, belonging to a particular class of the Trinidad and Tobago citizenry, who are themselves alleged members of the political establishment; most of whom claim to be patriots and servants of the country, but are in my personal opinion simply exploiting it to their own advantage.

I understand that they do so by allegedly partnering with the aforementioned politicians in alleged corrupt practices, for the sole purpose of financial self-enrichment and other gains.

Meanwhile, upstanding, hardworking, law-abiding citizens like myself, who simply refuse to compromise our values by refusing to be conformists and or participants in their alleged financial schemes, disguised as legitimate business dealings, are subjected to injustices that render us victims.

With all those thoughts then uppermost in my mind, I told myself that I would be a victim no more. And so, I decided that I would fight to the very bitter end, to get my just due.

It took Attorney number 2 14 months from the time I engaged his services, before he would finally file my claim in court. During that time and thereafter, he displayed such deplorable conduct, that it caused me to file a complaint against him with the Trinidad & Tobago Law Association.

Based on his conduct and information I received, it appeared that he had managed to carve out a career that was established on bullying and intimidatory tactics, and driven by an over inflated ego, more so than knowledge and professional decorum and acumen.

And that was eventually revealed; because as it turned out, even after all the pertinent information was provided to him, when he did finally file the claim in April 2018, he actually filed the claim against the wrong government entity.

In so doing, he generously provided the Attorneys for the government with a strong Nullity defense. Fortunately for me, the High Court Judge ruled against the government on their Attorneys Nullity defense. Unfortunately for me however, and as then expected, the Attorneys for the government appealed the High Court's decision, which they won in the Court of Appeal.

I subsequently requested and received the transcripts of the arguments from both sides from both the High Court and Court of Appeal to review them. In the transcript from the Court of Appeal, Attorney number 2 basically admitted that he messed up and appeared to be begging the Court's forgiveness for the unforgivable.

After making a number of court appearances on my behalf, and while I cannot possibly describe him as such a person or professional, he did do the honorable thing and came off record as my Attorney in the High Court.

He subsequently tried to extort a substantial sum of money from me, by threatening me in a letter that if I did not pay him the 6-figure amount that he was demanding by a certain date, he would apply for a Court Order to cease all of my assets. It was then that I understood the real reason behind his instruction at our very first meeting, for me to make the Will and e-mail it to him as a matter of urgency.

Attorney number 2 did not know which government entity to file my claim against; but he most certainly knew how to manipulate the corrupted, badly broken local judicial system well; because there was a reason that he came off record as my Attorney in the High Court only, and not in the Court of Appeal as well.

The entire experience, which included a fairly lengthy phone conversation on one occasion with an individual who had been working in the system for many years, also revealed an eye-opening dark side of the legal profession in my homeland.

My ongoing matter for payment owed to me by the Trinidad and Tobago Ministry of Sport, which I have been pursuing since May 2014, is still before the Trinidad & Tobago High Court. I have a new Attorney (number 3), whose services I was able to secure through "Spiritual Orchestration" in very early 2020.

I am trusting that whenever the matter eventually comes to its conclusion, it would be in my favor. I have since brought the matter to the attention of the Privy Council in London England. Following are the lyrics to a song I wrote that was inspired by my experience with "Attorney Number 2".

SONG TITLE: EXTORTION

Written by Alison Ayres © 2019 Alison Ayres All rights Reserved

VERSE 1
Ah was referred to ah Lawyer—For representation
In a serious legal matter—On ah Paradise Island
After de Lawyer man agree
To work on ah contingency arrangement
Screw up mih matter from de onset
Buh want ah six figure pay cheque

CHORUS
Extortion!!!!
Perpetrator—De white collar kind
Extortion!!!!
Perpetrator—Was on to you long time
Extortion!!!!
Perpetrator—Ah was smelling your grime
Extortion!!!!
Perpetrator—Read my lips—not one effin dime

VERSE 2
Threatening me in a letter—If he eh geh a cheque by a certain date
He go apply for a Court Order—all ah mih assets he go take
Another Con-human in disguise
In fancy suits and ties
Tried to live my life in peace
Buh now they finally wake de beast—**CHORUS—END**

LIFE CHANGING MOMENTS: LIFE CHANGING TIMES

I must now rewind to the start of 2018, when an absolutely terrifying life changing event occurred. I was then less than 12 months away from finally launching my NOSILA sports brand in the U.S. market with an online store. I had put in the time and completed most of the extremely hard work, that finally brought me to the point of doing so.

With the NOSILA logo since becoming an officially registered trademark, I had subsequently taken marketing courses; consulted with experts and sourced overseas suppliers. I had also taken courses in Adobe Photoshop, Illustrator and computer animation, so as to save me having to continue to depend on and pay outside providers for those services.

Since she was going to be my business partner, my wife also took the Photoshop course and also became quite proficient. She was then also bringing that skill to the business, which would have been much needed, and would have allowed me to focus on the other aspects.

She had steadfastly embarked on her own personal mission of self-improvement and self-growth since she had immigrated to the U.S. just over 3 years before, and was most certainly accomplishing it. But my wife had also been experiencing some serious medical issues in recent years, and had undergone major surgery since immigrating, and had continued to have ongoing tests done.

Then at exactly 7:35 p.m., Monday February 12th of the said year of 2018, my lifetime partner and I got the most devasting medically related news one can ever expect to receive. Both of our lives would be forever changed in that instant, upon the news being delivered by the medical specialist attached to the medical institution, that had been conducting the ongoing tests.

My wife was in a life and death situation. It had to be immediately addressed. Absolutely nothing else mattered then. The urgency was such that the very next day we were consulting a Surgical Oncologist. A couple of days later we were consulting a Medical Oncologist. A few days later we were at the Manhattan medical facility where she would undergo a CAT scan.

Our journey thereafter, would be filled with overwhelming, and sometimes seemingly insurmountable physical, emotional, mental, spiritual, and financial challenges to face and overcome. My wife's health then took absolute precedence over any and everything else.

Thus, my NOSILA business venture, as close as it was to being finally launched after many years of blood, sweat, stress and tremendous sacrifices, financially and otherwise once again, suddenly became unimportant. Still, I have not given up on it. I remain hopeful that it would become a reality, before I leave this earth. Following are the lyrics to a song I wrote that was inspired by our terrifying medically related experience.

WALK IN HOPE
Written by Alison Ayres © 2019 Alison Ayres All rights Reserved

INTRO:
Walk in hope! (4 times)

VERSE 1
7:35 pm—Monday 12th of February—2018
He delivered the news
Extremely serious health problem—Very scary—Gotta treat it right away
No time to lose
Dr Lewis said—go see Dr Deysine—Go see him tomorrow—He's on Ocean Avenue
I've already called him—arranged the appointment—he will be expecting you
Dr Deysine said—go see Dr Astrow—first we will do Chemo

See how much we could shrink that tumor
Since been on the journey! Sometimes on a gurney—I've since lost my sense of humor

CHORUS

You're my hero!
You inspire me the way you fight
You're my hero!
Every minute every day and night
You're my hero!
In so many ways you changed my life
You're my hero
You're my hero yes you are my wife

VERSE 2

7:35 pm—Monday 12th of February—2018
Was so confused
Couldn't wrap our minds around it then—excruciating memory—that pain of yesterday
Just lit a fuse—You are so very strong
You survived Chemo! Survived Vasovagal! Major surgeries!
You survived Chemo! You survived Chemo! Radiation Therapy!
Today not tomorrow! Today not tomorrow! Let's live in the here and now
Come on baby let's go! Come on baby let's go! Baby let's renew our vows

CHORUS—END

Then came a second medically related event; one that would not only change our lives even more, but forever change the lives of almost every human being throughout the entire world. Enter the year 2020; and the advent of the COVID19 pandemic. I do not think that anything more needs to be said about the absolutely dreadful virus.

EPILOGUE

Given the initial odds, I do consider myself to have been truly blessed to have had what I could only describe as an improbable life. I say that with the utmost gratitude.

I attribute it to the fact that it was a course charted by my sincere and overwhelming desire to fulfill my ultimate lifetime ambition with respects to my mother, and Spiritual Orchestration by "The Higher Power". Had it not been for finding in my mother's struggles very early on, which was the source that would provide the inspiration for me to live a purposeful life, I truly believe that my life would have turned out very differently; and not necessarily for the better.

Naturally, I have learnt many very important, painful and valuable life lessons, during the course of my journey. But none more important, painful and valuable than the lessons learnt from my experiences with "so called family and friends". And although it took getting burnt multiple times, I would like to think that I have learnt those life lessons well, or at least well enough, so as not to continue to repeat the related multitude of past mistakes the rest of the way.

I've met some really good people along my journey, several of whom have left a lasting impression. But on the other hand, I have also met some really devious, deceitful, pretentious, manipulative, heartless and simply evil human beings; some of whom profess to be "God Fearing".

It is said that experience is the best teacher; a theory that I happen to believe in. I will therefore be guided throughout the rest of my journey by my personal life experiences, as well as by my natural human instincts and keen sense of perception.

I will continue to be respectful to and be appreciative in those instances where it may apply, of those who are respectful to and in instances where it may apply, are appreciative of me, regardless of nationality, race, color, creed, social and or professional status, religion, gender or sexual orientation. I will continue to choose the option of distancing myself from, and or avoiding those choosing to treat me otherwise, be it so-called family, relatives, friends or acquaintances.

During the course of my journey, I strove for excellence in my professional life, and tried to make the right choices in my personal life, with the hope that in doing so, I would have fulfilled my true potential and ultimately my purpose during my time upon this earth. And that includes inspiring people in general, and young people in particular, who hopefully, would read my story and not only be inspired by it, but equally important, also learn from my personal life experiences.

Through the pursuit of my ultimate life goal, I realized my childhood dreams. Through the realization of those childhood dreams, I discovered life's possibilities. Through the discovery of its possibilities, life revealed itself to me. Until the inevitable event of death, I look forward to continuing to live the rest of it, as I lived the worst and best of it; simply and humbly; and most of all, without fear.

And so... I leave you with a song, and final words of inspiration.

SONG TITLE: CHAMPION "THE DREAMERS ANTHEM"
Written by Alison Ayres © 2015 Alison Ayres All rights Reserved

Verse 1
Don't give up on your dreams—of being a winner
Champion—Your dream of being a Champion
Never give up impossible as it seems—Saint or sinner
Champion—You can be a Champion
Cometh the moment! After chasing it for many years
Cometh the moment! That you finally overcome your fears
Cometh the moment! You lift your head and you begin to fly
Cometh the moment! You know your only limit is the sky

CHORUS
Cometh the day!—Cometh the moment!
You are a Champion!—You are a Champion!
Cometh the day! Cometh the moment!
Cometh the Champion!—Cometh the Champions—Of the world!

Verse 2
Don't give up on your dreams—to be a winner
Champion—our dream of being a Champion
Never give up elusive as it may seem—You've got it in yuh
Champion—You can be a Champion
Cometh the moment! When you can feel that's it's your time to shine
Cometh the moment! When you are first across the finish line
Cometh the moment! When you will hear all the applause and cheers
Come-ah cometh the moment!
Cometh the moment when you're brought to tears

CHORUS

BRIDGE
Chase your dream and don't stop
Never ever give up
Even when the ball drops—Never ever give up I say
Chase your dream...go get it
Don't live to regret it
Come-ah Cometh the day—**CHORUS—END**

"WHATEVER YOU VIVIDLY IMAGINE,

ARDENTLY DESIRE,

SINCERELY BELIEVE,

AND ENTHUSIASTICALLY ACT UPON...

SHALL INEVITABLY COME TO PASS."

Milton Keynes UK
Ingram Content Group UK Ltd.
UKHW050047120124
435873UK00005B/147/J